THEORY AND REFORM
IN THE EUROPEAN UNION

MANCHESTER
UNIVERSITY PRESS

SERIES EDITORS *Thomas Christiansen and Emil Kirchner*

Dimitris N. Chryssochoou, Michael J. Tsinisizelis,
Stelios Stavridis & Kostas Ifantis

THEORY AND REFORM IN THE EUROPEAN UNION

SECOND EDITION

MANCHESTER UNIVERSITY PRESS
Manchester and New York

distributed exclusively in the USA by Palgrave

First edition published 1999 by Manchester University Press

This edition published 2003 by
Manchester University Press
Oxford Road, Manchester M13 9NR, UK
and Room 400, 175 Fifth Avenue, New York, NY 10010, USA
www.manchesteruniversitypress.co.uk

Distributed exclusively in the USA by
Palgrave, 175 Fifth Avenue, New York, NY 10010, USA

Distributed exclusively in Canada by
UBC Press, University of British Columbia, 2029 West Mall,
Vancouver, BC, Canada V6T 1Z2

British Library Cataloguing-in-Publication Data
A catalogue record for this book is available from the British Library

Library of Congress Cataloging-in-Publication Data applied for

ISBN 0 7190 6385 X *paperback*

This edition first published 2003

11 10 09 08 07 06 05 04 03   10 9 8 7 6 5 4 3 2 1

Typeset in Minion with Lithos
by Northern Phototypesetting Co Ltd, Bolton
Printed in Great Britain
by Bell & Bain Ltd, Glasgow

To Dimitris K. Vardas
   Ioannis Tsinisizelis
   Spyros and Niki Stavridis
   Eugenia-Emmanuela and Ileana-Anastasia Ifantis

CONTENTS

LIST OF TABLES

LIST OF ABBREVIATIONS

ACLANT	Allied Command Atlantic
ACP	African, Caribbean and Pacific Countries
AFCENT	Allied Forces Central Europe
AFSOUTH	Allied Forces Southern Europe
AMT	Treaty of Amsterdam
CAP	Common Agricultural Policy
CEE	Central and Eastern European (Country)
CFE	Conventional Forces in Europe
CFSP	Common Foreign and Security Policy
CIS	Commonwealth of Independent States
CJPS	Combined Joint Policy Staff
CJTF	Combined Joint Task Force
COPS	Political and Security Committee
CoR	Committee of the Regions
COREPER	Committee of Permanent Representatives
COREU	Telex Network of European Correspondents
COSAC	Conference of European Affairs Committees
CSBMs	Confidence- and Security-Building Measures
CSCE	Conference on Security and Co-operation in Europe
CSO	Committee of Senior Officials
CTRP	Co-operative Threat Reduction Programme
DCI	Defence Capabilities Initiative
EAC	European Affairs Council
EAEC	European Atomic Energy Community
EBRD	European Bank for Reconstruction and Development
EC	European Community
ECB	European Central Bank
ECHR	European Convention on Human Rights
ECJ	European Court of Justice
ECSC	European Coal and Steel Community
EDC	European Defence Community
EEC	European Economic Community
EFTA	European Free Trade Area
EMS	European Monetary System
EMU	Economic and Monetary Union
EP	European Parliament
EPC	European Political Co-operation
ERDF	European Regional Development Fund
ERM	Exchange Rate Mechanism
ERRF	European Rapid Reaction Force

ESA	European Space Agency
ESC	Economic and Social Committee
ESDI	European Security and Defence Identity
ESDP	European Security and Defence Policy
ESF	European Social Fund
EUI	European University Institute
FSU	Former Soviet Union
GATT	General Agreement on Tariffs and Trade
HCNM	High Commissioner on National Minorities
IFOR	Implemention Force
IGC	Intergovernmental Conference
IMF	International Monetary Fund
INF	Intermediate-range Nuclear Force
JET	Joint European Taurus
JHA	Co-operation in Justice and Home Affairs
MAD	Mutual Assured Destruction
MEP	Member of the European Parliament
NAC	North Atlantic Council
NACC	North Atlantic Co-operation Council
NAFTA	North Atlantic Free Trade Agreement
NATO	North Atlantic Treaty Organisation
NIT	Treaty of Nice
ODIHR	Office for Democratic Institutions and Human Rights
OEEC	Organisation for European Economic Co-operation
OSCE	Organisation on Security and Co-operation in Europe
PCG	Policy Co-ordination Group (NATO)
PfP	Partnership for Peace
QMV	Qualified Majority Voting
R&D	Research and Development
REACT	Rapid Expert Assistance and Co-operation Teams
SACEUR	Supreme Allied Command Europe
SACLANT	Supreme Allied Command Atlantic
SDI	Strategic Defence Initiative
SEA	Single European Act
SGP	Stability and Growth Pact
SHAPE	Supreme Headquarters Allied Power Europe
SME	Small- and Medium-Sized Enterprise
TEU	Treaty on European Union
UK	United Kingdom
UN	United Nations
UNPROFOR	United Nations Protection Force
UNSC	United Nations Security Council
US	United States
USIP	United States Institute for Peace
WEU	Western European Union
WMD	Weapons of Mass Destruction

The events of 1989 unleashed a number of significant changes in European development, bringing in their wake consequences such as the dismantling of the Iron Curtain, the transformation of communist regimes, German reunification, dissolution of the Warsaw Pact and the Soviet Union, an end to the Cold War syndrome and the arrival of a host of new states. The consequences of these changes affect nation-states, the European Union (EU), and European security and stability. While Europe as a whole has moved from enmity towards friendship and from conflict to co-operation in economic, political and military fields, the internal stability and cohesion of many states has been adversely affected. The result has been civil wars, fragmentation, migration and economic and social hardship. Parallel to these developments are attempts by the Union for a larger and more integrated entity.

How Europe is responding to these changes and developments and their consequences is the focus of this series, appropriately entitled *Europe in Change*. Books in this series take both a historical and interdisciplinary perspective in order to compare the post-1989 situation with earlier periods in European history and benefit from the theoretical insights of different disciplines in analysing both events and developments.

Theory and reform in the European Union examines how the Union has changed since the events of 1989 and whether available theoretical and conceptual tools enable us to explain and predict future European integration. The authors highlight the uneven development both within EU policy areas and between EU policies and institutional settings, emphasising that, in spite of important breakthroughs in the form of the Treaty on European Union (TEU) and the Amsterdam and Nice Treaties, the political authority of the Union has not significantly increased. Nor, according to the authors, has there been a reliable integration theory as the basis for assessing the Union's future. They suggest that structural ways of understanding changing patterns of interaction, free from the inherently fragmented boundaries of micro-analysis, are needed to establish a more reliable theory. This would involve studying how intrastate policy-making intermeshes with that of large-scale polity formation, based on an interlocking structure of political authority – a transnational polity which lacks a single locus of decision-making. For the authors, such an entity would have to strike a balance between being the main locus of collective, binding decision-making for the constituent governments, and the dominant focus of popular identification.

By focusing on the Union as a joint-decision system and by incorporating the sociopsychological conditions of popular political identification, the authors offer some valuable insights into the European integration process. Their analysis enhances the understanding of the forces that form and reform the regional system, the relevance of Treaty development and the scope of EU policy expansion, as well as the context of the EU institutional and constitutional setting. It is a book which will be an important guide for students, teachers and researchers interested in the study of European integration.

Emil J. Kirchner

INTRODUCTION

Theorising about the structural conditions and operational dynamics of European integration has produced a wide-ranging 'laboratory' of concepts and ideas about what the European Union is, and towards what it is developing. Central to these analyses has been the search for conceptually refined paradigms and interpretations either on specific policy actors and processes, or on the dynamic institutional configuration of the larger management system. But what most analysts have concluded in the past in a more or less confident manner about the possible evolution of European governance has been trapped in the unpredictability of changing circumstances at both national and international level. Much to the surprise of the more supranationalist projections of European integration in the mid-1980s, a period described as a 'neofunctionalist comeback', the Union has managed to survive the tides of federalism and institutional centralisation. True, new patterns of interaction have emerged between the collectivity and its component parts. But considerable resistance became manifest on the part of national governing elites for substantive constitutional reforms to bring about a 'constitutive' European polity, whose citizens – presently in the form of separate national demoi, rather than in the shape of a transnational civic demos – are capable of directing their democratic claims to, and via, the central institutions of governance.

Put another way, a European 'civic space' is yet to emerge, and with it a more transparent, inclusive and participatory process of union. At the same time, however, 'conventional' intergovernmentalism, primarily concerned with the role and influence of national governmental actors, finds it equally difficult to provide an overall hermeneutic pattern of EU polity development. In many important respects, the current debate about the Union's political and constitutional physiognomy transcends the traditional analytical tools for studying its defining – and distinctive – properties and functions. Although a new 'conceptual consensus' (or even sufficiently convergent conceptual understandings) is still far from evident among its students, the conceptual apparatus developed in the 1990s, and particularly since the coming into force of the Maastricht Treaty, raises serious questions about the democracy, governance and polity of Europe. It also raises important concerns regarding the emerging forms of co-operative decision-making – themselves, product of a by now consolidated practice of political determination among the segment elites – and, in general, the relationship between theory-building and collective constitutional engineering.

How far, then, have the new conceptual lenses employed by contemporary scholarship to assess the state of European integration in the 1990s and early 2000s moved from the initial supranationalism–intergovernmentalism dichotomy? What is, or appears to be, distinctively new about the way in which the new theoretical approaches attempt to capture the dominant character of the relationship between national autonomy and regional institutionalisation or, alternatively, between state sovereignty and EU polity-building? Is it possible to discern an end state of the integration process – whether or not federal in kind – after almost half a century of continuous theoretical and empirical engagement in studying the policy processes and decisional outcomes of the general system? The answer to this last question remains as elusive as ever, albeit with an important qualification to be made: we do not know exactly what the end situation of the integration process might look like, but at least we can conclude with a degree of certainty what its final product will not come to resemble: a regional superstate subsuming the participating units – in the form of states, subnational political authorities and citizens – in its governance structures.

This is no easy conclusion, especially when looking at the political dynamics of the single European currency, the development of a common European Security and Defence Policy (ESDP) in the framework of a fast-changing international system, or even the federalist-inspired principles already embedded in the Union's primary law – i.e., dual citizenship, subsidiarity, proportionality and the like – and the reform package agreed in Amsterdam and, more recently, in Nice. So why is it that we dismiss the possibility of a regional superstate? First, because the Union is still composed of sovereign nation-states, whose dominant governing elites are still capable of managing the process of large-scale institution-building and – at least for the time being – treaty-making. Second, because since the 1990s state and regional organisations have found themselves bound in a mutually reinforcing relationship – what has been termed a 'symbiotic arrangement' – thus dismissing any zero-sum conception of the interplay between the collectivity and the constituent segments. Third, because the extension of the scope of integration, that is, the new policy arenas that gradually form part of the Union's policy *acquis*, does not necessarily coincide with the less dramatic extension of its level, namely, the actual way in which the new functional areas are managed – i.e., in a supranational or state-centric manner. Finally, the whole question of a 'democratic deficit' in EU and national political structures has revealed the growing democratic disjunction between the wishes of West European political elites and their respective publics, resulting in an acute legitimacy crisis.

All the above are issues with which this book deals. In particular, Chapter 1 provides a general introduction to the 'disorderly universe' of EU theorising, touching upon some methodological issues concerning the study of the regional process. In doing so it looks at the different theoretical approaches to European integration developed in the formative years of the process and up to the late 1970s. Chapter 2 directs its analytical *foci* to the examination of recent theoretical trends, as well as to the two treaty revisions which took place in the mid-1980s and early 1990s, giving birth to the Single European Act (SEA) and the TEU, respectively. Chapter 3 deals with the process of 'revising Maastricht', by assessing the politics of the Intergovernmental Conference (IGC) 1996/97 and the extent to which the outcome of the revision process – i.e., the Treaty of Amsterdam (AMT) – represents an advancement of the integration process or merely a consolidation of state competences. In a similar manner, Chapter 4 examines the politics of the IGC 2000 – a review process assigned the task of dealing with the so-called 'Amsterdam leftovers' – leading to the signing of the hotly debated and controversial Treaty of Nice (NIT), at least with reference to the way in which final agreement was reached and the growing dissonance between smaller and larger EU states during the final stages of the negotiations. Chapter 5 examines the extent to which change in the international system has produced political outcomes related to post-Cold War European security and defence. This analysis traces the definitional features of the 'new order' in Europe. Common themes involve debates about stability and instability, continuity and change, multipolarity and leadership, co-operation and discord, power capabilities and patterns of behaviour. It also incorporates an analysis of the post-11 September 2001 context, following the horrific terrorist attacks that shocked the international community. Chapter 6 directs analytical attention to the institutions which lie at the heart of the debate about European security and examines their interrelationship. A large part of the discussion deals with European integration from the perspective of foreign and security policy as well as with the issue of the Union's role in the post-Cold War world. Finally, Chapter 7 offers a critical summative account of the Amsterdam and Nice reforms and reflects on the Union's agenda post-Nice and the ongoing debate on the future of Europe.

1

The theoretical setting

Why theorise?

Forty years of theorising European integration have produced a situation where one might expect that little remains to be said. This is not an attempt to escape the intellectual responsibility of developing a greater understanding of the forces that constantly form and reform the regional system. It is only to state that the theory of such a polysemous concept as 'integration' appears to have reached a high plateau in its Western European context. Not that theorists of European integration should start looking for new regional experiments of comparable analytical potential. Rather, the idea is that the new challenges facing the study of regional integration in Europe (concerning both its theoretical boundaries and operational dynamics) do not take place in a theoretical vacuum: they are an extension, if not a refinement, of older ones. The task remains to discover a reliable integration theory as the basis for the future of he European Union (EU) and offer a convincing response to the challenges of large-scale polity formation.

Legitimately, however, one wonders whether Puchala's cynical prophecy that integration theory will amount to 'a rather long but not very prominent footnote in the intellectual history of twentieth century social science' will prove as accurate as the author would have us believe.[1] A first response might be that *theory matters*, whether or not its conceptual findings and qualifications are to be evenly appreciated by scholars and practitioners alike. For familiarity with theory helps to test our analytical tools and appreciate their relevance in real-life situations: According to Taylor: 'Each theory . . . leads to unique insights which are valid starting points for the purpose of comparison and evaluation.'[2] Or, as alternatively put by Keohane and Hoffmann: 'Attempts to avoid theory . . . not only miss interesting questions but rely on a framework for analysis that remains unexamined precisely because it is implicit.'[3] True, a great deal has still to be accomplished. But as long as theory-building is at the top of the academic agenda, there is good ground for thinking that important possibilities are deemed to be explored.

But what might constitute such 'possibilities'? How are they to be explored? What is the appropriate methodological line to that end? To start with, substantive progress in the field requires the transcendence of descriptive approaches about, on the one hand, the form and functions of the integrative process and, on the other, the resolution of fundamental conceptual problems confronting a discipline which has become subject to diverse interpretation. This requires, in Church's words, 'structured ways of understanding changing patterns of inter-action',[4] free from the inherently fragmented boundaries of micro-analysis: to project a macroscopic view of the Union based on systematic conceptual explanation. To that end, 'We need to be aware of the conceptions we use since they determine our perception of things'.[5] This methodological pathway to the study of European integration allows higher access to reality or, alternatively, offers the infrastructure from which 'a hierarchy of realities' might emerge.[6]

The analytical validity of these presuppositions is further justified when trying to establish a link between continuity and change within a system of multi-national shared rule; when attempting to identify the common values of distinct polities and the prospects for the emergence of new ones; when aiming at throwing some additional light on the dialectical and increasingly symbiotic union between a highly interactive society of independent nations and new sources of political authority; or even when engaging in a process of investigating the allegedly 'part-formed' and/or *sui generis* physiognomy of a composite 'union' comprising distinct culturally defined and politically organised units, where the dynamics of intrastate policy-making intermesh with those of large-scale polity-formation with enormous complexity, producing a new type of collective entity characterised by interlocking structures of political authority: a transnational polity, which lacks a single locus of authoritative decision-making.

But even more difficult is to evaluate critically an ever-expanding corpus of literature dealing with such a rich kaleidoscope of relations. And all this, while trying to make sense of a hidden political agenda concerning the future of the European state system itself and the viability of democratic arrangements within and across pre-established borders. Whatever the lessons stemming from the process of bringing together a number of democratic governments under the organisational logic of a larger management system, the work at hand will have made a contribution if it offers an opportunity to communicate the major concerns underlying the evolutionary nature of European governance and its functionally structured subsystems. Such a task represents, above all, a pragmatic challenge, confronting, on the one hand, the transformation of international behaviour and, on the other, the assertion of a new core set of values and principles of what might best be described as 'political co-determination': the forging of new co-operative arrangements for jointly managing the internal and external affairs of the nascent European polity. The perennial question to ask here is whether such a composite polity will strike a balance between its becoming the main locus of collective, binding decision-making for the constituent governments and the dominant focus of popular political identification.

To start with, there is a case to be made why existing theories of integration, even when taken in a complementary manner, fall short of capturing the dominant character of the relationship between the region (Union) and the subunits (states/substate system/citizens). A first attempt to answer this question is that Mitrany's functionalism, Haas' revised version of it (what was conveniently labelled as 'neofunctionalism') and the various federalist-inspired approaches to European integration, ranging from the American model of 'dual federalism' to the 'co-operative federalism' of the German political system, find it equally difficult to reconcile two apparently mutually exclusive principles: the preservation of high levels of segmental autonomy within a nascent, yet politically and constitutionally uncrystallised, system of mutual governance. That is, to capture the dynamics of two complementary objectives: strengthening the political viability of separate constitutional orders through the institutionalisation of joint sovereignty and with it the practice of political co-determination. The intellectual problem associated with such an endeavour is rooted in the different treatments and perceptions of 'general concepts' such as sovereignty, autonomy and interdependence, to mention only a few. Both normative and narrative interpretations of the integrative project, purporting to identify the logic of a distinct form of regionalism and its implications for the participating state and societies, often tend to overemphasise either the importance of the central institutions or, conversely, the role of national governments in setting the integrative agenda and then acting authoritatively upon it. This 'battle of theories' has produced zero-sum notions of transnational bargaining, coupled with unjustified confidence in how the system actually works and towards what it is developing. The 'elephant', however, to recall Puchala's colourful description, is not easy to manipulate in theoretical terms: it often turns into a 'chameleon', adjusting itself to the actual requirements of the day.[7]

Defining the Union

The conceptual problems mentioned above are further compounded by the fact that, on the basis of existing typologies, the Union still remains, almost by definition, an unsolved puzzle: a 'half-way house' between the worlds of 'federal state' and 'federal union of states'.[8] Although the Union is often taken to imply something more than the mere aggregate of its constituent parts, political authority has not yet moved towards a new regional centre. In this view, the Union is neither an international organisation as conventionally understood, nor is it becoming an ordinary state possessing a monopoly of law-making and law-enforcing powers. But equally puzzling remains the nature of its legal structure. For some, the Union rests upon a series of international treaty-based rules, while others prefer to speak of an incipient constitutional system driven by aspirations akin to those involved in traditional state-building. From an integration theory perspective, although the larger polity exceeds the Deutschian notion of a 'pluralistic security-community', it has failed to meet either the sociopsychological conditions of the older functionalist school or those related to the formation of a neofunctionalist-inspired European 'political community'.

Profoundly uncrystallised in its political superstructure, the Union remains an integrative venture whose final destination is yet to become discernible. Attributes such as 'partial polity' and 'part-formed political system' clearly demonstrate the lack of confident scholarly assertion,[9] while rendering the whole enterprise 'a challenge to the continuing separation of international relations from political science'.[10] But even without taking into account the series of neologisms invented over time to capture the distinctive properties that make up its governance structures, the intermeshing of federal principles, confederal structures and consociational processes (see Chapter 2) renders its institutional setting far from comprehensible. Simply to argue, however, that the Union is a polity *sui generis* and should thus be examined in terms of new conceptual paradigms or *ad hoc* theoretical interpretations, or even a combination of both, runs the danger of complying with undisciplined and often ill-founded formulations, while perpetuating its present stance in the grey, 'in-between' area of 'normal interstate' and 'normal intrastate relations': the two extreme poles of an analytical continuum on which political systems are conventionally located.[11] Herein lies perhaps the greatest intellectual challenge facing the contemporary student of European integration: to fill the existing gap between state-centric theory and federalist-driven approaches and develop a more profound understanding of what the Union actually is.[12]

To give a brief account of the complexity surrounding the issue of defining the regional system: Wallace notes that what has now been created by the constituent governments is 'a constitutional system which has some state attributes, but which most – or all – of its constituent governments do not wish to develop into a state, even while expecting it to deliver outcomes which are hard to envisage outside the framework of an entity which we would recognise as a (federal) state'.[13] He adds: 'The retreat from a federal objective for the European Community, while retaining a constitutional agenda which implied the need for a federal state-framework, has left a shadowy area at the center of EC construction.'[14] In this context, Sbragia asserts that it is perhaps more useful to think of the Community as 'an ongoing experiment in fashioning a new structure of governance, one that accepts a great deal of cultural diversity as well as incorporating politics based on the state-society model *and* politics based on relations between governments'.[15] Behind this statement lies the concept of *symbiosis* between the collectivity and the segments, adding credence to those employing co-operative federalism as a model for explaining current integrative arrangements, as well as to Taylor's understanding of the constitutional implications of the symbiotic process for the changing conditions of sovereign statehood in contemporary Europe.[16]

In attempting to explain the origins of political unions, McKay has put the issue thus: 'What we have witnessed in Europe . . . is a movement towards federation which has indigenous rather than external roots, over which there is near unanimity among elites and which has already produced real results in terms of the delineation of power between national and supra-national (or federal) authorities.'[17] Moravcsik, on his part, by developing a theory of 'liberal intergovernmentalism' (see Chapter 2), describes the Union as a regime that makes interstate bargaining more efficient, while enhancing the autonomy of national leaders;[18] a definition close to Puchala's understanding of the larger polity as a multilevel 'system of managed interdependence'.[19] But while Wallace accepts that the Union is 'more than an international regime but less than a fully-developed political system', questioning whether it can be seen as 'a political "community" in the widest sense',[20] Webb takes it to be 'a partially-integrated policy-making system at the regional level',[21] thus making Cameron's 'institutionalised intergovernmentalism' sound like a relatively specific analogy.[22]

Writing on the inappropriateness of classical statist, purely intergovernmental, and traditional federal forms of political organisation, Keohane and Hoffmann have captured the evolving European reality as 'an elaborate set of networks, closely linked in some ways, partially decomposed in others, whose results depend on the political style in the ascendant at the moment'.[23] But perhaps one of the most 'progressive' classifications has been Scharpf's conception of the then European Community (EC) as a 'joint-decision system', where the pathology of public policy-making is conditioned by a 'systemic tendency towards sub-optimal substantive solutions', exemplifying the notion of a 'joint-decision trap' or *politikverflechtungfalle*.[24] Embracing Wallace's dictum that the Community system is 'stuck between sovereignty and integration', while recognising that the effectiveness and implementation of common policies are greatly influenced by what Taylor had earlier called the 'interdependence trap', Scharpf argues that Europe 'seems to have become just that "middle ground between co-operation among nations and the breaking of a new one" which Stanley Hoffmann thought impossible'.[25] Although this statement contradicts the view that progress towards the formation of a European demos – conceived in civic rather than ethnocultural terms – should not be seen as a prelude to the emergence of a larger 'political nation', it adds something to the current debate. Other terms to be found in the *acquis académique* as means of conceptualising the larger entity include 'proto-federation', 'confederance', 'concordance system', 'quasi-state', '*Staatenverbund*', 'consortio', 'condominio', 'regulatory state', 'regional regime', 'mixed commonwealth', 'managed *Gesellschaft*', 'quasi-state', 'sympolity', 'federated republic', 'market polity', 'international state', 'confederal consociation', 'multilevel governance' and so on. If anything, the above definitional accounts suggest that the question of what the Union 'actually' is has yet to be sorted out.

Given the various conceptual and analytical difficulties in reaching an authoritative statement on the political physiognomy of the present-day Union, we suggest that, instead of placing undue emphasis on the peculiarities of its constitutive properties, it is perhaps more profitable to examine those aspects of its internal political organisation which can be paralleled, with a greater or lesser degree of accuracy, with already familiar forms of polity and/or models of governance. The underlying premise here is that a new theoretical thesis will not only have to take into account pre-existing classifications, but will also have to use them constructively so as to substantiate its findings both theoretically and empirically. As Groom has observed: 'There must be acknowledgment of the old Europe, but also a realisation that in building a new one, there are many original aspects that do not fit easily into the customary conceptual frameworks of integration theory.'[26]

The general thesis put forward in this book is that we are currently witnessing the reversal of the Mitranian logic of international integration: instead of 'form follows function',[27] it is increasingly the case that the structural properties of the larger management system dictate the pace and range of joint integrative schemes. Thus an additional concern has become manifest: the extension of the 'scope' (range) and 'level' (depth) of European integration do not necessarily coincide. Since the coming into force of the SEA in February 1987 and the TEU in November 1993, there is evidence to suggest that both the functional scope (new policy arenas) and territorial scale (new members) of the integrative process may well be extended, if not at the expense of the level of integration (ways of management), without either altering the locus of sovereignty or having any significant impact on the way in which the central institutions exercise political authority. The extension of QMV by these treaty revisions, as well as by the AMT in May 1999 and the more recent Treaty of Nice (signed in February 2001), on largely non-conflict-prone areas, helps to illustrate this point. But let us now turn to the way in which this ever-demanding exercise of EU theory-building has evolved over time.

Theorising integration

As already suggested, there are various ways of examining an inherently interdisciplinary object of study; arguably, as many as the constitutive bodies of theory which allegedly compose it. The process of European integration, revolving around the three-pillar structure of the Union – a structure which managed to survive any ambition to communitarise in any substantive terms its two intergovernmental components at the June 1997 and December 2000 Amsterdam and Nice Summits, respectively – is a good case in point. For since the early days of the process, students of European integration have applied a variety of methods and approaches in order to develop a more profound understanding of what the European 'body politic' looked like at the many different stages of its political and, in the wider sense of the term, constitutional, evolution. And yet, despite the many promising theoretical departures over the years, arguably only a few concrete theoretical arrivals have been achieved.

Different traditions of international relations theory, ranging from pluralist paradigms of interstate behaviour to (neo)realist interpretations of state-centric preferences and power, coupled with a plethora of approaches flowing from the domain of comparative politics 'proper' – in turn, seeking to link the domestic and international arenas of European governance – seem to have exhausted the analytical spectrum within which the study of European integration can bear fruits. More recently, however, a preference has emerged for the latter analytical pathway (the term 'comparativists' capturing this scholarly trend), although intergovernmentalism, or even modified schemes of co-operative interstate behaviour (at both treaty-formation and daily policy-making levels), have by and large survived the tides of supranationalism and institutional centralisation.

Doubtless, the initial supranationalist schemes were of considerable integrative potential, dominating the domestic policy arena of the Community during the formative years of the regional process. This was a period when Hallstein's Presidency of the newly founded Commission aimed at projecting a new structure of managing the affairs of the Community's nascent regime. Later, however, it was followed by a more balanced relationship between the Community's supranational/expansionist ambitions and intergovernmental realities. This was the beginning of what has been termed, after the 1966 Luxembourg Accords, the 'Second Europe': a transition stage leading to the 1969 Hague Summit, in turn hailed as the first significant *relance* of integration. The third integrative stage came about only a few years later, with the formal institutionalisation of the European Council at the 1974 Paris Summit. This top political institution was expected to provide the leadership needed to move the Community towards higher levels of integration, acting at the same time as a protective mechanism for sensitive (and often non-negotiable) national interests. Such a development signalled the inception of what was later to be termed as the 'Third Europe': a qualitatively different phase from the pre-1974 one, this time characterised by a more favourable version of intergovernmentalism as a method of promoting integration. The end result of this stage – itself a largely 'compromised structure' of the previous two – projected a symbiotic arrangement between national and European political (and even polity) dynamics.

The many different phases of European integration and the subsequent theoretical approaches devoted to their explanation point to the assumption that the formation of a European polity, as distinct from the making of a new regional superstate (a superordinate form of government beyond the nation-state), or for that matter from the construction of a purely confederal structure (a loosely institutionalised society of sovereign states), resembles an asymmetrical and often analytically incongruent synthesis of academic (sub)disciplines. Yet the rationale of studying the integrative phenomenon from the perspective of various, and often contending, schools of thought seems to be as relevant today as it was during the formative debate between functionalists and federalists (although this was a far less complicated one). But how are we to appreciate the enormous diversity embedded in the various theoretical approaches to the study of European integration in general, and its multifarious arenas of collective policy- and decision-making in particular? A first answer is to look at each particular theory of integration separately, placing at the same time its conceptual findings and analytical insights in a wider comparative context. Here, undoubt-edly, functionalism emerges as an appropriate point of departure.

Core theories of integration

Functionalism

In general terms, functionalism purports to explain why collective action in spe-cific, functionally linked areas of co-operation is a more attractive option than unilateral state action: group involvement in peaceful problem-solving schemes, supported by the necessary technical expertise, emanates as a real option. Nationalism and international anarchy are treated as the sources of the frag-mentation of the world community into rival groups, obstructing the creation of a 'working peace system'. International community-building is the function-alist remedy to these problems, centred on the resolution of basic welfare needs which transcend territorial considerations. Mitrany's understanding of 'the integrative dynamic', Taylor notes, 'is the learning process of citizens who are gradually drawn into the co-operative ethos created by functionally specific international institutions devoted to the satisfaction of real welfare needs'.[28]

This organic process is furthered by what may be described as 'management committee government', reflecting Mitrany's distrust of traditional assembly controls over complex policy-making. Guided by the quest to watch closely for the 'relation of things', Mitrany argued the case for replacing old-style, non-spe-cialist assemblies with new forms of representation and ways of obtaining public control, such as 'functional' assemblies composed of experts whose technical knowledge would guarantee greater and better efficiency in supervising govern-mental actions. In *The Functional Theory of Politics*, he reiterates that 'no one would share in power who did not share in responsibility' and that 'the func-tional structure could be made a union of peoples . . . directly concerned in any specific function, by giving them functional representation'.[29] Mitrany's under-lying rationale was that 'in acquiring formal representative status, [pressure groups] also assume a corresponding democratic responsibility'.[30] No doubt, however, this form of democracy, labelled by Mitrany himself as 'working democracy' (as opposed to 'voting democracy') is seen by those who perceive the institution of Parliament as the focal point of accountability as a hindrance to established notions of representative and responsible government.

The functionalist conception of 'union' is part of an evolutionary process of achieving functionally specific objectives, and not of a deterministic situation leading, immediately or necessarily, towards a federal state or even a state-like entity. Like other gradualist theories, the end product of the integration process is left deliberately vague (although some form of larger constitutional frame-work is not dismissed outright). One reason for this is that, according to Mitrany, 'form follows function' in that the actual needs of the integrative system will determine its structural properties. Although it would be false to assume that functionalist theory perceives federalism as an uncontrolled homogenising force eroding national diversity and/or identity, it maintains that it is in the interests of the integration process itself to proceed in an incremental, piecemeal fashion. Hence the idea of a modest 'step-by-step' approach as opposed to a federalist-inspired 'head-on' approach to European unity for fear that a federal surrender of sovereignty would be too big a sacrifice for national governments on the altar of their unification.

The key concept of the functionalist method is identified in the perception of a common interest among the various actors involved in the integration process, as well as a propensity to non-coercive means of problem-solving. This was judged to be vitally important for the European region to develop the necessary institutional machinery to produce common policies and decisions, not least due to its recent turbulent history. Thus the pursuit of common tasks was linked from the outset to the creation of common institutions possessing a responsibility of their own, albeit limited in scope. As Kitzinger has pointed out, the main difference between functionalists and federalists was that, whereas the former were preoccupied with defining the 'general interest' first, and then finding common answers to common problems, the latter sought joint action as a means for obtaining more efficient central institutions.[31] As a result, the functionalists sought 'to set up only that minimum of political institutions that was indispensable in order to direct the common action that was most urgently required'.[32] Supranationalism, as applied in a specific regional context producing a larger-scale territorial authority, is perceived as a potential source of replicating nationalist sentiments at a level beyond the nation-state.

Being confined to technical and economic areas, functional integration does not postulate the creation of a new sovereign power at a higher level. Instead, by trying to eschew politics, in terms of depoliticising communal issues rather than being inherently apolitical itself, it presents no immediate challenge to the sovereignty of states, which continue to survive as identifiable entities.[33] As Taylor states: 'the functionalist approach, indeed, allows the view that there is no point at which the state would *necessarily* lose its sovereignty, in the sense that power would now need to be finally transferred, or that the state would lose its legal right to act, if it so wished, against the wishes of the functional agency'.[34] In particular, the 'functional imperative', as the basic law governing the evolution of the integration process, rejected the inevitability of constitutional requirements and fixed divisions of political authority, instead focusing on problems which, although they cannot really be ignored, cannot be solved separately by each government acting alone. This has been termed as the 'unitary trap'.[35]

There seems to be a globalising, cumulative effect in the functionalist line of argument: once problems are recognised as common (or at least not essentially differentiated by the relevant community of actors), and solutions to these problems may arise from collective rational thinking, then there is a tendency to expand such co-operative behaviour to other relevant spheres of action. Does Mitrany's logic, however, necessarily avoid being trapped in the domain of conventional politics, where interests and preferences are shaped by traditional party political discourse and electoral considerations? The answer is that, despite certain elements of 'technical self-determination' embedded in the functionalist method, it does not always evade parameters of this kind. But there is another crucial point to be made about the political aspects of the functionalist logic, namely that functionalism is about the application of carefully examined, but not necessarily politically structured, strategies for transcending (national) territorial boundaries in tackling issues of a technical nature. Institution-building, in this regard, becomes conditional upon the (functionally determined) needs of the integrative system itself, rather than the preferred lines of action to be taken by national governments according to territorial interests.

However, it is not always easy to distinguish between 'non-territorial' and 'territorial' politics in the context of the Union's governance system, especially when a variety of actors pursues different, albeit not necessarily antithetical, interests and are motivated by different cultural traditions. In principle, however, not 'apolitical', but 'aterritorial', is a more appropriate term to describe the internal logic of functional arrangements. Functionalism in the Mitranian tradition is above all a theory of international society based on the principle of technical self-determination, reliance upon non-coercive means of international community-building, and an inherent mistrust of constitutional prescriptions of power-sharing. Mitrany's main concern was how to replace territorially defined structures of decision-making with international functional agencies, leading towards a 'working international system'.

Federalism

Federalism as an integration theory is much more relevant to the study of European integration than is often admitted. This is mainly owing to its increased concern about the dialectics of power-sharing in a compound political setting; its emphasis on in-built democratic arrangements linking different levels of governmental authority; its often flexible interpretation of the sovereignty principle; its focus on constitutional issues touching upon sensitive areas of individual and collective liberties, legislative representation and the allocation of competences; and its deeper concern about how to organise in a mutually reinforcing way the concurrent demands for 'unity in diversity'. Federalism, however, does not emanate from a single corpus of theory – a grand design, that is, which can be transplanted from one federal system to another without losing its internal (or systemic) relevance and cohesion. Rather, there can be different sets of principles and structures composing a federal polity. These, however, need to be seen in a wider symbiotic perspective: a creative co-existence of distinct but 'constitutive' units. Once one recognises these analytical constraints, it is possible to turn to the application of the various federalist designs to European integration and appreciate the diversity of their logic.

In general terms, federalism aims to reconcile the parallel demands for greater political union (but not necessarily unity) of the whole and adequate constitutional guarantees for the parts; namely, 'unity without uniformity and diversity without anarchy'.[36] Thus the appropriateness of federal arrangements 'would appear to lie in those instances where the existence and vigour of the forces that press both for wider unity and for autonomous regional diversity are relatively balanced'.[37] The striking of such a delicate balance emerges as the strongest catalyst for achieving overall 'federal cohesion' – itself a precondition for federations to survive the test of time. In Forsyth's words: '[Federal structures] establish a union but they simultaneously guarantee autonomy, and they fix or settle ratio or balance between the two.'[38] Or, alternatively: '[Federalism] is based on the existence of regional differences and recognises the claims of the component areas to perpetuate their individual characters.'[39] Here, democratic representation becomes a crucial factor for the political viability of federal units, highlighting the importance of accommodating territorial and non-territorial claims in nascent federal structures based on systems of common management such as the polity that is currently emerging in Europe.

Moreover, the representation of the people, either as a whole (when taken as a single entity) or as parts (when taken as a plurality of entities) becomes the prior object of the federation.[40] 'What is distinctive about federations', King notes, 'is not that "the people" are viewed as sovereign, but that the expression of this sovereignty is tied to the existence and entrenchment of regional, territorial entities'.[41] In fact, 'one of the characteristics of federalism that flows from its popular base is the reduction of the question of political sovereignty to an incidental one', with the federal principle representing 'an alternative to (and a radical attack upon) the modern idea of sovereignty'.[42] Consequently, there are two possible, but not antithetical, ways of perceiving 'the people': as united and as diverse, a duality which 'for the life of the federation, is implicitly inexpungible'.[43] In both equations, however, it is the federal demos as a whole, rather than primarily the dominant political elites representing the interests of each constituent unit, which is to be served by the central arrangements.

Although federations encompass a considerable range of purposes, identities, cultural traditions, organisational characteristics and power-sharing arrangements, as well as different means of protecting the constitution,[44] democratic representation of all participating communities emerges as a common defining property. The issue here is not so much about creating direct links between different levels of government but rather about establishing concrete and accessible avenues of communication between the demos and the central institutions. In speaking of such 'levels', one might assume that they are sharply separated from each other, 'like boxes piled on top of one another'.[45] In reality, however, these different levels are never thus sharply divided. But if one considers that in most federal systems the central authorities are free to exercise considerable power over the federal demos, it is easy to explain why these direct links are central to the democratic legitimacy of the federal polity.

Unlike a unitary state model, the degree of democratic participation in a federal system is linked to the extent to which legislative autonomy in the form of 'reserved powers' (powers not delegated to the federal level) has been con-ferred on each participating collectivity by the Constitution. Thus public par-ticipation in the affairs of the federation is intrinsically woven into the degree of autonomous action granted to each level of government in which the demos exercises its sovereign rights. Further, the extent to which democratic diversity, or 'a co-ordinated expression of it',[46] can be maintained without endangering the political cohesion of the federation is conditioned by the ability of the central arrangements to produce viable constitutional equilibria. Indeed, the intersec-tion between federalism and democracy passes through the capacity of the com-pound polity to generate a common commitment to federal unity, while preserving the integrity of the constituent units. This implies that the idea of federation emerges as a living, pluralist and organic political order which 'builds itself from the ground upwards'.[47] Hence federalism as a multilevel political arrangement is based on a constitutional system of delegated, reserved and/or shared powers between relatively autonomous, yet interrelated, structures of government whose multiple interactions aim to serve the sovereign will of the federal demos.[48]

With the postwar circumstances in Western Europe corresponding, in Bowie's words, 'to those which often in the past have led nations to undertake the initial steps towards federation', the federal solution emerged as an inspir-ing remedy for Europe's multiple organisational problems.[49] At the same time, the interposition of a central authority beyond pre-existing boundaries acquired, mainly thanks to Italian federalist thinking, the status of a desirable political ideology. Although the ideal of a united Europe predated the specific postwar attempts, what makes them unique is that 'the unity concept moved into the foreground of popular thinking with both an emotional and practical appeal'.[50] In a continent that was deeply shocked with the suicidal effects of nationalism, the federal impulse to postwar European unity rose as an attrac-tive alternative to a challenge that, in Bowie's words, 'went to the very founda-tions of social existence'.[51]

Far from conceiving the nation-state as an *a priori* fact of existence, the federalists regarded it as a 'historic accident' and proposed its transcendence by a process of 'rational federal development'.[52] As a Draft Declaration by the Euro-pean Resistance Movement in July 1944 put it: 'Federal Union alone can ensure the principles of liberty and democracy in the continent of Europe.'[53] Following this somewhat teleological line of thinking, any federal surrender of sovereignty seemed better than allowing the European state system to consolidate itself once more, especially after its 'great moral and material bankruptcy'.[54] Reflecting upon the 1944 Ventotene Manifesto, Bosco has observed: 'The real cause of international anarchy was seen as "the absolute sovereignty of national States", which is the source of power-politics in the international sphere and of totali-tarianism in the national one.'[55] Similarly, Spinelli has argued that the nation-state had become 'a compass which had ceased to give any bearings'.[56] These statements provided the moral justification of early federalist designs. The choice of European nations was one between federalism and anarchy, rather than between the former and some measure of interstate co-operation.

The federalists also argued their case by stressing the inability of states to provide new means of popular participation, and that an unprecedented 'legitimacy crisis' had shaken their once powerful structures: a deep-rooted structural crisis which prompted them to look above the nation-state itself as a means of resolving its acute legitimation problems. Underlying these criticisms is a belief that 'new loyalties will arise in direct conflict with the nation-state',[57] opening up much wider horizons than those afforded by the latter. This is exactly what European federalists had in mind: that these multiple pressures on the nation-state would lead to the recognition that new democratic arrangements would have to be devised so as to meet the challenges of the post-1945 era. Spinelli, for instance, had strongly opposed the idea proposed by national governments of a 'partial' European union without first creating a democratic infrastructure upon which common institutions would be based. In this sense, federalism provided the means not only to overcome the structural crisis of the nation-state itself, or even 'to transform the very essence of national statehood into a larger loyalty going beyond its territorial affinities',[58] but also a powerful stimulus to the extension of the democratic process.

Whatever the title ascribed to the envisaged polity, it was widely recognised that it would have to strike a balance between interdependence and autonomy, democracy and efficiency and, above all, unity and diversity. To convince the European peoples of the merits of federalism as a means of safeguarding their cultural and political traditions, the federalists stressed the representative character of the central institutions. It was maintained that the latter should be left free to exercise the political authority conferred on them by a written constitution in direct relation to the European public without having to rely upon the convergence of short-term national interests for the formulation of common policies. Herein lies federalism's greatest contribution to the cause of European unity: in the 'inclusive' political community, power and responsibility should be seen as being mutually supportive, rather than as a competitive tussle for political authority between the collectivity and the segments.

Writing on the strategic aims of the Federalist Movement, Levi refers to 'the objective of changing the character of exclusive communities which nation-states have and unifying them in a federal community thus transforming them into member states of the European Federation, in such a way that they can coexist peacefully though maintaining their autonomy'.[59] It was believed that federalism would encourage democratic diversity by establishing a system of co-ordinate but independent spheres of authority based on a division of power among state and federal agents. According to this scheme, the component legislatures would hold their executives accountable to their respective publics, while a European legislature would act as a potential barrier against the danger of central executive dominance. Resting upon a 'firm constitutional structure', the main powers of the federation were to lie in the sphere of defence, foreign affairs, commerce across state lines, international exchange, communication and, in Pinder's words, 'enough tax to sustain the necessary expenditure'.[60] On the whole, the envisaged pattern of federal–state relations was closer to the dualistic model of classical federalism, requiring a constitutional separation of powers between state and central authorities, rather than to a system of 'shared rule' based on concurrent competences, which were seen at the time as a potential source of internal disputes.

It soon became evident, however, that if the federal project was to be crowned with success it would have to overcome national governmental resistance to an immediate relinquishing of state sovereignty to a federal polity. The solution to this problem came from Spinelli, proposing a strategy based on a campaign of public persuasion for the drafting of a federal constitution. This task was to be carried out by a directly elected European Constituent Assembly.[61] The justification of Spinelli's 'constituent method' lay in the belief that such an assembly was the only acceptable body to transform the possibility of popular participation in the affairs of the federation into political reality. The constitution was to be based on a declaration of fundamental rights, democratic institutions and the separation of powers: it was believed that a balanced structure of national and federal competences based on the principle of dual federalism would preserve national identity and diversity in a way compatible with the democratic ethos. Thus it was agreed that the federation should have limited but *real* powers, with the remaining spheres of competence resting on state jurisdiction. In short, the gist of the federalist thesis was that 'federalism is the only international democratic bond which can create a reign of law among nations', as well as the only possible means for enlarging 'the sphere of democratic government from the ambit of the state to that of a group of states'.[62] As most federalists have acknowledged, however, the difficulty of the task lay not so much in convincing the European peoples of the need for a federation, but in convincing them that they, rather than their national governments, must create it. This brings us to the very limitations of European constitution-making, to which we now turn.

The first real test for the idea of creating a federal Europe came with the 1948 Hague Congress. Yet its end product, in the form of the Council of Europe, did not live up to federalist expectations. Rather, it represented 'a triumph of the unionists'.[63] As the Federal Movement was losing whatever popular appeal it initially displayed, an alternative method of institutional development started to consolidate its strength: Monnet's 'functional federalism'. Being functionalist in conception but federalist in prospect, this approach represented a new, albeit modest, integration philosophy. Convinced that European unification was not interested in 'end situations' as in evolutionary processes, the functionalists criticised the federal alternative for being totally impractical and idealistic, 'offering', in Harrison's words, 'merely the prospect of the unattainable'.[64] Instead, by recognising that integration had nothing to do with formal constitutional engineering, the functionalists stressed the point that Europe could not be unified 'by a stroke of the constitutional lawyer's pen'.[65] They criticised the federalists as advocates of an immediate objective which was largely overtaken by a naive sentimentalism, deceiving themselves with the illusion of radical political change. Likewise, Spinelli's pathway to unification was viewed as over-ambitious and legalistic, resting on the fallacious assumption that the termination of the war had also signalled the 'withering away of the nation state'. In general, the federal projects were believed to be consciously undermining the necessary gradualness of integration in order to achieve a rigid constitutional settlement, thus losing sight of the dynamics of 'functional incrementalism' as its major characteristic.

The early school of European federalism, by relying heavily on the American federal experience, seemed to have undermined the *sui generis* character of postwar European integration. In their unrestrained passion for a united Europe, Beloff asserts, federalists were misguided in looking to the US pattern for a promising analogy.[66] In Albertini's words, 'as a new form of the modern state, federalism is an American product. But the United States of America had not to overcome historically constituted nations to constitute itself.'[67] In contrast, the federal conception of Europe failed to recognise that such a vision was not the primary goal for a sufficient number of Europeans. Likewise, its constitutive principles did not acquire sufficient persuasive power to win the confidence of national governments. But it would be unjust not to reiterate the commitment of European federalists towards a democratic process of union, and their opposition to an essentially utilitarian form of interest convergence as a precondition for any substantive public loyalty transfers. For they unequivocally maintained that parliamentary democracy was too closely related to Europe's political culture to be denied beyond the state level. Finally, it was they who first stressed the importance of linking the idea of a European Constitution with the legitimation of the larger polity based on a parliamentary (bicameral) system of government.

Confederalism

Just as a federal state differs essentially from a unitary one, so does a confederation from a federation. Whereas the latter is based on a constitutive act which creates a higher, superordinate legal order, a confederation is based on a *foedus* or treaty among sovereign states. It thus represents a 'contractual union of states' in which the participants voluntarily decide to band together by way of 'mutual agreement' in order to transform their existing patterns of relations into something akin, yet not identical, to the internal relations of one state.[68]

Sharma and Choudhry have described the distinction between these models thus: 'a confederation is a loose union over confederating independent states, whereas a federation is a union deriving its authority from the citizens of the union'; 'a confederation is the outcome of an agreement or treaty made generally for a specific period . . . whereas a federation is the result of a true constitution supreme over all other instruments from which both [levels of] government[s] ... derive their respective powers'; 'in a confederation, the powers of the common body or authority are narrow and extremely limited, whereas in a federation the powers of the general government are wider, largely exclusive, and capable of being exercised through its own agencies'; 'in a confederation, the units are free to dissociate themselves from the union, whereas in a federation the units are united with the general government on a co-operative basis'; 'in a confederation the units retain their sovereignty, whereas in a federation the authority of government is shared by them with the general government'; and 'in a confederation the general government is subordinate to the regional governments, whereas in a federation the general government co-exists with the regional governments and is independent from them.'[69]

From a different perspective, in the case of the confederation, a plurality of previously independent states gives way to a 'treaty-constituted political body'[70] in which 'the condition of "the last say"'[71] rests with the partners to it, rather than with an independent authoritative entity having a monopoly of legislative and coercive powers. Hence Forsyth views confederation as being 'far more directly a contractual creature than the normal state', manifesting itself not as 'the constituted unity of one *people* or *nation*, but a unity constituted by *states*'.[72] He explains: 'the constitution of a confederation is not, by definition, the unilateral act of *one* people . . . considered as a homogeneous entity . . . a confederation is formed precisely because a nation or people in this sense is not deemed to exist, because the sense of identity and thus of trust between the citizens of each member state does not run to that depth.'[73]

In practice, a confederation takes the form of a 'half-way house' between 'normal interstate' and 'normal intrastate relations', with the constituent units reserving the right of self-determination: 'it is a union that falls short of a complete fusion or incorporation in which one or all the members lose their identity as states.'[74] Or, as defined by Elazar: 'Several pre-existing polities joined together to form a common government for strictly limited purposes . . . that remains dependent upon its constituent polities in critical ways and must work through them.'[75] This type of union, similarly to a 'mutual pact' among self-determining bodies politic, signifies a 'joint agreement to be independent'.[76] Forsyth explains: 'The contract which lies at its base is not a contract to abide by the will of the majority regarding the government to which all shall be subordinate, but simply a contract between equals to act henceforth as one.'[77] This is not to imply that a confederation possesses merely a 'legal' personality of the type of 'conventional' international organisations. Rather, it is capable of developing a 'real' personality of its own: 'an original capacity to act akin to that possessed by the states themselves.'[78] The underlying characteristic of a confederation as 'a system of governments' is that it provides the component parts with a variety of opportunities to achieve mutually advantageous co-operation without resigning their individual sovereignty, by focusing on intergovernmental relationships between a number of legally and politically equal centres of authority, rather than between them and a single federal government.

According to the German political theorist, von Treitschke: 'A Confederation of States . . . is recognised by international law as an association of sovereign States, who have bound themselves together, without resigning their independence, to further certain common goals . . . Consequently the members of a Confederation exercise their natural *liberum veto*.'[79] In other words, although confederations may have a considerable freedom in determining their internal organisational structures, 'they cannot as organisations make general rules or measures which are directly binding upon the states that create them'.[80] Forsyth makes the point well: 'Thus the individual states must give their express assent, or at the very least withhold their express dissent during a fixed period, before a convention, treaty, or any kind of general resolution made within or by an interstate organisation becomes binding upon them.'[81] All in all, confederations do not fundamentally challenge, at least in constitutional terms, the legal capacity of the constituent units to determine the fate of their own polities. In this context, the idea of a 'condominium of powers' in which the management of certain policy areas is voluntarily put into a limited but joint pool of sovereignty does not conflict with the above description.[82]

Moreover, Forsyth argues that 'the permanence accorded to a confederation is more than merely the standing "disposability" of the institutions of the typical international organisation'.[83] Instead, 'it is a profound locking together of states themselves as regards the joint exercise of fundamental powers', driven by a common determination to prevent hegemony and, hence, a monopoly of power.[84] Accordingly, confederation can also be seen as a *process* by which a group of separate states commit themselves by a treaty of union to mutually beneficial interaction which may well extend beyond the traditional patterns of international co-operation. And since it aims to reconcile the concurrent demands for preserving the sovereignty of the parts, and with it the integrity of their populations, and for maintaining high levels of co-ordination among them, this model is indeed capable of embracing a wide range of institutional possibilities. Thus it can be conceived, in line with Friedrich's dynamic model, as a 'federation-to-be',[85] or even taken to denote, according to Forsyth's theory, a 'genuine federal body', albeit of a looser kind, insofar as the constituent units become parts of a new whole.[86] In short, irrespective of whether the analytical dichotomy between the two forms of polity springs, as Friedrich believes, from 'the quintessence of the static and formalistic approach',[87] what seems to be certain is that the concept of confederation 'remains a useful part of the federal vocabulary'.[88]

The literature on confederation has impressed upon a number of scholars over the years in their attempt to classify the defining properties of the Union. The confederal character of the system has been pointed out by a number of scholars, summarised by Keohane and Hoffmann thus: 'If any traditional model were to be applied, it would be that of a confederation . . . since the central institutions are (a) largely intergovernmental, (b) more concerned with establishing a common framework than with networks of detailed regulations, and (c) apparently willing to tolerate a vast amount of national diversity.'[89] Similar descriptions of the Community are to be found, *inter alia*, in the subtitle of an article written by Brewin – 'A Union of States without Unity of Government'; in Church's prototypal term 'confederence' as a means of capturing its intrinsic confederal properties; and in Elazar's characterisation of the Community as a 'new-style confederation of old states'.[90]

The justification of the confederal approach to the study of European integration is that the evolution of the Community system has been shaped by arduous intergovernmental bargains among sovereign states, as well as by an attempt to accommodate their varying preferences in a mutually acceptable way, that is, without threatening what they have often perceived as their vital national interests. In this context, the idea that the larger entity is based on an international treaty, rather than a European Constitution, is also supportive of its essentially confederal character. What this view often fails to take into account, however, is the legal dynamics of integration and the political activism of the European Court of Justice (ECJ) in the process of 'constitutionalising' the treaties. Yet it is doubtful whether subsequent amendments to the founding treaties have brought about a higher constitutional order, at least when measured against the constitutional properties of the member nation-states. Rather, it seems that the larger political unit rests upon the separate constitutional orders of its component parts which, by virtue of their sovereign nature, continue to act as 'Masters of the Treaties' (*Herren der Verträge*). The mere fact that formal treaty change requires the unanimous consent of the member state governments underlines this point.

At the decision-making level, there is a case to be made against the confederal approach in so far as majority rule applies in the Council of Ministers. Yet, clear as it may be that states may well be outvoted in a number of policy areas, there is a tendency to treat the dissenting states with extreme caution when national interests are at stake. Hence the contention that more often than not it is the threat of invoking the right to veto, in accordance with the provisions of the Luxembourg Accords, that has a crucial impact in the negotiating process, resulting in most cases in 'package deals' of an accommodative nature. Another point which *prima facie* seems to contradict the confederal approach is that the European Parliament (EP) is the only directly elected international Parliament, possessing limited but effective co-legislative powers. Again, true as it may be that the EP acts as a source of the Union's democratic legitimacy, it remains far from being regarded as a Parliament in the conventional sense, since it still lacks the power to initiate legislation, to have a prominent role in setting the Union's legislative agenda, to hold collectively into account the Union's main legislative body (the Council) for its actions or inaction, to elect a single European Government, to hold its elections under a uniform electoral procedure, and so on. More importantly, there is evidence to suggest that the Union is characterised by a fragmented citizen body rather than a politically self-conscious European demos, capable of directing its democratic claims to, and via, the central institutions. This is a point that needs to be made in relation to the democratic properties of federal polities where a composite demos exists and forms the 'constitutive power' of the federation.

Transactionalism

The approach developed by Deutsch in his examination of the North Atlantic Area represented a shift in emphasis from the early theoretical endeavours of functionalists and federalists to a more empirically oriented framework of analysis. This was a systematic attempt to capture the relationship between international integration (largely seen as a process of community-formation) and social communication (changes in patterns of transactions), by focusing on the conditions which may bring about a large-scale 'sociopsychological community'. Deutsch defined integration as 'the attainment of a "sense of community" and of institutions and practices strong enough and widespread enough to assure, for a "long time", dependable expectations of "peaceful change" among its population'.[91] That could be achieved through processes of mutual transactions, cultural flows and social learning. Prominent in his argument was the idea of peaceful problem-solving through the intensification of avenues of communication among nations. This he called a 'security community': a framework of social interactions where war would eventually become in the relevant region both unthinkable and impractical. Deutsch's notion of 'security community' could be either 'pluralistic' or 'amalgamated', although he never really implied that there was an automatic forward linkage between these two different types of organisation.

Deutsch was not particularly concerned with the institutional configuration that the integration process would bring about. Nor was he especially interested in the allocation of authoritative power among different levels of decision-making. His research focused on the sociopsychological aspects of community-formation, which was seen as a result of increased and 'mutually responsive' transactions among its constituent parts. But it would be unfair to the logic of his approach to present the developments in transactions solely as an indicator of community-building. Taylor explains: 'It is also important to point out that it is the range and quality of changes in transactions that constitutes an indicator of community: too frequently Deutsch's ideas are criticised on the mistaken assumption that he sees *particular* transactions as *equivalent* to developing community.'[92] The end product of integration would take the form of an identifiable community of citizens – that is, a people – through a process of social learning. Although such an outcome would take a long time to materialise, in fact several generations as Deutsch suggested, what is important is that the 'uniting parts' would start to develop 'a sense of community' based on the power of common identities, shared values and belief systems, and a common perception of their destiny, and that certain norms and habits of societal interaction would emerge from the range and intensity of informal contacts. Community feelings, therefore, were seen as the result, rather than the cause, of closer links among the participating units.

The distinction made by Deutsch between a 'pluralistic' and 'amalgamated' security community warrants closer attention. The former was expected to produce a 'sense of security' among the relevant populations, whereby the resolution of conflicts through violent means would be replaced by mutually acceptable methods for their peaceful settlement. It was the particular attitudes of the actors involved that would create a certain culture of co-operation which, through the forging of further and closer communicative links among them, would make resort to war highly unlikely. On the other hand, Deutsch's idea of an 'amalgamated' security community was a more advanced form of political community, closer to the type of *Gemeinschaft* (or community) depicted by Tönnies in the late nineteenth century.[93]

In this type of association, as opposed to the more 'instrumental' notion of *Gesellschaft* (or society), one may perceive the embryo of a genuinely 'constitutive' community: 'a community that would constitute the very identity of the individuals.'[94] *Gemeinschaft* is more suitable for the prospering of mutually responsive relations since the individuals forming it have developed to a sufficient degree a 'sense of community', also known as 'community spirit' or 'community of attachment', strong enough to overcome, and even transcend, any potentially divisive issues which may arise as integration proceeds. Equally, where the 'community spirit' is less profound, integration will find it more difficult to cope with internal disputes. In this sense, the '*Gemeinschaft* factor' appears as one of integration's indispensable 'common spheres'.

Although no actual society or institution will ever conform completely to Tönnies' theoretical selections,[95] since they are conceptual entities representing two ideal types of social organisation, Deutsch was aware of the fact that a sociopsychological community would have to be based on 'a sense among the individuals forming it of belonging together, of having common loyalties and values, of kinship', so that the tasks performed within its structures would stem from 'a feeling of contributing something worthwhile to the good of the whole'.[96] Thus a *Gemeinschaft* is something qualitatively distinct and higher than the numerical sum of the private well-being of its members. In this type of community, people associate themselves together because they think of their relationship as valuable in the dual sense of being important both as ends *in* and *of* themselves. It is perceived as an internal, living and organic 'collective entity' – organic in terms of being considered and conceived of in relation to its parts[97] – whose 'norms of order' are based upon 'concord', as opposed to a *Gesellschaft* which rests on a contractual arrangement or 'convention'.

Resting upon relationships of mutual affirmation of a *federative* kind, the members of a *Gemeinschaft* gradually develop strong feelings of 'togetherness', 'we-ness' or even 'oneness', to the eventual framing of a collective consciousness. Accordingly, these individuals are bound together in symbiotic – that is, mutually reinforcing – relationships, thinking of their collective existence as dominating their respective individualism, while perceiving their close association as a means of improving their domestic conditions of living. In short, an entity which is formed through this positive type of relationship points to 'a lasting and genuine form of living together', as opposed to its counterpart form of 'human *Gesellschaft*', which is considered as a mere co-existence of people independently of each other.[98] Therefore, whereas the 'common sphere' of a *Gesellschaft* rests on the concept of contract, with its 'secret' lying in 'a rational coming together of ends that remain individual',[99] that of a *Gemeinschaft* rests on the concept of 'one people', with its 'secret' lying in an 'internally oriented relationship' developed among its members, rather than in a mechanical or artificial fusion of separate, private wills. Also, in *Gemeinschaft*-like relationships the ensemble of individual wills mutually direct each other towards an 'equilibrium of forces', with authority not being viewed as an all-powerful decision-making centre, but rather as a dialectical process of structuring civic relations.[100]

According to Taylor, Deutsch's sociological approach 'concentrated more on description and was more cautious about predicting the dynamic links between the various stages of the integration process'.[101] This distinguishes him from the analysis of neofunctionalism and the premium it placed on forward linkages. Being interested in the early stages of community-formation and the relationship between different conditions of the integrative process, Deutsch's analysis is also easy to distinguish from the early federalist school of thought and its emphasis on the constitutional prerequisites of European unification. In fact, Taylor notes, 'Deutsch's pluralistic security community contains no common decision-making centres ... but in some ways it is highly integrated'.[102] Institution-building, therefore, is not treated in mainstream Deutschian analysis as an end in itself or as a primary indication that integration has indeed taken place. Rather, the emphasis lies at a different level of analysis: the development of a sense of community at the popular level. In this, Deutsch shares a common belief with the older functionalists: the higher the level of sociopsychological community and, hence, of consensus in society, the greater the progress towards the integration of the segments into a larger purposive whole – i.e., 'a community of attitudes and values' – and the less controversial the process of transferring substantive powers to a new regional centre.

Neofunctionalism

Next comes neofunctionalism, which is often but mistakenly associated with Monnet's 'functional federalism'. The latter term has been employed as an analytical tool to explain the composite character of Monnet's gradualist approach to integration, amounting to a rather eclectic synthesis of elements of functionalism and neofunctionalism, without however being fully in accord with either. Neofunctionalism, therefore, should not be hastily classified as being – conceptually or otherwise – *in limbo* between functionalism and federalism. Although it shares some important elements of both schools (from functionalism the centrality of transnational actors and from federalism that of the central institutions) it has developed its own integrative logic, subscribing to certain principles and values of transnational interaction, dynamics of institution-building and styles of collective decision-making. In fact, the contribution of neofunctional-ism, an American-bred school of thought led initially by Haas,[103] has been unique in the study of European integration.

Most notably, neofunctionalist thinking inserted the element of conflict in the analysis of the regional process, as well as that of forward linkages among different, yet interrelated, policy arenas. Procedural mechanisms were seen as decisive, whereas the idea of a sociopsychological consensus at the popular level, a variable indirectly linked to Mitrany's philosophy of international integration, was not taken as a prerequisite for the transfer of authoritative decision-making power to a new regional centre. Rather, such a consensus, which in a way corre-sponds to the idea of a less polarised form of society, emerges as a latent prop-erty and/or a consequence of successful elite socialisation: the process by which influential factors of policy and decision-making from different national set-tings learn to work with each other under the institutional umbrella of a larger management system. In this context, a process of bureaucratic interpenetration or *engrenage*, emerged as the dominant *modus operandi* of the regional system. The idea is that different actors decide to shift their focus on collaborative action to the point that competences – functional and jurisdictional – become blurred, identities overlap and loyalties co-exist. Mutual reinforcement is a key to under-standing the logic of neofunctionalist 'spillovers' in functionally and/or politi-cally relevant policy arenas. Progressively, there will be a convergence of demands on the parts of governments and a propensity for further integrative action, facilitated by the new central authorities. The spillover effect may take three different forms: functional (technical pressures leading towards further integration), political (as a result of intensive levels of elite socialisation) and cultivated (through the role of the central bureaucracy).

An essential part of the neofunctionalist strategy was the identification of the Community Method as the new *modus operandi* of the integrative system. Such a 'method' consisted, *inter alia*, of high levels of elite socialisation, joint lobbying activities of organised interests, the Commission's right of legislative initiative, the involvement of national governments in complex negotiations at the European level, and a certain culture on the part of the Commission for upgrading the Community interest. It was not accidental, therefore, that in the early stages of the Community's development, neofunctionalism acquired the status of an ideology in Brussels. As Milward and Sørensen put it: 'the theory's technocratic elitism appealed strongly to European Community offi-cials who naturally saw the extensive theorizing about the workings of the Com-munity as a confirmation of their historical role as guardians of European integration processes.'[104] This line of argument chimes well with Monnet's phi-losophy of integration. According to Mutimer, 'neofunctionalism . . . provides relative rigorous formulation of the means of political integration developed *ad hoc* by Jean Monnet and his colleagues in the 1950s'.[105] Likewise, Monnet's pragmatic method was in line with Haas' dictum that 'functional integration requires pluralism'.

Taken as a dynamic process rather than a condition, the end product of integration remained an open-ended one. Even Haas' definition of 'political community',[106] as a possible end situation where loyalties are transferred towards a new centre, leaves much to be desired from an organisational point of view. The reason for this 'reluctance' to identify a terminal state of integration can be traced in the logic of neofunctionalism itself: having stressed the idea for an inner compulsion towards integration, 'in that the creation of common institutions would set in motion a process for the accumulation of wider functions', it would be too risky an endeavour to reach any authoritative conclusion on the political properties of the envisaged European polity. Neofunctionalists would often go as far as to state that the very incompleteness of the project would create the need for new central arrangements and, in time, for a directly elected EP to ensure democratic control over the larger, and by then federated, European 'community'. From the outset, however, direct democratic legitimacy was not viewed as a prerequisite for entrusting the new institutions with the political management of the larger entity. Attributes like 'political community', 'supranational authority' and 'federal union' add little to the precise institutional form the end product is expected to take. Perhaps the only relatively discernible outcome of integration in neofunctionalist terms is the creation of what Harrison called a 'self-regulating pluralist society'.[107]

Moreover, the neofunctionalists, by abandoning the central integrative role of attitudinal change while exhibiting a strong normative commitment to elite-driven integration, placed the emphasis on a 'procedural consensus' about the institutional rules of the game: they stressed 'the psychology of elites in an integration process ideally culminating in the emergence of a new political system'.[108] Further, they conceptualised integration as resulting from what Haas called an 'institutionalised pattern' of interest politics.[109] Such concentration on institutional developments had important implications for their conception of sovereignty. Taylor writes: '[neofunctionalists] implicitly accepted the view that sovereignty is strengthened by an expanding legal competence.'[110] Further, it was crucial for the common system to operate under conditions of economic and political pluralism, driven by what has been described as 'the expansive logic of integration'. The latter, once in train, was expected to transcend, and for the more optimistic even replace, existing nation-state structures. Implicitly, the neofunctionalists envisaged the development of a new regional government composed of a highly interactive community of actors.

But the important element remained firmly confined in the process of integration itself: successive spillovers would bring together previously unconnected policy arenas and demand a change in both the behavioural and operational attitudes of the 'relevant elites'. In this respect also, the Commission, in its function as a collegiate body, was to occupy the major role for European-wide policy change. It was assigned the task of acting as the motor of integration, the source of integrative initiatives and the centre of technical expertise for launching joint projects of a supranational character. The point to make here is that the Commission, in contradistinction to its predecessor (High Authority), was given a wide range of policy competences to influence, along with the Council, the common legislative process, and to be significantly involved in the process of setting the integrative agenda. This was especially true until the establishment of the European Council in the mid-1970s and the changing role and dynamism of the Presidency arrangements thereafter.

Although neofunctionalism stressed the importance of 'conflict' in the integrative process, it failed, initially at least, to distinguish between the 'scope' and 'level' of integration. The former refers to the range of the central arrangements in the form of policy arenas that become part of the region's integrative corpus – specific functions, that is, that are commonly managed at the larger level. On the other hand, the 'level' of integration refers to the ways in which such functional areas are managed, the involvement of supranational institutions in the shaping of common policies, and hence the extent to which the central institutions are capable of exercising political authority independently of national political institutions. Neofunctionalist thinking, certainly before Schmitter introduced the notion of 'spillaround', assumed that the scope and level of integration are mutual reinforcements: the more you bring into the common framework of interests and power new policy areas, the greater the involvement and, subsequently, the influence, of supranational institutions.

Consequent amendments to the original treaties, however, point in the opposite direction. For example, in the case of the SEA, although there existed a feeling of accomplishment among European leaders for overcoming some of the obstacles towards further market integration (in the sphere of negative integration), greater majority rule-making in the Council and more attention to issues of economic and social cohesion, the level of integration was not fundamentally altered to take the system closer to a federal polity. However, the scope of integration was significantly advanced to include new areas of transnational co-operation. A similar view may be adopted for the TEU, the AMT and the NIT which, taken together, do not alter the locus of sovereignty from national to supranational institutions of governance. These revisions add to the political dynamics of integration, but not to the formation of a European polity whose constitutional properties would present a direct threat to sovereign statehood.

Neofunctionalist theory has also been criticised on the following grounds: projecting a supranationally biased image of Community arrangements and dynamics; overestimating the role of the Commission as a policy initiator; overstressing the role and influence of organised interests at the larger level; offering an 'elite-driven' explanation of the Community's internal workings; not taking into account 'the logic of diversity' in the regional system; being overtaken by events, especially after the first major constitutional crisis of the Community in the mid-1960s; underestimating the viability of national polities; failing to distinguish between 'low politics' (spheres of technical co-operation) and 'high politics' (foreign policy and defence); ignoring the high levels of interdependence in the global arena, and so on. In the end, it was Haas himself who, in the mid-1970s, critically refined some of his earlier formulations, most notably the automaticity of the spillover effect.[111] As Church has rightly summarised the debate: '[neofunctionalist] predictions proved empirically wrong . . . the states of western Europe did not lie down and let supranationality walk over them.'[112] Yet he is equally right to point out that neofunctionalist theory 'was the first really deep and complex explanation of the Communities'.[113]

Theorising in the 1970s

International regimes

As neofunctionalism was gradually denounced in the late 1970s, a sense of renewed theoretical excitement was set in train by other, equally sophisticated, approaches, regime theory and interdependence theory being among the most prominent. The former brought into the debate the question of whether institutions really mattered in processes of internationalised governance – in the case of the Community, capable of producing publicly binding decisions – whereas the latter portrayed a dynamic system of increased interconnectedness, functional and structural, which set the pace and, to a certain extent, the depth of the regional management arrangements.

International regimes justify the separateness of states as constitutionally distinct entities. As Taylor put it: 'states do not cease to be states because they are members of a regime.'[114] At the same time, regimes allow states to 'socialise' with each other in a complex web of norms of behaviour, rules and procedures of decision-making that are commonly, if not *ex ante*, agreed upon by the participating actors. The emphasis is on informal routes of co-operative behaviour, patterned as much by specific political interests – although it has been argued that regimes imply 'a form of co-operation that is more than the following of short-run interests'[115] – as by a common tendency to pursue (but not necessarily explicitly set as such) reciprocal objectives. Regimes project a certain understanding of regional international co-operation: an 'inclusive' framework of multiple and, more often than not, complex interactions which reflect a given political reality. In the case of the Community, it could be argued that regime-creation, as in the case of the European Monetary System (EMS) in 1979, was directed at setting the limits of acceptable behaviour within a structure of collective, yet flexibly arranged, governance.

Although the influence of American-led international relations literature became immediately manifest in the discussion of the Community as an international regime (or as a system with significant regime characteristics), the latter concept remained conveniently vague as to embrace a multiplicity of different manifestations concerning the management of complex interdependencies, to the extent that almost every aspect of transgovernmental co-operation, whether stemming from a treaty-based mandate or from 'extra-treaty' arrangements, was classified as one type of regime or other. Cox's definition of regimes illustrates this point, '[Regimes] are . . . recognised patterns of practice that define the rules of the game',[116] as does Krasner, describing them as 'sets of implicit and explicit principles, norms, rules and decision-making procedures around which actors' expectations converge in a given area of international relations'.[117] A somewhat different account is offered by Young, who defines regimes as 'social institutions governing the actions of those involved in specifiable activities or set of activities'.[118] The emphasis here is on rules that are translated into 'well-defined guides to action' and on compliance mechanisms with the rules governing the regime. There is a certain procedural bias in this view, in terms of the actors' expected actions 'under appropriate circumstances'.[119]

Different interpretations of these elusive constructs come from authors who focus on the norms that regularise the behaviour of actors and guide their choices. Norms constitute 'standards of behaviour defined in terms of rights and obligations'.[120] The question here is: can norms transcend possible sources of tension among regime actors stemming from what Scharpf calls 'the self-interestedness of governments'?[121] If 'yes', then through which accommodationist mechanisms do actors reconsider their choices and decide to comply with a certain pattern of behaviour which is acceptable to their partners? This is no ontological issue; it is about the flexibility of the regime in question, the way in which it is valued by the participants, and the means by which norms can facilitate the reaching of agreements on the basis of mutualism and reciprocity. In a word, what are the limits of consciousness-raising that a regime can generate? These questions have serious theoretical implications when examining the major crises in the history of the Community, from de Gaulle's 'empty chair policy' in the summer of 1965, to the budgetary crisis of the early 1980s, to the negative Danish vote on the TEU in June 1992.[122] A common thread in these episodes was that the dissenting state did not seriously contemplate the possibility of withdrawing from the common regional system – an indication that regime analysis remains an important part of EU theorising.[123]

What regime theory found difficult to transcend, however, was the role of national establishments in dealing with issues relating to the level of integration, rather than merely its functional scope. Although the concept was capable of explaining why international co-operation does not necessarily take place within an anarchical environment, or even why it creates conditions conducive to structured interactions, regime analysis fell short of explaining the intensity of relations resulting from the regional process and the extent to which the structural properties of the system – that is, the treaty-based nature of the Community and the reality of mutual vetoes in the Council – could determine the level of integrative arrangements at certain points in time. True, regimes may account for the institutionalisation of multilateral relations in specific fields, but they do not offer any structured analysis of the nature of power-politics and interest differentiation among the participating actors. The conceptual lenses used by regime theory are often part of a largely normative interpretation of internationalised co-operation: namely, that states will play by the rules of the game, as of course set by themselves. Purely political considerations may then be subordinate to a functionalist explanation of collective action, overemphasising the actors' initial commitments.

In particular, where the degree of commitment exhibited by the constituent parts varies according to the stakes involved in the process, or in fields of co-operation where governmental activity rests primarily within the domestic arena, regime theory faces a difficult challenge: it has to take account of the more formalistic networks of relations developed by the Community (legal) system, where the influence of non-territorial institutions such as the Commission and the ECJ is of significance. Thus, like interdependence theory, regime analysis is often trapped in a rather dispersed or loose framework of exchanges among policy actors, undermining the impact of the Community's legal order (or its legal authority, for that matter) on shaping national patterns of behaviour and limiting their preferred options – that is, compliance with detailed Community regulations.

Another area of concern is that the Community is too fragmented a system of policy interactions to be treated as a single international regime: it needs to be differentiated according to the specific conditions of co-operation in its various policy sectors. Under this line of argument, the Community system could be seen as a multilayered structure of partial regimes, encompassing a multiplicity of different norms of behaviour and rules of the game (especially when different legislative procedures apply which determine the degree of involvement and strategy of the relevant actors). As Wallace put it with reference to the EC budget, 'the difficulties which the Community so far faced in agreeing on the objectives which the budget should serve . . . and the policies and priorities it should support, offer sobering evidence of the incompleteness and incoherence of the partially integrated policy-making system which it represents'.[124] Further, a partial conceptualisation of the Community's 'policy regimes' is not particularly helpful when assessing its cross-sectional, essentially political properties – that is, what defines it as a political system.

The proliferation of extra-treaty arrangements in the late 1970s stemmed from a deeper concern on the part of the national executives to reassert a considerable degree of national autonomy in the handling of their internal affairs within a sensibly arranged framework of complex interactions. In this respect, regime theory failed to take into account the relationship between the politicisation of issues that regional integration produced and the strategy employed by particular state actors to exercise managerial control over the integration process. These deeper concerns have as much to do with implied benefits from collective action (or regime maintenance) as with questions of an ideological nature about what kind of integration is allowed, or indeed prohibited. In fact, viewing the Community through the relatively modest lenses of international regime theory risks missing important points about the dynamics of formal interinstitutional linkages at the regional level and the importance of domestic politics in shaping transnational affairs. Perhaps this is the strongest critique of regime analysis as applied to the European integration process: politicisation and grassroots democratic concerns often determine the limits of regime formation at the larger level – they provide a clearly defined set of conditions about the legitimation of systems of common management.

Interdependence theory

'Interdependence' was put forward by students of the Community as a more analytically profitable term than 'integration', partly as a result of the unfulfilled objectives of political union in the mid-to-late 1960s, and partly due to the dominant role that national governments continued to enjoy in the management of Community affairs throughout the 1970s. In fact, one of the consequences of the Luxembourg Accords was not only the preservation of a decision-making culture in the Council of Ministers in favour of consensual outcomes, but also the gradual marginalisation of the Commission's influence over the domestic political orders of states. After the deterioration of the international economic environment in the early and late 1970s, a common thread emerged among the member state executives for the maintenance of a considerable degree of autonomy over their internal affairs against any potentially ambitious integrationist design, either in the field of institutionalised monetary co-operation or in those associated with the harmonisation (although the preferred term at the time was 'co-ordination') of the separate foreign policies of the segments.

The core set of relations determining the management, political or otherwise, of Community business was captured by the concept of interdependence: 'a condition (of intensive economic exchange) which may influence political relationships but does not necessarily elicit an integrative response from those most affected.'[125] Unlike 'conventional' neofunctionalist analysis, interdependence theory encapsulates the process of European integration in erratic rather than linear terms, emphasising 'the loss of control and sense of hopelessness which complex economic interactions can trigger, especially in governments whose fate turns on their ability to safeguard the welfare of their electorates'.[126] In a way, it sets the limits of a federalist-inspired political union since it shifts the focus from questions of institution-building and constitutional engineering to those associated with the management of pressing realities as a response to the changing conditions of market forces and the economy.

The application of interdependence theory to integration studies in the 1970s produced less concern about the conceptualisation of the Community as a political system, or for that matter as a form of polity with clearly defined boundaries of institutional development. This, in turn, diverted attention from the oft-raised question of whether the Community should follow an intergovernmental or federalist path to institution-building, to questions dealing more directly with the implications of policy co-ordination for the efficiency of the system as a whole. Policy outputs, in other words, were seen as much more interesting clusters of analysis – at both micro and macro levels – as compared with abstract models of collective governance based on ideologically defined rules and procedures of large-scale political organisation. Institutionalisation thus became of secondary importance to the student of interdependence theory in the Community: governments may well achieve a considerable degree of policy co-ordination and cohesion without being represented in a highly institution-alised framework of interactions. In this sense, perhaps, by diminishing any deterministic projections of the larger configuration, interdependence theory deviates from neofunctionalist-driven analysis, let alone federal macro-political aspirations. In Webb's words: 'Interdependence seems to be the answer for scholars and politicians who wish to keep their options open on the evolu-tion of the EC.'[127]

On the other hand, there is a common denominator where interdependence analysts converge when referring to the internal dynamics of the Community system – that is, the practice of mutualism in the management of complex rela-tions that results in a policy 'mix': a variety of costs and benefits to the partici-pating (interdependent) units. In this view, interdependence theory may be able to explain some, albeit certainly not all, aspects of the various negotiating games being played at the European level between national governments, transnational actors and non-territorial central institutions. The emphasis here is on a per-ceived diffusion of decision-making power among the major actors, as well as on expected utilitarian outcomes of intense interrelationships on essentially non-conflict-prone areas. Areas, that is, where state and non-state (transnational) actors pursue their strategic choices in view of pressing socioeconomic problems stemming from functional, and to a lesser extent structural, interdependence. Hence 'transnational coalitions' take shape within the Community's multi-layered setting, impinging with considerable rigour on its policy processes.

Moreover, by transcending the 'end product dilemma' of mainstream regional integration analysis – that is, federal state, confederation, union, and so on – interdependence theory claims to offer a pragmatic, ideologically free alter-native to the study of both the structural conditions and policy outcomes of intensive interactions – something that supranationalism, the argument has it, by its nature cannot offer. To quote again from Webb: '[Interdependence] encourages the analyst to focus on the policy issues first and foremost rather than be diverted by the particular and frequently parochial institutional prob-lems which infiltrate and obscure the policy debate in Brussels.'[128]

A fair amount of criticism directed against the interdependence school cen-tres around the basic, and, it needs saying, hard-won, political properties of the Community system: the role and influence of its supranational institutions *par excellence*; the dynamics of institutional 'spillovers' or forward linkages leading to further institutionalisation; and the impact of 'extra-treaty' arrangements on the conditions of joint decision-making, especially when sensitive issues are at stake for a particular state or group of states. The list could well be extended to cover interinstitutional relations, bargaining practices promoting national interests, issues of large-scale jurisdictional competence, the constitutional implications of Community law for the domestic legal orders of states, and so on. These issues, often due to their controversial nature, are dealt with more explicitly by *political* theories of regional international integration.

But more importantly, perhaps, interdependence should be seen as only one side of the coin. The other is the principle and practice of autonomy on the part of national political authorities. The interplay between the two has produced, as many theorists rightly expected, a 'flexible equilibrium', or even 'multiple flexible equilibria', where structural (mainly systemic) properties were in a position to determine the quality of functions performed by state agents (ways of management), be they bureaucrats, administrators or government representatives. In a way, and this is not an attempt to simplify an inevitably complex reality based on open-ended processes (also capable of producing unintended consequences), the problem confronting the interdependence approach is that it relies primarily on horizontal interactions whose decisional outcomes, however – that is, the process of regulating a policy arena where co-operative action applies – are based on a set of authoritative rules reached by joint decisions but applied vertically to the domestic orders of the participating collectivities. A functionalist understanding of sovereignty, therefore, as part of the interdependence vocabulary, is in need of further clarification.

Ideally, in a system of highly interdependent relations, territorially demarcated boundaries become of secondary importance to the expected fruits (or non-costs) of concerted action. Yet it is often the case that the management and, more accurately, the exercise of managing these relations, rests closely with 'executive-centred elites' which are often willing to compromise the wider interest – as resulting from the dictates of interdependence itself – to avoid the danger of intersegmental confrontation. Here, consensual politics prevail, whether or not specific treaty provisions may require a different course of procedural (decisional) action. Interdependence, in other words, does not guarantee that rational decisions prevail between actors who find themselves in the middle of a difficult dilemma: to strengthen the co-operative ethos of the regional arrangements or to resort to autonomous action under ideological or party political pressures (in fact the latter may be part of a single political package, as has often been the case in the history of interstate bargaining within the Community).

What interdependence theory cannot properly address, then, is the question of explicitly political choices on the part of dominant governing elites about the nature and extent of their involvement in joint co-operative schemes. This is something with which, much to the detriment of supranationalist-driven aspirations about the Community's political future, state-centric approaches are better equipped to deal. In conclusion, interdependence theory places Community politics in a wider pluralist perspective of post-industrial relations, diverging attention from a structured analysis of hierarchical conceptions of the regional process to a much more diffused system of policy co-ordination, transnational coalition-formation and economic management.

Concordance systems

More than thirty years have elapsed since Puchala's celebrated linking of the Community with the story of the elephant and the blind men. Although falling within the wider analytical framework of the interdependence school, Puchala's 'new thinking' about contemporary international integration is worth exploring in its own right, offering at the same time a thorough critical evaluation of conventional integration models. Indeed, in an attempt to break away from the classical theses of federalism and intergovernmentalism, Puchala discussed the integration phenomenon in terms of 'what it really is and is actually leading to'.[129] His main concern was that the pre-existing accounts of the relevant field, especially as applied in the case of Western Europe, had been characterised by conceptual confusion, stressing either the indispensability of national polities or that of the central institutions. As a result, normative theoretical preferences had exhausted the intellectual efforts of scholars, depriving the integration process of a descriptive model capable of conceptualising its distinctive properties and dynamics.

Puchala argued his case against the analytical validity of conventional approaches to the study of international integration such as federalism, functionalism, nationalism and what he called 'old-fashioned power-politics'. His criticism reflected the state of theorising integration in the early 1970s, a period when the Community's workings were characterised by a more favourable version of intergovernmentalism, but where no clear model of integration, or for that matter a wider conceptual consensus, had emerged among its students. Puchala was critical of the limited, predominantly economic, nature of the Community at that time, as well as of the autonomy of the Commission in representing the wider European interest being detached from the separate interests of the member states. His understanding of the Western European system also challenged the mainstream federalist approach, in that progress towards further integration was being equated with movement towards a central European government and the extent to which national political authorities had relinquished their sovereignty to an emerging federal state. The question he asked was 'to what extent does participation in an international integration arrangement actually enhance rather than undermine national sovereignty?'[130] This was something which effectively remained largely unspoken within the federalist camp.

However, Puchala was also critical of the view that equates international integration with nation-building processes. The point he made here was that Western European integration does not even closely approximate a model of political evolution where the measurement of its 'progress' or 'success' is conditioned by the extent to which the component parts that are being integrated move towards 'the social and cultural assimilation of [their] nationalities'.[131] In this respect, Puchala was particularly sceptical of the applicability of the 'nationalism model' in the study of international integration. His main argument was that such an approach lacked evidence of progress towards the envisaged process of assimilation among diverse peoples. Again, students applying the 'national-ism model' were asking, according to Puchala, the wrong questions: 'about people-to-people interactions and transactions, about similarities and differ-ences in people's life styles, value systems and cultural norms, and especially about their attitudes toward one or another and attendant perceptions of "we-ness".[132] In his view, the rather more interesting question to pose was about the relationship between peoples and their national governments, as well as between the former and international organisations and processes.

In his equally critical approach to Mitrany's functionalism, Puchala ques-tioned the extent to which his sectoral approach, for all its validity in locating the sources of international co-operation and the role of transnational (non-governmental) actors, had actually worked in the way in which the functionalist model originally intended. The point he made here was that in internationally integrating systems, '[l]eadership, initiative and prerogative have by and large remained with national governments',[133] rather than with newly formed techno-cratic agencies, large-scale bureaucratic entities and non-governmental actors. Moreover, functionalist theorising failed to predict the importance attached by national governments to pursuing 'welfare' objectives, rather than merely 'power' relations at the regional level. Equally, Puchala dismissed the function-alist claim about non-political aspects of international co-operation, arguing that no such issues really exist in interstate relations. He also pointed to another deficiency of the functionalist design in that, instead of being primarily preoc-cupied with sector-to-sector task expansion, 'there is possible expansion in the *political system* brought into being when functional sectors are integrated inter-nationally'.[134] Finally, he was concerned with the normative/hypothetical aspects of the functionalist analysis in that the end product of international integration would resemble a 'functional federation' or some sort of 'multi-sector merger'. In brief, functionalism in the Mitranian tradition failed, in Puchala's view, to ask 'how international co-operation is in fact achieved during international integra-tion in the very course of international politics'.[135] It has been 'partially strait-jacketed' by its own integrative assumptions.

Last in his 'critical list' comes the realist school of thought, perceiving inter-national integration as 'power politics'. This traditional international relations approach fails to understand what the phenomenon is all about, not least because it views international integration as 'a process of mutual exploitation wherein governments attempt to mobilise and accumulate the resources of neighbouring states in the interests of enhancing their own power'.[136] Such an account emphasises the self-interestedness of national governing elites which perceive international integration as an instrument towards the accumulation of greater power as 'international marriages of convenience, comfortable for all partners as long as self-interests are satisfied'.[137] The point that realist thinking is making is that international integration never really gets 'beyond the nation-state'. It stays confined within the dictates of international diplomacy, leading eventually towards disintegration: the participating actors are 'destined for divorce the moment any partner's interests are seriously frustrated'.[138] In general terms, Puchala noted, political realists are so convinced that international integration is played by traditional international relations rules – also set by traditional actors – that they never ask 'whether actors committed to international integration may be pursuing any other than the traditional inventory of international goals – autonomy, military security, influence and prestige'.[139] In brief, 'by assuming that international politics remains the same "old game" and that international integration is but a part of it',[140] the advocates of the realist analysis fail to take into account the possibility, if not reality, that international integration arrangements may in the end define the self-interests of states themselves, rather than *vice versa*.

So, with what did Puchala propose to replace the existing deficiencies in international integration analysis? His answer was that 'contemporary international integration can best be thought of as a set of processes that produce and sustain a Concordance System at the international level'.[141] Such a system of 'co-operatively interacting states' is based on the harmonisation of the actors' interests and on mutually beneficial interactions. The role of the nation-state remains central in the integration process but at the same time the institutions of the larger system possess their own organisational and operational logic. A Concordance System may include actors from different organisational levels or governmental arenas without producing a system of hierarchical authority structures. Rather, 'each of the actors remain[s] semi-autonomous . . . all are interdependent, and all interact in pursuit of consensus that yields mutual rewards'.[142] It is a complex international pluralist system with high levels of institutionalisation and various organisational networks, where international interactions are mainly channelled through bureaucratic, rather than diplomatic, means: 'a system of relations among sovereign states and separate peoples.'[143]

In the Concordance System, problem-solving and conflict regulation are facilitated via 'institutionalised, constitutional, precedential or otherwise standardised, patterned procedures which all actors commit themselves to use and respect'.[144] But it is not a state, national or transnational in kind. Rather, it takes the form of numerous functionally specific bodies, without having to rely upon federalist-inspired processes of institutional centralisation. More importantly, political conflict arises from different approaches to international co-operation, mainly in terms of the necessary procedural avenues to be pursued, rather than from 'fundamental incompatibilities in the interests of the various actors'.[145] Hence conflict may well be one of the system's functional aspects and not, as is often the case in various realist predictions, a move towards disintegration (or de-federation). Another important dimension of a Concordance System is the bargaining techniques used by the relevant actors to reach mutually reinforcing outcomes in international negotiations: coercion and confrontation should be excluded from the acceptable patterns of international (intrasystemic) behaviour. On the contrary, the rules of the system are determined by what Puchala calls a 'full information' game, where secrecy and deception are altogether unknown.

International interdependence – often seen as a result of 'national inadequacy' – emerges as a defining property of Concordance Systems. This does not amount, however, to a negation of the nation-state. Rather, 'nation-states can be preserved as distinct entities only through the international pooling of resources to confront problems that challenge their separate existence'.[146] Likewise, Puchala explicitly states that 'mass populations within the Concordance System need not be assimilated into a supranationality'.[147] However, they do confer legitimacy upon the system, comply with its authoritative decisional outcomes and, in general, support the integrative process.

In summary, the theoretical lenses employed by the Concordance Systems approach capture aspects of the structural, attitudinal and procedural conditions of international integration, while freeing the analyst from normative, hypothetical and ideologically defined interpretations of the integrative phenomenon. Thus it is a pragmatic approach aiming to reveal the underlying structure of relations between highly interdependent units and the way in which large-scale co-ordination projects, patterned on routinised procedures and standardised codes of conduct, transcend the ill-effects of adversarial politics in multiple policy arenas. It is these regime aspects of the Concordance System which are mainly responsible for the elimination of competitive tussles for political authority among the participants and the prevalence of positive-sum outcomes in multilateral negotiations. In conclusion, Puchala's approach to international integration attempted a fresh start by exploring the possibilities of consensus-formation, pragmatic politics, patterned procedures, institutionalised compromise, mutual responsiveness and co-operative behaviour. It is our contention that his analysis remains a valuable contribution in the field.

A final note

Having examined the core theories of integration both during the formative years of the regional process and throughout the 1970s, we can now turn to the relationship between the major constitutional revisions of the original treaties and the theoretical implications stemming from them, especially in the light of new approaches to the study of European integration in the 1990s, especially from the perspective of EU polity-building. Such an analysis will help us link the theoretical findings of Chapter 2 with the more detailed examination of recent treaty reforms, as epitomised in the Amsterdam and Nice outcomes, respectively (Chapters 3 and 4). It will also provide the analytical framework and normative basis from which we may develop a more penetrating understanding of the evolutionary nature of the integration process in general, and the qualitative transformation of the regional system from a policy-oriented enterprise to a transnational polity: a system of governance capable of producing authoritative political decisions, allocating values in European society, and transforming the traditional patterns of interaction among the component state/citizen parts.

Notes

1 Donald J. Puchala, 'The Integration Theorists and the Study of International Relations', in C. W. Kegley and E. Wittkopf (eds), *The Global Agenda: Issues and Perspectives*, New York: Random House, 1984, p. 198.

2 Paul Taylor, *International Co-operation Today: The European and the Universal Patterns*, London: Elek Books, 1971, p. i.

3 Robert O. Keohane and Stanley Hoffmann, 'Conclusions', in William Wallace (ed.), *The Dynamics of European Integration*, London: Royal Institute of International Affairs, 1990, p. 284.

4 Clive H. Church, *European Integration Theory in the 1990s*, European Dossier Series, No. 33, University of North London, 1996, p. 8.

5 *Ibid.*

6 Taylor, *International Co-operation*, p. 149.

7 Donald J. Puchala, 'Of Blind Men, Elephants and International Integration', *Journal of Common Market Studies*, December 1972, pp. 267–84.

8 For definitions of the terms see Murray Forsyth, *Unions of States: The Theory and Practice of Confederation*, Leicester: Leicester University Press, 1981, pp. 1–16.

9 Alberta M. Sbragia, 'Thinking about the European Future', in Alberta M. Sbragia (ed.), *Euro-Politics*, Washington, DC: The Brookings Institution, 1992, pp. 13, 257.

10 Thomas Christiansen, 'European Integration Between Political Science and International Relations Theory: The End of Sovereignty?', EUI Working Paper, No. 94/4, San Domenico: Badia Fiesolana, FI, 1994, p. 10.

11 On the distinction between these concepts see Forsyth, *Unions of States*, pp. 10–16.

12 Dimitris N. Chryssochoou, 'New Challenges to the Study of European Integration: Implications for Theory-Building', *Journal of Common Market Studies*, December 1998, pp. 521–42. See also Dimitris N. Chryssochoou, *Democracy in the European Union*, London and New York: I. B. Tauris, 1998.

13 William Wallace, 'Theory and Practice in European Integration', in Simon Bulmer and Andrew Scott (eds), *Economic and Political Integration in Europe: Internal Dynamics and Global Context*, Oxford: Basil Blackwell, 1994, p. 274. Likewise, Adonis has observed: 'It is fashionable to talk of a "democratic deficit", but that is but one aspect of a more chronic malaise: constitutional chaos.' See Andrew Adonis, 'Subsidiarity: Myth, Reality and the Community's Future', House of Lords Select Committee on the European Communities, London, June 1990, p. 11.

14 Wallace, 'Theory and Practice', pp. 274, 275.

15 Alberta M. Sbragia, 'The European Community: A Balancing Act', *Publius*, Summer 1993, p. 24.

16 See, respectively, Emil J. Kirchner, *Decision Making in the European Community*, Manchester: Manchester University Press, 1992, pp. 10–14; Simon Bulmer and Wolfgang Wessels, *The European Council: Decision-Making in European Politics*, London: Macmillan, 1988, pp. 8–11; and Paul Taylor, *International Organization in the Modern World: The Regional and the Global Process*, London: Pinter, 1993, pp. 80–111.

17 David McKay, 'On the Origins of Political Unions', paper presented at the 2nd ECSA-World Conference, 'Federalism, Subsidiarity and Democracy in the European Union', Brussels, 4–6 May 1994, p. 6.

18 Andrew Moravcsik, 'Preferences and Power in the European Community: A Liberal Inter-governmentalist Approach', *Journal of Common Market Studies*, December 1993, p. 507.

19 Quoted in C. Webb, 'Theoretical Perspectives and Problems', in Helen Wallace *et al.* (eds), *Policy-Making in the European Community*, Chichester: John Wiley, 1983, pp. 36, 40, n. 22.

20 William Wallace, 'Less than a Federation, More than a Regime: The Community as a Political System', in Wallace *et al.* (eds), *Policy-Making*, p. 410.

21 Quoted in *ibid.*, p. 406.

22 Quoted in George Tsembelis, 'The Power of the European Parliament as a Conditional Agenda-Setter', *American Political Science Review*, March 1992, p. 128.

23 Keohane and Hoffmann, 'Conclusions', p. 282.

24 Fritz W. Scharpf, 'The Joint-Decision Trap: Lessons from German Federalism and European Integration', *Public Administration*, Autumn 1988, p. 265.

25 *Ibid.*, pp. 257, 242. Cf. William Wallace, 'Europe as a Confederation: The Community and the Nation-State', *Journal of Common Market Studies*, September–December 1982, p. 67; Paul Taylor, 'Interdependence and Autonomy in the European Communities: The Case of the European Monetary System', *Journal of Common Market Studies*, June 1980, p. 373; and Stanley Hoffmann, 'Obstinate or Obsolete? The Fate of the Nation State in Western Europe', *Daedalus*, Summer 1966, p. 910.

26 A. J. R. Groom, 'The European Community: Building Up, Building Down, and Building Across', in Conference Proceedings, *People's Rights and European Structures*, Manresa, September 1993, p. 47.

27 David Mitrany, *A Working Peace System*, London: Royal Institute of International Affairs, 1943, pp. 72–3.

28 Paul Taylor, 'The Concept of Community and the European Integration Process', *Journal of Common Market Studies*, December 1968, p. 86.

29 David Mitrany, *The Functional Theory of Politics*, London: Martin Robertson, 1976, p. 119. Others, like Hirst, are partly in favour of these views, in so far as 'different forms of representation are not seen as a substitute for representative democracy, but rather as a supplement to it'. See Paul Hirst, *Associative Democracy: New Forms of Economic and Social Governance*, Cambridge: Polity, 1994, pp. 16–17.

30 *Ibid.*, p. 261.

31 Uwe Kitzinger, 'Time-Lags in Political Psychology', in James Barber and Bruce Reeds (eds), *European Community: Vision and Reality*, London: Croom Helm, 1973, p. 13.

32 *Ibid.*

33 This point is analysed further in Paul Taylor, 'Functionalism: The Approach of David Mitrany', in A. J. R. Groom and Paul Taylor (eds), *Frameworks for International Co-operation*, London: Pinter, 1990, p. 132.

34 *Ibid.*

35 Quoted in A. Bosco, 'What is Federalism?', paper presented at the 2nd ECSA-World Conference, 'Federalism, Subsidiarity and Democracy in the European Union', Brussels, 4–6 May 1994, p. 15.

36 R. L. Watts, 'Federalism, Regionalism, and Political Integration', in David M. Cameron (ed.), *Regionalism and Supranationalism: Challenges and Alternatives to the Nation-State in Canada and Europe*, London: The Institute for Research on Public Polity, 1981, p. 10.

37 *Ibid.*, p. 13.

38 Murray Forsyth, *Political Science, Federalism and Europe*, Discussion Papers in Federal Studies, No. FS95/2, University of Leicester, 1995, p. 12.

39 K. Robinson, 'Sixty Years of Federation in Australia', *Geographical Review*, 51:1, 1961, p. 2. Quoted in A. Murphy, 'Belgium's Regional Divergence: Along the Road to Federation', in Graham Smith (ed.), *Federalism: The Multiethnic Challenge*, London and New York: Longman, 1995, p. 75.

40 Preston King, 'Federation and Representation', in Michael Burgess and A.-G. Gagnon (eds), *Comparative Federalism and Federation*, New York: Harvester Wheatsheaf, 1993, pp. 95–6. Cf. Preston King, *Federalism and Federation*, London: Croom Helm, 1982, pp. 88–95.

41 *Ibid.*, p. 96.

42 Daniel J. Elazar, *Exploring Federalism*, Tuscaloosa: The University of Alabama Press, 1987, pp. 108–9.

43 King, 'Federation and Representation', p. 96.

44 Watts, 'Federalism', pp. 13–14.

45 Carl J. Friedrich, *Trends of Federalism in Theory and Practice*, London: Pall Mall Press, 1968, p. 3.

46 Reginald J. Harrison, *Europe in Question: Theories of Regional International Integration*, London: Allen & Unwin, 1974, p. 43.

47 Michael Burgess, 'Federalism as Political Ideology: Interests, Benefits and Beneficiaries in Federalism and Federation', in Burgess and Gagnon (eds), *Comparative Federalism*, p. 149.

48 On this issue see Dimitris N. Chryssochoou, 'Federalism and Democracy Reconsidered', *Regional and Federal Studies*, Summer 1998, pp. 1–20.

49 Robert R. Bowie, 'The Process of Federating Europe', in A. W. Macmahon (ed.), *Federalism: Mature and Emergent*, New York: Garden City, 1987, p. 497.

50 *Ibid.*, p. 496. For an account of past attempts to unite the Continent, see Sydney D. Bailey, *United Europe: A Short History of the Idea*, London: National News-Letter, 1948.

51 *Ibid.*, p. 497. Bowie writes: 'As important as [the nation-state's] economic and political decline was the spiritual malaise that affected much of its population.' See *ibid.*, p. 495.

52 Harrison, *Europe in Question*, p. 45.

53 As quoted in Uwe Kitzinger, *The European Common Market and Community*, London: Routledge, 1967, pp. 29–33.

54 Kitzinger, 'Time-Lags in Political Psychology', p. 8.

55 Andrea Bosco, 'The Federalist Project and Resistance in Continental Europe', in Andrea Bosco (ed.), *The Federal Idea: The History of Federalism Since 1945*, Vol. II, London and New York: Lothian Foundation Press, 1992, p. 52. See also Altiero Spinelli and Ernesto Rossi, *Il Manifesto di Ventotene*, Pavia, 1944, pp. 19–20. Cf. Mario Albertini, 'The Ventotene Manifesto: The Only Road to Follow', in Lucio Levi (ed.), *Altiero Spinelli and Federalism in Europe and in the World*, Milan: FrancoAngeli, 1990, pp. 127–40.

56 Altiero Spinelli and Ernesto Rossi, 'European Union in the Resistance', *Government and Opposition*, April–July 1967, pp. 321–9. Quoted in Ghita Ionescu (ed.), *The New Politics of European Integration*, London: Macmillan, 1972, p. 2.

57 Gordon Smith, 'The Crisis of the West European State', in Cameron (ed.), *Regionalism and Supranationalism*, p. 25.

58 Lucio Levi, 'Altiero Spinelli, Mario Albertini and the Italian Federalist School: Federalism as Ideology', in Bosco (ed.), *The Federal Idea*, II, p. 214.

59 Lucio Levi, 'Recent Developments in Federalist Theory', in Levi (ed.), *Altiero Spinelli*, p. 62. Cf. Watts, 'Federalism', p. 4.

60 John Pinder, 'The New European Federalism', in Burgess and Gagnon (eds), *Comparative Federalism*, p. 45.

61 Sergio Pistone, 'Altiero Spinelli and a Strategy for the United States of Europe', in Andrea Bosco (ed.), *The Federal Idea: The History of Federalism from the Enlightenment to 1945*, Vol. I, London and New York: Lothian Foundation Press, 1991, pp. 351–7. See also Michael Burgess, 'Federal Ideas in the European Community: Altiero Spinelli and European Union', *Government and Opposition*, Summer 1984, pp. 339–47.

62 Bosco, 'What is Federalism?', p. 2.

63 Denis De Rougemont, 'The Campaign of European Congresses', in Ghita Ionescu (ed.), *The New Politics of European Integration*, London: Macmillan, 1972, p. 25.

64 Harrison, *Europe in Question*, p. 48.

65 *Ibid.*

66 Max Beloff, writing in *The Times*, asserted that 'what one is struck with is not the parallel . . . but the immensity of the difference'. He concluded: 'those who believe in furthering European unity must seek elsewhere than in American federalism.' See Max Beloff, 'False Analogies from Federal Example of the United States', *The Times*, 4 May 1950. Cf. Roderick MacFarquhar, 'The Community, the Nation-State and the Regions', in Bernard Burrows *et al.* (eds), *Federal Solutions to European Issues*, London: Macmillan, 1978, pp. 17–24.

67 Quoted in Bosco, 'What is Federalism?', p. 13.

68 Forsyth, *Unions of States*, pp. 1–16.

69 B. M. Sharma and L. P. Choudhry, *Federal Polity*, London: Asia Publishing House, 1967, pp. 11–12. Cf. Paul Taylor, *The Limits of European Integration*, New York: Columbia University Press, 1983, pp. 270–5. Likewise, Watts has pointed out: 'The difference between the federal and confederal forms lies in the fact that in federal systems, the central institutions are free to exercise responsibilities assigned to them under the constitution in a direct relationship with the electorate, while in confederal systems the central agencies, operating as delegates of the regional governments, are dependent upon them for agreement to common policies.' See Watts, 'Federalism', p. 12.

70 Forsyth, *Political Science*, p. 16.

71 Robert A. Dahl, *A Preface to Democratic Theory*, Chicago: University of Chicago Press, 1956, p. 38.

72 Forsyth, *Unions of States*, pp. 15–16.

73 Murray Forsyth, 'Towards a New Concept of Confederation', European Commission for Democracy Through Law, Council of Europe, 1994, p. 12.

74 Forsyth, *Unions of States*, p. 1.

75 Daniel J. Elazar *et al.*, *Federal Systems of the World: A Handbook of Federal, Confederal and Autonomy Arrangements*, 2nd edn, London: Longman Current Affairs, 1994, p. xvi. The author defines the federation as 'a compound polity compounded of strong constituent entities and a strong general government, each possessing powers delegated to it by the people and empowered to deal directly with the citizenry in the exercise of those powers'.

76 Forsyth, *Unions of States*, pp. 11, 15–16.

77 *Ibid.*, p. 16.

78 *Ibid.*, p. 15.

79 Heinrich von Treitschke, 'State Confederations and Federated States', Book III, in Murray Forsyth *et al.* (eds), *The Theory of International Relations*, London: Allen & Unwin, 1970, pp. 330, 331.

80 Forsyth, *Unions of States*, p. 13.

81 *Ibid.*, pp. 13–14.

82 On this idea see Anthony D. Smith, *National Identity*, Harmondsworth: Penguin Books, 1991, p. 153.

83 Forsyth, *Unions of States*, p. 15.

84 *Ibid.* and p. 205.

85 Friedrich, *Trends of Federalism*, pp. 11–12. Friedrich defines federation as 'a union of groups, united by one or more common objectives, rooted in common values, interests, or beliefs, but retaining their distinctive group character for other purposes'. See p. 177.

86 Murray Forsyth, 'Federalism and Confederalism', in Chris Bacon (ed.), *Political Restructuring in Europe: Ethical Perspectives*, London and New York: Routledge, 1994, p. 58.

87 Friedrich, *Trends of Federalism*, p. 82.

88 Forsyth, 'Federalism and Confederalism', pp. 57–8.

89 Keohane and Hoffmann, 'Conclusions', p. 279.

90 See, respectively, Christopher Brewin, 'The European Community: A Union of States without Unity of Government', *Journal of Common Market Studies*, 26:1, 1987, pp. 1–24; Clive H. Church, 'The Not so Model Republic? The Relevance of Swiss Federalism to the European Community', Leicester University Discussion Papers in Federal Studies, No. FS93/4, November 1994, p. 15; and Elazar *et al.*, *Federal Systems*, p. xvi.

91 Karl W. Deutsch, *Political Community and the North Atlantic Area*, Princeton: Princeton University Press, 1957, p. 5.

92 Paul Taylor, 'A Conceptual Typology of International Organisation', in Groom and Taylor (eds), *Frameworks*, p. 18.

93 See Ferdinand Tönnies, *Community and Association*, translated and supplemented by Charles P. Loomis, London: Routledge & Kegan Paul, 1974.

94 Chantal Mouffe, *The Return of the Political*, London: Verso, 1993, p. 61.

95 Eugene Kamenka, *Bureaucracy*, Oxford: Basil Blackwell, 1989, p. 81.

96 Taylor, *The Limits of European Integration*, p. 3.

97 Tönnies, *Community and Association*, p. 160. Cf. R. M. MacIver, *Community: A Socio-logical Study*, London: Macmillan, 1936, pp. 22–8. MacIver states: 'A community is a focus of social life; an association is an organisation of social life . . . but community is something wider and freer than even the greatest associations.' See p. 24.

98 Tönnies, *Community and Association*, pp. 38–9.

99 Kamenka, *Bureaucracy*, p. 79.

100 On the relationship between *Gemeinschaft* and authority see Raymond Plant, *Community and Ideology: An Essay in Applied Social Philosophy*, London and Boston: Routledge & Kegan Paul, 1974, pp. 51–8.

101 Taylor, *International Co-operation*, p. 7.

102 *Ibid.*, p. 10.

103 Ernst B. Haas, *The Uniting of Europe: Political, Social and Economic Forces 1950–1957*, London: Stevens & Sons, 1958.

104 Alan S. Milward and Viebeke Sørensen, 'Independence or Integration? A National Choice', in Alan S. Milward *et al.* (eds), *The Frontier of National Sovereignty: History and Theory 1945–1992*, London and New York: Routledge, 1993, p. 3.

105 David Mutimer, 'Theories of Political Integration', in Hans J. Michelmann and Panayotis Soldatos (eds), *European Integration: Theories and Approaches*, Lanham: University Press of America, 1994, p. 33.

106 The term 'political community' is used here in accordance with Haas' definition, that is, as 'a condition in which specific groups and individuals show more loyalty to their central political institutions than to any other political authority'. See Haas, *The Uniting of Europe*, p. 5.

107 Reginald Harrison, 'Neo-functionalism', in Groom and Taylor (eds), *Frameworks*, p. 145.

108 Taylor, *The Limits of European Integration*, p. 7.

109 Ernst B. Haas, *Beyond the Nation-State: Functionalism and International Organization*, Stanford: Stanford University Press, 1964, p. 35. Quoted in Taylor, 'The Concept of Community', p. 87.

110 Taylor, 'The Concept of Community', p. 87.

111 Ernst B. Haas, *The Obsolescence of Regional Integration Theory*, Berkeley, CA: Institute of International Studies, 1975.

112 Church, *European Integration Theory*, p. 20.

113 *Ibid.*

114 Taylor, *International Organization*, p. 3.

115 Robert Jervis, 'Security Regimes', in Stephen D. Krasner (ed.), *International Regimes*, Ithaca: Cornell University Press, 1983, p. 173.

116 Robert W. Cox, 'Social Forces, States and World Orders: Beyond International Relations

Theory', *Millennium*, 10:2, Summer 1981, p. 128. Quoted in Groom and Taylor (eds), *Frameworks*, p. 202.

117 Stephen D. Krasner, 'Structural Causes and Regime Consequences: Regimes as Intervening Variables', in Krasner (ed.), *International Regimes*, p. 2.

118 Oran Young, *International Cooperation: Building Regimes for Natural Resources and the Environment*, Ithaca: Cornell University Press, 1989, p. 12. Quoted in Robert E. Breckinridge, 'Reassessing Regimes: The International Regime Aspects of the European Union', *Journal of Common Market Studies*, June 1997, p. 179.

119 *Ibid.*, p. 16.

120 Krasner, 'Structural Causes', p. 2.

121 Scharpf, 'The Joint-Decision Trap'.

122 Breckinridge, 'Reassessing Regimes', pp. 181–3.

123 *Ibid.*, p. 183.

124 Wallace, 'Less than a Federation', p. 408.

125 Webb, 'Theoretical Perspectives', p. 32.

126 *Ibid.*

127 *Ibid.*, p. 33.

128 *Ibid.*, p. 34.

129 Puchala, 'Of Blind Men', p. 268.

130 *Ibid.*, p. 271.

131 *Ibid.*

132 *Ibid.*, p. 272.

133 *Ibid.*, p. 273.

134 *Ibid.*, p. 274.

135 *Ibid.*, p. 275.

136 *Ibid.*

137 *Ibid.*, p. 276.

138 *Ibid.*

139 *Ibid.*

140 *Ibid.*

141 *Ibid.*, p. 277.

142 *Ibid.*, p. 278.

143 *Ibid.*

144 *Ibid.*, p. 279.

145 *Ibid.*, p. 280.

146 *Ibid.*, p. 282.

147 *Ibid.*, p. 283.

2

New directions in theory-building

Treaty reform in perspective

The SEA and beyond

In the mid-1980s, the whole scene became dominated by claims of a 'neofunctionalist comeback' – modified in nature, yet easily discernible in scope.[1] Processes of negative integration primarily at the market level were linked with the development of a wide range of policies covering almost all spheres of regional co-operation. Neofunctionalist 'spillovers' were envisaged for the transformation of a 'Business Europe' to a 'People's Europe': the functions of the larger management system seemed to have produced not only new expectations but also new pressures for further integration. But the institutional evolution of the Community was lagging behind its (re)emerging neofunctionalist ambitions. The SEA did not represent a qualitative leap towards a 'self-regulating pluralist society' at the regional level, or even towards high levels of political autonomy on the part of supranational institutions.

Although it needs to be pointed out that the Delors Commission did try to develop an independent strategy for managing the '1992 process' and to exploit its enormous publicity – a project supported at the time by even the most 'reluctant' Europeans including British Prime Minister Thatcher – the states once again found ways of resisting any substantive movement towards a profound transformation of the Community system: supranationalism championed in areas where the states wanted to see progress, such as the implementation of the single market programme (and even here there was to be a target date rather than a legally binding date for its completion). In those areas where national interests were, or appeared to be, at stake, such as European Political Co-operation (EPC) that was merely codified in a legal text, intergovernmentalism effectively prevailed as the dominant mode of decision-taking. Moreover, no subsequent alteration of the locus of sovereignty emerged as a result of the coming into force of the SEA in July 1987, although it did pave the way for higher levels of power-sharing in the Community system. An equally important line of criticism directed against resurgent neofunctionalist aspirations came from a number of scholars who stressed the fact that the theory did not take into account the wider international environment within which Community change was to flourish.[2]

So why did neofunctionalism, which had been obsolescent for some twenty years, emerge once again as the leading theory of European integration? A possible answer is that the SEA was hailed by many observers at the time as opening up new horizons for positive integration. Neofunctionalism was in fact the only theory that could place, if not justify, these claims in a dynamic, macropolitical perspective. After all, the analytical validity of the theory had been linked from the outset with the development of the Community political system and now there was a widespread sense of a renewed dynamism in the integration process. In particular, there was a feeling that the single market plan would not allow for any critical drawbacks. Instead, it was seen as constituting the 'motor' of integration, the long-needed integrative project that would accelerate the pace of the regional process by mobilising political elites, trade unions and the wider business community towards a commonly shared – and, crucially, feasible – objective. At the same time, there were mounting expectations that the dynamics of economic integration would soon spill over into the institutional sphere. Although new sources of possible pressure became manifest in a wide range of policy domains, neofunctionalist analysis concentrated on the stimulus rather than the outcome of the envisaged spillovers; that is, on the integrative dynamic rather than on the consequence of the newly generated impetus.

For instance, it was expected that increased trade and, albeit to a lesser extent, financial interdependencies would lead, in a somewhat deterministic fashion, towards a full-blown monetary union on the grounds that positive movement at one level of integration would set up problems that could only be resolved at another level. But there was no immediate link, nor was there any automatic mechanism to that end. On the contrary, much had to rely upon the convergence of interests among the dominant governing elites, which also had to take into account what such a move would entail for the sovereignty of their respective polities. The crucial question missed by 'new neofunctionalism' was how far can Community competences be extended beyond the traditional state level without raising the sensitive issue of national sovereignty? Even in the case of the SEA, for all the new dynamism and innovative strategy shown by the Delors Presidency, despite the existing political consensus among the national governing elites, and despite even the positive mobilisation of non-governmental actors around the '1992 project', the level of European integration cannot be said to have been significantly advanced.

However, it is equally difficult to assume that the member state governments decided to refocus, as Haas might have it, their loyalties, activities and political expectations on a new regional centre, for no such 'centre' ever came into being with the SEA. Moreover, neither the inherent technical characteristics of the vision of a 'Europe without frontiers', nor the utilitarian calculus of 'the cost of non-Europe', nor even the introduction of QMV in the Council (which was mainly aimed at speeding up European legislation in areas related to the completion of the single market) and of a new co-operation procedure upgrading (under certain conditions) the legislative role of the EP, can be said to correspond to what neofunctionalists originally had in mind: the regional centralisation of authoritative decision-making driven by the expansive logic of integration and, eventually, the emergence of a new European 'political community'.

Reflections on the TEU

This section considers the state of theorising European integration in the 1990s in relation to the political and constitutional physiognomy of the Maastricht Treaty. Such an inquiry is of particular theoretical interest as none of the previously dominant paradigms of regional integration in Europe provide an overall hermeneutic pattern. Rather, different theoretical accounts intermesh with enormous complexity as to the outcome of the twin Intergovernmental Conferences of 1990/91. A possible explanation is that from a phase of integration in the mid-1980s, when expected 'spillovers' monopolised the interest of the academic community, we moved into a situation where a process of 'overspill' became manifest:[3] the scope of integration – that is, the range of things that states decide to do together – had by then seriously expanded, whereas its level had become all the more difficult to dissociate from the control of state executives. Indeed, the component states were equally anxious to preserve the integrity of their respective polities, and hence to continue their existence as distinct sovereign entities and even reinforce their own autonomy, rather than be drawn into a system of uncontrolled institutional centralisation followed by advanced schemes of federalism and, as some may have it, regional state-building.

Art. A TEU states that 'The Union shall be founded on the European Communities, supplemented by the policies and forms of cooperation established in this Treaty'. Accordingly, the Union provides for a general umbrella under which the pre-established Communities continue to exist as separate legal entities. The EC is the more advanced component of a three-pillar structure complemented by the Common Foreign and Security Policy (CFSP) and Co-operation in Justice and Home Affairs (JHA). The latter pillars, by establishing two additional 'pluralist' arenas, reveal the limits of majority voting in still sensitive policy areas. The *locus decidendi* of the new competencies 'pooled' to the central institutions in these sectors rests firmly in the hands of the Council, the limited consultative role of the Commission and the EP notwithstanding. As Taylor put it: 'The whole was to be consolidated into a single package of activities linked in systems of common management.'[4] Owing to the cautiously designated stages of joint decision-making, the procedures operating in these pillars resemble an exercise in transnational regime formation: a co-operative venture based upon a commonly agreed set of principles, norms, rules and procedures, elaborate enough to promote a relatively high degree of horizontal interaction among the states, and elastic enough to be wholly consistent with the pursuit of a wide range of segmental interests in EU affairs.[5] As Bulmer and Scott put it: 'the two new pillars of the Union constitute an extension of the terrain of inter-state co-operation . . . a strengthening of the kind of intergovernmental arrangements which exacerbate the democratic deficit.'[6] This point is further supported by the perpetuation of a complex 'comitology' system which evades proper parliamentary control, national or European; the issue of extending the EP's co-responsibility over the Community's compulsory expenditure (agriculture); the question of a uniform procedure for European elections; and a wide range of issues relating to the openness, clarity and transparency of EU decision-making.

According to Art. E TEU, the four main institutions of the Union shall exercise their powers 'under the conditions and for the purposes provided for' by the provisions of the Treaty, while Art. N TEU renders all parts of the Treaty subject to the same revision rules. And since the TEU rests on two different sets of legal mechanisms – the Community Method and intergovernmental co-operation – the extent to which it has provided for a 'single institutional framework' is far from self-evident. However, Demaret recognises that 'the dividing line between the two types of mechanisms and between their respective fields of application is, in several instances, less than clear-cut'.[7] But even despite these reservations, the legal maze of the TEU has raised more questions than it originally sought to address, proving to be 'a source of controversy'.[8] As Wallace put it: 'the terms of Maastricht . . . can be interpreted as easily as making efforts to set a ceiling on, even a roll back of, the forces of supranationalism as they can be seen as crossing a new threshold on the route towards a European transnational polity.'[9] It is thus conceivable that the Union does not possess a legal personality of its own. Rather, 'it must be considered a new international organization *sui generis* and thus as a subject of international law'.[10] If by the term 'international organisation' we mean 'a formal, continuous structure established by agreement between members . . . from two or more sovereign states with the aim of pursuing the common, interests of membership',[11] then challenging this view is no easy task. Suffice it to stress that the confusion surrounding the 'constitutionality' of the TEU is supportive of the fact that for many scholars the question whether the Union has moved closer to a federal type of polity remains largely unanswered.

What is also remarkable in the central arrangements brought about by the TEU is the insistence of sovereignty-conscious states to protect their own cultural, political and constitutional features; a point clearly made in Art. F(1) TEU: 'The Union shall respect the national identities of the Member States, whose systems of government are founded on the principles of democracy.' This is indicative of the need to sustain a pluralistic form of society at the regional level, implying that any challenge to constituent identities would be legally and practically unacceptable. The search for unity through an 'uneasy compromise' between federalism and confederalism implies a series of interstate concessions to meet the challenges of joint decision-making, without losing sight of the growing quest for national autonomous action. Both points seem to substantiate the view that, owing to the premium it places on preserving (territorial) segmental autonomy within a sensibly arranged 'union', the TEU is characterised by a unique blend of consensual mechanisms for accommodating segmental diversity within a nascent, yet fragile, political unity. Joining together diverse entities in a regional union that respects their individual integrity, the constitutional structure of the Union challenges the organic theory of the polity, without relying entirely on the properties of 'segmented differentiation'. From this stems its greatest merit as a system of mutual governance, but also its strongest concern: to provide equality of status to its members while allowing for a less rigid understanding of sovereign statehood. In fact, the TEU offers an advanced conception of the practice of political co-determination. This has been achieved so far by applying a mixed system of consensus and majority government, consistent with what Forsyth had earlier defined as 'unanimity at the base, majority voting in the superstructure'.[12]

The political fragility of the new arrangements was clearly manifested not only during the negotiations leading up to the signing of the TEU in February 1992, but also during its arduous course of ratification and the subsequent 'opt-outs' secured by the more sceptical members as a *quid pro quo* for consenting to the Union project. Against the background of an ever more cynical electorate, any residual touch of optimism from the mid-1980s seemed to have evaporated by the conclusion of the ratification process in October 1993. Although the TEU finally managed to survive the new tides of Euroscepticism, a new 'democratic disjunction' became manifest between the wishes of national leaders and popular political sentiments.[13] As in past treaty revisions, the TEU reflected in a most tenacious way the ongoing tussle between those defending the rights of states (as sovereign units) and those projecting an independent legitimacy for the Union (as an composite polity). In Neunreither's words: 'It is a text for insiders, not only in being difficult to read and to digest, but even more because of its paternalistic approach – everything is done *for* the people, not very much *by* the people.'[14] Thus the lesson to be learned from the Maastricht process is that unless there is a sufficient area of consensus at the elite level, no viable outcome(s) can exist. This accords with what most students of integration had implicitly assumed: over the 1990s, the weight of the evidence is that the extension of the scope and level of European integration has exploited a crucial property of consensual politics: the capacity to reconcile the challenges of institutional innovation with the need for systemic continuity. The conclusion to be drawn is that 'the burden of proof' lies more on federalism than on intergovernmentalism as a method of organising both the internal and external affairs of the general system. This view is further supported by the rather moderate, and certainly unimaginative, reform packages agreed in Amsterdam and Nice in June 1997 and December 2000, respectively, which will be examined later in this study.

Having examined some crucial aspects of the TEU, it is time to consider in greater detail some of the stimulating theoretical attempts to (re)conceptualise, largely from a political systemic perspective, the emerging properties and functions of the regional system. Of particular interest here are liberal inter-governmentalism, the fusion thesis, new institutionalism, multilevel gover-nance, the international state thesis, the concepts of condominio and consortio, the examination of the Union's state-like properties in comparison with other forms of state, the confederal consociation thesis, as well as new normative per-spectives on EU theorising, such as neo-republicanism and constructivism.

New theoretical approaches

Liberal intergovernmentalism

The approach developed by Moravcsik in the early 1990s aimed at widening the spectrum of scholarly debate about the evolution of the EU system, its internal decision-making procedures and, more importantly, the relationship between domestic politics and international co-operation – the latter is achieved mainly by using Putnam's analogy of the two-level games.[15] Liberal intergovernmental-ism, in attempting to restore the superiority of state-centric approaches to the study of regional integration, purports to explain, on the one hand, the interac-tion between states and international organisations and, on the other, the rela-tionship between national preference-formation, coalitional behaviour and interstate bargaining. What is distinctive in this approach is that it offers a range of intellectual opportunities for moving beyond 'unicausal theorising', by inte-grating three important subdisciplines of general international relations theory: regime analysis, negotiation theory and intergovernmentalism. The wider the-oretical concern revolves around an understanding of the dynamic interplay between a liberal interpretation of national preference-formation, the rational-ity of actors pursuing their interests at the central level and the distinct nature of intergovernmental bargaining within the Community system.

The welcoming aspect of this analysis is that it links the domestic political orders and economic agendas of states to joint decision-making, as well as to coalition-formation in the Council. Moravcsik argues that Community institu-tions, which are generally taken as highly reactive agents operating within a 'pas-sive structure', strengthen the power of national governments in two important respects: 'they increase the efficiency of interstate bargaining', often by acting as 'facilitators of positive-sum governing', and they 'strengthen the autonomy of national political leaders vis-à-vis particularistic societal groups within their domestic polity'.[16] The point being made in the latter case is that state executives mediate between domestic interests and Community action: integration out-comes are shaped by the relative bargaining power of national governments and by the distribution of preferences among them. The Community's transaction cost-reducing function, its highly institutionalised policy co-ordination envi-ronment and the institutional delegation (pooling of sovereignty) that take place at the larger level (mainly through the application of majority rule) are important factors towards a viable negotiating order: 'a successful inter-governmental regime designed to manage economic interdependence through negotiated policy co-ordination.'[17] In brief, despite its many critics (who are particularly sceptical of the theory's working assumptions on state rationality and its tendency to downplay the impact of decision rules and institutional preferences), Moravcsik's 'new intergovernmentalism' represents a attempt to bridge the gap between neofunctionalist pre-theorising and 'substantive' theorising, by proposing a challenging research agenda, which places the emphasis on the primacy of interstate bargaining in determining the pace and range of the regional arrangements.

The fusion thesis

Wessels' analysis on the subject projects a dynamic macropolitical view of the integrative process.[18] The argument he puts forward is that European integration is characterised by an 'ever closer fusion' of 'public instruments from several levels linked with the respective Europeanisation of national actors and institutions'.[19] Wessels stresses the development and importance of institutionalised patterns of joint problem-solving between national and European governance structures for the fulfilment of public needs. This makes the larger system part of the evolution of West European statehood itself. In Wessels' words: 'it is a crucial factor and dynamic engine of the fundamental changes in the statehood of western Europe'; thus attributing to the Union a much more complex role than that of merely 'rescuing the nation state' in the Milwardian sense.[20] Conceptually, the term 'fusion' is taken to mean something more than merely a 'horizontal pooling of sovereignties' as understood by mainstream realist state-centric analyses. Rather, it bears a strong resemblance to the functioning of the German political system of 'interlocking' federalism or *Politikverflechtung*, which in turn refers to a continuous process of negotiation between state and federal agents in the determination of national policy. In fact, this particular form of interlocking authority structures becomes part of Wessels' explanatory variables for the patterns of political systemic growth and differentiation in the Union.

Applied to the Union's composite polity, 'fusion' refers, according to Wessels, to the 'merger' of public resources located at several levels of governance, including substate structures. This, however, has as a result the blurring of responsibilities among the actors involved and, by extension, an increased difficulty in tracing the accountability of diffused policies. This kind of 'messy federalism', to borrow a phrase, is also reminiscent of the way in which politics operates in the German system, where an apparent 'accountability deficit' stems from the complexity and composite nature of national policy-making in determining which particular actor or set of actors is responsible for which decision(s). In general terms, the Union is treated as 'the logical product of fundamental choices by member governments', operating through 'package deals', without however undermining the role of central institutional actors, which remain important 'in shaping the perceptions of national actors'.[21] In short, the fusion thesis purports to explain the new challenges confronting the evolution of West European states and the way in which they, as the basic units constituting a larger polity, 'try to achieve an increased effectiveness in applying public instruments by using efficient procedures on the one hand, while maintaining a major say through broad and intensive participation on the other'.[22]

New institutionalism

Leaving aside the apparent methodological sophistication of new institutionalism, many of its explanations rely upon a rather uncomplicated (and until recently largely unqualified) assumption that institutions make a difference in the process of organising public life: whether formal or informal in kind, institutions are not merely epiphenomena: they form a constitutive part of a fuller and for that matter more profound understanding of complex social reality. Indeed, the revival of institutional analysis as an indispensable element in conducting political science research is partly to do with an attempt to tackle new challenging questions about the changing conditions of the liberal constitutional polity and of novel processes of socioeconomic governance, and partly to do with the equally demanding task of providing better explanations about the causal impact different institutions have on specific policy outcomes, by means of influencing – i.e., systematising, structuring, constraining, etc. – the formation of actors' preferences and the pursuit of their interests. New institutionalist accounts also assert that institutions, conceived as non-neutral arenas of human governance, facilitate the exchange of information among actors, offer the possibility of informal contacts, assist the internalisation of norms, enhance the quality of communicative action, promote patterns of co-operative behaviour (often by means of shaping the behaviour of those working within their structures), and map the expectations of actors on issues of social and political change. In particular, institutions are capable not only of promoting change, but also of constraining it, as well as touching upon sensitive issues of actors' identity, rather than merely acting as neutral or passive instruments for aggregating societal interests and claims.

The arguments mounted in support of new institutionalism in the discussion of the EU political system can be summarised as follows: supranational institutions have an impact on the behaviour of national governing elites and domestic policy actors, while becoming important venues for conflict resolution; the present-day Union offers the most advanced form of regional institutionalisation based on both formal and informal mechanisms of rule-making and norm-setting; post-SEA, there is a notable re-embrace of institutional analysis, treating institutions as meaningful, autonomous actors in the European policy setting, often by means of imposing constraints on rule-based state behaviour; systemic growth in the Union has often led to a series of 'unintended consequences' regarding the influence and competence acquisition of supranational institutions at the expense of state executives which can no longer act as gatekeepers; explaining and understanding the evolution of the integrative system can no longer rely on an analysis of 'grand episodes' and 'history-making' decisions through formal interstate negotiations; supranational institutions limit the capacity of states to exercise effective and/or ultimate political control in either setting the integrative agenda or in determining integration outcomes; the emergence of new policy norms and regulatory practices influencing EU policy-making.

Focusing on the impact of the central institutions on integration processes, Bulmer analyses the transformation of European governance from a comparative public policy perspective,[23] offering a new institutionalist account that goes beyond both purely descriptive empiricism and reductionist political analysis. In doing so, his illuminating analysis has placed EU institutions 'in a context which allows differentiation between formal political institutions, informal conventions and the norms and beliefs embedded within those institutions'.[24] The underlying assumption here is that institutions matter: 'that political struggles are mediated by prevailing institutional arrangements.'[25] New institutionalism treats institutions as instruments capable of shaping 'the pattern of political behaviour', going 'beyond the formal organs of government' to include 'standard operating procedures, so-called soft-law, norms and conventions of behaviour'.[26] Both the SEA and the TEU, Bulmer notes, can be understood from a historical institutionalist perspective, for they created and extended the competences of the Community and have generated changes in the conventions and norms embedded in the central institutions.[27] Bulmer's analysis does not point either to a holistic or a unifocal approach, but rather complements other theoretical endeavours in their examination of EU politics and governance in the 1990s.

In general, the new institutionalist political science raises challenging research questions about the institutional dynamics of macropolitical order-building; the consequences of institutional reform (through formal or informal means and procedures); the impact on constitutive norms on actual policy performance; the ways in which institutions structure the interaction between different actors, shape their choices and influence their behaviour; the relationship between continuity and change in a system of institutionalised rule; the interplay between institutional affirmation and transformation; the intrinsic and extrinsic importance of institutional settings, and so on. Having said this, however, it is still imperative to qualify further the central institutionalist tenet, namely that institutions matter. Here, a promising research agenda drawn from the domain of comparative politics has recently emerged, examining not only the question of whether or not institutions are important, but also for what, while touching upon issues of regime or system-wide performance and institutional causality. It is almost a certainty, at least for the foreseeable future, as well as a very welcoming aspect in EU theory-building, that institutional approaches to the study of European integration will grow stronger and that its students will be better equipped to deal in a more insightful and systematic manner with such intricate issues as the impact of less formalised arenas of governance on integration outcomes, the role of institutional values in everyday policy-making and, crucially, the normative context within which the constitutive actors and governance arrangements of the European polity operate as norm-setting forces.

Multilevel governance

In stark contrast to state-centric approaches to European integration like liberal intergovernmentalism (which generally perceive the EU system as a means of enhancing state sovereignty or autonomy), the 'multilevel governance' school aims to inform our understanding of an emerging European polity that is increasingly characterised by overlapping competences and structures of political authority. In this context, Marks, Hooghe and Blank have directed their *foci* to the study of the Union as a system of 'multilevel governance'.[28] Being critical of (realist) state-centrism, this group of scholars looks at the 'polity-creating process' that is currently emerging in Europe, leading to a situation whereby 'authority and policy-making influence are shared across multiple levels of government', and where national governments 'have lost some of their former authoritative control over individuals in their respective territories'.[29] The point the authors make is that 'the locus of political control has changed' – state executives do not monopolise decision-making competencies any longer – and that '[i]ndividual state sovereignty is diluted in the Union by collective decision-making among national governments' and by 'the increased autonomy and independent influence that EU institutions have come to enjoy'.[30]

There are indeed limits to both individual and collective state executive control: increased majoritarianism in the Council and the regression of its (once dominant) 'veto culture'; the mistrust among state executives; the role of interest group organisations and transnational actors in the actual policy process; the intensified interconnection of different political arenas, the increased complexities and specialisation of collective public policy-making (requiring detailed regulation); the co-legislative rights of the EP; the agenda-setting role of the Commission along with its substantive informational capacity and policy implementation influence; the political dynamics of the ECJ's legal activism; domestic party political competition; subnational mobilisation, national constitutional constraints on formal treaty change, and so on, are only a few factors to mention. From this school of thought, EU policy-making 'is characterised by mutual dependence, complementary functions and overlapping competencies'.[31] The Union is thus taken as a 'multilevel polity' composed of interlocked arenas for political contest, where direct links are established among actors in diverse political arenas, where political control is diffuse – often leading to 'second-best' policy outcomes, in turn resulting from Scharpf's notion of a 'joint-decision trap' or *Politikverflechtungsfalle* – and where 'states no longer serve as the exclusive nexus between domestic politics and international relations [or intergovernmental bargaining]'.[32] Although it is not claimed that supranational institutions will eventually supersede the member state executives, multilevel governance theorists argue that no single locus of accumulated political authority exists, or for that matter is likely to come into being, owing to the largely 'post-sovereign' character of the Union, in that authority cuts across traditional state boundaries and domains of policy action. A major difference between liberal intergovernmentalism and the multilevel governance approach is that, according to the former, governments bargain the interests of domestic actors in state-dominated arenas, while the latter acknowledges the mobilisation of domestic actors directly in the transnational arena through their involvement in multilevel policy networks, where they represent one out of many competing actors.

Multilevel governance carries at least two important meanings in relation to national sovereignty. First, there is a notion of a single, albeit pluralistic and asymmetrical, regional polity, within which sovereignty is dispersed among competing political actors which chose to bypass their central national authorities in their dealings with Brussels. The European polity thus transcends the traditional bond between territory, function and, increasingly, identity, and becomes a new venue for conflict resolution, interest articulation and the representation of claims stemming from 'smaller', diverse, but politically organised units. This perspective, which in large measure leads to a postmodern approximation of EU reality, stresses the limits of state sovereignty in advanced processes of union and the penetration of diverse social and political settings. A second meaning to national sovereignty denotes a new type of collective action that recognises the constitutional foundations of sovereignty as resting on the member state polities, but challenges the capacity and, hence, the functional autonomy of states to respond effectively to pressing socioeconomic realities. In this sense, subnational mobilisation becomes an additional vehicle for the re-allocation of authoritative problem-solving capacity to constitutive entities within a polity that remains dependent in critical ways on its subsystems, but which also allows for new structures of political opportunity to emerge. This implies a dynamic understanding of governance, not so much as the political capacity to steer, but as a practical means for domestic actors to influence large-scale policy-making by hitting several access points directly. To summarise the two conceptions of sovereignty: in the first case, contrary to the hierarchical order of the Westphalian sovereignty regime, there is an explicit acknowledgement of the structural transformation of the nation-state, which now becomes an integral part of a new multilevel polity of diffused public authority and governance functions. In the second case, the state retains *de jure* sovereignty but loses its autonomy – its capacity rather than authority to control events – in performing its tasks as the principal actor for the articulation of domestic interests, as well as in projecting its political domination of collective problem-solving.

International state

In an illuminating analysis about the 'post-ontological' stage of contemporary EU studies (the emphasis being on explanation rather than categorisation), Caporaso sheds light on the character of the European polity and the possible ways of conceptualising its evolving institutional structure from the theoretical perspective of different 'forms of state'.[33] His insightful research encourages the analyst to develop a deeper and, comparatively speaking, historically informed understanding of the Union as a 'regional international state': 'an international structure of governance based on the extrusion of certain political activities of its constituent units.'[34] Caporaso is also critical of the view that equates the emergence of EU authority structures, however novel or difficult to conceptualise in traditional political systemic terms, with a direct loss of national autonomy. Instead, he urges the analyst to focus on 'the ongoing structure of political authority and governance', that is, the complex interaction of economic and political relations among the member states, which are mediated by supranational institutions.[35]

Drawing on three stylised 'forms of state' as 'conceptually possible expressions of political authority organised at the national and transnational levels'[36] – the Westphalian state, the regulatory state and the postmodern state – Caporaso makes the point that each of these distinct governance structures captures a significant part of the evolving EU reality. After clarifying, however, that his analysis represents a 'comparative exploration of three metaphors rather than a test of three theories', he argues that the first ideal state form helps us to perceive regional integration as 'a re-enactment of the traditional processes of state-building from the seventeenth through to the twentieth centuries'; the second encourages us to think of the present-day European polity as 'a supranational state specialising in the control and management of international externalities'; and the third directs us to an understanding of the general system as a 'polymorphic structure', which is characterised by the absence of a strong institutional core, is increasingly fragmented, has no clear public sphere as compared to its domestic counterparts and where 'process and activity become more important than structure and fixed institutions'.[37]

In general terms, Caporaso's understanding of the Union as an 'international state' is closer to the regulatory and postnational forms of polity than to the traditional Westphalian state model. Such an understanding of the EU system, while remaining historically informed, marks a shift away from vertically defined end products such as 'political community', 'federal state', 'constitutional union' and the like which, to borrow from Haas, 'foreclose real-life developmental possibilities'. Instead, Caporaso's preferred lines of investigation and resulting conceptual understanding are able to incorporate different visions and ideal-type (normative) orientations of European political order. Notwithstanding the view that statist analogies to the study of the European polity are only partly justified, and that hypothetical integration outcomes are, at best, 'mere provisional points in the future', Caporaso's international state thesis encourages contemporary integration theorists to focus more closely on 'the ongoing structure of political authority and governance', that is, the complex interaction of economic and political relations among the subunits that are mediated by the central institutions. In short, his examination contributes to a 'post-ontological' account of the emerging European polity informed by a novel instance of social formations, interests and interactions that are embedded in an international structure of governance.

Consortio and condominio

Schmitter's examination of 'some alternative futures for the European polity' through the projection of novel forms of political organisation constitutes a welcome contribution to the debate about the evolution of the Union.[38] Arguing that the latter already represents 'the most complex polity that human agency has ever devised', Schmitter rejects the idea that the end state of integration will be 'a "re-run" of the processes and policies that earlier made the nation state the predominant political institution of Europe'; instead, he claims that the Union, presently lacking a locus of clearly defined authority, a central hierarchy of public offices, a distinct sphere of competence, a fixed territory, an exclusive recognition by other polities, an overarching identity, a monopoly over legitimate coercion and a unique capacity to impose its decisions, 'is well on its way [to] becoming something new'.[39]

What might this 'new' entity be? Two possible suggestions from Schmitter, presented as ideal-types, warrant our attention. The first refers to the notion of a 'consortio', defined as 'a form of collective action . . . where national authorities of fixed number and identity agree to co-operate in the performance of functional tasks that are variable, dispersed and overlapping'.[40] In it, the segments retain their respective territorial identities and 'accept positions within a common hierarchy of authority, but pool their capacities to act autonomously in domains they can no longer control at their own level of aggregation'.[41] Another possible, albeit less imaginative, integration outcome is the emergence of what Schmitter calls 'condominio', referring to a complex regional arrangement based on 'a variation in both the territorial and the functional constituencies'.[42] He explains: 'Instead of a Eurocracy accumulating organisationally distinct but politically co-ordinated tasks around a single centre, there would be multiple regional institutions acting autonomously to solve common problems and produce different public goods . . . Moreover, their dispersed and overlapping domains . . . could result in competitive, even conflictual, situations and would certainly seem inefficient when compared with the clear demarcations of competence and hierarchy of authority that (supposedly) characterise existing nation states.'[43]

At present, Schmitter concludes, the idea of a condominio-type outcome, somewhat reminiscent of Haas' multivariate integration scheme termed 'asymmetrical authority overlap', emanates as the most probable trajectory of the European polity. Schmitter's analysis is not a-historical. For all the novelty of his alternative integration scenaria for the future of Europe, he offers a general conceptual justification for applying the terminology of pre-existing forms of polity to the study of contemporary Europe. In particular, he embraces the view that, in the interests of conceptual refinement and historically informed comparisons, one has to turn to the past to recapture a more diverse language about political units. Revisiting European history, especially its early modern phase, where the continent witnessed the emergence of 'composite states' characterised by a system of shared sovereignty, overlapping political arenas and multiple points of contention, offers scholars the opportunity to draw valuable insights and categories of analysis in order to get their bearings in a present that is in flux. Rethinking the present Union in light of past experiences of polity-building is a productive way of sparking scholarly imagination in studying processes that have also evolved through different phases, and which are reminiscent of those currently under way. More importantly, such lines of inquiry provide the cognitive resources necessary not only for the framing of intriguing hypotheses, but also for functional analogies of recent developments to be tested. At the same time, Schmitter's analysis helps integration scholarship to become familiar with an otherwise nebulous image of EU polity-building, by allowing for the transfer of assumptions and ideas from novel political formations, which can in turn offer a useful conceptual laboratory for insightful comparative investigations to be drawn.

Confederal consociation

The concept of 'confederal consociation' was first introduced in the mid-1990s, drawing on Taylor's earlier work, as a means of capturing the dialectic between fragmentation and stability in the EU polity. The point made was that the TEU gave birth to an advanced form of regional organisation, which can best be defined as a compound polity whose distinct culturally defined and politically organised units are bound together in a consensually prearranged form of 'union' for specific purposes, without losing their sense of forming collective national identities or resigning their individual sovereignty to a higher central authority.[44] Confederal consociation emanates as a promising analogy in filling the existing gap between state-centric and federalist-inspired approaches to European integration, suggesting that the constituent governments have discovered new ways of strengthening their positions both regionally and internationally. Indeed, the three-pillar structure created by the TEU, similar to an ancient Greek temple, and the moderate reforms brought about by its recent revisions, help to maximise the states' influence in deciding upon matters of common concern, while allowing them to enjoy what Lijphart described earlier as 'a high degree of secure autonomy in organising their own affairs'.[45]

Segmental autonomy, therefore, supported by an accommodative mutual veto, a proportional representation of all states to the central institutions, and an increased propensity of national leaders to rely on what Taylor called 'government by alliance'[46] via *reversible dissensus* practices in joint decision-making, highlights the determination of states to exercise managerial control over integration, even if this implies the striking of less ambitious settlements among them. Confederal consociation has an interesting analogue with a system of horizontal *Kooperative Staaten*, in that the collective power of component parts is well preserved by making progress towards further formal integration dependent on the convergence of national preferences, as in the workings of the European Council which represents the Union's 'grand coalition' forum for striking interstate compromises. This polycentric and multilogical pattern of federalism co-exists with a more favourable version of intergovernmentalism as a method of promoting unification, and is based on the premise that the defence of each separate interest coincides with the need to strike a deal in the context of an intersegmental positive-sum game. It may best be defined as a case of 'inverse federalism': a situation in which political authority tends to be diffused as much as possible to the segments and away from the central institutions of governance.[47] This mode of interaction may be seen as a discernible integrative stage, where the dynamics of elite-led governance shape the forms that EU federalism is allowed or indeed prohibited from taking. In brief, territorial politics is becoming stronger in the larger system as the scope of joint decisions is being extended, thus bringing the *locus decidendi* of the central political system closer to the domain of state agents.

The last property of confederal consociation, that of 'controlled pluralism', highlights the elite-dominated character of EU decision-making, in that the members of the elite cartel are induced to adopting the working principles of 'joint consensual rule'. This co-operative dynamic conflicts with the 'winner-takes-all' ethos which subsists in majoritarian systems, deviating also from normative democratic theory and its insistence on 'rule by the many'. But it accords with the development of consensus politics at the leadership level, supported by a transnational political culture among the national governing elites. By dismissing an 'either/or' conception of EU politics, confederal consociation makes the point that the extension of central competences is compatible not only with the very idea of statehood itself, but also with further national state-building, subnational community-strengthening and multiple identity-holding. It also contains a suggestion both of the non-conflictual character of EU power-sharing and of the means through which the separateness of the segments, in the form of well consolidated democracies, is compatible with processes of 'institutionalised compromise'. Hence, the preservation of 'pluralism-within-unity' is conditioned by an overarching concern at the elite level for meeting the conditions of stable governance.

Finally, by emphasising elite-driven, as opposed to demos-led, integration, the model suggests that the dialectical co-existence of a plurality of forces pressing simultaneously for a more centralised or decentralised, loose or coherent, technocratic or democratic Union, passes through the capacity of states to retain ultimate control over both European constitutional choice and change. This system of consensus elite government, in which high levels of interconnectedness co-exist with segmental autonomy, approximates the type of community detected by Taylor as 'managed *Gesellschaft*': 'a decentralised though coordinated system of political interaction in which the segments . . . are characterised by high levels of interdependence with each other, but nevertheless preserve and even augment their autonomy.'[48] What is striking in this unique interplay between co-ordinated interdependencies and diffuse political authority is that the interests of the 'territorial state' co-exist with those of the central institutions insofar as they are products of consensual inter-elite negotiations.[49] This last observation, which has important and, one might argue adverse, implications for the emergence and consolidation of a European civic demos *ab intra*,[50] brings us to the final part of our theoretical inquiry, asking an oft-raised question: where do we go from here?

Constructivism

This strand in EU theorising, heavily drawing from constructivist approaches to international relations theory, has arguably come closer to instituting a systematic 'second-order discourse' in the study of the European polity. In 1999, a special issue of the *Journal of European Public Policy* was devoted to the 'Social Construction of Europe', recognising the value of a normatively informed, metatheoretical research context to EU polity-building, by investigating, *inter alia*, the impact of constitutive norms and rules; the role of ideas and communicative action; the uses of language and deliberative processes; the interplay of routinised practices, socialisation, symbolism and institutional interaction; and the interplay between agent identity and interests. The whole exercise was meant to herald a 'constructivist turn' in EU studies, aiming 'to go beyond explaining variation [in politics and policy] within a fixed setting' and to stress 'the impact of "intersubjectivity" and "social context" on the continuing process of European integration . . . [in brief, to call attention to] the constructive force of the process itself'.[51]

The starting point of this emergent research trend is an aspect of change, in that integration has 'a *transformative* impact on the European state system and its constituent units', as well as a firm belief in taking the logic and methods of social science inquiry seriously and incorporate into the process of understanding social reality 'human consciousness' and 'ideational factors' with a normative as well as instrumental dimension.[52] The gist of the argument is that there exists 'a socially constructed reality' as an expression of what Ruggie calls 'collective intentionality'.[53] Keeping in mind that there is both a realist and an idealist component in constructivist thought, constructivism represents a social theory with a strong interdisciplinary reach, straddling the lines between the various subfields of social science research. This interdisciplinary trend is exemplified in the writings of Shaw and Wiener, whose aim is 'to track norms from "the social" to "the legal" . . . [and] trace the empirically observable process of norm construction and change . . . with a view to examining aspects of "European" constitutionalism [and citizenship practice]'.[54] Their core set of conclusions is that EU constitutional politics as 'day-to-day practices in the legal and political realm as well as the high dramas of IGCs and new Treaties' is about 'fundamental ordering principles which have a validity outwith the formal setting of the nation state', that 'norms may achieve strong structuring power . . .

[and] are created through interaction', and that '[t]he processes of norm construction and rule-following are mutually constitutive'.[55]

The general question posed by constructivist theorists in EU studies is 'to what extent, and in which ways, a new polity is being constructed in Europe'.[56] The principal aim is to problematise the changing social ontologies of European polity-formation. It is on this premise that middle-range constructivist theorising becomes well suited to the study of the European polity, directing its research *foci* to 'the juridification and institutionalization of politics through rules and norms; the formation of identities and the construction of political communities; the role of language and discourse'.[57] Although it would be rather difficult, as it would be unfair, to reach an authoritative conclusion on the overall contribution of constructivism to the field, for it is both a recent and an ongoing attempt 'to enlarge the theoretical toolbox of EU studies',[58] a multitude of useful analytic and epistemological insights can be drawn from an interdisciplinary constructivist research programme that places metatheoretical thinking at the centre of understanding the social ontology of the European polity, thus creating 'an arena in which ontological shifts and meta-theoretical moves can be debated'.[59]

Particularly with reference to issues of polity and democracy, constructivism represents a critical normative turn in integration studies, in that the means and ends of the Union's social legitimation are increasingly becoming the object of analysis. In this context, the emphasis has not been exhausted, as in other approaches, on the question which body of theory can best explain the constitutive norms and rules of European governance *per se*, but rather which type of theorising offers a deeper understanding of the European polity in relation to the sociopsychological conditions of European identity-building. Whether this metatheoretical approach will contribute to the emergence of a conceptual consensus about the construction of a democratic theory of European integration – a task requiring the refinement of integration theory and the development of 'transcendent perspectives' on a range of conventional dispositions that existing theories and approaches hold – is difficult to foresee. Yet, the point is clearly made in constructivist discourses that familiarity with metatheory is a two-way process: it helps to develop 'overarching theoretical perspectives' and appreciate their relevance to 'first-order theorising'.

(Neo)republicanism

In its basic conception, a *res publica* aims at fulfilling three fundamental ends: justice through the rule of law; the common good/public interest through a mixed and balanced constitution; and liberty (or civic freedom) through active citizenship. Overall, *Omnia reliquit servare rempublicam* captures the republican imagination of a virtue-centred life, defined in civic terms. It is worth noting that, even 2510 years since the founding of the Roman republic, an anniversary that passed largely unnoticed by present-day Europeans, the above features constituting the *raison d'être* of the *res publica* continue to mark their impact in the interminable search – scholarly and otherwise – for 'the good polity'. Recently, republican thought managed to infiltrate the disorderly universe of EU theorising, by yielding some valuable new insights into an already voluminous *aquis académique* on how best to conceptualise the evolving Union. Such approaches, however, have become more than simply 'trendy': new republican perspectives on the Union sought not only to revive, but also to nurture a paradigm of social and political organisation founded on a new 'civic partnership' among distinct historically constituted demoi. Indeed, republican conceptions of Europe are part of a demanding intellectual current: the search for a reliable as well as democratic theory of integration able to capture the dialectic between strengthening the viability of the component public spheres through the institutionalisation of a mixed sovereignty regime. The point being made here is that, absent a formal (or material) European constitution, and given the inchoateness – at best – of a European civic demos (and corresponding lack of an input-oriented European legitimacy), there is urgent need for a substantive restructuring of the Union's civic arenas with a view to engaging its citizens in its governance structures. This philosophy accords fully with a civic conception of the European polity that aims to assess the relationship between the Union and 'the civic'. Such normative explorations have been recently brought into focus, often by employing the language of 'second-order discourse', especially in the sphere of collective norm-orientation and political constitutionalism. Their distinctive contribution to the field is that they have given rise to a 'normative turn' in contemporary EU studies, signalling at the same time a paradigm shift from 'policy to polity', or from 'diplomacy to democracy' – or, more accurately, 'from democracies to democracy'.

Pace the view that, for all the richness of recent normative investigations, the Union will continue to be, at least for the foreseeable future, 'an ongoing social scientific puzzle', Bellamy and Castiglione have attempted to capture the Union's complexity, pluralism and hybridity – in that its political system displays a 'baffling mixture' of federal and intergovernmental properties – through a theory of 'democratic liberalism' based on 'a pre-liberal conception of constitutionalism that identified the constitution with the social composition and form of government of the polity'.[60] This amounts to a political system capable of dispersing power within civil society, while encouraging dialogue between the component parts of the polity. 'Instead of the constitution being a precondition for politics', Bellamy and Castiglione note, 'political debate becomes the medium through which a polity constitutes itself'.[61] Being highly critical of any territorial and/or hierarchical distribution of power, democratic liberalism brings the constituent groups of the polity into an equilibrium with one another, aiming at dispersing power so as 'to encourage a process of controlled political conflict and deliberation [as a way of filtering and channelling preferences] . . . moving them thereby to construct and pursue the public good rather than narrow sectional interests'.[62] The theory goes that, within this pluralist polity characterised by a differentiated social context, there can be different forms of representation employed for different purposes. Differentiation is crucial to the kind of political constitutionalism advocated by democratic liberals, as it links together justice, the rule of law and the democratic dispersal and division of power, while providing a balanced mix of social forces and levels of authoritative decision-making.

From a similar prism, by reviving the usage of an eighteenth-century term, MacCormick suggests that the European polity can be best defined as a 'mixed commonwealth', within which the subjects of the 'constitution' are not homogeneous, but rather represent a mixture of political agents that share in the sovereignty of the larger political entity.[63] Bellamy and Castiglione explain this point well: 'The polycentric polity that is therefore emerging is a definite departure from the nation state, mainly because it implies a dissociation of the traditional elements that come with state sovereignty: a unified system of authority and representation controlling all functions of governance over a given territory.'[64] MacCormick's notion of a lawfully constituted European commonwealth of post-sovereign states, whose normative validity stems largely from the existence of a well-established legal order (supported by foundational norms, basic doctrines, and general principles), allows the regional polity to conduct itself as a *Rechtsgemeinschaft* but not as a *Rechtsstaat*. Within it, and absent 'a single power-structure with a single normative frame',[65] or, to borrow from Lindberg and Scheingold,[66] in the context of an 'ambiguous pluralist system', political authority is neither proportionately nor symmetrically vested in an overarching centre, but is rather distributed through overlapping arrangements, with the polity being characterised by various degrees of decentralisation and 'infinitely tiered multiple loyalties'.[67] Informed by an associative understanding of governance, this pluralist depiction of the European polity as an essentially heterarchical order within which sovereignty is dispersed across and between a variety of actors and public domains, and where a 'balanced constitution' emerges as the ultimate protective mechanism against the danger of domination – political, judicial, constitutional or otherwise – is fully in line with Tarrow's insightful and historically informed definition of the Union as a 'composite polity': 'a system of shared sovereignty, partial and uncertain policy autonomy between levels of governance, and patterns of contention combining territorial with substantive issues'.[68] Tarrow's conceptualisation largely draws from the work of historian Wayne te Brake on the formation of 'composite states' in early modern Europe, where people 'acted in the context of overlapping, intersecting, and changing political spaces'.[69]

Republican theory embodies a strong normative commitment to democratic deliberation for the promotion of the public interest, as opposed to factional demands, and to the setting up of a particular kind of constitutional ordering based on the idea of 'balanced government'. Such ordering, in the form of a constitutional state, is dedicated to offering citizens 'undominanted' (or quality) choice. But it is not the latter that causes liberty. Rather, liberty is constituted by the legal institutions of the republican state. In this context, democratic participation is not taken as an end in itself, but rather a means of ensuring a dispensation of non-domination or non-arbitrary rule. Another republican variation on the theme of *vita activa* takes civic participation 'as a process of constructing politics, not merely one means among others to secure something else'. In brief, the rule of law, opposition of arbitrariness and the republican constitution are constitutive of liberty, conceived in republican terms as civic freedom. With reference now to the idea of 'balanced government', Craig argues that it was forged in two related ways: negatively, by associating the constitution of 'a proper institutional balance' with the aim of preventing tyranny; and positively, by ensuring a deliberative form of democracy, 'within which the different "constituencies" which made up civil society would be encouraged to treat their preferences not simply as givens, but rather as choices which were open to debate and alteration'.[70] More than that, liberty was expected to be best preserved under 'a mixed form of republican governance' through certain constitutional practices or provisions, whereby no single component part of government would be privileged over the others; such normative issues, claims Craig, are of relevance when considering the actual distribution of authority within the Union.[71] Here, republicanism claims to strike a balance between participation in the European legislative process and the attainment of the general public good, by allowing for 'a stable form of political ordering for a society within which there are different interests or constituencies'.[72] In institutional terms, the idea of a 'balanced constitution' in the Union is reflected in the Commission's exclusive right to initiate legislation and its interaction with civil society, the EP's co-decision rights in fostering more deliberative outcomes and the relationship between the Council's indirect democratic mandate and the fact that the Union rests on a system of treaty-based rules.

But there also exist other facets of republican thinking relevant to a civic conception of Europe. Lavdas, for instance, draws on Pettit's seminal study on freedom as non-domination – as opposed to a negative conception of liberty as non-interference, or to a positive conception of it as self-mastery – to argue that the larger polity may develop in the future the democratic functions of institutionalised public deliberation (and a corresponding concern with active or participatory citizenship), which are necessary, but not sufficient, conditions for a more 'democentric' process of union.[73] Given the absence of an engaging European demos, a republican mode of governance emanates as an appropriate means of disentangling 'the issue of participation in an emerging polity from the cultural and emotional dimensions of citizenship as pre-existing affinity and a confirmation of belonging'.[74] The point here is that 'some elements of the real and symbolic *res publica*, may sustain a degree of political motivation *vis-à-vis* the Union and its relevance for peoples' lives while also allowing for other and more intense forms of motivation and involvement at other levels of participation'.[75] But given the apparent lack of organic unity among Europe's constituent demoi, the republican challenge is one of institutionalising respect for difference and group rights (in line with the dictates of multiculturalism), while sustaining a shared sense of the public good. This is more likely to be achieved through Pettit's third concept of freedom (as non-domination), in that it 'enables a view which aims to combine the recognition of the significance of the pluralism of cultural possibilities for meaningful choice and a framework based on a minimal set of shared political values'.[76] From these neo-republican expositions, one could imagine a European *res publica*, within which a multitude of commitments may generate higher levels of civic engagement, while enhancing the possibilities of meaningful choices on the part of the composite demos through the institution-alisation of a deliberative, rather than aggregative, model of governance.

Concluding note

Every theoretical journey has its own rewards. These may stem either from a plurality of intellectual formulations exploring the nature of complex political phenomena, or indeed from wider methodological and/or epistemological concerns. The theoretical examination of the Union *qua* polity or system of governance, and of European integration processes more generally, is no exception. On the contrary, it is through the conceptual and analytical lenses offered by a rich corpus of regional integration theory that one may develop a more profound understanding of the structural properties, behavioural characteristics and operational dynamics of what is frequently referred to as 'the emerging European polity'. The term 'polity' constitutes an appropriate point of reference for two significant reasons: first, it is ideologically free from the narrow and often analytically vulnerable insights offered by classical (realist) state-centric approaches to European integration; second, it is capable of avoiding the equally biased interpretations of a supranationalist conception of the larger system.

On the other hand, that no present theoretical account of recent developments in the Union claims to represent the nucleus from which a new 'grand theory' of regional integration might emerge, that is, one with widely applicable comparative insights, is almost self-evident. Likewise, none of the prevailing interpretations of the Union in general, and of EU polity-building in particular, is capable of predicting with a degree of confidence the future evolution of the regional system. On the contrary, prediction is altogether treated as a risky exercise and has thus been avoided by most contemporary analysts, Schmitter's imaginative research on alternative and often unprecedented integration outcomes notwithstanding. But there is something inherently fascinating and rewarding in undertaking such risks – especially when there is no reason at all for integration scholarship to be narrowly confined in the domain of traditional descriptive analyses and exegetic patterns of real-life events.

With this in mind, and from a rather optimistic interpretation of European polity dynamics, it is possible to suggest that a shift in paradigm has taken place since the mid-1990s, namely 'from policy to polity' or, somewhat differently, 'from diplomacy to democracy'. This new transition stage is best captured by the term 'nascent *Gemeinschaft*'. Leaving aside for the moment the moderate reform packages agreed in Amsterdam and Nice, especially with reference to the process of democratising the Union, the post-Maastricht phase can be seen as part of a wider political evolution – even constitutional if one were to describe the formal treaty framework as the EU's 'political constitution' – towards a European 'public sphere', comprising citizens capable of being simultaneously conscious of their separate existence as distinct entities and of their collective existence as a composite demos. In particular, nascent *Gemeinschaft* aims at distancing current integration practices from the logic of consensus elite government by means of stressing the democratic potential of European citizens. Instead of large-scale decisions being the result of intensive interelite accommodation mostly through *in camera* bargaining, they should be subjected as closely as possible to the conditions of the democratic process, the most crucial of which refers to the notion of European 'civic competence': the institutional capacity of EU citizens to be actively involved in the governance of the larger polity.[77] Nascent *Gemeinschaft* focuses on the process of turning an aggregate of electors into a politically responsible demos whose members feel part of a larger purposive whole and are capable of directing their democratic claims to, and via, the central institutions, thus opening the way towards a new democratic *civitas* in Europe.

In this sense also, nascent *Gemeinschaft* can be seen as both a conceptual position and a new point of departure for citizens to develop a more profound sense of civicness within an 'inclusive' European polity. Here, the term 'polity' refers to a system of governance capable of engaging its component state/citizen parts in the making of authoritative political decisions which have implications for the allocation of values in the transnational society. The characterisation of the Union as an 'emerging polity', compound yet easily identifiable as a collectivity, refers to no less. In fact, it is now possible to contemplate the idea of replacing the rather deterministic concept of 'integration', whose teleology is closely linked to the 'directionality' of the general system, with that of 'polity-formation': the making of a large-scale political system composed of highly interdependent states and demoi, characterised by overlapping, intersecting and often competing policy arenas, public spheres and civic spaces. Although 'integration' remains useful in the vocabulary of EU studies, insofar as it purports to explain the joining together of previously autonomous units under a new regional centre, 'polity-formation' is better equipped to capturing the constitutive nature of European governance. In short, for a polity that is constantly under the scrutiny of international scholarship, but where no substantive consensus or even convergent conceptual understandings exist on its social and political ontology, the search for clear answers (and questions) is no easy task. Such problems, however, will be compounded even further should we fail to investigate the normative implications that polity-building generates for the future of Europe.

Keeping these theoretical notes in mind, we can now move on to the politics of the IGC 1996/97, and the extent to which the resulting AMT represented a significant step towards furthering the democratic properties of the EU system, or whether it corresponded to a largely managerial type of reform designed to preserve the intrinsic nature of the Union as a confederal consociation, and with it the premium it places on consensus elite government and the practice of political co-determination. We will then examine, in Chapter 4, the Nice process and outcome, following the conclusion of the IGC 2000 and the subsequent signing of the NIT in February 2001. In both case studies, our previous theoretical analysis will act as a wider laboratory of concepts and ideas so arranged as to help us throw some additional light on the dynamics of European governance since the late 1990s. It is to this demanding but no less exciting task that we now turn.

Notes

1 J. Tranholm-Mikkelsen, 'Neo-Functionalism: Obstinate or Obsolete? A Reappraisal in the Light of the New Dynamism of the EC', *Millennium*, Spring 1991, pp. 1–22.

2 See Robert O. Keohane and Stanley Hoffmann, 'Institutional Change in Europe in the 1980s', in Robert O. Keohane and Stanley Hoffmann (eds), *The New European Community: Decisionmaking and Institutional Change*, Boulder: Westview, 1991, pp. 1–39.

3 Paul Taylor, 'Prospects for the European Union', in Stelios Stavridis *et al.* (eds), *New Challenges to the European Union: Policies and Policy-Making*, Aldershot: Dartmouth, 1997, pp. 13–41.

4 Paul Taylor, *International Organization in the Modern World: The Regional and the Global Process*, London: Pinter, 1993, p. 99.

5 This formulation draws on Stephen D. Krasner, 'Structural Causes and Regime Consequences: Regimes as Intervening Variables', in Stephen D. Krasner (ed.), *International Regimes*, Ithaca: Cornell University Press, 1983, p. 2.

6 Simon Bulmer and Andrew Scott, 'Introduction', in Simon Bulmer and Andrew Scott (eds), *Economic and Political Integration in Europe: Internal Dynamics and Global Context*, Oxford: Basil Blackwell, 1994, p. 8. Cf. Stelios Stavridis, 'The "Second" Democratic Deficit in the European Community: The Process of European Political Co-operation', in F. R. Pfetsch (ed.), *International Relations and Pan-Europe: Theoretical Approaches and Empirical Findings*, Münster: Lit Verlag, 1993, pp. 173–94; and M. Anderson, M. den Boer and G. Miller, 'European Citizenship and Cooperation in Justice and Home Affairs', in Andrew Duff *et al.* (eds), *Maastricht and Beyond: Building the European Union*, London: Routledge, 1994, pp. 104–22.

7 Paul Demaret, 'The Treaty Framework', in D. O'Keeffe and P. M. Twomey (eds), *Legal Issues of the Maastricht Treaty*, London: Wiley Chancery Law, 1994, p. 6.

8 Roy Pryce, 'The Maastricht Treaty and the New Europe', in Duff *et al.* (eds), *Maastricht and Beyond*, p. 3.

9 Helen Wallace, 'European Governance in Turbulent Times', *Journal of Common Market Studies*, September 1993, p. 294.

10 George Ress, 'Democratic Decision-Making in the European Union and the Role of the European Parliament', in D. Curtin and T. Heukels (eds), *Institutional Dynamics of European Integration: Essays in Honour of Henry G. Schermers*, Vol. II, Dordrecht: Martinus Nijhoff, 1994, p. 156.

11 Clive Archer, *International Organisations*, 2nd edn, London: Routledge, 1992, p. 37.
12 M. Forsyth, 'Towards a New Concept of Confederation', European Commission for Democracy Through Law, Council of Europe, 1994, p. 14.
13 For details see Stelios Stavridis, 'Democracy in Europe: West and East', in Conference Proceedings, *People's Rights and European Structures*, Manresa, September 1993, p. 130.
14 Karlheinz Neunreither, 'The Syndrome of Democratic Deficit in the European Community', in G. Parry (ed.), *Politics in an Interdependent World: Essays Presented to Ghita Ionescu*, Aldershot: Edward Elgar, 1994, p. 96.
15 Andrew Moravcsik, 'Preferences and Power in the European Community: A Liberal Intergovernmentalist Approach', *Journal of Common Market Studies*, December 1993, pp. 473–524. See also Robert D. Putnam, 'Diplomacy and Domestic Politics: The Logic of Two-level Games', *International Organization*, 42:3, 1988, pp. 427–60.
16 *Ibid.*, p. 507. See also Ben Rosamond, *Theories of European Integration*, London: Palgrave, 2000, p. 143.
17 *Ibid.*, p. 408.
18 Wolfgang Wessels, 'An Ever Closer Fusion? A Dynamic Macropolitical View on Integration Processes', *Journal of Common Market Studies*, June 1997, pp. 267–99.
19 *Ibid.*, p. 273.
20 *Ibid.* and p. 274. See also Alan S. Milward, *The European Rescue of the Nation State*, Berkeley, CA: California University Press, 1992.
21 Wessels, 'An Ever Closer Fusion?', p. 274.
22 *Ibid.*, p. 287.
23 Simon Bulmer, 'The Governance of the European Union: A New Institutionalist Approach', *Journal of Public Policy*, 13:4, 1993, pp. 351–80.
24 *Ibid.*, p. 353.
25 *Ibid.*, p. 355.
26 *Ibid.*
27 *Ibid.*, p. 370.
28 Gary Marks, Leisbet Hooghe and Kermit Blank, 'European Integration from the 1980s: State-centric v. Multi-level Governance', *Journal of Common Market Studies*, September 1996, pp. 341–78.
29 *Ibid.*, p. 342.
30 *Ibid.*, pp. 342–3.
31 *Ibid.*, p. 372.
32 *Ibid.*
33 James Caporaso, 'The European Union and Forms of State: Westphalian, Regulatory or Post-Modern?', *Journal of Common Market Studies*, March 1996, pp. 29–52.
34 *Ibid.*, p. 33.
35 *Ibid.*
36 *Ibid.*, p. 29.
37 *Ibid.*, pp. 35, 39, 45.
38 Philippe C. Schmitter, 'Some Alternative Futures for the European Polity and their Implications for European Public Policy', in Yves Mény *et al.* (eds), *Adjusting to Europe: The Impact of the European Union on National Institutions and Policies*, London and New York: Routledge, 1996, p. 25.
39 *Ibid.*, p. 26.
40 *Ibid.*, pp. 30–1.
41 *Ibid.*, p. 31.
42 *Ibid.*
43 *Ibid.*
44 For further details see Dimitris N. Chryssochoou, 'Democracy and Symbiosis in the European Union: Towards a Confederal Consociation?', *West European Politics*, October 1994, pp. 1–14.

45 Arend Lijphart, 'Consociation and Federation: Conceptual and Empirical Links', *Canadian Journal of Political Science*, September 1979, p. 506.

46 Paul Taylor, 'The Politics of the European Communities: The Confederal Phase', *World Politics*, April 1975, p. 346.

47 This has been described elsewhere as an 'inverse pyramid'. For further details see Michael J. Tsinisizelis and Dimitris N. Chryssochoou, 'From "Gesellschaft" to "Gemeinschaft"? Confederal Consociation and Democracy in the European Union', *Current Politics and Economics of Europe*, 5:4, 1995, pp. 1–33.

48 Taylor, 'The Politics of the European Communities', p. 336.

49 Dimitris N. Chryssochoou, 'European Union and the Dynamics of Confederal Consociation: Problems and Prospects for a Democratic Future', *Journal of European Integration*, 18:2–3, Winter/Spring 1996, pp. 279–305.

50 See Dimitris N. Chryssochoou, '"Europe's Could-be Demos": Recasting the Debate', *West European Politics*, October 1996, pp. 787–801. Cf. Dimitris N. Chryssochoou, 'Rethinking Democracy in the European Union: The Case for a "Transnational Demos"', in Stavridis *et al.* (eds), *New Challenges*, pp. 67–85.

51 Thomas Christiansen, Knud E. Jørgensen and Antje Wiener, 'The Social Construction of Europe', *Journal of European Public Policy*, 6:4, 1999, pp. 528–9.

52 *Ibid.*, p. 529.

53 Quoted in *Ibid.* For the original argument see J. G. Ruggie, *Constructing the World Polity: Essays on International Institutionalization*, New York: Routledge, 1998, p. 33.

54 Jo Shaw and Antje Wiener, 'The Paradox of the "European Polity"', in M. Green Cowles and Michael Smith (eds), *State of the European Union, Volume 5: Risks, Reform, Resistance, and Revival*, Oxford: Oxford University Press, 2000, pp. 67–8.

55 *Ibid.*, pp. 75, 87.

56 Christiansen *et al.*, 'The Social Construction of Europe', p. 537.

57 *Ibid.*, p. 538.

58 *Ibid.*, p. 543.

59 Shaw and Wiener, 'The Paradox', p. 68.

60 Richard Bellamy and Dario Castiglione, 'Democracy, Sovereignty and the Constitution of the European Union: The Republican Alternative to Liberalism', in Z. Bańkowski and A. Scott (eds), *The European Union and its Order* London: Blackwell, 2000, p. 181.

61 *Ibid.*, p. 182.

62 *Ibid.*, p. 181.

63 See Neil MacCormick, 'Democracy, Subsidiarity, and Citizenship in the "European Commonwealth"', *Law and Philosophy*, 16, 1997, pp. 331–56.

64 Richard Bellamy and Dario Castiglione, 'Building the Union: The Nature of Sovereignty in the Political Architecture of Europe', *Law and Philosophy*, 16:4, 1997, p. 443.

65 MacCormick, 'Democracy', p. 338.

66 See Leon N. Lindberg and Stuart A. Scheingold, *Europe's Would-Be Polity: Patterns of Change in the European Community*, Englewood Cliffs, NJ: Prentice-Hall, 1970.

67 Ernst B. Haas, 'The Study of Regional Integration: Reflections on the Joy and Anguish of Pretheorising', *International Organization*, 24:4, 1970, p. 635.

68 Sidney Tarrow, 'Building a Composite Polity: Popular Contention in the European Union', Institute for European Studies Working Paper, No. 98/3, Cornell University, 1998, p. 1.

69 Wayne te Brake, *Shaping History: Ordinary People in European Politics, 1500–1700*, Berkeley and Los Angeles: University of California Press, 1998, p. 278.

70 Paul P. Craig, 'Democracy and Rule-making within the EC: An Empirical and Normative Assessment', *European Law Journal*, 3:2, 1997, p. 114.

71 *Ibid.*, p. 115.

72 *Ibid.*, p. 116.

73 Kostas A. Lavdas, 'Republican Europe and Multicultural Citizenship', *Politics*, 21:1, 2001,

pp. 1–10. See also Philip Pettit, *Republicanism: A Theory of Freedom and Government,* Oxford: Clarendon Press, 1997.

74   *Ibid.,* p. 4.

75   *Ibid.,* p. 5.

76   *Ibid.,* p. 6.

77   See Dimitris N. Chryssochoou, 'Metatheory and the Study of the European Union: Capturing the Normative Turn', *Journal of European Integration.* 22:2, 2000, pp. 123–44.

3

The Amsterdam reforms
Partial offsets and unfinished business

Introduction

As a result of the IGC 1996/97, the member governments of the Union signed in Amsterdam, in June 1997, the Treaty which partially reformed the Maastricht Treaty. All those who linked the outcome of the review conference with the construction of a democratically organised European polity, or even regarded it as an opportunity for a more or less permanent clarification of the physiognomy of the Union, have no real grounds for celebration as realism, in the end, seems to have had its way. Indeed, the changes introduced by the new Treaty, if anything, failed to deliver the much-needed clarification of the properties of the system towards more familiar models of governance and political organisation. It is probably fair to suggest that the outcome of the prolonged negotiations that led to the AMT, as well as the nature of the new Treaty itself, relates to the well-known French saying, *plus ça change, plus c'est la même chose*. As the *Economist* put it, the Amsterdam Summit 'produced more of a mouse than a mountain'.[1] Or, as the *Guardian* reported: 'Europe is much the same this week as it was last week.'[2]

The AMT represented the third formal reform of the original Treaties of Paris (1951) and Rome (1957). Compared, however, with the two intervening revisions, namely the SEA (1986) and the TEU (1992), it will most likely go down in the history of European treaty reform as the 'unnecessary Treaty' or the 'uncourageous' one, since none of the major issues in its political agenda were really touched upon. Contrary to the two earlier treaty-amending processes, the AMT is characterised by a generalised lack of vision as to the political and constitutional future of a Union about to embark on further enlargements. Perhaps that was the reason behind the rather uncontroversial process of its ratification, at least as compared with the TEU, which allowed the Treaty to come into force on 1 May 1999.

The IGC 1996/97

From the outset, the review conference was greeted with mixed feelings: some member states showed extreme caution, others thought it was too soon to engage themselves in a process of reforming Maastricht, while others were hesitant to disturb an already delicate balance brought about by the TEU. The IGC opened its workings on 29 March 1996 in the north Italian city of Turin under the auspices of the Italian Presidency, followed by the Irish and then the Dutch Presidencies, while the Dublin European Summit of October 1996, known also as Dublin I, stipulated that the Conference should be concluded at the Amsterdam European Summit of June 1997. The reform process evolved via no less than forty meetings at the level of the representatives of Foreign Affairs Ministers, sixteen meetings of the Ministers, and five Summits of the heads of state and government.

Although there is no doubt that important issues were indeed at stake during the reform process given the prospects for further EU enlargement, it would be even more accurate to note that what was not formally discussed in the context of the IGC, intentionally or not, proved to be more significant, or even consequential, for the future development of the Union. The adequacy of the Maastricht provisions on Economic and Monetary Union (EMU) by 1999 in relation to questions of economic and social cohesion, and the prospects for a well-thought-out reform of the central institutions in relation to questions of democratic legitimacy are good cases in point, and so are the extension of European citizenship rights, the need to bring national parliaments closer to the European legislative process, as well as the problem regarding the allocation of competences among different levels of governance. With the benefit of *a posteriori* knowledge, however, the fact that the IGC did not discuss EMU, considering that the Maastricht decisions in that regard were final, could be considered a wise choice, although the same cannot be said for the remaining set of problems that were confronting the internal political organisation of the Union. Instead, such issues formed part of a hidden political agenda concerning, *inter alia*, the future of the European welfare state system, the economic costs of eastward enlargement, the social and political integration of European citizens, questions of institutional equity, efficiency and legitimacy, as well as issues of interinstitutional accommodation, to mention only a few.

Moreover, the rationale behind Art. N TEU had also to do with the need to take stock of the CFSP in general and the role of the Western European Union (WEU) in particular, a delicate subject upon which there was disagreement during the twin IGCs of 1990/91. As the agenda of the IGC was expanding rapidly, almost Summit after Summit, the December 1993 Brussels European Council decided that the Conference should expand its agenda to include such issues as the size of the Commission and the weighting of votes in the Council, while the Corfu European Council opened the issue of QMV. In general, the TEU came for re-negotiation in accordance with the procedural pattern that forms part of the *acquis communautaire*. More specifically, the IGC 1996/97 was based on the following combination of Treaty articles and Declarations attached to the Treaty:[3]

- The fifth case of Art. B TEU which states that 'with a view to considering, through the procedure referred to in Art. N(2), to what extent the policies and forms of co-operation introduced by this Treaty may need to be revised with the aim of ensuring the effectiveness of the mechanisms and the institutions of the Community'.
- The eighth paragraph of Art. 189b EC, through which the co-decision procedure may be extended.
- Arts I.4 paras 6 and I.10, which provide for the revision of those articles dealing with the CFSP.
- The attachments to Declarations 1 and 16.[4]

Following Wessels, the following four options seemed feasible during the review conference: implementing Maastricht; reforming Maastricht; renationalising Maastricht; and abandoning Maastricht.[5] Essentially, this clarification of the available options for European treaty reform was a task assigned to an *ad hoc* group of representatives of the Foreign Affairs Ministers of the member states, which was set up following a decision by the June 1994 Corfu European Council,[6] and became known as the 'Reflection Group'. The Group was mandated to contribute to the review process, functioning as it were as a forum for discussion, thus reflecting upon and elaborating, but not negotiating, issues and options to be included in the IGC agenda. Chaired by Westendorp, the then Spanish Secretary of State for the European Communities, the Group presented its findings in two documents, the Interim Report of August 1995,[7] and the Final Report of December 1995.[8]

The reports of the Reflection Group

The Final Report was submitted to the December 1995 Madrid European Council.[9] In it, the Group had defined its tasks as being the improvement of the workings of the Union, and the expansion of the capabilities of the Union to enable it to rise to both internal and external challenges (including the new rounds of enlargement towards the countries of Central and Eastern Europe (CEE)). The Final Report was structured around three dimensions, namely flexibility, efficiency and democracy.

'Flexibility' or 'variable geometry' or 'enhanced co-operation' or else
As discussed in Chapter 2, Schmitter had suggested an institutional transformation of the Union which he termed 'condominio'.[10] This form of governance is based, in his words, on 'a variation in both the territorial and the functional constituencies', and in our view draws heavily on Mitranian functionalism, save for the fact that Schmitter's approach is influenced by the 'end of history' thesis,

rather than the by then not clearly defined 'end of ideology' thesis. More importantly perhaps, Schmitter's integrative outcome also represents a reversal of the Mitranian logic to integration, in the sense that 'function follows form' (see Chapter 1). Notwithstanding the theoretical discussion of the Union as a condominio-type organisation, and despite the fact that 'flexibility' or 'enhanced co-operation' between the member states has been hailed as a major operational principle of the Union, clarifying such concepts within the latter's multilevel and plurifunctional system of governance has time and again proved problematic. These principles involve some 'variable geometry' practices such as those of the EMS/Exchange Rate Mechanism (ERM) arrangements in the 1970s, the Shengen Agreement before the AMT, and the Eureka programme. The Final Report was quick to point out, however, that such an outcome could be perceived only as a temporary arrangement and that it would not lead to a 'Europe *à la carte*' or similar forms of functional integration. Flexibility might have become all the more important as an organising principle of European governance in view of 1999, when the final stage of EMU commenced. Were this type of organisation to prevail, *ceteris paribus*, a pattern of differentiated participation in integration schemes, albeit for the medium term, would emerge. EU members would find themselves split into different groups according to each other's domestic or other priorities. Some of them would not adopt certain policies; others would not participate in the EMU arrangements, or would remain outside the WEU, especially in the eventuality of the latter emerging as the military branch of the Union, and so on. The above scenario would only strengthen the intergovernmental features of the general system, giving it a strong confederal bearing, and thus bringing it closer to a Europe of 'concentric circles'.

Moreover, the debate on flexibility, in either the workings of the Reflection Group or the meetings of the IGC *per se*, and the desire of the original members of the Community and the Commission to include the principle in the revised Treaty in the form of an article, draws an analogy with the inclusion of subsidiarity in the TEU and the legalistic debate that surrounded its introduction.[11] The rationale for the inclusion of a flexibility clause in the AMT was threefold: first, as a reaction to the observed behaviour of certain member states and the rights of opting-out that have been granted to them; second, owing to the unwillingness of some member states and the inability of others to attain the qualification criteria for entry in the third stage of EMU; and third, owing to the urgent need to take into account the institutional accommodation of the EU's eastward enlargement, given that the latter would create a Union too large and too heterogeneous to act in unison. On the other hand, flexibility entailed a strong dose of political realism, particularly concerning the hidden agenda of convergence, economic or otherwise. The dilemma that emerged in the IGC 1996/97 was between a pragmatic (rational), a normative (radical), and a mixed approach. Table 3.1 summarises the alternatives that were open to the member states.

Table 3.1 A typology of European constitutional choice

	Approach		
Properties	*Pragmatic*	*Normative*	*Mixed*
End result	Confederation	Federation	Confederal consociation
Modus operandi	Flexibility/ effeciency	Demos formation	Controlled pluralism
Locus of sovereignty	State rule	Civic rule	Consensus elite government
Central arrangement	Constitutions	Constitution	Constitutional engineering

Flexibility was finally included in the new Treaty, though in a way that precludes the creation of a Europe *à la carte* by introducing scores of strict conditions. In particular, Art. 1 of the general clauses to be inserted as a new Title in the AMT reads thus:[12]

> Member states which intend to establish closer cooperation between them may make use of the institutions, procedures and mechanisms laid down in the Treaties provided that the cooperation aims at the furthering of the objectives of the Union and the protection and servicing of its interests, respects the principles of the Treaties and the single institutional framework of the Union, is only used as a last resort . . . concerns at least a majority of the member states, does not affect the acquis communautaire, does not affect the competencies, rights, obligations and interests of the member states which do not participate therein, is open to all member states . . . [and] is authorised by the Council .

In addition, Art. 2 states that the new flexible arrangements will be governed by the same decision-making rules as in the TEU/EC adjusted accordingly for membership, and that the EP will be regularly informed by the Commission and the Council (Art. 3). However, additional conditions are to apply if flexible cooperation is introduced under the EC Treaty.[13] In particular, Art. 5a EC precludes member states from initiating flexible arrangements in the areas which:

- fall within the exclusive competencies of the Community;
- affect the Community policies, actions or programmes;
- concern the citizenship of the Union or discriminate between nationals of member states;
- fall outside the limits of the powers conferred upon the Community by the Treaty;
- constitute discrimination or restrict trade and/or distort competition between member states.

Furthermore, an additional condition is inserted in Art. K12, paras 1, 2 and 3 (all of which are subject to the jurisprudence of the ECJ) of the Treaty,[14] insofar as this stipulates that the new 'flexible' arrangements aim at enabling the Union to become an area of freedom, security and justice. Authorisation for the creation of these arrangements will be granted by the Council acting by QMV after an opinion by the Commission and the EP. Any objection, however, by a member state on grounds of 'important and stated reasons' results in the whole decision being referred to the European Council for a decision by unanimity. This provision accords fully with the consociationalist nature of European decision-making when vital national interests are at stake (see Chapter 2).

Efficiency and democracy

Efficiency was the second major organising principle of the Union to be included in the Report of the Reflection Group; arguably, a rather nebulous concept that was badly in need of further clarification. In conjunction with the flexibility principle, it might have addressed the potential of the general system to producing policy outcomes without any reference to their quality, or the number of the participating states for that matter. The Report, however, did not hint at an institutional set-up capable of satisfying the conditions of flexibility and efficiency. It did state, however, that the IGC should also preserve the single institutional framework of the Union, in that the composition of the ECJ, the Commission and the EP would be fixed, but that of the Council and the procedures therein would vary.

The picture was further complicated by the introduction in the Report of the issue of democracy and the oft-quoted 'need to bring the Union closer to its citizens', as a third major organising concept. This might have been a reference to the 'democratic deficit' of the Union, one of its celebrated structural shortcomings, but the emphasis of the Report was rather on the third pillar of the Union than on the interinstitutional balance of power within the first pillar. There was no consensus in the Group on the extension of the competences of the EP and only marginal modifications were considered. On the other hand, the Commission, in its Report on the TEU, has pointed to the importance of and the need to take measures to bring the Union nearer to its citizens. As the Report stated: 'Democracy comprises the very essence of the Union, while effectiveness is the precondition for the future.'[15] Regardless of the above discussion, however, the outstanding issues in the institutional agenda of the IGC were as follows:

- the Union and its citizens (including issues related to the transparency of its workings, the need to strengthen its democratic legitimacy, and a possible revision of the principle of subsidiarity);
- the introduction of a flexibility clause;
- the hierarchy of Community Acts;
- the Comitology phenomenon;
- the rationalisation of the decision-making processes and decision-taking arrangements in the Council in view of future enlargement;

- the composition of the Commission and the EP, and the latter's electoral system;
- Common Foreign and Security Policy;[16]
- Justice and Home Affairs.

Transparency and subsidiarity

These issues are dealt with together since they tend to have overlapping consequences. At any rate, they are part of the package, which is linked to the relationship between the Union and its citizens. The AMT has elevated the importance of the issue by including ten chapters dealing with various relevant subjects. Increased transparency is vital if the Union wishes to close the gap between the functioning of its institutions and the way in which its citizens can identify with its emerging governance structures. The term was linked to a right of information of Union citizens and the need for a more simplified and thus more comprehensible Treaty. In its report on the functioning of the TEU,[17] the Commission stated that there have already been steps in that direction, which should nevertheless be improved. There were twenty-two meetings of the Council of Ministers that were held in public – mostly during the Danish Presidency during the first half of 1993 – which dealt, however, with secondary and manifestly insignificant matters. By the same token, the Commission received 220 applications requesting access to its documents, 53.7 per cent of which were accepted, 17.9 per cent rejected, and 28.4 per cent concerned documents already in circulation or published by another EU institution.[18] The AMT acknowledged the need for increased transparency in the workings of the Union by including a special chapter (Chapter 10) and a new Art. 191a, whereby 'any citizen of the Union . . . natural or legal person shall have a right of access to European Parliament, Council and Commission documents',[19] subject to certain rules and conditions as specified on the Declaration to the Final Act on Art. 191a.[20]

The principle of subsidiarity is found in Art. 3b TEU. We have had the opportunity to comment elsewhere on its various shortcomings.[21] The topic is by now well documented and it suffices to point out that there is a need for further clarifications for the principle to become operational. The majority in the Group, however, wished that Art. 3b should remain unchanged. The Commission, in its Report on the TEU, suggested that: 'The concepts of the directive, of mutual recognition or that of the partnership [in the case of regional policy] reflect the principle of subsidiarity.'[22] This probably reveals that there is a misunderstanding of the meaning of the principle or that this is used in a way that suits the interests of EU institutions. In federal systems, the principle refers to concurrent competences defined by Toth as the 'authority of two different bodies to intervene with the same authority at the same time'.[23] Community law does not recognise 'concurrent powers' given that the powers of the Community are in principle exclusive in nature. In addition, the legal community resented the inclusion of the principle in the Treaty on the grounds that it could not be properly checked by the ECJ. The necessity for the conception of a specific body to examine the employment of the principle was reflected in the Group's Report, where it was intended that a 'higher consultative body' should be set up. But its composition and functions were not designated and there was an interesting reference made to a new role envisaged for national parliaments, since this new body would have been composed of their representatives.

In the end, however, a Protocol and a Declaration were attached to the AMT, providing guidelines for the application of the principle by Community institutions. Para. 5 of the Protocol stipulates as a prerequisite that any action by the Community has to be *a priori* justified on the grounds that such action cannot be achieved by the member states alone, and also that it can be better achieved by the Community. Strict guidelines were also set before the Commission initiates its policies: the issue under consideration must have transnational aspects; it has to be demonstrated that action by member states alone or lack of Community action would conflict with the Treaty; and that Community action would produce benefits of scale.[24] There is an attempt in the Protocol to refine the meaning of this dynamic yet elusive concept, although it sets some strict conditions for its application. Thus, each institution must respect the principle of subsidiarity and that of proportionality (sustained by qualitative and, if possible, by quantitative indicators; see Art. 4), according to which any action by the Community shall not go beyond any action necessary for the attainment of the objectives of the Treaty (Art. 1). The application of these principles must respect the *acquis communautaire* and the institutional balance, the powers of the ECJ and Art. F(3) TEU, according to which 'the Union shall provide itself with the means necessary to attain its objectives and carry through its policies' (Art. 2) and will be applied in the areas where the Community does not have exclusive competences (Art. 3). *Ceteris paribus*, directives should be preferred to regulations and framework directives to detailed measures (Art. 6), thus leaving as much scope for national decisions as possible (Art. 7). The Commission must act cautiously in this context, preferring as much prior consultation as possible before initiating legislation, except in cases of urgency or required confidentiality (Art. 9); minimise administrative or financial burdens on national or subnational institutions; and submit an annual report to the European Council, the Council of Ministers and the EP on the application of the principle.

The rationalisation of the decision-making process

The TEU has created a complicated institutional structure under the heading 'European Union', in the form of an ancient Greek temple based on three separate pillars – the EC, the CFSP and JHA.[25] Under Art. C TEU, the three pillars share a common institutional framework under the aegis of the European

Council. A closer examination, however, reveals that this framework is not so common after all, as the TEU has brought about a rather messy institutional setting, whereby the members states and the central institutions intermingle in no less than twenty-nine different decision-making procedures, depending on the policy area and/or the pillar in question: some procedures may or may not require consultation with the EP and/or other EU bodies depending on the issue at hand, a proposal from the Commission, a simple or qualified majority in the Council, and so on. This has become even more messy after the so-called 'Ioannina Compromise' of July 1994, whereby, under certain conditions, the minority veto in case the Council operates under QMV is not the normal twenty-three votes, but instead twenty-six.

The co-operation and co-decision procedures in Arts 189b and 189c EC were hailed as the procedures that were instituted to bridge the Union's 'parliamentary deficit' (with reference, however, to direct legislative involvement of the EP, as such a 'deficit' also has an important national component). As we have argued elsewhere,[26] these procedures help to co-opt the EP closer to the *locus decidendi* of the Union, in spite of their use in only fourteen and fifteen policy areas, respectively. The Interim Report suggested that a near-consensus was formed in favour of preserving the *status quo* and only of marginal modifications in the EP's role were considered. Hence, a clear majority was recorded in the Group against any changes in the position of the EP within the interinstitutional balance of power. In any case, it is our contention that the evolution of the Union towards a federal-like polity would require the introduction of a republican system of 'checks and balances' as an interim arrangement on the way to fully blown demos control. This view is justified further, by considering the marginal influence national parliaments and subnational assemblies have in the determination of EU legislative outcomes.

The AMT, however, introduced changes in the co-operation and co-decision procedures as a move towards the declared aim of simplifying EU decision-making. In particular, the following changes were introduced in Art. 189b EC regarding co-decision. The procedure starts off with the submission by the Commission of a proposal to the Council and the EP, as was previously the case under the TEU. Here, a new stage is introduced before the adoption by the Council of its Common Position requiring first the EP to deliver an opinion before the Council acts. If the Council approves the amendments of the EP, if the latter has tabled amendments, or if the EP does not propose amendments in the Council's opinion, then the Council adopts the act by QMV. Otherwise the Council adopts a Common Position and sends it to the EP. (Under the original procedure in the TEU, the EP had the opportunity to indicate that it intended to reject the Council's Common Position. Under the new procedure this has been dropped.) If within three months of such communication the EP approves the Common Position or does not reach a decision, the act is deemed to have been approved. If the EP rejects the Common Position by an absolute majority of its members, the act fails. Otherwise, the EP sends its amendments to the

Table 3.2 Areas in the Treaty requiring co-decision

Art. 49	Free movement of workers
Art. 54	Right of establishment
Art. 56	Right of establishment
Art. 57	Right of establishment
Art. 66	Services
Art. 100a	Internal market
Art. 100b	International market
Art. 126	Education
Art. 130s. 3	Environment
Art. 129d	Trans-European networks
Art. 129	Public health
Art. 129a	Consumer protection
Art. 128	Culture (+ unanimity)
Art. 1301	Research

New Articles in the AMT

Art. 5	Employment
Art. 119	Social policy – equal opportunity
Art. 191a	Transparency (general principles)
Art. 209a	Countering fraud
New article	Customs co-operation
Art. 213a	Statistics
Art. 213b	Authority on data protection

Added to co-decision from other procedures

Art. 6 (*from co-operation*)	Discrimination on grounds of nationality
Art. 8a(2) (*from assent*)	Free movement
Art. 51 (*from consultation*)	Internal market (rules on social security for immigrant workers)
Art. 56(2) (*from consultation*)	Right of establishment of forein national
Art. 57(2) (*from consultation*)	Right of establishment of self-employed persons. Conditions of access for natural persons
Art. 75(1) (*from co-operation*)	Transport policy
Art. 84 (*from co-operation*)	Transport policy
Art. 2(3) (*from co-operation*)	Social policy
Art. 125 (*from co-operation*)	European Social Fund
Art. 127(4) (*from co-operation*)	Vocational training
Art. 129d (*from co-operation*)	Other measures (trans-European netowrks)
Art. 130E (*from co-operation*)	European Regional Development Fund
Art. 130o (*from co-operation*)	Research
Art. 130w (*from co-operation*)	Development co-operation

Council. If the Council approves Parliament's amendments by QMV, and by unanimity those for which the Commission has expressed a negative opinion, then the Common Position is adopted thus amended. Otherwise, the Conciliation Committee is convened within six weeks. At this stage, a *prima facie* substantial change has been introduced which seems to be adding weight to the co-decision procedure: for an act deemed to have been approved, a joint text has to be approved by the Council and the EP; otherwise, the act fails. Thus, the Council no longer has the opportunity to reaffirm its Common Position by unanimity and have the act adopted. Instead, agreement on the joint text of the Conciliation Committee is a *sine qua non* for the adoption of the act. As the new paragraph 5 of Art. 189b EC states:

> If within six weeks of its being convened, the Conciliation Committee approves a joint text, the European Parliament, acting by an absolute majority of the votes cast, and the Council, acting by a qualified majority, shall have each a period of six weeks from that approval in which to adopt the act in question in accordance with the joint text. If either of the two institutions fails to approve the proposed act within that period, it shall be deemed not to have been adopted.

In addition, para. 6 reads thus: 'Where the Conciliation Committee does not approve a joint text, the proposed act shall be deemed not to have been adopted.'

Table 3.2 shows all the areas in the AMT that fall within co-decision (in all thirty-seven areas). As the table indicates, after the AMT, the co-operation procedure of Art. 189c EC has been almost eradicated from day-to-day decision-making, save only for two cases relating to EMU. The main decision-making procedures are now reduced to three: assent (five cases), consultation and co-decision. The co-decision procedure has been simplified and extended in its use to twenty-three more issue areas under the Treaty. The much discussed Art. 138B concerning the right of initiative of the EP and its interpretation has not found any support in the Reflection Group. The Commission, in its Report on the TEU, explained the meaning of Art. 138B, in that such requests do not require the Commission to put forward a proposal;[27] the Commission has only to take the 'greatest possible account of them'.[28] Accordingly, any such request by the EP is not legally binding on the Commission as is the case with Art. 152 EC, when the Council requests the Commission to put forward a proposal. The AMT did not in the end alter Art. 138b and, hence, yet another opportunity was clearly missed for further democratisation.

QMV

The voting mechanisms in the Council have also been altered with the AMT. In particular, QMV has been expanded into new policy areas, while decisions requiring unanimity have been reduced in a modest attempt to unify and simplify the relevant procedures. QMV was extended to sixteen new areas of the Treaty, as illustrated in Table 3.3. The general assessment to be made here is that,

Table 3.3　New areas in the Treaty where Qualified Majority Voting (QMV) is applicable

Article	Subject
	Amsterdam Treaty provisions
Art. 4	Employment guidelines
Art. 5	Incentive measures
Art. 118(2)	Social exclusion
Art. 119(3)	Equality of opportunity
Art. 129(4)	Public health
Art. 191a	Transparency
Art. 209a	Countering fraud
Art. 213a	Statistics
Art. 213b	Authority on data protection
Art. 227(2)	Outermost regions
New article	Customs co-operation
	Previous treaty provisions
Art. 45(3)	Aid on imports of raw materials
Art. 56(2)	Right of establishment of foreign nationals
Art. 130i(1)	Research framework programme (adaptation and supplementation
Art. 130o	Joint undertakings in R&D

similarly to the extension of QMV in previous treaty reforms, majority decisions are allowed in non-controversial and, by extension, non-conflict-prone areas, rather than in areas where the states want to speed up legislation.

The hierarchy of Community Acts

This is hardly a novel issue since it was raised during the twin IGCs of 1990/91 on Political Union and EMU that led to the signing of the TEU in February 1992. In reality, it has been an issue waiting to be settled since 1984, when it was first presented in the EP's Draft Treaty on European Union.[29] During the IGCs 1990/91, it was rejected on the grounds that such a system refers to a *de facto* classification of levels of governance as well as a *de jure* classification of institutions involved in policy-making top-down. Nevertheless, Declaration 16 attached to the TEU proclaims that 'The IGC agrees that the IGC to be convened in 1996 will examine the degree to which it is possible to revise the classification of the Community Acts so as to arrive at a hierarchy in the various Community Acts'.

　　The source of the following classification of Community Acts was the EP's Institutional Affairs Committee and the Italian government during the IGCs, when four types of Community Acts were suggested: Constitutional Acts, refer-ring to the process of treaty reform; Organic Laws, referring to the functioning of EU institutions; Regular Laws, referring to the formal decision-making process of the Union; and Regulations, referring to policy implementation. Dif-ferences between these types reflect mainly the differences in the decision-taking mode for each category, since the required majorities get lower as one moves down from Constitutional Acts to Regulations. There was a slight modification of this proposal in the Group's Interim Report where Regulations and Regular Laws were merged into one. The Reflection Group did not seem to have dis-cussed this issue in any great detail and referred the whole subject to the IGC. Differences between the member states seem to have been a mere reproduction of those at previous Conferences. In the end, nothing of this sort was included in the AMT.

Table 3.4 summarises the positions of the member states on the general theme of 'a Union closer to its citizens'. The table is exhaustive on the issues that were discussed in the context of the IGC 1996/97. Some explanation of this table, however, is in order. One of the seemingly key issues in the IGC agenda was the legal personality of the Union. Its non-existence runs counter to the overall objectives of the Treaty and is a real obstacle to the Union's role in international affairs. In the Reflection Group there was a clear preference in favour of grant-ing the Union with legal personality, which was abandoned at the last moment. Thus, as a result of the AMT, the Union does not possess a legal personality of its own; does not have the capacity to enter into binding agreements; is not recognised as a subject under international law; does not possess institutions or a budget of its own, but rather continues to rely on those of the Community. Similarly, on the question of nationality, there was a clear majority during the negotiations for Union citizenship not to replace national citizenship, and this was reflected in the amended Art. 8: 'every person holding the nationality of a member state shall be a citizen of the Union. Citizenship of the Union shall com-plement and not replace national citizenship.' Likewise, the attempted dropping in the TEU of the requirement on Art. 8e was not successful. The Council will still need unanimity if it wishes to strengthen the common citizenship provi-sions. Art. 8d TEU was also amended to enable citizens of the Union to address EU institutions in one of the official languages and receive a reply in the same language. Finally, an addition to the Preamble of the Treaty exhorts the virtues of education and its continuous upgrading. Culture and sport were also included in the AMT in recognition of their special significance for citizens' identities and welfare.

For the Union to become part of the European Convention on Human Rights and Fundamental Freedoms (ECHR), an amendment to the TEU was required. But this never materialised and the Union after the AMT is still not part of the Convention, in spite of a clear majority to the contrary during the negoti-ations (see Table 3.4). However, Art. F TEU was amended to include para. 1, according to which 'the Union is founded on the principles of liberty, democracy,

Table 3.4 A Union closer to its citizens

	COM	EP	B	DK	D	GR	E	F	IRL	I	LUX	NL	A	P	SF	S	UK
Chapter on fundamental and human rights in the Treaty	y	y	y	y	y	y	y	y	np	y	y	y	y	n	n	np	n
Become part in ECHR	y	y	y	np	np	y	y	n	R	y	y	np	y	y	y	y	n
Equal treatment and non-discrimination clause	y	y	y	np	y	y	y	y	y	y	y	y	y	y	y	y	n
Add social rights	y	y	y	np	np	np	y	n	n	n	np	np	np	y	np	n	n
Direct effect for Art. 8A	np	y	np	np	np	y	n p	n	n	np	np	np	y	np	np	n	n
EU citizenship does not replace national	y	y	y	y	n[	y	y	y	np	y	y	np	y	y	np	y	np
No unanimity for Art. 8E	np	y	n	np	n	y	n	n	n	np	n	n	y	np	n	n	n
Public meetings of Council	np	y	R	R	np	np	n	n	y	np	np	y	n	y	y	y	n
Equality clause for women	y	y	y	np	np	np	y	y	np	y	y	y	y	np	y	y	n
Protection by the ECJ	y	y	y	np	y	np	n p	y	np	y	y	y	np	y	np	np	np
Political control: suspension of certain rights	np	y	y	np	y	y	y	np	y	np	y	y	np	np	np	y	n
Political control: exclusion from EU meetings	np	n	n	np	np	n	n	np	np	np	np	np	n	np	np	n	np
Right of information on EU affairs	y	y	y	y	y	y	y	y	y	y	y	y	y	np	y	y	y
Development of nationality	np	y	np	np	np	y	y	y	np	y	y	y	y	np	y	n	n
List on fundamental rights	n	y	y	np	y	y	np	np	np	y	n	np	y	y	np	np	n

Source: European Parliament, the Secretariat, JF/bo/234/96, p. 1.
Key: y, affirmative; n, negative; R, reserve position; np, no position.

respect for human rights and fundamental freedoms, and the rule of law, principles which are common to the member states'. A new Art. Fa provides, under rather strict conditions, for penalties to those member states that are found in breach of the principles in Art. F(1) above. A new Art. 236 EC has also been inserted to expand penalties under the TEU to the EC Treaty as well. Both articles seem to be outward-looking, in that they were included in the AMT with the eastward enlargement in mind. The only amendment to the TEU, which is directly related to enlargement, concerns the supplement of the first sentence of Art. O TEU, according to which 'any European state which respects the principles set out in article F(1) may apply to become a member of the Union'. Note should also be taken of the new Art. 6a EC, which prohibits discrimination based on sex, racial or ethnic origin, religion or belief, disability, age or sexual orientation. A unanimous Council is foreseen to be taking measures to combat discrimination on the above grounds.

Section II of the AMT, concerning the 'Union and the Citizens', consists of nine chapters and deals with such diverse issues as consumer protection, quality of legislation, social policy, public health, subsidiarity, transparency and employment. A new Title VII on employment has been added to the Treaty in response to the widespread belief that some action on that front was urgently required, not least because the EMU arrangements, as well as the general economic philosophy spread in the TEU, have been increasingly identified as one of the reasons leading to the current poor employment situation in the Union. The Title consists of six articles and two declarations, constituting a rather loose framework of co-operation, with the Union in a primarily co-ordinating role. A new Employment Committee (Art. 6) is also introduced, consisting of thirty-two members with an advisory role, but overall responsibility for action rests firmly with the member states. According to Art. 4, each year the Council and the Commission will draw up a joint report on the employment situation in the Union to be discussed at Summit level. On the basis of the conclusions to be reached at the Summit, the Council, acting by QMV, will draw up guidelines for the member states. The latter will each year provide the Council and the Commission with an annual report of their activities in the light of the guidelines which, if necessary, may lead to the issuing of Council recommendations to the member states, after a recommendation by the Commission. Finally, the circle is squared, in that the Council and the Commission, on the basis of the national reports, will draw up reports to the European Council on employment. Art. 5 foresees the possibility for adopting incentive measures via the co-decision procedure to encourage co-operation between the member states, by providing incentives aimed at developing exchanges of information and best practice, offering comparative insights and advice, as well as promoting innovative approaches and evaluating experiences by recourse to pilot projects. The duration of these incentive measures may not exceed five years, and the maximum amount of their financing should always be specified.[30] Whatever the merits of the new Title, its inclusion in the AMT cannot but be considered a positive step towards confidence-building between the Union and its citizens.

The Protocol on Social Policy attached to the TEU,[31] together with the annexed Agreement on Social Policy, have been inserted in the AMT, with the UK becoming part of it. Simultaneously, the Protocol and the Agreement are repealed from the Treaties. According to Art. 117 the objectives to be attained include the promotion of employment, the improvement of living and working conditions, the establishment of proper social protection, dialogue between management and labour, the development of human resources and the combating of social exclusion. Art. 118 lists the areas in which the Community shall support and complement the activities of the member states, introducing concurrently changes in the decision-making arrangements. Table 3.5 shows which areas of action in the field of social policy require unanimity and co-decision, and which minimum standards are to be introduced so as to avoid adverse effects to medium-sized enterprises.

Table 3.5 Areas of action by the Community: co-decision and unanimity in social policy

Co-decision	Unanimity
1 Improvement of the working environment to protect health and safety	1 Social security and social protection of workers
2 Working conditions	2 Protection of workers where their employment contract is terminated
3 Information and consultation of workers	3 Representation and collective defence of the interests of workers and employers, including co-determination
4 Integration of persons excluded from the labour market	4 Conditions of employment for third-country nationals legally residing in the Community
5 Equality between men and women with regard to labour market opportunities and treatment at work	5 Financial contributions for promotion of employment and job creation, without prejudice to the provisions related to the ESF

Note: Pay, right to strike, right to impose lock-outs, right of association are excluded.

An interesting case of macrocorporatist arrangement seems to have been instituted with para. 4 of Art. 118, foreseeing the possibility, on a joint request by labour and management, allowing member states to entrust the organisations of management and labour to implement any directives of the issues included in Table 3.5. Were such a situation to arise, member states would only have to guarantee to the Community that the required directives would be implemented. Last but not least, the provisions of Art. 118 do not apply to pay, rights of association, the right to strike or the right to impose lock-outs.

Arts 118a and 118b in the new Title seem to be quite significant. The AMT, in its Art. 118a (para. 14), instructs the Commission to promote the consultation of management and labour at Community level before drafting any proposals in the field of social policy. Management and labour not only have the right to forward an opinion but, if so required, to issue a recommendation as well. This is a clear institutionalisation of the social partners at the larger level. The organisations of management and labour, if they so wish, may demand the Council to conclude an EU-level agreement on the issues provided for in the Table 3.5 (Art. 118b) with due regard to the specified exceptions. However, member states are neither obliged to apply the agreements, nor to work out rules for their transposition, nor even to amend existing national legislation to facilitate their implementation.[32] Well, so near and yet so far!

Art. 118c entrusts the Commission to encourage co-operation between the member states, by conducting studies, delivering opinions, and arranging consultations in social policy issues, including:

- employment;
- labour law and working conditions;
- basic and advanced vocational training;
- social security;
- prevention of occupational accidents and diseases;
- occupational hygiene;
- the rights of association and collective bargaining between employers and workers.

The principles of equal pay, equal opportunities, and equal treatment for men and women are strengthened in the AMT by virtue of Art. 119, and the meaning of the term 'equal pay' is clarified beyond doubt. Finally, and courtesy of Art. 120, the Commission shall draw up each year a progress report on Art. 117 concerning the developments in the field of social policy.

The Preamble of the TEU and Arts B and 2 EC were amended to include references to the need to attain the objective of sustainable development. A new Art. 3d in the AMT integrates environmental protection in all sectoral policies with the view to promoting such development. Paras 3–5 of Art. 100a EC have been replaced by paras 3–9 in the revised Treaty, introducing escape clauses regarding harmonisation measures on the environment. Member states may retain national policies and avoid the harmonisation measures decided by the Council or by the Commission on the grounds of major needs referred to in Art. 36 or may adopt national policies based on new scientific evidence. They only have to notify the Commission of their intentions. The Commission may in turn accept or reject the national provisions within six months after having verified that such policies do not constitute a form of disguised discrimination, restriction to trade or an obstacle to the functioning of the internal market. If the above possibilities are ruled out in the process, it follows that the national measures stand. The same applies if the Commission reaches no decision within the period of six months.

Art. 129 EC was amended with the view to enabling the Community to take measures on the issue of public health which, after the eruption of the BSE disease and the criticisms directed towards the Commission, received a top place in the agenda of the IGC. According to the amended Art. 129, Community action will be complementary to that of the member states and will attempt to strengthen co-operation between member states towards the improvement of public health, the prevention of human illness and diseases and the obviation of sources of danger to human health. Finally, consumer protection was included in the AMT through the amendment of Art. 129a. In para. 1, the Community pledges to protect the interests of consumers and to promote their rights to information and education as well as to organise themselves so as to safeguard their interests, given that consumers represent the least organised interest not only in the majority of member states but at the Community level as well. Of greater consequence seems to be para. 3 of Art. 129a, which states that the Community shall contribute to the objectives stated above through measures adopted in the context of the completion of the internal market, as well as measures supporting, supplementing and monitoring national policies. Politically though, para. 4 may prove to be more relevant for the interests of consumers, as the measures in para. 3 will be taken on the basis of the co-decision procedure, with a keen EP to act in the direction of consumer protection.

Decision-making and enlargement

The Union seems to be in trouble as it is confronted with the effects of the 1989 '*annus mirabilis*'[33] in its internal institutional equilibria, and is forced to expand eastwards for a variety of reasons and motives. It has been suggested that the real task of the IGC 1996/97 was to provide for the necessary mechanisms to prepare the Union for a smooth accession of CEE countries,[34] and others in its Mediterranean periphery like Cyprus and Malta. On that account, the AMT was disappointing given that the decisions on this issue were thrown *ad calendas Graecas*. The Treaty itself suggests that this issue should be addressed one year before membership of the Union exceeds twenty, but without specifying any further concrete timetable. In particular, a specific Protocol attached to the Treaty,[35] consisting of two articles and a declaration to the Final Act, provides for the institutional accommodation of the prospective rounds of enlargement. Art. 1 of the said Protocol states that:

> on the date of entry into force of the first [fifth][36] enlargement of the EU the Commission shall comprise one national of each of the member states provided that, by that date, the weighting of the votes in the Council has been modified, whether by reweighting of the votes or by dual majority, in a manner acceptable to all member

states, taking into account all relevant elements, notably compensating those member states which give up the possibility of nominating a second member of the Commission.

Art. 2 in the same Protocol reads thus:

At least one year before membership of the European Union exceeds twenty, a conference of the representatives of the member states shall be convened in order to carry out a comprehensive review of the provisions of the Treaties on the composition and functioning of the institutions.

The whole issue of institutional reform eventually became subject to the successful outcome of yet another IGC, which was convened in February 2000 (see Chapter 4). Institutional accommodation of the prospective rounds of enlargement presents potentially insurmountable problems in a Union of twenty-seven or so members. Flexibility and efficiency, as major operational principles of European governance, might have been in support of this appendage. Equally, the third stage of EMU might also have helped in the same direction in view of the fact that, *ceteris paribus*, a number of member states may not participate (either willingly or necessarily) in its structures. It was thus expected that a variable geometry scheme would again be established in 1999, on the occasion of the final stage of EMU. The issue, however, is complicated not only because the present institutional set-up of the Union is dated, as it was originally designed for six members, but also by the fact that the vast majority of the prospective newcomers are small states which, if added to the existing small EU states, will upset an already delicate balance in joint decision-making in favour of the smaller and weaker states. Hence, a new decision-making formula should be so devised as to ensure that, after enlargement, neither the larger nor the smaller states become alienated.

Perhaps, a system of double concurrent majorities may be required on the lines suggested by Vibert.[37] According to Tables 3.6a–c, after the forthcoming waves of enlargement, the Union will consist of thirty members. A system of double concurrent majorities means that for a decision requiring a qualified majority vote (70 per cent), 70 per cent of the member states representing 70 per cent of the population will also be required. This is facilitated with the grouping of the member states by size (Table 3.6b), whereas the minority veto will consist of states from each size group (Table 3.6c). In this context, and for the purpose of accommodating future rounds of enlargement, membership of the Commission and the EP was also discussed in both the Reflection Group and the IGC. The discussions led to the introduction of an amendment to Art. 137 EC, according to which the number of MEPs will not exceed 700. As to the membership of the Commission, it became plain earlier on that such an issue was part of an unsuccessful trade-off with the voting arrangements in the Council and any decision had to be postponed. Table 3.7 summarises the main terms of discussion within the Group.

Table 3.6a Concurrent majorities

Majorities	No. of countries	Share of population (%) (minimum)	Share of population (%)	Minimum no. of countries	No. overruled
Simple	16	(12.7)	51	(4)	14/49
2/3	20	(21.8)	66	(6)	10/34
3/4	22	(24.8)	75	(8)	8/25
4/5	24	(32.6)	800	(11)	6/20
Unanimity	30	(100.0)	100	(30)	

Table 3.6b Categories

	Category A (up to 10 m pop.)	Category B (11–40 m pop.)	Category C (above 40 m pop.)
No. of states	22	4	4
Population (m)	120	116	249
% population	25	24	51

Table 3.6c Voting thresholds

	No. countries needed	% of population needed
Simple concurrent majority (50% + 1)	16	51
Ordinary qualified majority:		
Two measure (2/3)	20	66
Three measure	(8/4/2)	75–85)
High qualified majority:		
Two measure (4/5)	24	80
Three measure	(5/3/1)	85–94)
Unanimity	30	100

Source: F. Vibert, 'A core Agenda for the 1996 Intergovernmental Conference', European Policy Forum, London, 1995, pp. 54–5.

Table 3.7 Main items discussed within the Reflection Group

CFSP	Mutual assistance for the defence of the external frontiers of the Union
CFSP	Gradual incorporation of the WEU in the EU
CFSP	Representation of the Union through 'Mr or Mrs FSP'
CFSP	Vital national interests to block common action
General	Enlargement negotiations six months after the IGC
General	Discussion on the relationships between resources and costs in view of enlargement
Commission	One member per member state
Decision-making in the Council	No to the criterion of the population
Presidency	Yet to rotation on a six-monthly basis
National Parliaments	Increased role
Institutional set-up	No to *à la carte* Europe

Justice and Home Affairs

JHA is the third pillar of the Union and an almost purely intergovernmental construction, although a majority in the Group was in favour of its further integration with the Community pillar. Under its auspices come crucial subjects such as immigration, the protection of human rights, police and customs co-operation and co-operation in civil and criminal matters. As Art. K1 TEU stipulates, there are nine policy areas attended to in JHA, all of which touch upon the 'hard core' of national sovereignty. The structure is a pyramid-like form, at the top of which is the Council of Ministers, and below it three committees (asylum, police and customs, and judicial co-operation) and twenty working groups, with the K4 Committee – the CoR (COREPER) equivalent of the third pillar – as the overall co-ordinator.[38] As in the second pillar (CFSP), JHA falls outside the jurisdiction of the ECJ, while the policy input of the Commission and the EP is very limited, if non-existent. The purely intergovernmental disposition of the third pillar is of great importance for the political physiognomy of the Union as, without doubt, if third-pillar issues were to be included in the Community Method, this would be a serious push towards the impending transformation of the Union into a federal-like polity. Arguably, this largely state-centric pillar may become the master key to the integration puzzle in the not-too-distant future.

The creation of JHA as a separate pillar consisting of ten articles, and its inclusion in the TEU (Title 6) – mainly on Chancellor Kohl's insistence, owing to the single market programme – was hailed as an important new integrative element. Previously, these areas were covered by a plethora of *ad hoc* groups (such as the 1986 *ad hoc* group on immigration, the 1988 Rhodes group, the mutual assistance group, the horizontal group, the European Committee to combat drugs, the Trevi group, and the Schengen Secretariat). Its inclusion also owes much to the collapse of the communist bloc, the economic degeneration of the CEE countries, and the demographic trends and poor economic conditions in the Maghreb and Mashreq countries, as well as those of the sub-Saharan region. The acknowledgement of the significance of the third pillar was a more recent development, first with the report of the Reflection Group, and second with the revised Draft Treaty presented by the Dublin Presidency in December 1996. The following points summarise the workings of JHA since its original inception with the TEU:

1   Title VI of the TEU has had the least possible productivity since 1993. Only two Joint Actions and one convention have gone past the institutional impediments of the pillar.
2   The provision of Art. K.9 (passerelle) has been virtually ignored.
3   Title VI is full of institutional rigidities with obvious consequences for its workings.
4   Unanimity was the rule in the workings of the pillar, adding further obstacles to the production of legislation.
5   The right of legislative initiative in the pillar was divided between the Commission (Arts K1–K6) and the member states (Arts K7–K9).

An area of freedom, security and justice

The debate in the IGC, as depicted in Table 3.8 summarising the positions of the member states, has found some expression in the AMT, which produced a whole new Chapter 2 on the 'Progressive establishment of an area of Freedom, Security and Justice'. The fourth indent of Art. B TEU was amended so as 'to maintain and develop the Union as an area of Justice, in which the free movement of persons is assured in conjunction with appropriate measures to respect border controls, immigration, asylum and the prevention and combating of crime'. A new Title is also inserted in the AMT concerning the 'free movement of persons, asylum and immigration', and consisting of nine articles and several declarations to the Final Act. According to Art. A of the new Title, within a five-year period, measures aimed at ensuring the free movement of persons, measures in the fields of asylum, immigration and the safeguarding of the rights of third-country nationals, and measures in the field of judicial co-operation in civil matters and police, as well as in criminal matters, will be introduced. These measures will, at least, provide for the same level of security as in the Schengen Agreement according to a Declaration attached to the Treaty.[39] Art. B provides for the legal authorisation for the adoption of measures that will ensure the free movement of European citizens and the same treatment of third-country

Table 3.8 Negotiations on the third pillar

	COM	EP	B	DK	D	GR	E	F	IRL	I	LUX	NL	A	P	SFSF	S	RU
Third pillar in the EC	y	y	y	y	y	np	np	np	np	np	y	y	y	np	n[	np	n
Partially in the EC	np	np	np	np	np	y	y	y	y	np	np	np	np	y	y	y	n
Not in the EC	np	np	np	y	np	np	np	np	np	np	np	np	np	np	np	np	y
Improved third-pillar instruments	y	y	y	y	y	y	y	y	y	y	y	y	y	y	y	y	y
Improved K9 process	y	y	y	y	np	y	y	y	np	np	y	y	y	y	y	np	y
Policy on visas in the EC	y	y	y	np	y		y	y	y	y	y	y	y	y	y	y	np
Policy on asylum in the EC (K1.1)	y	y	y	y	y	y	y	y	y	y	y	y	y	y	y	y	np
Immigration policy in the EC (K1.3)	y	y	y	y	y	y	y	y	y	y	y	y	y	y	y	y	n
Rules of franchising external frontiers in the EC (K1.2)	y	y	np	np	np	np	y	np	np	np	y	np	y	y	np	np	np
Fight against internal fraud in the EC (K1.5)	y	y	np	np	np	np	np	np	np	np	y	np	y	np	np	np	np
Fight against drugs in the EC (K1.4)	y	y	y	y	np	np	np	np	y	np	y	np	np	n	np	np	n
Judicial co-operation in civil matters in the EC (K1.6)	y	y	np	np	y	np	np	np	np	np	np	np	np	n	np	np	np
Police co-operation (K1.9)	n	y	n	np	y	np	np	np	np	np	np	np	np	n	np	np	n

Source: European Parliament, JF/bo/234/96, p.3.
Key: y, affirmative; n, negative; np, no position.

nationals when crossing the frontiers of the Union, including the regime governing the issuing of visas. This article, however, is followed by a Protocol and a Declaration to the Final Act on Art. B(2)(b), by which the application of Art. B(2)(b) seems to be negotiated, provided that 'due consideration shall be taken in the application of the said article [of] the general foreign policy considerations of the member states', and that its application will be 'without prejudice to the negotiation or conclusion (by individual member states) of agreements on related matters'. Furthermore, according to Art. C of the revised Treaty, within five years of its entry into force, the Council, acting unanimously (and through the co-decision procedure after the five years) will introduce sets of minimum requirements on asylum, measures on refugees and displaced persons, measures on immigration policy (issuing of long-term visas and residence permits, illegal immigration and illegal residence) and measures defining the rights and conditions under which third-country nationals who are legally residing in one member state may reside in another. With a Declaration attached to the Final Act on Art. C(3)(a), member states may negotiate and conclude agreements with third countries in the domains of the said article, as long as such agreements respect Community law. Moreover, measures by individual member states are foreseen if confronted with an emergency situation stemming from a sudden inflow of refugees. In such cases, Art. D(2) stipulates that the Council, on a proposal from the Commission, may adopt temporary measures (but not for more than six months) for the benefits of the member states concerned.

Britain, Ireland and Denmark, the countries of the Community's second wave of enlargement, have been granted an opt-out from the provisions of this new Title in the AMT and the Schengen Agreement. Protocols Y and X concern the positions of Britain and Ireland, and Protocol Z that of Denmark. According to Protocol Y, Britain and Ireland maintain full control of their external borders. According to Art. 8 of Protocol Y, Ireland may at any point notify the President of the Council that it no longer wishes to be part of this Protocol, a clear indication that this country was 'forced' into opting out so as to have its bilateral relations with Britain undisturbed, and particularly with reference to 'the common travel area', as stated in the Declaration by Ireland to the Final Act on Protocol X. As for the position of Denmark, Art. 5 of Part 1 of Protocol Z, as if opting out were not enough in itself, gives this country the right to become part in the new Title and the Schengen Protocol in the future under the terms of international but not Community law! In this case it seems that Denmark will not participate in the decision-making structures nor will it accept the jurisdiction of the ECJ when acting under the terms of the new Title, if and when of course the country decides to join in these provisions.[40]

With the AMT a revised Title VI has been inserted on police and judicial co-operation in criminal matters. Title VI under the TEU consisted of ten articles referring to JHA. Six new articles (Arts K1, K2, K3, K4, K7, K10) are inserted in the Title in order to 'provide citizens of the Union with a high level of safety within an area of Freedom, Security and Justice'. Art. K1 stipulates that, in order to attain the above objectives, measures should be introduced for the prevention and combating of organised crime, terrorism, arms- and drug-trafficking, offences against children, corruption and fraud. For these reasons, closer co-operation between judicial authorities, police forces, customs authorities and other competent agencies, either directly or through Europol, should be furthered and accompanied by measures to approximate legislation on these matters if and when appropriate. The Council shall lay down the conditions and limitations under which the competent authorities of one member state or Europol may operate in the territory of another member state (Art. K4). The Council, according to Art. K6 and at the initiative of one member state or the Commission, can adopt: common positions to define the approach of the Union in a particular matter; framework decisions for the approximation of national laws and regulations which are binding as to the end result; binding decisions with no direct effect, for any purpose under this Title; and conventions entering into force when ratified by at least half of the member states concerned. This last instrument is an interesting example of 'flexibility' in practice.

The AMT spells out in detail the meaning of common action in the area of police and judicial co-operation. In the new Art. K2, police co-operation is taken to include operational co-operation in relation to the prevention, detection and investigation of criminal offences; the collection, storage, analysis and processing of the relevant information through Europol; co-operation and joint initiatives in training; exchange of liaison officers; secondments; the use of equipment and forensic research; and the common evaluation of particular investigative techniques. Five years after the entry into force of the AMT the Council will develop a new supportive role for Europol, with new leadership capabilities but subject to the appropriate judicial review from the member states, by allowing Europol to ask the competent national authorities to conduct and co-ordinate their investigations in specific cases, to promote, in co-operation with it, liaison arrangements between prosecuting/investigating officials in the fight against organised crime, and finally to establish a cross-border database on organised crime.

Common action on judicial co-operation in criminal matters (Art. K3) is taken to facilitate and accelerate co-operation between ministries and judicial authorities in relation to the enforcement of decisions; facilitate extraditions between member states by ensuring compatibility in the rules between them; prevent conflicts of jurisdiction between member states; and develop minimum rules relating to the definition and penalties in the fields of organised crime, terrorism and drug-trafficking. According to Art. K7, the ECJ may offer preliminary rulings on the validity and interpretation of decisions, framework decisions, and on the measures for their implementation. This process, however, does not seem to be 'automatic', for acceptance by any member state of a preliminary ruling by the ECJ is also subject to that state's acceptance of the jurisdiction of the ECJ through a special declaration (Art. K7(2)). This is a practice long established for the International Court of Justice in The Hague. According to Art. K7(5), the ECJ will not have jurisdiction to review the validity or proportionality of operations carried out by the police or other law-enforcing agencies of the member states, or the exercise of responsibilities incumbent upon member states with regard to the maintenance of law and order and the safeguarding of internal security. And all that in spite of the fact that the Ombudsman is entitled to receive complaints under this Title (Art. K13, para. 1).[41] Instead, under Art. K7, para.6, the ECJ shall have jurisdiction to review the legality of decisions and framework decisions for lack of competence, breach of an essential procedural requirement, infringement of the Treaty or of any rule of law relating to its application, or misuse of powers. The ECJ can also rule on any dispute between member states on the condition that the Council has not managed to settle that dispute after six months of its having been referred to it by one of its members. Finally, the ECJ will have jurisdiction to rule on any dispute between member states and the Commission regarding the interpretation and application of conventions. The extension of the ECJ's jurisdiction in JHA can only be considered as a development to be welcomed, considering the past state of the play under the TEU, where the ECJ was almost totally excluded. A little more courage to have its jurisdiction extended to the realm of private citizens would have done a world of good to the credibility of the new Title VI. But let us now turn to the recent reforms introduced by the NIT.

Notes

1 *Economist*, 'Mountains Still to Climb', 21 June 1997, p. 37.
2 *Guardian*, 'The Real Lesson of Amsterdam', 18 June 1997.
3 See Final Report of the Reflection Group, SN 520/95 REVI, Brussels, 5 December 1995, p. 1.
4 Declaration 1 of the TEU concerns civil protection, energy and tourism. Declaration 16 concerns the hierarchy of Community acts.
5 See Wolfgang Wessels, 'The Modern West European State. Democratic Erosion or a New Kind of Polity?', in S. S. Andersen and K. A. Elliassen (eds), *The European Union: How Democratic Is It?*, London: Sage, 1996, pp. 57–69.
6 See Corfu European Summit Conclusions, June 1994.
7 Interim Report of the Chairman of the Reflection Group, 24 August 1995, SN 509/95.
8 Final Report of the Reflection Group, Madrid, 5 December 1995, SN 520 REV.
9 *Ibid.*, p. 3.
10 Philippe C. Schmitter, 'The European Community as an Emergent and Novel Form of Political Domination', Estudio Working Paper, 26, 1996, p. 1.
11 See, for example, Andrew Adonis, 'Subsidiarity: Myth, Reality and the Community's Future', House of Lords Select Committee on the European Communities, London, June 1990. Also A. G. Toth, 'The Principle of Subsidiarity in the Treaty of Maastricht', *Common Market Law Review*, 29, 1992.
12 Draft Treaty of Amsterdam, 19 June 1997, CONF/4001/97, p. 139.
13 *Ibid.*, p. 141.
14 *Ibid.*, pp. 40–1.
15 See European Commission, 'Report on the Functioning of the Treaty on the European Union', SEC (95)73/1 Final, 10 May 1995, pp. 4–5.

16 The EFSP is dealt with in Chapter 6 in this volume and is not discussed in this section.

17 See European Commission, 'Report on the Functioning of the Treaty', Appendix, No. 10, p. 110.

18 Toth, 'The Principle of Subsidiarity', p. 1079.

19 See Draft Treaty of Amsterdam, p. 92.

20 *Ibid.*, p. 92. The Declaration to the Final Act on Art. 191a stipulates that a member state may ask the Commission or the Council not to communicate documents originating from that member state.

21 Michael J. Tsinisizelis and Dimitris N. Chryssochoou, 'From "Gesellschaft" to "Gemeinschaft"? Confederal Consociation and Democracy in the European Union', *Current Politics and Economics of Europe*, 5:4, 1995, pp. 1–33.

22 See European Commission, 'Report on the Functioning of the Treaty', pp. 29–30.

23 See Toth, 'The Principle of Subsidiarity', p. 1079.

24 See Draft Treaty of Amsterdam, p. 89.

25 The literature since the entry into force of the TEU is voluminous. See, *inter alia*, the comprehensive account by Clive H. Church and David Phinnemore, *European Union and European Community. A Handbook and Commentary of the Post Maastricht Treaties*, London: Harvester Wheatsheaf, 1994.

26 Tsinisizelis and Cryssochoou, 'From "Gesellschaft to Gemeinschaft"?', pp. 10ff.

27 See European Commission, 'Report on the Functioning of the Treaty', p. 14.

28 *Ibid.*, p. 14.

29 See *Making Sense of the Amsterdam Treaty*, The European Policy Centre, Brussels 1997, p. 110, para. 153. This publication offers a comprehensive account of the new Treaty.

30 Declaration to the Final Act on incentive measures referred to in Art. 5 of the new Title on Employment.

31 Treaty on European Union, Office for the Official Publications of the European Communities 1992, pp. 196–201.

32 Declaration to the Final Act on Art. 118b (2).

33 The term is borrowed from Ralph Dahrendorf, *Reflections on the Revolution in Europe*, Boulder: Westview, 1991.

34 See on this issue, *inter alia*, Christopher Preston, *Enlargement and Integration in the European Union*, London: Routledge for UACES, 1997. The Copenhagen Summit of June 1993 set out the criteria that the new applicant countries have to attain: 'membership requires that the candidate country: (1) Has achieved stability of institutions guaranteeing democracy, the rule of law, human rights and respect for and protection of minorities. (2) Has a functioning market economy as well as the capacity to cope with competitive pressure and market forces within the Union. (3) Has the ability to take on the obligations of membership, including adherence to the aims of political, economic and monetary union.'

35 *Ibid.*, p. 114.

36 Our emendation. The first round of enlargement took place in 1973 to include in the Community the United Kingdom of Great Britain and Northern Ireland, Ireland and Denmark; the second in 1981 to include Greece; the third in 1987 to include Spain and Portugal; and the fourth in 1992 to include Sweden, Austria and Finland.

37 See Frank Vibert, *A Core Agenda for the 1996 Intergovernmental Conference*, European Policy Forum, London, 1995, pp. 28ff.

38 The whole JHA structure is similar to that of the North Atlantic Free Trade Agreement (NAFTA) of 1994. For a detailed account see Bill Tupman and Alison Tupman, *Policing in Europe: Uniform in Diversity*, Exeter: Intellect, 1999.

39 See Draft Treaty of Amsterdam.

40 The point raised in para. 182, p. 116 of *Making Sense of the Amsterdam Treaty*.

41 *Ibid.*, p. 116, para. 186.

4

The Treaty of Nice and its critics

Introduction

In February 2000, yet another IGC, the fourth since the entry into force of the SEA in 1987, inaugurated its workings with the explicit objective to arrive at a resolution on the so-called 'Amsterdam leftovers'. That is to say, on those decisions that should have been decided upon during the June 1997 Amsterdam Summit, where a pronouncement had not proved possible. This was no easy task given the animosity of the deliberations during the Amsterdam process and the high stakes drawn in case of breakdown and, by extension, a likely collapse of the integration process: the next round of enlargement involving up to twelve new member states from Central and Eastern Europe, Malta and Cyprus. A special Protocol attached to the AMT on 'the enlargement and the institutions of the Union' stated thus:

> On the day of the entry into force of the enlargement of the Union and in spite of the provisions of Articles 157.1 TEC, Article 9.1 of the ECSC Treaty and Article 126.1 of the EAEC Treaty, the Commission shall include one citizen per member state provided that, by that date, the weighting of votes in the Council would be modified either through reweighting or through a double majority system, in a manner acceptable to all member states . . . Ministers who are members of the General Affairs Council will assume full responsibility for the Conference.[1]

At the second Part of the said Protocol it was stated that:

> One year before the number of the member states of the European Union exceeds twenty, an IGC will be convened in order to proceed to a comprehensive reform of . . . the composition and functioning of the institutions.[2]

The decision to convene the IGC 2000 was taken at the Cologne European Summit on 4 June 1999. In the resulting Presidency Conclusions, it was stated that:

The European Council confirms its decision to proceed with an Intergovernmental Conference of the representatives of the member states early in 2000 in order to solve the institutional questions that remained open during the Amsterdam process . . . which must be decided upon before enlargement. The IGC must conclude . . . at the end of 2000.[3]

As possible items in the IGC agenda, the Cologne Summit proposed the composition and size of the Commission, the reweighting of votes in the Council and the extension of QMV.[4] The Presidency Conclusions did not fail to point out, however, that other items related to the institutions should have been included, which were not specified at that stage. This was rectified immediately afterwards and, as a result, the IGC agenda expanded. In particular, the December 1999 Helsinki European Council concluded that the

Conference will examine the size and the composition of the European Commission, the weighting of votes in the Council as well as any other necessary changes in the treaties related to the institutions and the implementation of the Treaty of Amsterdam. The next Presidency [Portugal] will report to the European Council on the progress of the Conference and may propose additional items in the agenda of the IGC.[5]

As the report of the Portuguese Presidency to the European Council in Santa Maria de Feira stipulates,[6] the IGC 2000 should have reached a conclusion on eight issues with the view to preparing the Union for its subsequent round of enlargement. These issues concerned the composition of the major EU institutions (including the Economic and Social Committee (ESC) and the CoR), the weighting of votes in the Council, the extension of QMV, improvements in the procedures on enhanced cooperation[7] and various minor issues.

Outside the formal confines of the IGC two more issues were taken up: a proposal for a Charter of Fundamental Rights (see Chapter 7) and the common European Security and Defence Policy (see Chapter 6), both of which could have had much more serious and lasting ramifications on the physiognomy of the general system and, more generally, on the future direction of the integration process. It is worth recalling that other important issues were also discussed on the sidelines of the IGC, mainly at the initiative of the Commission, such as the hierarchy of Community Acts and the simplification of the Treaties (see below).

The Commission and the Nice process

The views of the Commission

On 1 September 1999, the Commission appointed an *ad hoc* working group chaired by the former Prime Minister of Belgium, Dehaene, the preceding German President, Weizsäcker, and Lord Simon of Haighbury, chairman of the British Petroleum. The task of the group was to report on institutional reform in view of enlargement. The Dehaene Report was published on 18 October 1999. It was structured around a number of initiatives. More specifically, it wished for the broadening of the Cologne agenda to incorporate questions of Treaty simplification and reorganisation, a step of substantial consequence which, had it be taken, it would have led to an altogether different reform outcome (see Chapter 7). It also suggested ways to improve the workings of all the institutions of the Union. Its recommendations on the Commission included the strengthening of the powers of its President and the organisation's overall political direction. Moreover, it was stated that the deficient democratic legitimacy of the larger system entailed that QMV should be generalised and accompanied by parliamentary co-decision in the first pillar and, gradually, in the remaining two. According to the Report, the Amsterdam provisions on enhanced co-operation have not been used owing to an overabundance of built-in inflexible requirements and should therefore be taken up for reform. Transparency and the ensuing enlargement, suggested the Report, point to the reorganisation of the Treaties. This should be done by dividing the existing Treaties into two parts: the first would contain a Basic Treaty, enlisting the general orientations and objectives of the Union, citizens' rights and provisions on the institutional framework. A second, separate part, would include all the other provisions – i.e., common policies – which could be reformed only by a unanimous Council or by a super-qualified majority, after however an opinion of the EP was taken by a reinforced majority. Overall, the Report favoured a substantial simplification of the reform procedures.

The Commission, in its report on institutional adaptation to enlargement,[8] took on board the Dehaene proposals, pointing out that the issue of the reorganisation of the Treaties had been taken up during the IGC 1996/97, but without success. This issue was also met with the support of the EP.[9] The simplification of the reform procedures could follow the logic of Art. 95 (2 and 3) of the ECSC Treaty that provides for reform of the Treaty provisions without the interference of national parliaments. This so-called 'small reform' facility in the ECSC Treaty, under which the EP must give its approval by a 2/3 or 12/15 majority, was also suggested by the first Report of the European University Institute (EUI), in a study undertaken at the Commission's request.[10] Briefly, the EUI Report suggested the following (see also Chapter 7): first, that Treaty simplification makes sense only in the cases of the TEC and the TEU. Second, that the TEU, as reformed by the AMT, should be replaced by a Basic Treaty, which would include only the fundamental provisions of the TEC and the TEU. The rest of the provisions would be attached to the Basic Treaty in the form of Protocols. In this way, Treaty simplification becomes a straightforward exercise. A second EUI Report considered whether a possible simplification of the Treaties might also require a change in the reform procedures themselves. Here, the EUI suggested that unanimity should be abolished during the reform process and be replaced by a super-qualified majority with a right of opt-out to those member states that would find themselves in a minority position. The Report also recommended the strengthening of 'autonomous' reform procedures – i.e., the

ECSC small-reform model; the need for organising better the work of European Councils at the end of review conferences to improve the quality of its decision-taking; and that the Convention model, as applied in the case of the Charter of Fundamental Rights, be used as a vehicle for formal treaty change.

Discussions in the IGC on the Commission

During the IGC 2000, those negotiations that were of consequence to the Commission focused on the need to find suitable ways to preserve the fundamental principle of its working method – i.e., collective responsibility – in view of prospective enlargements and the resulting increase in its membership. In its opinion on the IGC, the Commission emphasised this very point by stating that

> The Commission reaches thousands of decisions each year . . . approximately 200 per week . . . is embarking upon a reorganisation of its internal services . . . because after the enlargement the preservation of its collective responsibility will be a far more difficult exercise.[11]

The Commission suggests that in a Union of twenty-five–twenty-seven members, a Commission of thirty-three–thirty-five members would find it all the more difficult properly to exercise its leadership and, hence, the IGC should reach an agreement on its future composition. The Commission itself has put forward two alternative scenarios: the first referred to a system of rotating membership, whereby the order of membership had to be explicitly mentioned in the Treaties and under which every member state would have one Commissioner in every five out of seven Commissions.[12] The second scenario involved a system whereby each member state would have the right to nominate one Commissioner. This would lead to a Commission of thirty-five members in a Union of twenty-eight (including Turkey) – or, a Commission of thirty-three members were Turkey to be excluded – under the existing system in which the bigger member states have two Commissioners each. This scenario was advanced with the proviso that there would be a massive reorganisation of the Commission to enable it to offset any possible functional difficulties resulting from an increase in its size.[13]

The Commission Report also emphasised the need to increase the powers of its President and the way of his/her election. In particular, it was suggested that the President should be able to dismiss individual Commissioners for serious misconduct or inefficiency during their term of office. This would strengthen the position of the President and would allow him/her to apply his/her political leadership function more efficiently than presently. A different way of electing the Commission President was also in order according to the Report with the view to bestowing the political system of the EU with a higher degree of democratic legitimacy. Table 4.1 shows the Treaty provisions related to the Commission that were discussed in the IGC 2000.

In the IGC discussions, significant changes in Arts 219 (para. 2), 217 and 215 were tabled even if the results obtained were more modest than originally hoped for by the Commission. To give an example, a change common to the Law

Table 4.1 Treaty provisions related to the Commission

Article	Subject
219 TEC first paragraph	The Commission functions under the political guidance of its President
219 TEC second paragraph	The Commission decides with the majority of its members
217 TEC	The Commission elects two Vice-Presidents from among its members
218 (2) TEC	The Commission decides on its Rules of Procedure

Table 4.2 Proposed changes in Art. 217

Art. 217	Proposed new Article	IGC Conclusion
The Commission may elect two Vice-Presidents from among its members.	The President will determine the political orientation of the Commission.	The Commission works under the political guidance of its President who determines its internal organisation, and that it functions efficiently on the basis of collective responsibility.
	The President may appoint two vice Presidents from among its members.	The functions of the Commission will be structured and allocated to its members by the President. The President during the Commission's term of office may reshuffle portfolios. On the agreement of the Commission, the President may appoint Vice-Presidents from among its members.
	The President may entrust members of the Commission with special duties and responsibilities for part or the whole of their term of office.	On the agreement of the Commission, the President may demand the resignation of individual members.

Table 4.3 Member state positions on the Commission

Member state	Position
Belgium	One Commissioner per member state, appointment of the Commission by common accord of national governments, strengthening of the President, no hierarchy of Commissioners
Denmark	One Commissioner per member state, more Vice-Presidents, internal reorganisation of the Commission
Germany	Limit to the size of the Commission
Greece	One Commissioner per member state, more Vice-Presidents, internal reorganization of the Commission
France	Limit to the size of the Commission
Ireland	One Commissioner per member state, more Vice-Presidents, internal reorganisation of the Commission
Italy	Limit to the number of Commissioners
Luxembourg	One Commissioner per member state, appointment of the Commission by common accord of national governments, strengthening of the President, no hierarchy of Commissioners
Netherlands	One Commissioner per member state, appointment of the Commission by common accord of national governments, strengthening of the President, no hierarchy of Commissioners
UK	Limit to the number of Commissioners
Spain	Limit to the number of Commissioners
Portugal	One Commissioner per member state, more Vice-Presidents, internal reorganisation of the Commission
Austria	One Commissioner per member state, more Vice-Presidents, internal reorganisation of the Commission
Sweden	One Commissioner per member state, more Vice-Presidents, internal reorganisation of the Commission
Finland	One Commissioner per member state, more Vice-Presidents, internal reorganisation of the Commission

of Associations was suggested, that the Commission may reach a decision by a majority of its members but in case of a split vote, the side including the vote of its President wins through.[14] This addition, however, was not accepted by the IGC. More significant still were the changes proposed for Art. 217,[15] according to which the President of the Commission would have acquired more powers *vis-à-vis* the rest of the Commissioners and would have been elevated from his current *primus inter pares* status. Table 4.2 shows the proposed changes to Art. 217 by the Commission and the IGC conclusions.

Table 4.3 supplies information on the positions adopted by the member state representatives during the IGC on the Commission. On the basis of the data presented by Table 4.3, it seems that the bigger countries demanded a limit to the number of Commissioners. In most cases in the positions of the bigger countries there is no mention on the internal reorganisation of the Commission as a serious enough issue to warrant attention in the official documents produced during the IGC. On the contrary, the smaller members made an issue of the size and the political role of the Commission, being unanimously behind the initiative on its internal reorganisation, insisting on the principle of one Commissioner per member state, while rejecting any limit to the size of the Commission. The smaller members also rejected the hierarchy among Commissioners, but on the whole supported an increase in the number of Vice-Presidents.

Changes with the Treaty of Nice
The result of the IGC deliberations and the negotiations that took place during the December 2000 Nice Summit are shown in Table 4.4.

Table 4.4 Summary of the provisions on the Commission in the Treaty of Nice

Subject	Arrangement	Time
Size of the Commission	One Commissioner per member state	1 January 2005
Powers of the President	Increase in the powers of the President	With ratification of the Treaty of Nice
	Responsibility for the internal organisation of the Commission	
	On the Commission's accord, the President can ask a member to resign	
Rotating membership	When the 27th member joins the Union	Unknown
Internal reorganisation		In progress

In the Protocol on the 'enlargement of the Union',[16] and particularly in its Art. 4, it is stated that Art. 213 TEC would be amended to reflect the changes decided at the IGC 2000 and the Nice Summit. More specifically, it was decided that Art. 213(1) would be so revised so that the Commission would consist of one Commissioner per member state, effective on 1 January 2005. Such a decision was accompanied with an unspecified system of rotation – with the explicit task of ensuring both geographical as well as demographic balance in the college of Commissioners – which will be effective for the first Commission appointed after the twenty-seventh member joins the Union. The Council, acting unanimously, will decide on the number of Commissioners and the system of rotation, with due attention to the preservation of a working equilibrium between the member states. More important, though, proved the changes inflicted upon the process of electing the new Commission and its President. The whole system now evolves in four phases and has been aptly communitarised. The new Art. 214 TEC specifies that the new President will be elected by QMV by the European Council acting as General Affairs Council. This is Phase I of the new and quite lengthy process. Phase II involves the EP, which must approve the Council's choice. Were that to be the case, then (Phase III) the chosen President and the General Affairs Council, acting by QMV, will draw up a list of the members of the new Commission on the basis of proposals received by the member states. The President and his/her Commissioners must be approved *en bloc* by the EP. Finally (Phase IV), following the approval of the EP, the new Commission and its President must be appointed by the General Affairs Council (with the European Council again acting as General Affairs Council) on the basis of QMV.

Changes were also introduced in Art. 215 TEC regarding the powers of the Commission President. Under the revised arrangement of Art. 215 (para. 2), any member of the Commission who resigned, was forced to resign, or died will be replaced by the Council acting by QMV. It should be noted though that under the revised Art. 215 (para. 4) it becomes feasible for a unanimous Council to decide not to replace a member of the Commission who does not fulfill his/her duties on the above-stated grounds. Under the revised Art. 217, the position of the Commission President is strengthened, although not at the extent originally desired by the Commission. The President is now responsible for the internal organisation of the Commission in order to protect its principle of collective responsibility, as well as its internal effectiveness and cohesion. Para. 2 in Art. 217 offers the President the opportunity to reshuffle the responsibilities of individual Commissioners during their term of office. This is an important development and is expected to lessen the intergovernmental grip upon the Commission, and in particular the horse-trading associated with the allocation of Commission portfolios among the member state governments. Moreover, the President, after obtaining the Commission's agreement, can appoint Vice-Presidents whose number is not specified, thus increasing his/her margin of manoeuvre in the allocation of competences in the body. Finally, para. 4 of the same Article stipulates that the President, after obtaining the agreement of the Commission, may request the resignation of a member of the Commission. Overall, therefore, the hold of the President is strengthened as a result of the NIT.

Decision-making in the Council

Reweighting of votes or a different voting system in the Council (double majority system) was the demand put forward by the AMT, as mentioned earlier in this chapter. This was probably the more important element in the institutional package that became subject to an extensive and arduous negotiation during the IGC 2000 and the Nice Summit. In general terms, the deliberations in the IGC evolved along two alternative scenarios: reweighting of votes in favour of the bigger member states, which might have lost their second Commissioner, or a system of double majority voting. In each system, there are pros and cons, as will be discussed below. The Report of the Portuguese Presidency at the Santa Maria de Feira European Council mentioned that there was convergence in the IGC on the following five points:[17]

- Any chosen system should reflect the double nature of the Union, in the form of a union of states and a union of peoples.
- The chosen system should guarantee equity between the member states, transparency and effectiveness in the workings of the Council, and should also be simple and easily comprehensible by the citizens of the member states.
- Any chosen system should represent at least 50 per cent of the population of the Union.
- The reweighting of the votes is part and parcel of the issues of the composition of the Commission and the allocation of seats in the EP.
- Any chosen system should facilitate decision-making in the Council.

Table 4.5 illustrates the existing weighting of Council votes and the population of the member states as reported by Eurostat in 1999.

Table 4.5 Weighting of votes and population of the member states

Member state	Population (m)	Number of votes
Germany	82,038	10
UK	59,247	10
France	58,966	10
Italy	57,612	10
Spain	39,394	8
Netherlands	15,760	5
Greece	10,533	5
Belgium	10,213	5
Portugal	9,980	5
Sweden	8,854	4
Austria	8,082	4
Denmark	5,313	3
Finland	5,160	3
Ireland	3,744	3
Luxembourg	429	2
Total	375,325	87

On the basis of the data provided by Table 4.5, a decision by the Council requires 62 out of 87 votes. These 62 votes in percentage terms represent 71.26 per cent of the total votes in the Council and require the votes of at least eight member states. This is the minimum number of states required for a decision to be reached. This minimum number also represents 58.16 per cent of the combined population of the fifteen members. Conversely, 26 votes cast are required for the rejection of a proposal by at least three member states representing 12.38 per cent of the Union's population. In theory, only three of the bigger member states with 10 votes each may form a blocking minority. Table 4.6 shows the informal population threshold as it has evolved in the EU since 1958.

Table 4.6 shows that in every instance since 1958 any decision taken by QMV was always the expression of the majority of the member states and, more importantly, of the majority of the population. Tables 4.7–4.9 project the current QMV system to an EU of twenty-seven or twenty-eight members.

Table 4.6 Informal population threshold since 1958

EEC 6 (%)	EEC 9 (%)	EEC 10 (%)	EEC 12 (%)	EU 15 (%)
67.71	70.49	70.1 4	63.27	59.83[a]
			58.18	

Note: [a] This was after German reunification.

On the basis of the data provided in Table 4.7, under the existing decision-making system – i.e., before the entry into force of the NIT – for a decision to be blocked it requires 43 votes cast by at least five member states representing 10.45 per cent of the combined population of the member states. Moreover, according to the same data, a blocking minority can be formed by eight new enlargement member states, for example by Turkey, Poland, Rumania, the Czech Republic, Bulgaria, Lithuania, Hungary and Malta (total votes 44). Turkey alone could cover the minimum required population threshold! In an Union of twenty-seven members, the danger of blocking minorities formed exclusively by the new member states is more remote because of the absence of Turkey. In the system under discussion there is no compensation for those member states that lose their second Commissioner. The double majority systems discussed in the IGC exhibit a number of interesting features and advantages. Table 4.10 offers the necessary information.

Population weights add up to 1,000 and thus become easy to verify whether a decision taken carries the necessary population support, as expressed by the percentage of the combined population of the member states supporting a particular decision. For the approval of a proposal, a majority of the member states is required – i.e., fourteen member states in an EU-27 and the satisfaction of the existing population threshold of 58.2 per cent. For the rejection of a proposal,

Table 4.7 Existing QMV system projected for EU-27 and EU-28

Member state	Number of votes	Population
Germany	10	82,038
Turkey	10	64,385
UK	10	59,247
France	10	58,966
Italy	10	57,612
Spain	8	39,394
Poland	8	38,667
Romania	6	22,489
Netherlands	5	15,760
Greece	5	10,533
Czech Rep.	5	10,290
Belgium	5	10,213
Hungary	5	10,092
Portugal	5	9,980
Sweden	4	8,854
Bulgaria	4	8,230
Austria	4	8,082
Slovakia	3	5,393
Denmark	3	5,313
Finland	3	5,160
Ireland	3	3,744
Lithuania	3	3,701
Latvia	3	2,439
Slovenia	3	1,978
Estonia	3	1,446
Cyprus	2	752
Luxembourg	2	429
Malta	2	379
Total EU-28	144	545,566
Total EU-27	134	481,181

Table 4.8 EU-28

	Votes	% of votes	Minimum number and (%) of member states	Minimum % of population
QMV	102	70.83	14 (50.0)	51.36
Blocking minority	43	29.86	5 (17.9)	10.45
Total	145			

Table 4.9 EU-27

	Votes	% of votes	Minimum number and (%) of member states	Minimum % of population
QMV	96	71.64	14 (51.85)	50.20
Blocking minority	39	29.10	4 (14.81)	10.50
Total	135			

Table 4.10 Double majority systems

Member state	Population weight EU-28	Population weight EU-27
Germany	150	169
Turkey	118	–
UK	109	123
France	108	123
Italy	106	120
Spain	72	82
Poland	71	80
Romania	41	47
Netherlands	29	33
Greece	19	22
Czech Rep.	19	21
Belgium	19	21
Hungary	18	21
Portugal	18	21
Sweden	16	18
Bulgaria	15	17
Austria	15	17
Slovakia	10	11
Denmark	10	11
Finland	9	11
Ireland	7	8
Lithuania	7	8
Latvia	4	5
Slovenia	4	4
Estonia	3	3
Cyprus	1	2
Luxembourg	1	1
Malta	1	1
Total EU-27	1,000	1,000

again a majority of the member states is required or, alternatively, four member states whose population adds up to 419 units $(1{,}000 - 582 = 418 + 1 = 419)$ representing 11.62 per cent of the combined population in the Union. A simple majority is required for the adoption or the rejection of a particular proposal. There is no weighting of votes and *each member state has only one vote.* The paradox in this approach relates to the fact that the higher the population threshold for the approval of a proposal the smaller it becomes for its rejection. The difficulty here is self-evident: there is no compensation to the bigger member states for the loss of their second Commissioner. In addition, such a system does not take into account the differences in the political weight of the member states, thus making it less popular with some of them. Had the political problem of the physiognomy of the Union been resolved, this system would have been a front-runner. A version of a double majority system which combines features from the existing QMV arrangements was also discussed in the IGC as shown in Table 4.11

Table 4.11 Double majority system with features of existing QMV arrangements

	Votes		Population weight	% of votes	Minimum number and (%) of member states	Minimum % of population
QMV	102	and	582	70.83	14 (50.00)	58.20
Blocking minority	33	or	419	29.86	4 (14.29)	10.45
Total	135					

The difference between this and the previous system has to do with the fact that this system requires a weighted instead of a simple majority for the rejection or approval of a decision. Thus, this system takes due account of the differences in political (and economic) weight between the member states. The population threshold is the same as in the previous system – i.e., 58.2 per cent, that under the QMV system currently in force. Adoption of a proposal requires 102 out of 135 votes cast by at least fourteen member states which gather between them 582 units (58.2 per cent population threshold required). The blocking minority consists of 33 weighted votes $(135 - 102 = 32 + 1 = 33)$ or, alternatively, by 419 units from four member states. The QMV threshold is at normal levels inside the 1958–2000 average (70 per cent). The 'deficiency' of this version of a double majority system is that there is no compensation for the loss of the second Commissioner on the part of the bigger members, although a version taking account of just that could have been easily recommended.

Changes in the weighting system with the Treaty of Nice
The issue was finally resolved in the December 2001 Nice Summit. After a marathon session, the Summit concluded in favour of a system resembling the last system discussed above with some interesting features borrowed from the double majority models; Table 4.12 supplies the details. In Art. 3 of the Protocol on the enlargement of the Union, which was attached to the NIT, it is stated that the above changes will come into force on 1 January 2005.[18] In effect, this is the necessary transitional stage required for the smooth accession of the new members. When the Council decides on a proposal from the Commission, the QMV is set at 169 out of 237 votes cast by at least the majority of the member states (eight), expressing at least 62 per cent of the population of the Union, which is a specific Treaty requirement (see below). The blocking minority is set at 69 out of 237 votes, which can be formed by at least three member states representing 30.6 per cent of the combined population of the Union (Italy, Spain and the Netherlands are used in the above example – i.e., 29 + 27 + 13 = 69). The point is that this blocking minority can be easily formed by a number of combinations between the member states. Three bigger member states can reach the required level of votes ($29 \times 3 = 87$), which is something that may happen at the existing QMV system as shown in Table 4.12. On the whole the votes of the bigger member states nearly tripled, from 10 to 29, those of the medium-size member states more than doubled (for example, Belgium, Portugal and Greece moved from 5 to 12 votes with the Netherlands winning an additional vote, moving from 5 to 13). The countries of the northern EU enlargement moved from 4 to 10 votes with the exception of Finland (and Ireland), which moved from 3 to 7

Table 4.12 EU-15: new weighting of votes in view of enlargement

Member state	QMV in force	New QMV	Population
Belgium	5	12	10,213
Denmark	3	7	5,313
Germany	10	29	82,038
Greece	5	10	10,533
France	10	29	58,966
Ireland	3	7	3,744
Italy	10	29	57,612
Luxembourg	2	4	429
Netherlands	5	13	15,760
UK	10	29	59,247
Spain	8	27	39,394
Portugal	5	12	9,980
Austria	4	10	8,082
Sweden	4	10	8.854
Finland	3	7	5,160
QMV	62/87 (26)	169/237 (69)	

votes and seem to be on the losing side in that regard. The bigger gains seem to be those of Spain, which moved from 8 votes at the current system to 27 at the new one. In fact, Spain demanded during the IGC to have the same number of votes as Germany, France, Italy and the UK, while France contributed to the near-collapse of the Nice Summit by refusing to have fewer votes than Germany. Table 4.13 shows the allocation of votes in the Council as agreed at Nice for the enlarged Union.

Table 4.13 EU-27: weighting of votes

Member state	Population	New weighting of votes
Germany	82,038	29
UK	59,247	29
France	58,966	29
Italy	57,612	29
Spain	39,394	27
Poland	38,667	27
Romania	22,489	14
Netherlands	15,760	13
Greece	10,533	12
Czech Rep.	10,290	12
Belgium	10,213	12
Hungary	10,092	12
Portugal	9,980	12
Sweden	8,854	10
Bulgaria	8,230	10
Austria	8,082	10
Slovakia	5,393	7
Denmark	5,313	7
Finland	5,160	7
Ireland	3,744	7
Lithuania	3,701	7
Latvia	2,439	4
Slovenia	1,978	4
Cyprus	752	4
Luxembourg	429	4
Malta	379	3
Total EU-27	481,181	
QMV EU-27	258/345	

In both cases shown above, it seems that the Nice European Council did not accept the introduction of a double majority system, but only elements of it in the form of a required population threshold for the taking of a decision in the Council (62 per cent) instead of the far simpler and more legitimate versions discussed during the IGC. This population criterion though is not a condition for the taking of a Council decision. It becomes one only if one or more member states demand verification, in that any taken decision in fact reflects the 62 per cent population requirement. Even so, this system does not include a weighting of the population like the double majority systems discussed during the IGC and as such the verification process may run into difficulties. As the Protocol on the Enlargement and the Final Declaration of the review conference states:

> When the Council acts on a qualified majority, one of its members may demand verification that the qualified majority consists of 62 per cent of the total population of the Union. If this condition is not met the decision will not be taken.[19]

Overall, the new system resembles the one discussed during the IGC, a system on the lines of the existing one, but with adjustments in favour of the bigger states, compensating them for their eventual loss of their second Commissioner. It should be reminded that the new QMV system will come into force on 1 January 2005 at the same date as the provisions on the Commission (see above). The system itself, which in fact represents a neorealist triumph, bears some marks of a compromise struck in the Nice Summit with reference to the population threshold, thus adding a double majority perspective in the agreed system. The QMV threshold set at nearly 75 per cent, mainly at the insistence of Germany, brings the whole system one step backwards towards the direction of unanimity, and is expected to complicate the taking of decisions in the first pillar. Overall, it seems that the bigger member states (the 'big four' plus Spain) increase their influence under the new system disproportionately in comparison with the rest of the member states. It also seems that the bigger states during the Nice negotiations acted in concert to achieve a reweighting of votes in their favour. The informal institutional implications of such a practice, if sustained, are pretty obvious: the bigger member states occupy the driving seat in the general system.

If we attempt to judge the new system using the criteria mentioned in the Feira Report, it is possible to conclude that not a single condition was fulfilled: the chosen system only partially reflects the double nature of the Union as a union of states and a union of peoples, and it adds little to the need for more transparency and effectiveness in the workings of the Council; in fact, it can be safely argued that it does exactly the opposite. Moreover, it is not a system that can claim the simplicity required to be easily comprehensible by the citizens of the member states and does not seem to be facilitating decision-making in the Council. Wessels makes the same point, stating that there are still 38(!) different ways for the Council and the EP to interact in decision-making and 11(!) different ways of decision-making in the Council.[20] In summary, the new system in a Union of twenty-seven or more states consists of three interrelated qualifications: the majority of the member states, a qualified majority, and a population threshold.

The other institutions and the Nice process

The EP

The EP formally presented its views on the basis of Art. 48 (2) TEU.[21] They were structured around three main lines of argument: first, the EP called for a more democratic process of union on rather conventional lines, with its membership not exceeding the Amsterdam threshold and a transitional period for accommodating the MEPs from the new member states. Second, it suggested that there should be a provision inserted in the Treaty related to the 2009 Euro-elections, according to which 10 per cent of the EP's membership will be elected in a single constituency with two lists, one European and one national. This means that the EP is proposing a limited transfer of the German electoral system at the larger level. The pro-federal features of this suggestion are evident and need no further comment! Third, regarding both the operation and organisation of EU-level political parties, the EP proposed the following change in the wording of Art. 191:

> The European political parties contribute to the development of a European consciousness and the expression of the political will of the peoples of Europe. On a proposal from the Commission, the EP and the Council, on the Article 251 procedure, will lay down the criteria, the rules and the procedures for financing (including Community financing) the European political parties.[22]

It is clear that the debate on European political parties is closely linked to their financial links with the national level, an issue with serious political ramifications in some member states such as Germany, Greece and Italy, among others. In any case, there should be greater transparency on this issue given that the EU experiment cannot afford further legitimation crises. The financing of political parties at the European and national levels must be two altogether separate issues. Moreover, it is a well-documented fact that the EP lacks a permanent seat. Its plenary sessions are held in Strasbourg and Luxembourg and its committees meet in Brussels. Apart from the South African Parliament during the period of Apartheid it is the only other Parliament whose seat is different from the seat of the Executive. To address this long-standing problem, the EP has suggested the following new provision in the NIT: 'The EP with an absolute majority of its members will decide on the location of its permanent seat where all its meetings would be taking place.'[23]

As far as the structure and workings of the Council are concerned, the EP proposed its reorganisation along federal lines, again without any serious prior debate on the justification of these proposals. As such, the Council should decide on the basis of a double majority system, should become accountable for its acts or its omissions to act on the EP and should be divided into an executive and a legislative Council.[24] The Commission President should be elected by the EP from a list drawn up by the Council and should have sufficient power to dismiss individual members of the Commission for serious misconduct during their period of office. The same right, the EP suggests, should be given to the EP on the basis of Art. 216, that is after the EP's application to the ECJ.[25]

On the issue of the reorganisation of the ECJ, the EP suggested that it should consist of a number equal or higher to the number of the member states. The Court of First Instance should be given the right to deliver opinions on the basis of the Art. 234 procedure (preliminary ruling). The jurisdiction of the ECJ should be extended to all the issues in Title VI of the TEC (visa, asylum, free movement of persons including migration) and Title VI of the TEU (Judicial and Police Cooperation). The EP should be given the same right afforded to the Council and the Commission to appeal in front of the ECJ by reforming the provisions of Arts 230 and 232 TEU.

Unanimity in the Council should be limited to all issues of constitutional nature with parliamentary co-decision being the main decision-making mechanism in the Union. The Treaties should be simplified on the basis of the EUI Reports (see above), the Charter of Fundamental Rights should be incorporated into the Treaties (see Chapter 7), and a hierarchy of Community Acts be duly established. The enhanced co-operation provisions in the AMT should be reformed to enable a smaller number of states to take the initiative for flexible integration schemes and the various restrictions attached in the AMT should be eased. Finally, the EP called for the setting up of a new institution, the European Prosecutor's Office, to combat fraud in the EU.[26] Table 4.14 summarises the position of the EP during the IGC 2000.

Table 4.14 Views of the European Parliament (EP)

Hierarchy of Community Acts	Yes
Incorporation of the Charter of Fundamental Rights in the Treaties	Yes
Unanimity in the Council abolished	Yes
Loosened enhanced co-operation provisions	Yes
Double majority system in the Council	Yes
Co-decision and QMV main decision-making mechanisms	Yes
Reform of the ECJ and of the Court of First Instance	Yes
One Commissioner per member state	Yes until 2010
Simplification of the Treaties	Yes
Gradual abolition of the pillar system	Yes
Generalisation of the ascent procedure	Yes

Table 4.15 shows the results of the negotiations during the Nice Summit on the allocation of seats in the EP in an EU-27. It reflects the third element in the package deal agreed in the Nice Summit besides the size and composition of the

Commission and the weighting of votes in the Council. The French refusal during the negotiation for the reweighting of Council votes to accept more votes for Germany preordained that from the 'big four' countries only Germany managed to come out of the negotiations without any losses in the new allocation of seats in the EP. Indeed, all current EU members lose seats, save for Germany and Luxembourg, who retain the same number of seats. France, Italy and the UK lose 15 seats each and Spain loses 14. The four bigger states and Spain lose 59 seats between them, whereas the other members lose from 3 to 6 seats each. It seems that in the new EP, and especially that of 2009–14, one-seventh of all Members of the European Parliament (MEPs) will be coming from Germany. Hungary and the Czech Republic are the losers in the new system, having fewer seats than countries with similar population sizes. The total number of seats is

Table 4.15 Allocation of seats in the EP

Member state	EU-27: New allocation of seats	EU-15: Current allocation of seats	Difference between EU-15 and EU-27
Germany	99	99	0
UK	72	87	−15
France	72	87	−15
Italy	72	87	−15
Spain	50	64	−14
Poland	50	–	–
Rumania	33	–	–
Netherlands	25	31	−6
Greece	22	25	−3
Czech Rep.	20	–	–
Belgium	22	25	−3
Hungary	20	–	–
Portugal	22	25	−3
Sweden	18	22	−4
Bulgaria	17	–	–
Austria	17	21	−4
Slovakia	13	–	–
Denmark	13	16	−3
Finland	13	16	−3
Ireland	12	15	−3
Lithuania	12	–	–
Latvia	8	–	–
Slovenia	7	–	–
Estonia	6	–	–
Cyprus	6	–	–
Luxemburg	6	6	0
Malta	5	–	–
Total EU-27	732	626	91

732, well beyond the limit of 700 set at Amsterdam, courtesy of the new Art. 189(2). Article 2 of the Protocol on the Enlargement attached to the NIT states that the total number of MEPs for the period 2004–9 will be equal to the number of seats specified in Art. 190(2) TEC plus a number of MEPs from the member states that will sign their Accession Agreements to the Union. If the total number of MEPs is less than 732 it will be corrected in such a way so that it will be as close to that number as possible. The correction will be made by the Council and the total number of MEPs may be temporarily higher than 732 if new members accede after the corrective decision of the Council.

The new Art. 300(6) offers the EP the same right as the other major EU institutions, namely the right to appeal in front of the ECJ for questioning the compatibility of international agreements with the EU legal order. If these agreements are found by the ECJ to be incompatible with the Community's legal order, then these can enter into force with the procedure specified in Art. 48 TEC, that is, after ratification by national parliaments. Other changes related to the EP include Art. 191 on European political parties, which has been changed so that 'a legal basis for the financing of the political parties could be created' according to the reasoning offered by the Commission.[27] In the new Art. 191, a paragraph was inserted under which the Council and the EP (co-decision) are authorised to issue regulations on the financing of political parties after observing certain conditions. The EP, by virtue of the reformed Art. 190(5), is given the right to draw the statute (regulations and general conditions governing the performance of the duties of its members) of the MEPs requiring also QMV in the Council and an opinion by the Commission, although the taxation issues of the MEPs will require unanimity in the Council.

The ECJ

The ECJ, in spite of the pro-integration activism that characterised its rulings over time, was very careful to avoid addressing the political issues in the agenda of the IGC 2000, preferring instead to focus on issues directly involving its organisational set-up, improvements in its workings, the creation of special bodies – Judicial Panels, to take up cases involving the employees of EU institutions – and the allocation of the workload between itself and the Court of First Instance.[28] All in all, the ECJ tabled five proposals in the IGC, three of which were of major importance. First, the ECJ and the Court of First Instance asked to acquire the right to modify their Rules of Procedure as is the case with the European Court of Human Rights and the International Court of Justice in The Hague, in the place of the present arrangement under which this is the task of the Council acting unanimously. The Nice Summit granted the ECJ the right to draw its Rules of Procedure to be decided by the Council acting on QMV. As a result, Arts 223 and 224 were modified accordingly. Second, the ECJ asked for the introduction of a screening system on the choice of cases to be addressed to it, involving annulment of decisions by the Court of First Instance. The Treaty was thus modified to give the latter the right to hear at second degree decisions by the Judicial Panels (Art. 225(2)). It also granted the ECJ the right to hear at second degree decisions by the Court of First Instance. After the entry into force of the NIT, the Court of First Instance acquires the right to hear cases under the following Articles:

- Art. 230, legality of Acts adopted jointly by the EP and the Council, of Acts of the Council, of the Commission and of the European Central Bank (ECB), other than recommendations and opinions, and of Acts of the EP intended to produce legal effects *vis-à-vis* third parties.
- Art. 234, preliminary ruling giving under conditions the right to the Court of First Instance to refer to the ECJ, and to the ECJ the right to review, under conditions, decisions by the Court of First Instance.
- Art. 230, direct action.
- Art. 238, arbitration.
- Art. 236, employment differences involving employees of EU institutions.
- Art. 225(2), decisions of the Judicial Panels. Successive declarations by the governments of the member states attached to the Treaty clarify the details in the implementation of this Article.
- Art. 229a, the ECJ acquired the right to review cases related to industrial property.

Overall, this is a major review of the EU judicial system, which is expected to have significant consequences in the future direction of the integration process. Students of European integration should be aware of such developments, principally because they are expected to contribute further to the political activism of the ECJ.

The ESC and the CoR

In its opinion on the IGC 2000,[29] the ESC presented a shopping list designed to improve its status in the interinstitutional balance of power within the Union. In fact, it tabled four main demands. First, it should be stated clearly in the new Treaty that the ESC is an important forum of social dialogue. Second, the ESC should acquire the role of a moderator in cases where the Treaty requires its opinion on complex issues. Third, the obligatory consultation of the ESC by the Commission when the latter prepares its legislative proposals. Fourth, the term of the ESC should be five years, to coincide with those of the Commission and the EP. All of the above demands were rejected by the Nice Summit. For its part, the CoR in effect adopted the positions of the EP as stated above and demanded that the regions be acknowledged as having equal status with the national and Community levels,[30] by reforming Art. 5. Such a demand was also rejected by the Summit. There was, however, a reallocation of seats in both institutions in order to take into account the prospects for further enlargement, as shown in Table 4.16. All of the current member states retain the same number of seats after Nice and the total membership in both institutions increases from the current 222 to 344 (not more than 350 in the wording of the NIT) after enlargement (EU-27).

Table 4.16 New allocation of seats for the Economic and Social Committee (ESC) and the Committee of the Regions (CoR)

Member state	New allocation after Nice	Current allocation
Germany	24	24
UK	24	24
France	24	24
Italy	24	24
Spain	21	21
Poland	21	–
Rumania	15	–
Netherlands	12	12
Greece	12	12
Czech Rep.	12	–
Belgium	12	12
Hungary	12	–
Portugal	12	12
Sweden	12	12
Bulgaria	12	–
Austria	12	12
Slovakia	9	–
Denmark	9	9
Finland	9	9
Ireland	9	9
Lithuania	9	–
Latvia	7	–
Slovenia	7	–
Estonia	7	–
Cyprus	6	–
Luxembourg	6	6
Malta	5	–
Total EU-27	344	222

Unanimity, QMV and co-decision

Table 4.17 sums up the modest results of the IGC 2000 and the Nice Summit. All in all, forty-nine provisions came up for negotiations including some representing a clear procedural anomaly such as that of Art. 42 (measures of social protection in the context of the free movement of persons) or Arts 62, 63 and 67, which require simultaneously unanimity in the Council and co-decision with the EP. The Commission proposed that unanimity should be preserved in

Table 4.17 From unanimity to QMV

Article	Subject	Notes
7.1	Establishment of a breach of fundamental rights by a member state	4/5 Council special super-qualified majority
23.2	Nomination of special representatives of CFSP	
24	Binding international agreements CFSP/JHA	
13.2	Measures to promote non-discrimination	QMV and co-decision
18.2	Free movement of persons	QMV and co-decision
65	Judicial cooperation in civil matters excluding family law	QMV and co-decision
67	Common rules on asylum policy	Unanimity and co-decision
100	Emergency aid for natural disasters	EP informed
111.4	International representation in economic and monetary policy	
123.4	Introduction of the Euro to new member states	
133	Trade in services and commercial aspects of intellectual property (with exceptions)	
137	QMV and co-decision may be used for protection of sacked workers, co-determination and collective protection of workers and employers and conditions of employment of legitimate third-country nationals	
157	Measures to support action in industrial policy	QMV and co-decision
159	Action to support economic and social cohesion outside structural funds	QMV and co-decision
161	Reform of structural and cohesion funds	QMV and assent of EP as from 2007
181–	Economic, financial and technical co-operation with third countries	
190.5	MEPs statute except taxation	
191	Statute of political parties	QMV and co-decision
207.2	Appointment of Secretary General and Deputy Secretary General of the Council	
210	Salaries and pensions of Court of First Instance	
214	Nomination appointment and replacement of members of the Commission	
223	Rules of Procedure of ECJ	
224	Rules of Procedure of the Court of First Instance	
247	Appointment of the Court of Auditors	
248	Adoption of Rules of Procedure of the Court of Auditors	
259.1	Appointment of ESC	
263	Appointment of CoR	
279	Financial regulation for EU budget	As from 2007

five groups of decisions and that QMV should become the dominant *modus decidendi* in the EU;[31] these were:

- In the case of Arts 22, 190(4) and 269, according to which any decisions taken have to be ratified by national Parliaments.
- In thirteen cases related to institutional issues affecting the political equilibrium between the member states (Arts 67(2), 100(1), 100(2), 104(14), 107(5),123(5), 202, 221, 222, 225(2), 245, 290, 308).
- In three cases related to taxation and social policy not related to the internal market (Arts 93, 95, 137(3)).
- In three cases related to deviations from the internal market rules (Arts 57(2), 72, 88(2)).
- In four cases of unity of law between international agreements and internal legislation (Arts 111 (1), 187, 300, 310)).

However, reactions by a number of member states but principally from the UK, Sweden and Denmark and to a lesser extent from France, Ireland, Spain and Luxembourg, resulted in the decision of the Nice Summit which is shown in Table 4.17, according to which twenty-seven provisions move to QMV,

Enhanced co-operation

The debate about 'flexibility' or 'enhanced co-operation' is old enough to be traced back to Dahrendorf, who proposed an *à la carte* arrangement of the Community as early as 1979 and continued with Giolliti in 1982,[32] who suggested that differentiation should become a principle of the Community's future evolution. Stubb undertook the useful task of explaining the jargon used on this issue in several European languages.[33] The term 'variable geometry' refers to a situation in which several member states co-operate in order to satisfy specific objectives in a more or less exclusive fashion, in the knowledge that the rest of the members cannot participate lacking the necessary know-how (and know-why) prerequisites. Examples of this kind of co-operation are abundant during recent years. The Eureka project, the JET project, the Airbus or the ESA,[34] all involve interstate co-operation outside the formal confines of the Treaties and are all more or less permanent and exclusive forms of international co-operation. In an *à la carte* co-operation scheme, the member states are allowed to choose the kind of co-operation to be associated with and accept their participation in the attainment of a limited number of common objectives. The idea of 'multispeed co-operation' involves several member states in a less exclusive fashion than before, in which other members will be allowed to join in whenever they find it advisable.[35]

The AMT (see Chapter 3) introduced the 'flexibility' provisions in Arts 11 TEC, 43 and 44 AMT. The relevant provisions have not been used up to now, principally because it was felt that such provisions were introducing scores of strict requirements that were not facilitating the development of such forms of co-operation. The French Presidency circulated a questionnaire to the representatives of the member states in the IGC that attempted to pinpoint the reasons for the non-use of the flexibility clauses.[36] Returns from the questionnaire almost unanimously blamed the plethora of requirements in the AMT. The flexibility clauses became part of the IGC agenda during the Portuguese Presidency. The latter's Report to the Santa Maria de Feira Summit revealed that during the IGC two alternative scenarios were discussed for changing the flexibility clauses: the Report calls the first scenario 'the enabling clauses scenario', drawing from the situation in the first and third pillars; the second scenario is referred to as the 'predetermined model', rooted in the Schengen and EMU provisions and experience and attempted to built on the AMT provisions.[37] It was the latter scenario that effectively prevailed. The reasons advanced in the Report relate to the challenge of further enlargements and in particular the avoidance of the impression that the changes in the flexibility clauses were taking place with the prospective members in mind. Possible areas of enhanced co-operation were also mentioned in the Report such as the CFSP and defence, police and judicial co-operation, the environment, research and development (R&D), and industrial co-operation. The EP through the Delgado Report also supported the envisaged changes in the AMT provisions.[38]

Changes with the Treaty of Nice

There were two important changes in the clauses on enhanced co-operation: the first involved a change in the minimum number of member states to embark on such projects, from the majority of the member states in the AMT to *eight* in the new Treaty. Second, the 'emergency brake' procedure was abandoned, according to which the whole issue could be referred to the European Council to make a unanimous decision (see Chapter 3). This was replaced by a provision whereby a proposal for enhanced co-operation may be deferred to the European Council by the Council of Ministers acting on QMV, which will discuss the proposal, but no vote will be taken. The proposal will then go back to the Council of Ministers to decide by QMV.

According to Art. B, any enhanced co-operation will be regarded as a solution of the 'last resort' in the sense that any decision to that effect will be taken only if it becomes plain that the required majorities in the Council will not be forthcoming and the Union cannot move *in toto* towards new areas of co-operation. Art. C gives the opportunity to any member state to join in an enhanced co-operation scheme at any time, provided that they 'respect the basic decision and the decisions taken herewith'. Moreover, Art. D asserts the institutional procedures to be adopted in the context of enhanced co-operation. All Council members are allowed to take part in the deliberations, but only the participating members have a right to vote. Decisions will be taken by QMV defined for the purposes of the enhanced co-operation as a proportion of the weighted votes and as a proportion of the number of the participating states. Unanimity consists exclusively of the latter, whereas the decisions adopted within an enhanced co-operation will not form part of the *acquis communautaire* and will be binding only on the participating states. Consistency between the policies of the Union and those involved in an enhanced co-operation is left to the co-operation between the Council and the Commission.

In the first pillar, the interested member states must submit an application for enhanced co-operation to the Commission. The latter may submit a proposal to that effect to the Council or notify the applicant member states for the reasons of not doing so. In the first pillar, the whole process rests decisively with the Commission. If it chooses not to submit a relevant proposal to the Council, then the whole process stops right there since there is no alternative open for the applicant member states. The Council, acting by QMV on a proposal from the Commission and after consulting the EP (or with its assent if the proposal concerned relates to an issue area covered by co-decision), will give authorisation to set up such flexible integration schemes. Any operating expenditure will be borne by the participating members, whereas the expenditure associated with EU institutions will be borne by the general budget.

There is also a provision in Art. E giving the opportunity to a unanimous Council to decide that all costs associated with enhanced co-operation is covered by the general budget of the Union. According to clause H, any member state wishing to participate in an enhanced co-operation in the first pillar must notify the Council and the Commission of its intentions. The latter will give its opinion on the subject to the Council within three months and will reach a decision on the member state's request within four months of its submission. Clauses I–M refer to the conditions for establishing a framework of enhanced co-operation in the second pillar. This must respect the principles, general guidelines and consistency of the CFSP and the decisions taken in this context, the powers of the Community, and must observe that there is consistency between the policies of the Union and its external activities.

According to clause J, the foundation of enhanced co-operation in the second pillar relates only to the implementation of a common action or a joint decision and is forbidden *expressis verbis* in matters having military or defence implications. The new Treaty, in its clause L, assigns to the High Representative of the CFSP – the Secretary General of the Council – the task, if not duty, of fully informing all members of the Council on the implementation of enhanced co-operation in second-pillar issues. Clause M specifies the procedure allowing other member states to join in an enhanced co-operation scheme in the CFSP framework. These must notify the Commission and the Council of their intentions. Within three months the Commission shall give its opinion to the Council, which will decide by QMV within four months, unless it decides to hold the member states' request in abeyance, though specifying a date for the re-examination of the issue.

Clause O specifies the procedure for enhanced co-operation in the third pillar. Again, the interested member states must address a request to the Commission, which in turn must decide whether to submit a proposal to the Council. If the Commission decides not to submit a proposal, it must notify the member states concerned of the reasons of not doing so. Contrary to the arrangements in the first pillar, in the third pillar, interested members are given the option to initiate a discussion in the Council which, after consulting the EP and acting by QMV, may concede authorisation. Other member states wishing to join an enhanced co-operation scheme in the third pillar (Clause P) will have to go through a procedure similar to that described in the case of the CFSP. Table 4.18 summarises the situation in each pillar.

Table 4.18 Enhanced co-operation

Pillar	Initiative	Proposal	Decision
EC	Member state (min. 8)	Commission	Commission
CFSP	Member state (min. 8)	Commission	Council/ QMV
CJHA	Member state (min. 8)	Commission or member states	Council/QMV

Concluding remarks

The negotiations during the IGC and the Nice Summit were successfully concluded, in the sense that a compromise was eventually struck, leading to a new institutional equilibrium. The bigger member states, above all Germany and to a lesser extent Spain, seem to be on the winning side if we reflect on the new equilibrium in each of the EU institutions. But the decision-making system in the Council has become less citizen-friendly, if not more complex and conspicuously less efficient. It comes as no surprise, therefore, that a Final Declaration attached to the NIT calls for yet another reform process leading to an IGC in 2004, which may in turn lead to a new Treaty (see Chapter 7). The rationale for further reform attempts to face the 'real' issues of the EU's evolving agenda: democratic participation, openness and transparency in decision-making, civic rights and duties, the wider issue of the constitutional identity of the Union and, in short, the perennial issue of legitimising its political constitution. Before moving on to these themes, Chapters 5 and 6 attempt to assess the international post-Cold War environment and the new European security architecture.

Notes

1 See Treaty of Amsterdam, Protocol No 7, p. 111.
2 *Ibid.*
3 Presidency Conclusions of the European Council in Cologne, SN 150/99, para. 52, p. 20
4 *Ibid.*, p. 53.
5 Presidency Conclusions of the European Council in Helsinki, SN 300/99, 10–11/12/1999, paras 15–18.

6 See CONFER 4750/00, 14 June 2000, p. 5 ff.

7 Added at the Santa Maria de Feira Summit.

8 See 'Adapting the Institutions to make Success of Enlargement' COM (99) 592 Final, November 10 1999.

9 See European Parliament, A5-0086/2000, 13 April 2000, point 31.1.

10 European University Institute, 'A Basic Treaty for the European Union', Robert Schumann Center for Advanced Studies, 15 May 2000.

11 See COM (2000) 34 Final, paras 11–26, 26 January 2000.

12 *Ibid.*, para. 12.

13 Indeed, the new Commission President Romano Prodi, who took over after the resignation of the Santer Commission in 1999, set up a plan ending in 2002. This plan was published in COM (2000) 200 Final, Vols 1 and 2 (Action Plan), 'Reforming the Commissin: A White Paper'. The internal reorganisation of the Commission was based on five principles: independence from sectional, national or other influences; responsibility; control, promoting a culture of co-operation between the stuff of the Commission; efficiency and simplification of administrative processes; and transparency, internally and towards the citizens of the Union.

14 See Revised Summary CONFER 4815/00, 30 November 2000, pp. 64–5.

15 *Ibid.*

16 SN 533/00, p. 76

17 Report of the Portuguese Presidency, p.18 and especially the attached Annexes.

18 SN 533/00, Treaty of Nice, Annex 1, pp. 74 ff.

19 SN 533/00, Treaty of Nice, Protocol on the Enlargeent of the European Union, 12 December 2000, pp. 74 ff.

20 See W. Wessels, 'Nice Results: The Millenium IGC in the EU's Evolution', *Journal of Common Market Studies*, 39:2, 2001, pp. 197–219.

21 See 'Report on the European Parliament's Proposals for the Intergovernmental Conference', A5-0086/2000 Final, 27/3/2000 Part 1.

22 *Ibid.*, p. 6

23 *Ibid.*, p. 7.

24 *Ibid.*, pp. 7–8

25 *Ibid.*, p. 8.

26 *Ibid.*, p. 9.

27 See COM (2000) 444 Final, 12/7/2000, Communication from the Commission. Additional Commission Contribution to the Intergovernmental Conference. Regulations Governing Political Parties.

28 See 'Contribution of the Court of Justice and of the Court of First Instance to the IGC'. The document can be found at the EU/ECJ Internet site 'europa'.

29 Opinion of the ESC, 'IGC 2000 and the role of the ESC', Brussels, 1 March 2000.

30 See 'Opinion of the Committee of the Regions on the IGC', 17 February 2000, Committee on Institutional Affairs/005, 32A.

31 See COM (2000) 34 Final, 26 January 2000.

32 Reported by W. Wallace, 1982, p. 433.

33 See C.-G. A. Stubb, 'A Categorization of Differentiated Integration', *Journal of Common Market Studies*, 34:2, 1996, pp. 283–95.

34 Stubb, 'A Categorization', p. 286

35 *Ibid.*

36 CONFER 4758/11, July 2000. Note of the French Presidency.

37 CONFER 4750/00, p. 51

38 See EP 2000/2162 (INI), Committee on Constitutional Affairs, 12 October 2000.

5

Geopolitical imperatives of system change
Order and security in post-Cold War Europe

Introduction

This chapter addresses the question of how change at the international system level has produced those political outcomes related to European security and defence design post-Cold War. It is both a description and an evaluation of the way in which Europe's security arena has changed, as well as an attempt to come to terms with the process that led to the 'internalisation' of system change. By 'internalisation' we mean the process – or better, the causal relationship – between system change and policy response. Our argument is that the nature of the post-Cold War systemic reality has been instrumental in sustaining and even increasing actors' faith in co-operative frameworks and in further advancing rule-governing state behaviour and interaction in the European region. The discussion aims at assessing not only the impact of change on the Union *per se*, but also the way change has been translated into policies and strategies that led to the further transformation of the European institutional environment in the field of security and defence. In particular, the argument put forward is that the nature of the new systemic reality in Europe, contrary to realist and neo-realist predictions, can be conducive to the efforts of EU member states to formulate norms and rules which can promote co-operative state behaviour and advance the integration process – slowly and painfully – in foreign and security policy. The analysis deals with the theoretical debate in the field and aims at tracing the defining features of the 'new European order'. Concepts such as globalisation, multipolarity, anarchy, national interests, roles and identities are examined, albeit briefly, in an attempt to understand the structure of the European regional subsystem in relation to state behaviour and interaction.

Although highly unoriginal, there is no other way but to indicate, right from the beginning, that the geopolitical earthquake of 1989–91, which entailed the demise of communism and ignited a process of dissolution of the CEE order, has also eliminated the basic elements of the postwar global as well as regional structure. History and geography, which tight bipolarity had kept *in limbo* for over forty years, have re-emerged as factors reconstituting Europe's identity. The scope of political change, the rapidity with which events become known at the global scale, and the complexities involved in trying to understand the new security challenges, have been and continue to be discussed. Our traditional conception of the classic factors of power in analysing and explaining the changing security environment is still relevant. The difference today, as Dewitt put it, is 'the reach of impact, the complexity of the causal process, the range and capabilities of actors involved, and the acknowledgement that threat and response are no longer within the sole or even primary purview of the military'.[1]

Against this background, the discussion in the following pages addresses two important dimensions of current international concern. The first is the evolution of the European security system in the new millennium, taking account of the changing properties of world politics since the collapse of bipolarity and attempting to assess the extent to which structure, power and actors have been assigned new meanings under the impact of uncertainty and unpredictability following the tectonic shifts in world affairs. Second is the extent to which the strategic ramifications of the new geopolitical realities and the new security challenges, although lacking a unified concept of threat, can adequately 'provide' rules for state interaction and, crucially, for reinforcing the 'institutionalisation' of security. Moreover, can process and institutions be instrumental in redefining identities and interests towards a less competitive and even non-conflictual European system, especially when – as in the case of the Union – the negative impact of international anarchy is neutralised by the long-term experience of co-operative institutional frameworks of normative interaction? In the context of the latter, the analysis in this and in Chapter 6 is directed towards the examination of (not only) EU institutional response and adaptation to the new structural elements, but also towards assessing the development of strategies, both national and institutional, as well as the formulation of effective policies.

The overall question is one of *rationale* in the context of security elusiveness in a turbulent world. A discussion of key components of national and institutional policy-making and of the key transformation elements that crowd the new European security agenda contributes to this overall understanding. Common themes involve debates about stability and instability; continuity and change; multipolarity and leadership; co-operation and discord; power capabilities and patterns of behaviour.

Rethinking security

The dramatic change of international systemic polarity clearly reflects the development of new structural variables as products of trends aiming at revising institutional entities and state policies. These trends can be seen as directly linked to problems and challenges of redefining basic tools of analysis: structure and the nature of the system, national interest, state sovereignty and power. In this context, any discussion about the prospects of a new system of collective security in Europe – as they have been expressed through the decisions taken in Maastricht, Amsterdam, Berlin and Madrid – should take account of the constituent elements of change that produced the 'new order'.[2]

With respect to the international system, the term 'structure' refers to the ordering of principles and priorities, as well as to the distribution of capabilities among units that lead to the various forms of polarity. Among the several uncertainties arising from the new structure, there is one persisting 'certainty': the anarchical nature of the international system. Anarchy has been constant throughout the history of the interstate system. At the same time, the range of options available to any state is constrained by the international distribution of power.[3] That a multipolar order has succeeded the bipolar one is clear, and so is the fact that the emerging multipolarity will differ markedly from the multipolarity of previous eras. Whereas the multipolarity of the 1970s and 1980s took on meaning within the broader context of persisting bipolarity, the multipolarity of the 1990s and (possibly) beyond does not do so.[4] During the Cold War, the Union and Japan were great powers when judged by their economic productivity, trade balances and financial surpluses; but they were scarcely such when judged by their continued security dependence on the US. Post-1989, these actors could be great powers not only in the economic sense, but also because the political impact of their economic power will no longer be qualified by a security dependence that imposes substantial constraints on their freedom of action in foreign policy.

The 1991 Gulf War had complicated things, for in the midst of the dust and fire, the rhetoric of American politics turned to talk of a 'new world order'. This phrase has come to symbolise, for many, a set of expectations and hopes, few of them terribly clear or well articulated, and even fewer so far fulfilled. If there is to be a new order, it will have to emerge not simply out of the ashes of the old, but rather in a dynamic tension with the powerful legacy of great-power war and resulting international institution-building during this century. There is, therefore, a critical evaluation problem, which is linked to the need for conceptualising the changing European order. It is of paramount importance to identify the nature of the post-Cold War order in Europe, and at the same time to trace the implications of systemic change both for the order itself – as a structural construction – as well as for the state units that lend legitimacy to that order.

According to Smith, there are essentially four dimensions to this *problématique*. The first has to do with the nature and character of 'order' in general. The second has to do with the concept of change. The third concerns the response(s) to the process and the products of change, and the fourth addresses 'the issue of impact, and the ways in which changes in the order and in the actions of major participants feed into further processes of change', which influence both the nature of the whole (system) and the behaviour of the parts (state or other units).[5] At an empirical level, the changing nature of the order can be linked to a series of important developments. First and foremost, it is the existence of structural change that produces a rearrangement of European state relationships, especially in the field of world economy. More and more, 'globalisation' enhances the interdependence of national economies and undermines the traditional relationship between state power and the market. Globalising production and global finance transform global economy into a system of 'governance without government'.[6] As noted briefly by Cox:

> there is a transnational process of consensus formation among the official caretakers of the global economy. This process generates consensual guidelines, underpinned by an ideology of globalisation, that are transmitted into the policy-making channels of national governments and big corporations ... The structural impact on national governments of this global centralisation of influence over policy can be called the internationalising of the state. Its common feature is to convert the state into an agency for adjusting national economic practices and policies to the perceived exigencies of the global economy.[7]

An important implication of Cox's argument is that the state becomes a transmission belt from the global to the national economy, 'where heretofore it had acted as the bulwark defending domestic welfare from external disturbances'.[8] As he points out, 'different forms of state facilitate this tightening of the global/local relationship for countries occupying different positions in the global system'.[9] In this context, Held argues that relations of economic, political and cultural interdependencies across the globe – and more so in Europe – are undermining the sovereignty and autonomy of states in all aspects of their security (and elsewhere).[10] Closely linked with this process is the emergence of new states in Europe, and hence the need to trace the components of the new European system. At the same time, revision of the economic and security status outside Europe has raised questions about the boundaries of the system and the interests of European state actors. More often than in the past, there are new and sometimes unexpected linkages between political, security and economic concerns that increasingly undermine the capacity of states, as foreign policy actors, both to recognise and to respond to new challenges and needs for (collective) action. Finally, there has been a major institutional challenge relating to the adequacy of existing institutions for concerted international action, as well as to the potential for co-ordination between state and non-state forces, transnational or subnational.

This last issue is of paramount importance for Europe: European transnational forces, combined with fragmenting subnational ones, create ambiguity and fluidity; the Union forms an 'island of peace': a unity of transnational networks and a common retrenchment from a violent periphery. Paradoxically, however, these processes are also reproduced within the single state with national networks, security zones and areas of violence. Transnational forces and the growth of cosmopolitanism have weakened the nation-state, but this challenge has led to the emergence of nationalist reactions and the legitimation of subnational secessionist forces. As Hassner put it, 'the nation-state is both obsolete and obstinate'.[11] In Western Europe, the challenge to the nation-state comes primarily from the process of integration and globalisation; in the historically imperial Eastern Europe, the challenge comes from a reconstructed national–romantic ethic primordialism, which could lead to the disconnection of the assumed unity of state and nation. As the locus of international security shifts in practice from state to nation, the unchallenged, and uncritical, acceptance of the unity of state and nation has become problematic. The amalgam of state/sovereignty is contested within and across international boundaries, as it is confronted by a competing amalgam: nation/identity. The implication is that, although the state remains a central actor in the international system, it is not the sole actor in the area of security. Ethnonationalism and identity politics also have system-transforming effects in international relations.[12]

In attempting to respond appropriately to the new conceptual and, eventually, policy challenges, we must do more than merely add new issues to the global agenda. Our thinking about the nature and pursuit of security must change. The attempt to understand the new European order and security should take account of its geographical and functional scope, its degree of institutionalisation, its strength and fragility and its ideological and normative elements. While the collapse of the Soviet bloc and accelerating globalisation have fundamentally altered the structure of geopolitics, 'our conceptual frameworks and menu of policy prescriptions are indelibly infused with a Cold War political logic'.[13] The definition of security issues, the way in which they were analysed, and the policies that resulted were the products of the dominant geopolitical and ideological environment. Consequently, security was understood primarily in military terms, and security studies fixated on the problem of achieving and maintaining a stable balance of nuclear and conventional forces between two ideological–political blocs. The militarised conception of security that grounded international relations during the Cold War is being challenged simultaneously both by multifaceted and holistic conceptions.[14]

The collapse of communism, and with it of Soviet hegemony in CEE, removed the immediate military threat. A threat to national security no longer necessarily evokes images of invading armies. The concepts, labels and even norms to which those in the Western security community have grown accustomed over the past fifty years are no longer so clearly applicable. While the military dimension of security is no less important in the post-Cold War environment, there are clear limitations on the application of conventional interstate-level analysis to the examination of international security in general, and European security in particular. Strategic studies are now viewed as focusing on more than the use of military force; security no longer presumes a principal concentration on challenges to a government and country from outside its borders; conflict no longer necessarily means only the violence of armed force;

central governments are no longer viewed as the sole legitimate authorities for the use of coercive means; and defence no longer presumes that military force is either the first or the most appropriate instrument for action.

All this amply proves that Laidi is right in stressing that the 'reconstruction of meaning or purpose' and its linking up with the exercise of (military) power cannot be settled through 'any ideological or teleological deintoxication which the proponents of Popper's *open society* seem to be advocating at times'.[15] For all that, the divergence between meaning and power cannot be reduced to the tension between the integrative logic of the economy and the disintegrative dynamic of identity. It triggers off a 'chain' reaction affecting all the factors related to the exercise of political sovereignty, the most important being the military instrument. Russia provides the best example: while it remains by far the leading military power in Europe, the way we view the collapse of Russian power is governed less by its inherent weaknesses than by the fact that, today, there is no underlying plan to this power. This leads us to the commonplace but nonetheless essential observation that a military power, no matter how large, suffers a considerable loss of meaning the moment it is unable to connect power with a military policy.[16] The divergence between military power and military policy affects not just Russia but also, albeit to a lesser extent, the US and the other European powers.

Moreover, the replacement of the major military threat from the East by multilevel and multidirectional threats, though admittedly of lower tension, has lent great fluidity and instability to the European security system, which was not well equipped, in terms of policies, competences and institutions, to deal with it. The avalanche of change has clearly demonstrated the difficulties in meeting the new problems that have arisen from the debris of the old order. Instability and a perception of insecurity have resulted from the change in the power structure and ideological configuration of the international system caused by the collapse of the entire deterrence regime as previously defined; namely, the encompassing of those norms, rules and procedures, which provided for the system's governance. It may well be true that the end of the Cold War provides an opportunity to raise the strategic threshold and thereby reduce substantially the possibility of a global conflict; and while this may be true for Europe, one should not be too sanguine about the prospects for a 'peace dividend' in many parts of the world, some of them being worryingly close to or even inside the 'European perimeter'.

For all that, the new Europe makes prediction about the course of international politics difficult. Ambiguity and the dynamics of transformation pervade the immense and unique problems posed in the post-Cold War world by the challenge of achieving security. In the 1990s, policy-makers confronted circumstances that were more diffuse, multiple and uncertain than those faced by earlier generations. The ending of the Cold War has loosened the bonds of patron–client politics, thereby giving licence to the rise of micronationalisms, encouragement to narrow sectoral interests, and legitimacy to unilateral efforts to redraw subnational, national and even international boundaries. The rules are yet to be defined, where the true nature of threats remain shrouded by their multiplicity and complexity, and where it is hard to judge what constitutes winning and losing.[17] In straightforward terms, the end of the Cold War has removed the *ultima ratio* for crude distinctions not only between friends and foes, but also between primary and secondary conflicts. The result has been a structural modification of the international stakes, from a vertical pattern (conflicts are not all of equal importance) to a more horizontal logic (conflicts are too complex and too specific for their settlement to be fungible).[18]

Security challenges become even more complex when one turns to those issues that may not directly challenge the viability of the state in traditional terms, but that may nevertheless undermine its sovereignty, compromise its ability to control the penetrability of its borders, and exacerbate relations, whether between groups within the polity or between states within the regional or global system. Increasingly, it is argued that individual and collective security are dependent on our ability to confront the new challenges. Among the new factors that transcend boundaries and threaten to erode national cohesion, the most perilous are the so-called 'new risks': drug trafficking, transnational organised crime, nuclear smuggling, refugee movements, uncontrolled and illegal immigration, and environmental risks.[19] These are not new sources of potential conflict. They all existed to some extent or another during the Cold War, but were largely subsumed by the threat of military conflict between the North Atlantic Treaty Organisation (NATO) and the Warsaw Pact countries.

Responding to these threats, especially to wide environmental degradation in the former communist states, will be an important dimension of preventive defence. The political and economic costs of environmental degradation and mismanagement, such as the high disease rates and safety shortcomings in nuclear plants in the former Soviet Union (FSU), are proving to be formidable challenges to economic development and stability. The simple recognition of such problems, however, has not always elicited effective responses from the international community. Instead, nations have frequently opted to focus their energies on the more manageable manifestations of pending conflicts, such as arms build-ups, that result from disagreements between nations over non-traditional security issues.[20] Because Europeans face so many difficult security challenges, all of which compete for attention and resources, it will be difficult to tackle these kinds of non-traditional threats. Yet, they cannot simply be ignored for long: the environmental threats posed by the aging nuclear infrastructure in CEE and the former Soviet states, inadequate controls over highly enriched uranium and other nuclear materials (including weapons-grade materials) in Russia, and the deterioration of nuclear-powered vessels (some of which literally are rotting in port), could all soon reach crisis proportions.[21] Although these problems have not gone unreported, much more needs to be accomplished if future disasters are to be avoided.

Refugee movements and illegal immigration represent additional layers of non-traditional threat to Europe's security and stability. While the most publicised refugee flows in the past few years have occurred in Central Africa, more than 800,000 Bosnian refugees remain in Germany and other European states, and almost 500,000 Albanians have entered Greece and Italy. Many other refugees have resettled in Europe after fleeing or emigrating from former colonies. The economic and social burdens these refugees place on government services have become substantial. As a result, numerous countries in Europe are beginning to re-examine their immigration policies and enforce more stringent standards. This could have a destabilising effect on the less economically advanced European nations and could threaten interstate relations. It could also lead to domestic unrest if more is not done soon to regulate the flow of refugees and expedite safe repatriation of those not accepted for long-term residence. In the interim, Europe is experiencing an increase in crime rates and hate crimes, any of which could lead to instability and thence to conflict and insecurity.[22]

These factors, probably as much as the proliferation of weapons of mass destruction (WMD) (nuclear, chemical and biological), their means of delivery, and human rights abuses, pose profound challenges to the viability of a new global order, as they are more than capable of contributing to violence and other forms of coercion. Contrary to other global challenges (the communications revolution, water shortages, access to energy resources, financial flows), they call directly into question the very authority of the state and are therefore potentially, if not openly, subversive. This multifaceted conception of security entails a multifaceted approach to security itself. While an exclusively state-centred analysis is capable of illuminating some facets of discord and conflict in the 1990s (e.g., proxy wars and irredentism), it is limited by its one-dimensional optic: the distribution and character of military power.[23] This multifaceted/multidimensional security concept means that there is no rigid link between a comprehensive concept for understanding a new situation and the quality of the response. On the contrary, a broad concept allows a flexible, tailored policy in which force is only one of the various means employed.[24] In the final analysis, security is a politically defined concept. It is open to debate whether the widening of security might be a good or a bad political choice, but security is not intrinsically a self-contained concept, nor can it be related to military affairs only. If political priorities change, the nature and means of security will inevitably follow and adapt to the different areas of political action.[25] Security is also multidimensional, in that individual welfare is more central to policymaking than it was fifty years ago. Individual security can no longer be satisfied only through military measures; it needs a multidimensional understanding. As Politi notes, 'individual security and international stability are becoming increasingly interwined and a security threat is anything that hampers any relevant organisation in ensuring individual security'.[26] This means that security is elusive; more than ever, it is embedded in the interaction of localising and globalising forces. The axes of conflict in the shadow of the Cold War will probably be more complex, not less, and more difficult to manage. Policies begin to blur traditional dividing lines, both between jurisdictions and between concepts that once were discrete.

What does the above discussion mean for the prospects of co-operation in Europe? Contrary to Mearsheimer's predictions, and the ever-heightening complexity and unpredictability of world politics, today's anarchy and multipolarity do not necessarily undermine such prospects, especially in Europe and the Atlantic arena. World politics should not be viewed as a historically frozen realm of power-hungry states, but rather as a dynamic process of interaction among individuals, groups, states and international institutions, all of which are capable of adapting their sense of self-interest in response to new information and changing circumstances. Under the proper conditions and adaptive foreign policy responses, multipolar systems, not bipolar ones, can produce relatively greater stability. This observation does not ignore the fact that the multipolar systems of the eighteenth and nineteenth centuries were structurally unstable. Far from avoiding war, they used it to preserve the essential variables of the system, primarily the rights of the major powers, in a status of greater or lesser dynamic equilibrium. The latter was subject to much erosion at the edges and uncertainty as to the growth and decline of relative power positions. Europe's security *problématique* has changed too much in the 1990s and possible responses are too different to expect that future security dilemmas will be clones of those that plagued Europe in the past. In the eighteenth, nineteenth and much of the twentieth century, the essential action in the global balance of power had taken place in Europe. Since the end of the Cold War, the European Continent is no longer necessarily the focus of shifting alignments and multilateral security. A balance of power could still be maintained in Europe but disorderly developments in Asia, the Middle East, and elsewhere, could negatively affect the stability of the European subsystem. In other words, although a stable Europe may be a necessary condition for world peace, it is by no means a sufficient one.[27] Thus, the connection between multipolarity and European instability is rather simplistic, as it is only when bipolarity is combined with other systemic conditions that European instabilities are exacerbated. In that sense also, it is not polarity but *polarisation* that can lead to conflictual situations. And there is no evidence that such a process will occur in the European subsystem, at least in the foreseeable future.

On the contrary, as the analysis that follows illustrates, the European protagonists (the US included), while still part of an anarchical environment, have not pursued a relatively simple process of behavioural adaptation to post-Cold War systemic realities. Rather, they have embarked upon a more complex process of an *ab intra* redefinition of their identities, roles and, to an extent, interests, mainly by protecting and on many occasions reinforcing the *sui generis* European institutional environment that has proven instrumental in stabilising their expectations. In one sense, the European 'model' represents a fusion between liberal and realist visions of the international system: it retains states as the basic units, but contains the security dilemma within a non-conflictual, if not co-operative, culture. In this context, the analysis in the following two sections focuses on the changing roles, structures, power capabilities, strategies and patterns of behaviour of the main actors as a response to systemic change.

The issue of leadership: the US in the new Europe

Although security concerns have been fundamentally influenced by changes in the European and international state system and by the reallocation of power on a structural level, security and defence policies will continue to be defined by traditional 'constituent elements': the Atlantic connection (which will remain of fundamental importance to Europe even if the US reduces its involvement); independent national strategies and choices; and a densely institutionalised environment. As a result, the internal distribution of roles will probably remain unclear because of overall systemic uncertainties. The foundations, however, will remain broadly the same, at least in the short and medium run. Perhaps the most important issue is the extent to which American power and behaviour should and could influence the course of events and the shape of European developments.

What might be called 'structural heterogeneity' is one of the main features of the new international system; it refers to the existence of different international structures corresponding to the different kinds of power: military, monetary, trade, industrial, energy, and so on. This formation has given rise to a major academic debate about US power capabilities. It could be argued that the present and likely future distribution of capabilities will take new forms in different spheres. The military sphere is dominated by the US and is expected to be so in the foreseeable future. The economic sphere, on the other hand, is multipolar, with a high degree of transnational interdependence and a profound trend towards power diffusion. This phenomenon has resulted in an even more significant decline of US effectiveness to 'arrange things' according to its own perception of world order. Viewed in historical perspective, the Europe of the Cold War was distinctive not so much because it was stable – Europe had experienced nearly comparable periods of stability before – but because the US was the linchpin of Europe's order. That state of affairs became natural to most Americans actively involved in international affairs, and public opinion polls suggest that it became part of the US foreign policy landscape.[28]

Throughout the history of Atlantic relations, the question of 'leadership and followership' has dogged the steps of policy-makers and has constrained the lines of policy itself. While it might be argued that during the 1950s and 1960s the sheer preponderance of US power rendered such issues redundant, it was by no means clear that structural power could eliminate the diversity of national role conceptions and perceptions of stakes which inevitably underlay the developing EU–US relations. It was apparent by the 1960s that American leadership was often mercurial and increasingly questioned within the US itself, and that the role of follower was not attractive to some EU members. Perceptions of the costs and benefits arising from adherence to the Atlantic norm were certainly not uniform, as shown by the tangled history of trade and monetary relations. During the 1970s and 1980s, the underlying diversity and contention in this area became increasingly apparent, although it is open to question how far they fundamentally modified the structure of Atlantic relations.

It could be argued that with the decline of the US *vis-à-vis* the Union in non-military matters, vestiges of American hegemony in EU–US relations appeared anachronistic. Politically, the Nixonian definition of the US as an 'ordinary country' during the early 1970s was disingenuous to say the least, but it did express an important perception held by US policy-makers and the attentive public: that Americans were asked to sacrifice their natural interests and instincts for the benefits of their allies (especially those in Europe) who were no longer incapable of fending for themselves. This perception persisted and has strongly influenced the spirit in which the development of the Union and its political presence have been received. Alongside this went the tendency for the US to attempt periodic redefinitions of the Atlantic relationship and thus, by implication, relations with the Union and Western Europe more generally. Perceiving the Union as a predominantly regional economic actor, and the Europeans as 'partial partners', was indicative of the American unease with developments in Europe, leading the US to castigate the Europeans for not acting politically, and then to reprimand them for their more assertive actions through EPC or other channels. For their part, the Europeans found the role of followership increasingly irksome as their collective consciousness progressed; a development fostered, in large measure, by the erratic nature of US leadership itself. As Featherstone and Ginsberg have put it: 'The hegemon tried to hold on to its outdated prerogatives in an increasingly interdependent (as opposed to dependent) world, while the former client did not initiate a new, more rounded relationship with its former patron but instead moved toward greater economic and foreign policy independence from it.'[29]

The developing security relationship between the US and Western Europe also reflected the tensions between structure, stakes and role that have been identified above. One key feature of the 1970s and 1980s was the questioning of the foundations of US security policies – questions which led to wide oscillations around the central adherence to multilateral structures; key amongst them, NATO. Unilateralism and Soviet–American bilateralism cast doubts over the ability of the US leadership to reflect the needs and aspirations of Western Europe, from SALT I to Reykjavik and beyond. At the same time, for the US, the Europeans' self-identification as a 'civilian', if not a 'civilising', power was suggesting the very kind of free-riding behaviour which Americans were increasingly ready to identify. Since the late 1980s, EU–US relations have been very different from any previous period post-1945. In the 1990s, not only did an era pass but also a way of thinking. As noted elsewhere, profound international events have raised questions at the very heart of our understanding of international politics. America's place in the world is debated and old thinking will not suffice. In 1991, Roberts noted that the specific intellectual agenda within the debate about US foreign policy after the Cold War is defined by three challenges.[30] The first is to evaluate how long-standing policy priorities and instruments carry over into the new era. The second is to identify new foreign policy issues that have emerged in the shadow or wake of the Cold War. The third is to pose the larger, transcendental questions about what the US stands for in the world and what Americans want to accomplish as a nation. Without answers to these questions, the evaluation of priorities and policies is sterile and impractical. Not since the late 1940s has the policy research community faced such an all-encompassing task. The US cannot simply carry forward the strategies, policies and concepts of the past into a quite different future. One clear lesson of the 1990s, though, is that very little concerted international action is indeed possible without American leadership. The reunification of Germany, the liberalisation of world trade arrangements, the Gulf War and strong intervention in the former Yugoslavia – military and otherwise – all required the US to articulate policies, as well as to convince and sometimes pressure others into joining.

The Gulf War and the admittedly impressive US exhibition of 'capacity to go to war' shows that military power is not obsolete. However, the assumption that the military victory of the US in the Gulf implies that the US has become once again 'hegemonic' would be simplistic.[31] In the twentieth century, the US was forced to intervene in Europe in order to rescue a faltering balance of power from aspiring hegemons. The post-Cold War multipolar balance of power, unlike those of the past, cannot rely on war as a cheap means by which the strong restrain those who aspire to join the majors' club. Nuclear and high-technology weapons make even small-scale wars unacceptably costly for developed democracies. And those weapons will be of limited value in deterring and coercing non-state actors who engage themselves in micro-wars within and across state borders.[32] Within the subsystem of the advanced capitalist and ever-globalising, if not already globalised, world, where the Union and the US act and interact without the presence of the communist threat, the significance of military strength is being reduced. Threats or promises concerning force are very difficult to make on issues of trade barriers or macroeconomic policy co-ordination. Estimates of future power will be more than ever based on the power of state-supported trade, finance capital, investments and other non-military aspects of power. The diffusion of effective power resources between the Union and the US (and Japan) has resulted in power becoming multidimensional and difficult to exercise. In that respect, the promise contained in President Bush's concept of a 'new world order' should not be viewed as a new *Pax Americana*, for no such US dominance can either be effective or viable in the long run, without support from international coalitions including West European states. If there is 'order', it will surely not be premised on the primacy of the US alone, save where, as in the Middle East, military power can still be a major arbiter of events with implications far beyond the region.[33] The concept of a 'new world order' was born at a time when the US had put together an unprecedented coalition of states to act for a common purpose. The coalition's rationale in 'Operation Desertstorm' was not military: the US possessed the necessary capacity of its own, although it welcomed the efforts of key European allies. Instead, it served political purposes: to convince Americans that the US was not acting alone to secure an asset (oil) that was more important to other countries; and to counter Iraq's charges that it was championing the cause of the downtrodden against the 'enemies of Arab people'. Also, the situation in the Soviet Union meant that the ample US forces still in Europe could be withdrawn without fear.

The coalition's success does not necessarily set a precedent, however. There is, in fact, no other place on earth about which so many countries care so much, because of oil. As Calleo observes: 'the conditions in the Gulf War did provide a near perfect occasion to demonstrate American power . . . Militarily and geopolitically, however, these were not conditions that could be generalised into a new American-dominated world order.'[34] Likewise, Yugoslavia and the 1998 Iraqi mass destruction weapons crisis have shown that, important as it may be for the US to take the lead, it is unlikely that military power alone will be offered as a solution, at least not without 'objections'. Europe after the Cold War has new security problems, with new complex political and economic dimensions for which the US does not seem well prepared nor much disposed to take the lead in addressing. Nor did the major Western European powers seem eager to legitimise a renewed American hegemony, without some share in the power of decision in terms of defining problems, suggesting remedies, creating strategies and assigning roles. The emotional and psychological adjustments that the US faced in the 1990s is not limited either to changes in the agenda or in the tools most likely to be prominent in conferring power and influence. By the end of 1990, the Soviet threat to American and Western European interests had been replaced by less focused fears of economic and political disruption in Eastern Europe. One might have thought, on the basis of either 'balance of power' or 'balance of threat' theory, that European alignments with the US would have weakened more than they did in the 1980s. Signs of tensions in EU–US relations over trade, the international role of the Union, and relations with the East, had begun to mount in the later years of the Reagan administration. Changes in America's relative position in influencing and, to the extent possible, determining great events had affected its hegemonic role.

This prospect caused confusion regarding America's post-Cold War role. The confusion, however, did not express itself with the familiar dichotomy of the 1930s, that is, between imperialism and isolationism. Rather, it reflected the fact that identifying interests, setting goals and choosing instruments in contemporary US foreign policy had become a more formidable task than ever before. Kissinger was quick to point out that the end of the Cold War, in a manner similar to the end of Second World War, has produced a great temptation to recast the international system in America's image.[35] Kissinger, however, rejects the notion of a 'unipolar' or 'one-superpower' world, as power has become more diffuse and America's ability to shape the rest of the world has actually decreased.[36] This means that the American exceptionalism, which was the basis for a Wilsonian foreign policy, appears less relevant for the coming years. For Kissinger, the nineteenth-century concept of 'balance of power' is the way forward for the US, whose foreign policy-makers have to articulate a notion of the national interest that is served by the maintenance of an equilibrium in Europe and in Asia, as America cannot 'remedy every wrong and stabilise every dislocation'. But at the same time, it cannot afford to 'confine itself to the refinement of its domestic virtues' because that would lead to American security and prosperity being dependent upon decisions made by others, of which the US would progressively lose control.[37] Kissinger's preference for a 'Congress of Vienna'-like framework for American post-Cold War strategy says little about how the US and the rest of the major international players (Europe, Russia, China and Japan) will achieve this kind of interaction in the world arena, when their governments and societies are facing enormous challenges domestically. As Miller has indicated, 'state-to-state balancing is also more complicated when there are no significant adversarial relationships among these five. Such balancing provides no guidance when non-state actors and functional topics crowd agendas.'[38]

Nevertheless, the US has attempted to make its policies compatible with its relative decline in power and the expansion and globalisation of interdependence, but this process of change has been undermined by a lack of strategic vision. Adopting a realist perspective, Krasner argues that US behaviour is constrained by its own capabilities and the distribution of power in the international system.[39] The external environment will inevitably pressure the US to move towards congruity between commitments and capabilities. In short, because the US is the main loser (in relation to its Western European allies) from structural change in world politics, it is bound to adjust its foreign policy behaviour. There has been, therefore, an undercurrent of disorientation in American foreign policy resulting from difficulties in translating the abstract of military might into actual political success. Having claimed credit for winning the Cold War, US policy-makers have been faced with the equally daunting task of managing peace. Building constructive relations among all the emerging great powers has been a challenge exacerbated by the co-existence of military and economic competition. Because both the issues as well as the hierarchy of power are different in each of these spheres, solutions on one level are likely to pose problems on the other and *vice versa*.

Although international policy co-ordination was never more difficult, there is evidence to support the thesis that the US foreign policy-making elites are attempting to craft policy by pursuing a strategy that promotes American power, position and primacy in order to enhance the capacity of the US to exercise influence abroad. The issue here is one of continuity and/or change. American actions in the Gulf (both in the early 1990s and in 1997–98), Somalia, Haiti, the Korean Peninsula and Yugoslavia, although problematic and incoherent, represented the continuation of Washington's commitment to an active international agenda, even without a geopolitical and ideological rival. A global foreign policy inspired by *Realpolitik* efforts to prevent other states from 'renationalising' their foreign and security policies is a clear manifestation of continuity. This policy framework is based on the conviction that America's prosperity depends on the preservation of an interdependent global political economy, and that the precondition for economic interdependence is the geopolitical stability and reassurance that flows from US security commitments. Policies of renationalisation would destroy this reassurance and stability upon which US interests are presumed to rest. The assumption is that, if Washington cannot or will not solve others' problems for them, the world order strategy will collapse. Compelled to provide for their own security, others would have to emerge as great or regional powers and behave as independent geopolitical actors.[40]

This American globalism, then, is compatible with a set of principles that have come to be associated with world order, stability and, hence, vital US interests. Three principal objectives remained as they had for forty years: to maintain a strong European defence capacity, led by the US; to encourage a process of European integration that remained compatible with a 'US-made' liberal international political economy; and to continue global liberalisation of trade and investment on terms favourable to American interests. To attain all three objectives, the US had to maintain a strong influence in Europe, and either co-operation on economic and security issues had to be mutually reinforcing or, at worst, conflicts in one area (especially economic) had to be prevented from contaminating relations in the other. The fact that the US sought to institutionalise its relationship with the Union almost at the same time as the collapse of the General Agreement on Tariffs and Trade (GATT) talks in 1990 is a case in point. The 1990 Transatlantic Declaration can be interpreted as the institutional recognition of the changing nature of the EU–US relationship, in which the US is coming to terms with its reduced capability to influence EU behaviour within the old and outdated structures of the 'hegemonic era'. The Declaration not only formalised pre-existing linkage processes between the two, but it also confirmed the weakening of US leverage. Growing and intensifying interdependence forced the US to seek to formalise the process of co-operation with the Union, in the face of important changes both within the Union – the completion of the single market programme, the Maastricht process (especially EMU) and further reforms to accommodate prospective enlargements – and in the new Eastern Europe. The Declaration was an important, though modest, step in the direction of 're-fashioning' EU–US political relations.

The ancillary objectives of US foreign policy in Europe also displayed a degree of continuity: to secure European support, where possible, for American actions outside Europe (e.g., in the Gulf), and to avoid increased financial or military obligations on the Continent. Fiscal pressures in the US made the latter objective even more important and reinforced American interest in European initiatives for greater burden-sharing in defence, preserving at the same time the centrality of NATO with a new command structure, albeit at lower force levels. American attitudes towards increased European defence co-operation had always been ambivalent, with the US willing to see greater co-operation in order to reduce its own burden, but not to the point of undercutting NATO. That is why the American reaction to the Franco-German initiative of reviving the WEU as an exclusively European defence capability was one of concern. However, the policy outcome of Maastricht, Amsterdam and Berlin, which left the WEU subordinate to NATO, the inability of the Union to develop a common position on the Gulf and Yugoslav crises, and the *de facto* effective co-operation of the US, Britain and France in the Gulf War, diminished American concerns about NATO's role, even though it played no official part in out-of-area crises (until 1994 in the former Yugoslavia). The issue here is that the decline of American hegemony does not suggest that American leadership is on the wane. To be sure, the US overall material capabilities and power position have declined significantly since the early postwar years. But the political institutions and structures of relations that were built under American sponsorship after the Second World War still provide channels and routines of co-operation. America will not (and probably cannot) play the leadership role it did a generation ago, but that leadership has been reinvented in the form of a dense set of institutional and transnational linkages among major actors and regions in the world. Conflicts and disputes are as ubiquitous as ever, but they have become more domesticated and contained. Ikenberry summarises this argument most succinctly:

> Those who believe that American leadership is unlikely, if not impossible, look at past cases, particularly the end of World War II and a mythical version of the nineteenth century, to argue that the necessary conditions are missing: the hegemony needs overwhelming power, a clear purpose, and a large reservoir of political will. The error in the reasoning is not in failing to see that these factors are absent, but rather in failing to understand that they are not necessary in the current conditions, which call for a quite different kind of influence that relies on different instruments and that can thrive in the absence of these factors.[41]

While the actual record of US foreign policy in the late 1990s had by no means been a great showcase of global or Western leadership, the habits and institutional foundations of American leadership were still in place. For Ikenberry, the widespread worry about the end of US leadership is partly a result of a misunderstanding of what leadership is and the changing conditions in which it must operate. If leadership means the ability to foster co-operation and commonality of social purpose among states as well as the ability to reinforce institutionalisation at a systemic level, then American leadership and its institutional creations will long outlast the decline of its postwar position of military and economic dominance; and it will outlast the foreign policy stumbling of particular US administrations.[42] In this regard, the far-flung political institutions, rules, norms and relations that the US built during the Cold War are still in place, and these overall macro-structures can be seen to work despite the steady decline in

America's hegemonic position and the failings of its leaders. Indeed, the overall US-shaped system is still in place. It is this macropolitical system, a legacy of American power and its liberal polity, that remains crucial in generating agreement in the post-Cold War international relations.

Brzezinski goes further in arguing that American global power is exercised through a global system of distinctively American design that mirrors the domestic American experience.[43] Although America's international preeminence unavoidably evokes similarities with earlier imperial systems, the differences are more essential. They go beyond the question of territorial scope. As the imitation of American ways gradually pervades the world, it creates a more congenial setting for the exercise of the indirect and seemingly consensual American hegemony. And as in the case of the domestic American system, that hegemony involves a complex structure of interlocking institutions and procedures, designed to generate consensus and obscure asymmetries in power and influence. American global supremacy is thus buttressed by an elaborate system of alliances and coalitions that literally span the globe.[44] As Nye and Keohane have commented, American influence in Europe was greater in the 1990s than during the 1980s.[45] During the Cold War, international institutions such as NATO, GATT, and the Union were essential instruments in the implementation of American global strategy. The US successfully sought to prevent further loss of influence by maintaining a congenial political–economic order in Europe. Successful institutions tend to create interests that support them: even if NATO and GATT could not have been formed *ab initio* under the conditions of the 1990s, they were able to persist under these conditions.[46] Although the Bush administration implemented a 25 per cent reduction in the US force structure, including a sharp cutback of American troops in Europe under strong Congressional pressure to cut the defence budget in the spring of 1990, it succeeded in maintaining the centrality of NATO in European defence and was, by and large, able to keep US policy, preferences and interests intact. NATO remained central to the American internationalist strategy post-Cold War, and emphasis on the alliance was consistent with the US position throughout the Cold War years. By adapting NATO doctrine and structure, and by fending off French efforts to replace it as the central focus for the organisation of defence, the US was able to maintain its long-standing interest in NATO as the central focus for European defence, and thus to maintain its own influence as a central participant in the European security debate. Also, continuing US support for greater European integration must be interpreted as a realisation that the Union can act as a stabilising force in Western Europe and a catalyst for smooth democratic transition in the East. It is interesting, as the following section shows, that even the EU member states chose 'institutionalisation' as a response to systemic transformation: Germany sought to use institutions to reassure its neighbours as it regained a central role in Europe, and Britain tried to retain institutions such as NATO that magnified its influence. Washington viewed reliance on a web of international institutions (especially NATO) as the best way to preserve a strong position in the tactical bargaining with both Russia and West European powers. The process of institutional adaptation which has been the outcome of interstate bargaining is at the heart of the new European security architecture.

The post-11 September 2001 context

Nobody can credibly deny the fact that the terrorist attacks against the US have in effect ushered in a new era in international politics. The priorities of international relations, the nature of regional politics, the shape of political alliances, the driving purpose of US foreign policy, the nature of international cleavages, the evolving role of military forces and the risks of WMD were all affected by the epoch-making events. The terrorist attacks have altered the Western strategic threshold but they have not really challenged the American position in the world, although the impact on the US strategy debate is profound. In terms of international distribution of power, the overall international security paradigm remained reasonably clear-cut. The US occupies a dominant place in the post-Cold War international system, especially in those aspects of the system dealing with national and international security. Again, one clear lesson of the Afghanistan campaign – like Bosnia and Kosovo – is that all major post-Cold War 'strategic projects and challenges' require effective US leadership.

In the campaign against international terorism, the US – once more – took the lead. By exercising its right of self-defence, it built a varied coalition in support of that right and has sought to develop a strategy to defeat terrorism with a global reach. A new strategic era has thus dawned. The US has a newly defined enemy, which is neither the old Soviet Union nor a, potentially, resurgent China, but international terrorism and terrorist sponsored states.[47] The pursuit and defeat of these enemies has become the overarching goal of US President G. W. Bush and his administration. It has, therefore, become a defining feature of international relations today. Countries formerly having difficult relations with the US, ranging from Russia, to Pakistan, to Iran, have an opportunity to develop a new strategic framework for themselves. New relationships, even alliances, will be built on the campaign against global terrorism, and these may endure well into the future. These radical and, in large measure, structural changes in the international political scene will have a considerable impact on the domestic context in which foreign policy is being conducted. Grand strategy, in the difficult circumstances of the ever-globalising information age, has returned to the fore with the US adopting a strategy of large-scale coalition-building.

Indeed, American diplomacy, since 11 September 2001, has been predicated on the need to build a large coalition of sorts, in order to fight the campaign against terrorism on many fronts and by employing a multitude of means. It is a coalition of sorts, because it is essentially one of variable geometry. Britain has been involved from the outset in all elements of the campaign; broad political support, direct military involvement, military assistance, intelligence sharing, co-operation on financial controls, collaboration in UN Security Council (UNSC) diplomacy, co-ordination of national diplomatic efforts, development of long-term geopolitical strategy (and capacity for co-ordinated action), humanitarian and refugee policy, consultation on macroeconomic dimensions and sundry work. Other countries are involved in a subset of these activities. Moreover, the coalition is not merely led by the US but cannot be much influenced by others precisely because it is of such varied and inconsistent participation. These realities mean that there has been no major change, despite what some have suggested, in the instincts that animate the present US administration of G. W. Bush. Despite the latter's decision to pay United Nations (UN) dues and consult widely, US foreign policy has not embraced multilateral diplomacy in the traditional meaning of the phrase, nor found a new affection for international treaties. Indeed, the anti-terrorist campaign shows that the US has been adapting a more traditionalist view of international politics and taking harsher judgements about the relevance to its own security of actual or proposed international instruments and will be more, rather than less, vigorous in ensuring that it is not constrained by them when it seeks to act in self-defence. This could lead to a zero-sum struggle for power between the US and those that could threaten its territory, allies, friends or interests. According to Daalder, 'this is a view ... that places military–security issues on the top of the US foreign policy agenda and focuses on threats to security as the main rationale for American engagement abroad'.[48]

At the level of scholarly debate, after the tragedy of 11 September, a stream of analysts were quick to criticise Fukuyama's 'end of history' thesis.[49] Rather emphatically, some went as far as to declare that history has only taken a break or even that that was the end of the end of history! For his part, Fukuyama responded by saying that such an unprecedented attack on thousands of civilian lives constituted in itself a historical event, while pointing out that the way in which he used the word 'History' in 1989 referred to the progress of humankind toward modernity, namely the institutions of liberal democracy and capitalism, in that it was difficult at the time to discern a viable alternative type of civilisation that people wanted to live in after the demise of communism, monarchy, fascism and the like. Such views were opposed by Huntington who, by dismissing the idea of a single global system (or of world-wide progress toward it), pointed out that the world was mired in a 'clash of civilisations', with several major groups, defined in cultural terms, constituting the new fractures of world conflict.[50] In particular, although he admits to the emergence of non-state actors on the global scene, holding however that nation-states will remain the most powerful actors in world affairs, Huntington argued that conflict will continue to occur within civilisations, but also that the most dangerous conflicts of all will occur on the fault-lines between civilisations. His *The Clash of Civilisations*, however, may well have raised the question of the cultural dimension of security, in that the 'clash' occurs along the lines of religiously inspired militancy against Western liberal values, but missed the underlying causes of Islamic resurgence itself, as it was obsessed with the cultural symbols or the retrieval of collective historical memories. A related criticism to his work was that, by rewriting Muslim history, he failed to encourage intelligent dialogue between the two opposing cultures, thus fostering fragmentation and prolonging historical stereotypes.

Fukuyama, on the other hand, sees the end of the Cold War as evidence of the triumph of liberal democracy over any oppressive and/or authoritarian type of regime: liberalism, in short, reigns triumphantly as the only remaining ideology. While Fukuyama admits that certain internal conflicts exist within liberalism, for instance, among classes, he dismisses these conflicts on the grounds that they are manageable. Conflict is central to his view of the future of international politics, its most important sources being ideological. Although he posits two possible ideological challenges to liberalism – religion and nationalism – he dismisses the threat posed by religion by claiming that religion is ill-suited to the realm of politics, suggesting at the same time that the liberal political process may help to resolve nationalistic tensions. In both cases, Fukuyama's faith in liberalism is overly optimistic. Irrespective of whom of the two wins the argument – and it is too early to even speculate on that – it is worth noting that, although they both see religion as threatening either the so-called 'Western civilisation' or for that matter 'liberalism' as its major constitutive feature, each seems to be employing a rather different approach. More specifically, Huntington rejects ideology and focuses on culture, while Fukuyama emphasises ideology. The fact that these apparently different perspectives lead to similar insights is not coincidental, as both theorists find religion as an inherently non-rational, pre-modern phenomenon. Yet, the question persists: is there a distinction to be drawn between, on the one hand, a generalised image of modernity based on an evolutionary model projected by the West to the outside world and, on the other, the way in which the institutions of modernity – formal and informal, political and economic – are sufficiently enough developed or indeed well enough established to be exported (at any rate of success) to non-Western polities? Be that as it may, we claim that such a distinction is of relevance to developing a more penetrating understanding of the form – or, better, forms – Western 'domination' currently takes in global politics, as well as to the very process of theorising, albeit mostly at the normative level, whether or not Western-style liberalism has reached a posthistorical stage. Before we bring this *problématique* to a close, Fukuyama's observations on the endurance of modernity post-11 September 2001, merit our attention:

> We remain at the end of history because there is only one system that will continue to dominate world politics, that of the liberal-democratic West. This does not imply a world free of conflict, nor the disappearance of culture as a distinguishing characteristic of societies ... But the struggle we face is not the clash of several distinct and equal cultures struggling amongst one another like the great powers of 19th-century Europe. The clash consists of a series of rearguard actions from societies whose traditional existence is indeed threatened by modernisation. The strength of

the backlash reflects the severity of this threat. But time and resources are on the side of modernity, and I see no lack of a will to prevail in the United States today.[51]

European national visions, preferences and strategies

In the framework already described, the process of systemic transformation lends new salience to the factors outlined in this chapter. In the first place, the notions of leadership and followership in EU–US relations, based on the learning of the past fifty years, demand redefinition if not reconstruction. Within Europe, the leadership role in many areas seems at last partly to be falling to the Union, either by default or by design. For example, in 1989 the US and the EU were the major actors in establishing a co-ordinated Western response to the collapse of communism in Eastern Europe. The Western Economic Summit in Paris in July 1990 agreed on a programme to aid Poland and Hungary, with the Union acting as the chief co-ordinator. The European Bank for Reconstruction and Development (EBRD) began operating in 1991, in part to service the programme. The initial subscribed capital of the Bank was ECU 10 billion, borne by thirty-nine nations plus the EU institutions. Just over half the Bank's capital was committed by the twelve EU nations (45 per cent) and the EU institutions (6 per cent) combined. The US contribution was 10 per cent.[52] The programme was later extended to cover Bulgaria, Czechoslovakia, East Germany (prior to German reunification), (former) Yugoslavia and Romania.

However, the overall picture of the Union's role after the Cold War is much more complex and challenging. The war in the former Yugoslavia revived visions of a Europe racked by discord and ancient rivalries.[53] For the Union, the conflict exposed its lack of unity and will to act as a custodian of European security. The important issue here is the fact that the Balkan conflict has sapped the Union's confidence and undermined its credibility, thus contributing to the crumbling of popular support for the TEU, which was already diminishing as a result of the economic recession of the late 1980s and early 1990s. The eventual ratification of the Treaty did not repair the image of the Union as incapable of shouldering the responsibility of acting as the principal stabiliser in a meta-communist European context. At the same time, the Union's evolution and search for a role were, and still are, burdened by the reality of a reunified Germany, which threatens the tacit bargain that has been at the heart of European integration: Germany's acceptance of French political leadership in the Union, in return for a preponderant voice on economic affairs. Germany was thus tied to the West through US leadership on security matters within the NATO structure and French leadership on political issues within the Union. In the 1990s, Germany was suddenly transformed from a middle power contained in a variety of constraining structures and institutions into a major player, given its new size, economic might and geostrategic location in the new Europe. As Hoffmann asserts, 'within the EC, the relative equilibrium among the "big three" – France, the Federal Republic, and Britain – has broken in Germany's favor'.[54]

Mearsheimer argues that nationalism, German reunification and the likely reduction of American involvement in Europe will lead to intensified political rivalry and conflict among the major European powers, essentially as a result of the persistence of anarchy and multipolarity.[55] Yet, breaking out of this kind of realist straitjacket, it should be noted that the existence of international institutions shows that anarchy does not necessarily prevent co-operation.[56] In the absence of institutional stabilisers such as the Union and NATO, multipolarity and nationalism could be fatal, as the First World War demonstrated. In a case such as this, expectations play a crucial role. States and leaders will expect conflict and seek to protect themselves through self-help, and by seeking relative gains the potential of conflict will increase. International institutions, however, exist, in large measure, because they facilitate self-interested co-operation by reducing uncertainty and, hence, by stabilising expectations.[57] Post-unification German policies, like those employed post-1945, are closely linked to international institutions. A united Germany did not revert to old-fashioned nation-state manoeuvring. Genscher regarded his 'policy of responsibility' as a practice beyond the traditional balance of power politics.[58] This does not imply that Germany does not pursue what it perceives as its national interests (see the former Yugoslavia), only that it demonstrates a clear preference for co-operation forging multilateral structures like the Union, WEU, NATO or the Organisation on Security and Co-operation in Europe (OSCE). The account of Anderson and Goodman shows that the German post-Cold War strategies reflected the instrumental role of these institutions for a German policy that depended on reassuring both adversaries and allies.[59] As in the half-century since 1945, it is crucial for Germany to remain a reliable partner, ready, willing and able to shoulder responsibilities with its allies. To remain an influential partner Germany must fulfil its international obligations. A strengthened multilateralism in the European security environment is of vital importance for Germany, which not only has more neighbours than any other European nation, but lies on the dividing line between the affluent West and the fledgling democracies in CEE. It was, therefore, in Germany's interest to promote both integration and ever closer co-operation in NATO and the Union, while simultaneously stabilising Central and Eastern Europe. Germany had a vital interest in keeping the US involved in European security affairs through a transformed and reinvigorated NATO, and a WEU organically linked to the former.

For France, the demise of the Cold War order provided a test for the validity of a set of assumptions and attitudes towards European security, which have constituted the French security model for almost three decades.[60] The French reaction has been one of confusion and ambiguity. French policies have been mostly dictated by immediate perceptions and concerns, particularly those dealing with German reunification and its consequences. The most striking feature of these policies has been the French preference for deepening European integration as the best response to new systemic challenges. The implicit motive was that further integration would alleviate the risk of a hegemonic Germany.

But faithful to its Gaullist tradition, French foreign policy has also attempted to preserve a degree of independence. According to Hoffmann, 'it is the difficult combination of anxiety about Germany and worry about French independence which explains the subtleties and contradictions of France's European policy'.[61] While the deepening of integration was seen by French elites as the best way to restrain Germany's 'operational sovereignty', the very same process was seen as potentially leading to a situation in which Germany might dominate the institutions designed for its containment. The dilemma for French policy-makers was over integration and independence. The idea of an 'organic link' between the WEU and the Union as independent from NATO as possible, while allowing space for the preservation of French military independence, proved impossible to realise, and led to unsuccessful initiatives and inconsistent attitudes. It is indicative of the French confusion and inconsistency that while the rhetoric used had a strong federalist colouring, the proposals submitted in the IGCs of 1990/91 and 1996/97 were compatible with intergovernmental premises. French policy thus allowed the US to rally Britain and Germany behind the reform of NATO's force structure, which was endorsed in June 1991. The British plan that prevailed increased the role of the Europeans (minus France) within NATO, especially through the creation of a rapid reaction force integrated in NATO's command structure.[62] While the British position was consistent with the basic principle of keeping the US involved in Europe, what kept Germany from endorsing the French 'vision' over NATO was not only the stabilising role of the Alliance in Europe as well as its attraction to Eastern European governments, but also France's own reluctance to abandon its autonomy for the construction of a truly collective European security system.

For Britain, the most important objective in the post-Wall period has been to preserve its 'special relationship' with the US. The view has been that NATO is the best vehicle for the preservation of the US commitment to Europe, which was viewed as essential to European security. Moreover, the continuation of US involvement was seen by London as the best way to neutralise the threat that German reunification presented to the European balance of power and, hence, to Britain's position. Britain perceived NATO as the *conditio sine qua non* of the post-Cold War settlement. Britain insisted throughout the '2 plus 4' negotiations that a unified Germany would have to be a NATO member and that NATO should remain the linchpin of European security. Throughout the Cold War, British defence policy had become so integrated with NATO policy that it was difficult to separate the two.[63] In the mid-1990s, the British view started shifting towards supporting moves to strengthen a European pillar in security and defence. However, this did not signal a fundamental change in British attitudes. For Britain:

> NATO must remain the bedrock of Europe's security and its capabilities should not be duplicated. However, we also need a stronger WEU so that European countries can take on their proper share of the burden and act effectively in situations in which the US may not wish to be involved . . . We need to take high-level decisions

of policy and military action involving Western European countries at summit level. That would keep co-operation on an intergovernmental basis, and not on the basis of Community competence.[64]

This seemingly new British approach has been the result of US reluctance to become involved in issues that do not constitute vital American interests, and of the need to work out ways that foreign policy decisions by the Fifteen can be translated into defence action by the WEU. For Britain, this will not mean a European army or for that matter duplication of NATO. As Douglas Hurd has observed, 'some things will not change. Defence against invasion – defence of our vital interests: these are NATO's essential tasks. But Europeans can and must respond to other demands in Europe and beyond: peace keeping, crisis management, humanitarian operations, sanctions enforcement.'[65]

The foregoing discussion shows that European national responses to the end of the Cold War were conditioned by the highly institutionalised European environment. Not only that, but European governments promoted 'institution-alisation', albeit in different forms (adaptation, reform, consolidation, etc.). This, however, does not mean that institutions have dictated policies. Rather, they have been used to accommodate national interests and to promote national power and policy preferences in well-known co-operative frameworks. It should not escape our attention that national positions and policies reflect deeper antitheses, which relate to fragile balances, national visions and external orientations and interests, both within and outside the EU system. These antitheses derive from the lack of homogeneity of geopolitical perspectives, differing concepts or evaluations of external threat and differing national strategies. The result has been a divergence among fundamental interests and, consequently, the development of divergent national strategic orientations and foreign policy preferences and approaches.

Entering into the security realm is not uncontroversial considering that the Union for a long time professed to be a 'civilian power', lacking military might and ambitions in the military sphere. The European political system on the 'high politics' level is still fragmented into nation-state units, which, throughout its history, either used intergovernmental co-operation with participation in the Atlantic Alliance or developed bilateral co-operation, like France and Germany. This means that the European countries have almost always had the will to integrate trade and economic policies, but not to abandon their authority and autonomy in the vital areas of security and defence, which allow them to behave as independently as possible in the international system. The European defence system was built – at both collective and national levels – on the basis of an 'Atlantic' rather than a 'European' logic. The presence of the US in Europe 'undermined' the need for excessive defence armaments, thus eliminating the systemic causes of past European conflicts. The historical significance of the US presence lies in the fact that it contained the traditional competitive and conflictual tendencies in Europe as well as a developed network of Euro-American institutions and processes, within which defence and security policies were inter-nationalised. What should be clear is that American involvement and the Soviet threat led to 'Atlanticism' rather than the 'Europeanisation' of defence. The reactions of the major European powers to the tidal changes of the 1990s are testament to this thesis. The calls for a more autonomous European defence system that could be subject to supranational processes should not ignore national strategies and preferences. Successful implementation of the CFSP, as well as of a common defence policy, will continue to depend, as the Amsterdam outcome clearly showed, less on legal obligations and more on favourable political and strategic variables and factors in the European regional and global arenas.

In that context, implementation of the decisions made at Maastricht and Amsterdam could not only be painful but may actually dampen European foreign policy activism and threaten the whole *acquis communautaire*. Joint security policies backed by military options are likely to be possible only when all the member states' interests are under threat. Alternatively, they might refuse to comply with the agreed guidelines. Amsterdam revealed that a modern European strategy document is not easy to write, given the very different foreign policy traditions of the different EU members and the uncertainty of the contemporary world. What treaty reforms have done in the 1990s is to identify defence as essential to EU construction. In such a context, a common security organisation becomes a means to a compelling political end. Given this, imperative practical issues such as military planning, command structures, effectiveness and efficiency are in danger of becoming subordinate considerations. This is against all historical experience. The history of international relations since the Greek–Persian Wars has showed that states band together to meet perceived security threats; they do not forge defence structures to achieve a preconceived political federation. The implementation of Amsterdam stands this logic on its head. The accelerated move to create a more than intergovernmental defence regime as an (implicit) precondition for eventual political union seems to ignore the fact that no functional equivalent to US strategic leadership exists in Europe, nor is one likely to emerge in the foreseeable future. Moreover, regimes should not be viewed as progenitors of regional security communities that supplant national governments. This outcome is highly improbable and might in the end prove to be dangerous. If states perceive that regimes are being constructed around and under them, they are apt to withdraw their co-operation, with adverse consequences for peace and stability in Europe. Instead, the regime-building process should draw from states their common interests in redefining the terms of an interstate security community in Europe, recognising non-state actors as critical supports for the process.

Moreover, successful regime-building requires identification and definition of the threat. NATO experience has shown that there is a linear relationship between the internal cohesion of an alliance and the way in which members perceive external threats and challenges. The nature of European interstate relations post-1989 has changed to such an extent that the definition of a specific and identifiable threat is very difficult. The Soviet threat has been replaced by a complex of fluid and 'secondary' dangers: local or regional instability, civil and identity-based conflicts, revisionist tendencies in the regional subsystems, nuclear proliferation, and even potential resurrection of past dangers such as nationalist groups and parties in Russia. Failure of EU members to define the nature and character of post-Cold War threats could not only undermine attempts to transform the CFSP into 'defence policy', but could endanger the integration process in other fields. The evolution of the European security institutional map in the 1990s confirmed that the compelling task was not to create structures that derive from member states' compulsions to assuage anxieties about the future, which will erode further the EU's credibility in defence and foreign policy by ignoring the heterogeneity of the European system, but to renovate the transatlantic security arrangements by shifting from a US-led system to a multilateral and more EU-involved one. It should be noted once more that 'institutionalisation' was chosen as *the* principled European security policy: the Treaty on Conventional Forces in Europe (CFE), the Confidence- and Security-Building Measures (CSBMs) agreements, the Paris Charter, the creation of the North Atlantic Co-operation Council (NACC), the strengthening of the Conference on Security and Co-operation in Europe (CSCE)/OSCE's conflict prevention and peacekeeping machinery, NATO's 'Partnership for Peace' (PfP) initiative, together with the decisions taken in Berlin for a European Security and Defence Identity (ESDI) and a Combined Joint Task Force (CJTF), and in Madrid for NATO's enlargement, have already laid the foundations of a new cooperative security order in place. It is to these developments that we now turn, in an attempt to yield some further insights into the institutional and political evolution of European foreign, security and defence policy.

Notes

1 David B. Dewitt, 'Introduction: The New Global Order and the Challenges of International Security', in David Dewitt, David Haglund and John Kirton (eds), *Building a New Global Order: Emerging Trends in International Security*, Toronto: Oxford University Press, 1993, p. 1.
2 By the term 'order' we mean a formal or informal sum of relations which produces regular and expected patterns of behaviour and in which commonly accepted views on issues of hierarchy, legitimacy and normative interaction prevail. See, for example, Robert Cox, *Approaches to World Order*, Cambridge: Cambridge University Press, 1996, especially Chapter 6. For a historico-sociological approach, see John A. Hall, *International Orders*, Cambridge: Polity Press, 1996, especially Chapter 1.
3 Stephen D. Krasner, 'Power, Polarity and the Challenge of Disintegration', in Helga Hoftendorn and Christian Tuschhoff (eds), *America and Europe in an Era of Change*, Boulder: Westview, 1993, p. 22.
4 R. W. Tucker, '1989 and All That', *Foreign Affairs*, 69:4, Autumn 1990, pp. 96–7.
5 Michael Smith, 'Beyond the Stable State? Foreign Policy Challenges and Opportunities in the New Europe', in Walter Carlsnaes and Steve Smith (eds), *European Foreign Policy:*

The EC and Changing Perspectives in Europe, London: Sage, 1994, p. 24. Smith attempts to approach the problems of foreign policy analysis in the framework of change in Europe. He discusses the implications of change for the 'European state' by looking for the linkages between the tools of foreign policy analysis and state theory. In this exercise, the primary sources are those provided by John Ikenberry and his work on 'The State and Strategies of International Adjustment', World Politics, 39:1, 1986, and Robert Cox and his work on 'States, Social Forces and World Order: Beyond International Relations Theory', in Robert Keohane (ed.), Neorealism and its Critics, New York: Columbia University Press, 1986, as well as 'Multilateralism and World Order', Review of International Studies, 18:2, 1992.

6   On this notion, see James N. Rosenau and Ernst-Otto Czempiel (eds), Governance Without Government: Order and Change in World Politics, Cambridge: Cambridge University Press, 1992; Susan Strange, Casino Capitalism, Oxford: Basil Blackwell, 1986.

7   Robert Cox, 'Global Restructuring: Making Sense of the Changing International Political Economy', in Richard Stubbs and Geoffrey R. D. Underhill (eds), Political Economy and the Changing Global Order, London: Macmillan, 1994, p. 49.

8   Ibid.

9   Ibid. 'At one time, the military–bureaucratic form of state seemed to be optimum in countries of peripheral capitalism for the enforcement of monetary discipline. Now, International Monetary Fund-inspired "structural adjustment" is pursued by elected presidential regimes (Argentina, Brazil, Mexico, Peru) that manage to retain a degree of insulation from popular pressures. India, formerly following a more autocentric or self-reliant path, has moved closer and closer toward integration into the global economy. Neo-conservative ideology has sustained the transformation of the state in Britain, the United States, Canada, and Australasia in the direction of globalisation. Socialist party governments in France and in Spain have adjusted their policies to the new orthodoxy. The states of the former Soviet empire, insofar as their present governments have any real authority, seem to have been swept up into the globalising trend.'

10   According to Held, 'states, including new states, operate in a complex international system which both limits their autonomy and infringes even more upon their sovereignty. Any conception of sovereignty which interprets it as an unlimited form of public power is undermined. Sovereignty itself has to be conceived today as already divided among a number of agencies, national, international and transnational, and limited by the very nature of this plurality.' See David Held, Modern State and Political Theory, Stanford: Stanford University Press, 1992, p. 16.

11   Pierre Hassner, 'Obstinate and Obsolete: Non-Territorial Transnational Forces versus the European Territorial State', in Ola Tunander, Pavel Baev and Victoria Ingrid Einagel (eds), Geopolitics in Post-Wall Europe: Security, Territory and Identity, London: Sage/Oslo: International Peace Research Institute, 1997, p. 58.

12   Kenneth D. Bush and E. Fuat Keyman, 'Identity-Based Conflict: Rethinking Security in a Post-Cold War World', Global Governance, 3:3, September–December 1997, p. 314.

13   Ibid., p. 311.

14   See, for example, Kenneth Booth, 'Security and Emancipation', Review of International Studies, 17, 1991, pp. 313–26; Helga Hoftendorn, 'The Security Puzzle: Theory-Building and Disciple-Building in International Security', International Studies Quarterly, 35, 1991, pp. 3–17; Edward Kolodziej, 'Renaissance in Security Studies? Caveat Lector!', International Studies Quarterly, 36, 1992, pp. 421–38; Barry Buzan, People, States and Fear: An Agenda for International Security Studies in the Post-Cold War Era, 2nd edn, New York: Harvester Wheatsheaf, 1991; and Michael Klare and Daniel Thomas (eds), World Security: Challenges for a New Century, New York: St Martin's Press, 1994.

15   Zaki Laidi, 'Introduction: Imagining the Post-Cold War Era', in Zaki Laidi (ed.), Power and Purpose After the Cold War, Oxford: Berg, 1994, p. 2.

16 *Ibid.*, p. 3.

17 James N. Rosenau, 'New Dimensions of Security: The Interaction of Globalising and Localising Dynamics', *Security Dialogue*, 25:3, September 1994, p. 255.

18 See Zaki Laidi, 'Power and Purpose in the International System', in Laidi (ed.), *Power and Purpose*, p. 11.

19 WEU, *European Security: A Common Concept of the 27 WEU Countries*, WEU Council of Ministers, Madrid, 14 November 1995, pp. 8–14.

20 The most prominent recent reminder of the need to take such threats seriously has been the Chernobyl nuclear reactor disaster in Ukraine. The Ukrainian government today still allocates nearly 15 per cent of its national budget to managing the environmental after-effects. The total economic and social costs incurred across Europe, including increased health care expenditures and declining life expectancies, will probably never be accurately determined. However, the threat of future Chernobyls is real. The problem of environmental degradation in Eastern Europe is not limited to unsafe nuclear plants, however. It already extends to polluted rivers, toxic dumping, unproductive farm lands, non-existent emission controls and a myriad of other threats to life. Like Chernobyl, these threats must be addressed because their consequences are far-reaching and unacceptable, not only to the populations of the independent Central, Eastern European and newly independent states, but to the whole of Europe. See Ralph A. Hallenbeck, Thomas Molino and Kevin Roller, *Preventive Defence: A New Framework for US–European Security Cooperation?*, Wilton Park: The Center for Global Security and Cooperation, July 1997, p. 40.

21 For several years the US has been attempting to address these problems through the Cooperative Threat Reduction Programme (CTRP). Through the CTRP, the US has helped to destroy ballistic missiles and silos, and has even purchased some highly enriched uranium from the former Soviet Republics and assisted in setting up improved nuclear safety, security and safeguard procedures. To date, however, the CTRP has not eliminated the problems posed by nuclear materials. Indeed, many experts believe that too much attention has been paid to dismantling missiles and silos, and far too little has gone to safeguarding nuclear weapons, military and civilian reactors and loose materials. This comment appears to have substantial merit. If preventive defence policies are to be taken seriously as a framework for addressing these kinds of non-traditional threat to European security, US, Russian and European governments must do more. See *ibid.*, p. 41.

22 WEU, *European Security*, p. 13.

23 The best example is John J. Mearsheimer, 'Back to the Future: Instability in Europe after the Cold War', *International Security*, 15:1, Summer 1990, pp. 5–56. He argues that the demise of the Cold War order is likely to increase the chances that war and major crises will occur in Europe: 'The next decades in a Europe without superpowers would probably not be as violent as the first 45 years of this century, but would probably be substantially more prone to violence than the past 45 years. This pessimistic conclusion rests on the argument that the distribution and character of military power are the root causes of war and peace' (p. 6).

24 According to Politi, 'only in short-term lobbying battles is an alternative between prevention and repression seen'. See Alessandro Politi, *European Security: The New Transnational Risks*, Chaillot Papers, 29, WEU Institute for Security Studies, October 1997, p. 13.

25 *Ibid.*, p. 14. See also Barry Buzan, 'Rethinking Security After the Cold War', *Cooperation and Conflict*, 32:1, 1997, pp. 5–28.

26 Politi, *European Security*, p. 16.

27 Fergus Carr and Kostas Ifantis, *NATO in the New European Order*, London: Macmillan/St Martin's Press, 1996, pp. 44–5.

28 Gregory F. Treverton, 'America's Stakes and Choices in Europe', *Survival*, 34:3, Autumn 1992, p. 119.

29 Kevin Featherstone and Roy H. Ginsberg, *The United States and the European Community in the 1990s: Partners in Transition*, London: Macmillan/St Martin's Press, 1993, p. 14.

30 Brad Roberts, 'Introduction', in Brad Roberts (ed.), *US Foreign Policy After the Cold War*, Cambridge, MA: MIT Press, 1992, p. vii.

31 Robert O. Keohane and Stanley Hoffmann, 'The Diplomacy of Structural Change: Multilateral Institutions and State Strategies', in Hoftendorn and Tuschhoff (eds), *America and Europe*, pp. 44–5.

32 Stephen J. Cimbala, *US Military Strategy and the Cold War Endgame*, London: Frank Cass, 1995, p. 127.

33 Robert E. Hunter, 'Starting at Zero: US Foreign Policy for the 1990s', in Roberts (ed.), *US Foreign Policy*, p. 15.

34 David P. Calleo, 'America's Federal Nation State: A Crisis of Post-imperial Viability', *Political Studies*, 42, 1994, pp. 26–7.

35 Henry Kissinger, *Diplomacy*, New York: Simon & Schuster, 1994, p. 805.

36 *Ibid.*, p. 809.

37 *Ibid.*, p. 833.

38 Linda B. Miller, 'The Clinton Years: Reinventing US Foreign Policy?', *International Affairs*, 70:4, October 1994, p. 624.

39 Krasner, 'Power, Polarity', p. 29.

40 C. Layne and B. Schwartz, 'American Hegemony – Without an Enemy', *Foreign Policy*, 92, Autumn 1993, p. 15.

41 G. John Ikenberry, 'The Future of International Leadership', in Demetrios James Caraley and Bonnie B. Hartman (eds), *American Leadership, Ethnic Conflict, and the New World Politics*, New York: The Academy of Political Science, 1997, p. 2.

42 *Ibid.*

43 Zbigniew Brzezinski, *The Grand Chessboard: American Primacy and its Geostrategic Imperatives*, New York: Basic Books, 1997, p. 24.

44 According to Brzezinski, 'American supremacy has thus produced a new international order that not only replicates but institutionalises abroad many features of the American system itself. Its basic features include: a collective security system, including integrated command and forces, e.g., NATO; regional economic co-operation and specialised co-operative institutions; procedures that emphasise consensual decision making, even if dominated by the US; a preference for democratic membership within key alliances; a rudimentary global constitutional and judicial structure.' See *ibid.*, pp. 28–9.

45 Joseph S. Nye and Robert O. Keohane, 'The United States and International Institutions in Europe After the Cold War', in R. O. Keohane, J. S. Nye and S. Hoffmann (eds), *After the Cold War: International Institutions and State Strategies in Europe, 1989–1991*, Cambridge, MA: Harvard University Press, 1993, p. 105.

46 *Ibid.*

47 See the remarks by John Chipman, Director of the International Institute for Strategic Studies, 'The Military Balance Press Conference', 18 October 2001.

48 Ivo H. Daalder, 'Are the United States and Europe Heading for Divorce?', *International Affairs*, 77:3, July 2001, p. 559.

49 See F. Fukuyama, 'The End of History?', *National Interest*, 1:3, 1989, pp. 3–18; and his *The End of History and the Last Man*, New York: Free Press, 1992.

50 See S. P. Huntington, 'The Clash of Civilizations?', *Foreign Affairs* 72:3, 1993, pp. 22–49; and his *The Clash of Civilizations and the Remaking of World Order*, London: Touchstone, 1996.

51 See F. Fukuyama, 'History is Still Going Our Way: Liberal Democracy will Inevitably Prevail', *Wall Street Journal*, 5 October 2001.

52 Featherstone and Ginsberg, *The United States and the European Community*, p. 106.

53 Michael J. Brenner, 'EC: Confidence Lost', *Foreign Policy*, 91, Summer 1993, p. 24.

54 Stanley Hoffmann, 'America and Europe in an Era of Revolutionary Change', in Hoften-dorn and Tuschhoff (eds), *America and Europe*, p. 63.
55 Mearsheimer, 'Back to the Future'.
56 See Robert O. Keohane, *After Hegemony: Cooperation and Discord in the World Political Economy*, Princeton: Princeton University Press, 1984, especially Chapter 6.
57 Robert O. Keohane, 'The Diplomacy of Structural Change', p. 52.
58 R. G. Livingston, 'United Germany: Bigger and Better', *Foreign Policy*, 87, Summer 1992, pp. 165–6.
59 Jeffrey J. Anderson and John B. Goodman, 'Mars or Minerva? A United Germany in a Post-Cold War Europe', in Keohane, Nye and Hoffmann (eds), *After the Cold War*.
60 Frederic Bozo, 'French Security Policy and the New European Order', in Colin McInnes (ed.), *Security and Strategy in the New Europe*, London: Routledge, 1992, p. 197.
61 Stanley Hoffmann, 'French Dilemmas and Strategies in the New Europe', in Keohane, Nye and Hoffmann (eds), *After the Cold War*, p. 138.
62 *Ibid.*, p. 131.
63 Luise Richardson, 'British State Strategies After the Cold War', in Keohane, Nye and Hoffmann (eds), *After the Cold War*, pp. 158–9.
64 Speech by John Major, House of Commons, 1 March 1995.
65 Speech by Douglas Hurd to the German Society for Foreign Affairs, Berlin, 28 February 1995.

6

Institutional imperatives of system change
The evolving European security architecture

Introduction

The European landscape is changing rapidly, not least owing to a series of decisions taken in the second half of the 1990s. In June 1996, NATO's foreign ministers decided to adopt ESDI 'within the Alliance' and to develop the CJTF concept. In May 1997, NATO and Russia agreed to establish a Joint Permanent Council. In June 1997, EU leaders reached agreement on the AMT. In July 1997 in Madrid, NATO agreed on the admission of three new members (Poland, Hungary and the Czech Republic), while the Commission published its Opinion on CEE candidates and presented its Agenda 2000 report on the implications of enlargement. In 1998 and 1999 the Union began accession negotiations with twelve countries: Bulgaria, Cyprus, the Czech Republic, Estonia, Hungary, Latvia, Lithuania, Poland, Romania, Slovakia, Slovenia and Malta. In December 1999, the Union also re-affirmed Turkey's candidacy status although no negotiations have begun owing to the long path towards democratisation that Turkey must embark upon if it is to fulfil the political side of the Copenhagen Criteria. Economically, in late 2000 and early 2001, Turkey experienced massive financial crises which means that meeting the economic criteria also has a long way to go. In December 2000, the Nice European Council meeting formalised rapid developments in European security and defence, by creating within the CFSP context an ESDP with new institutional arrangements in Brussels and a planned European Rapid Reaction Force (ERRF), which was declared 'operational' at the Laeken European Council in December 2001. Apart from the Union and NATO, institutions like the WEU and OSCE also experienced developments, including, in the case of the WEU, its own demise. This chapter considers the institutional responses to the geopolitical and geostrategic challenges of system change in the fields of European foreign policy, security and defence. It looks at the four institutions which lie at the heart of the debate about European security after the

Cold War: the Union, NATO, the WEU and (to a lesser extent) the OSCE. It examines their development and analyses their interrelationship: what we have learned to call the European 'security architecture'. The final section of the chapter deals with the issue of the Union's role in world politics post-Cold War.

European foreign and security policy

This section presents a detailed analysis of European foreign and security policy as it has emerged after nearly fifty years of efforts by the EC/EU, dating back to the early 1950s with the European Defence Community (EDC) saga, and bringing us up to the Amsterdam and Nice reforms of October 1997 and February 2001, respectively. Attention is given not only to the CFSP itself, but also to its predecessor, EPC, which spanned nearly a quarter of a century (1970–93) before it was replaced by the CFSP with the coming into force of the TEU. One needs to stress a fundamental difference in the efforts at foreign and security policy cooperation before and after the Cold War, as the latter offered (Western) Europe two fundamentally different scenarios, one prior to, and one after, its demise. The dominant view from 1947 until 1989 was one favouring integration in an effort to protect the free Western side of Europe from succumbing to the communist threat of the Soviet empire (accompanied by similar economic and social efforts against the internal threat of communism, especially in France and Italy). This created a 'West versus East' divide that coloured all integration efforts in 'high politics' areas prior to 1989.

After 1989, the security challenge has become one of integrating the East into the existing foreign and security structures of the West and, of course, of adapting them to this new international environment. Whereas the first phase was one of 'exclusion', the second, and current, phase is one of 'inclusion'. The implications are enormous for integration theory and practice as they address totally different requirements. Pre-1989, defence meant that integration efforts were geographically limited to Western Europe and best served in practice by NATO thanks to American leadership and capabilities. Post-1989, we are facing the prospect of a Continent-wide security and defence system that may or may not include the US. That is to say, the European security agenda is now one of creating an overarching architecture that would include all European states and all the many institutions on the Continent dealing with international affairs (the Union, WEU, NATO, OSCE, and the Council of Europe). In practical terms, this means that the future of the CFSP/ESDP is clearly linked to the institutional reforms required to render the Union more efficient as it enlarges. This became visible in recent treaty reforms, where future changes to the number of Commissioners have been made dependent on a reweighting of votes in the Council. Amsterdam, in particular, also extended the scope of QMV in the CFSP, making it clear that treaty reforms would take into consideration not only the 'old' argument about the international interests and duties of the big states, but also the fact that Germany is now a fully fledged actor in international politics (as it is now reunited, fully sovereign, and its Constitution is being re-interpreted to allow for a more active international role, seeking a seat on the UN Security Council) and that the Union could consist of nearly twenty-seven or so members in the not-too-distant future.

All this has of course impacted on the very definition of what 'Europe' actually means. In other words, where will the borders of the current Union end in the longer term? This question goes beyond the mere geographical definition of the Continent and will undoubtedly have implications for what kind of Union and what international role for the Union will ensue. The nature of the EU political system has been discussed earlier in this book (Chapter 2), whereas the question of what type of actor the Union is in international affairs is covered later. Before dealing with this issue, however, one needs to assess the impact of the initial debate on integration theory and developments in European foreign and security policy, as what is debated today is a continuation of a much longer discussion.

The initial debate

The fundamental question of the first two decades of European integration, that is, up to the mid-1960s, had two main dimensions: federalism versus intergovernmentalism, and big versus small states. This particular debate first occurred in the late 1940s and early 1950s and culminated in the EDC saga of 1950–54.[1] Such a debate was then repeated in the slightly different environment of the 1960s with the Fouchet Plans. The latter period was dominated by Gaullism and was part of a wider malaise which culminated in the first major institutional crisis of the Community in 1965, which was resolved by the Luxembourg Accords of January 1996. The same year, however, also witnessed the French withdrawal from NATO's integrated military command.

The questions of West European economic reconstruction and collective defence had been temporarily settled with the 1947 Marshall Plan (OEEC) and the creation of NATO in 1949. The sheer dominance of the US in both organisations meant that immediate concerns had been dealt with. But foreign and defence co-operation, both in more general terms and with a view to deepening integration, remained largely unanswered all the same. The setting up of the Council of Europe in 1949 had shown the limits of European federalism but the debate carried on with the creation of the ECSC and, more importantly for our purposes, with the EDC, where a clearly federal defence structure had been proposed by the Pléven Plan in 1950. Important to note here is that the EDC project eventually failed in 1954, and with it the prospects for the establishment of a European Political Community. The key feature of the debate at the time was, in our view, the question of sovereignty, which brings in the British stance on the matter but, crucially, adds the issue of how to balance the national interests of big states with those of small(er) ones, preferably within a structured, institutionalised framework. The question of 'efficiency versus accountability', which reappeared later and has dominated European foreign and security policy since the 1970s, contained then a different dimension to the current debate, which mainly deals with democracy (see below). The older debate amounted to how much power big states should have in the aftermath of the Second World War in general, and before (EDC) and after (the Fouchet Plans) the Suez *débâcle* of 1956 in particular. More recently, however, and in part owing to the relative small size of most applicant states (either engaged in current accession negotiations or future ones), this debate has re-emerged, even if one must note that not only the international context – political and economic – is different, but also the very nature of the Union itself.

All this had normative and descriptive implications for the kind of structure the integration process would allow in the fields of foreign and defence policy, with the federalists offering a supranational entity and the intergovernmentalists adamantly opposing it. The main arguments in favour or against a federal structure have been described at some length elsewhere (see Chapter 1). All that needs to be added here is that the federalists favoured a constitutional solution to all the problems of European foreign policy and defence at a stroke. The federalisation of Western Europe would have automatically created a common foreign and security policy with a common defence (European armed forces). In order to make the whole process politically acceptable, the EDC would have been part of the European Political Community tied to the EDC plan, comprising a common government, Parliament, and so on; that is, a federal political union. At the other end of the spectrum, the intergovernmentalists basically argued that the collective defence of Western Europe had been taken care of by the creation of NATO, and that defence and foreign policy should remain within the exclusive remit of national control and traditional military alliances. In terms of which EC states favoured which alternative in the 1950s and 1960s, a distinction can be made between, on the one hand, the federalists in Italy, (West) Germany, and the Benelux countries, and, on the other, France and Britain (the latter initially as a non-member and then as a potential member), which favoured a more intergovernmentalist approach.

As no compromise could be found between the two extremes, partly because of fundamental differences and partly because Britain refused to join initially and then was prevented from joining by the French in 1963 and 1967, no further progress was achieved in foreign and defence matters within a strictly European framework. As a result, the continuing debate over the desirability and feasibility of such a project was dominated by the French and were linked to developments in their polity. Indeed, domestic changes in Paris altered the overall European landscape when the EDC plan was overturned by an unholy alliance of Gaullists and communists in the *Assemblée Nationale* in 1954, and, once the Fifth Republic had been established in 1958, de Gaulle dominated European politics. As a non-member, Britain was not directly involved in the debate and did not gain much credibility or sympathy by trying to undermine the Community (the creation of the European Free Trade Area (EFTA) in 1960) and by signing agreements with the US on military (including nuclear weapons) and intelligence issues. Germany was geographically divided, politically impaired at the international level (Basic Law and later WEU restrictions on arms production and possession), and with a foreign presence on its soil (with both divided Berlin and divided Germany as symbols of limited sovereignty). All this meant a stalemate as far as European foreign and security policy was concerned. Only bilateral intergovernmental efforts succeeded – most notably, the Franco-German Treaty of 1963 – and NATO's predominance remained unchallenged, despite increasing problems with US foreign policy in South-East Asia. However, the economic successes of the Community in general, and those of the Customs Union and the Common Market in particular, meant that there was an impact that extended well beyond the Community's internal borders. Accordingly, efforts to find a way of integrating and co-operating on the political side of economic affairs did not go away, both internally (political union) and externally (foreign affairs). Hence the setting up of EPC in 1970, following the December 1969 Hague Summit.

From EPC to the CFSP and . . . the ESDP

The main foundations of European foreign policy co-operation were laid down by the EPC framework following the 1970 Luxembourg Report, and were developed throughout its history with the 1973 Copenhagen Report, the 1981 London Report, and more recently with Title III of the SEA. We contrast here EPC with the failed attempts of the 1950s and 1960s, and identify the reasons for a different outcome and its implications for integration theory.

The main reason for the successful development of EPC was ironically that the previous failures had shown the limits of supranationalism in 'high politics' areas central to national prerogatives and, ultimately, sovereign statehood. But even successive Gaullist attempts at a more confederal, big-powers, Concert of Europe-type arrangement had their own limitations. Those same failures, however, had also shown the existing resolve of smaller states to push ahead with integration in all domains of policy action.[2] The international environment had also changed, with the consolidation of *détente* and the emergence of new leaders in all key members of the Community and in Britain (Brandt, Pompidou, Heath). All these changes at the domestic, European and international levels led to the setting up of EPC in 1970 and the first enlargement of the Community in 1973. In fact, the new members actively participated in foreign policy discussions even before they formally joined the EC/EPC framework.[3]

The principal reasons for EPC's success can be attributed to its intergovernmentalism, flexibility, pragmatism and its built-in room for adaptation. The EPC arrangements also coincided with a stagnation phase in other areas (especially the economy following the oil crises of 1973 and 1979), and it can be argued that, to paraphrase Taylor, such arrangements 'saved' the overall process of integration by allowing intergovernmentalists to be seen as possible integrationists for the first time.[4] A similar case has been made more recently by

Øhrgaard, arguing that there is clear 'affirmative' evidence that 'integration can occur in an intergovernmental setting'.[5] But where this book parts company from Øhrgaard is on his conclusion that Haas' neofunctionalism must be reassessed in that new light. Instead, we argue that confederal consociation offers a better alternative (see below). Despite its limitations from a classical federalist prism,[6] it was thanks to EPC that foreign policy co-operation was occurring for the first time within an institutionalised framework, albeit distinct from the Community's and more flexible than it (no formal role for the Commission and no jurisdiction for the ECJ). Moreover, one needs to link progress in foreign policy with the enlargement process at the time, which was to include a leading international country, Britain. Finally, while EPC showed that political leadership had been reinstated as a key element in any integrative move (thus presenting a setback for the automatic spillover thesis), it also confirmed that some momentum does take place on its own and that the success of economic integration in the 1950s and 1960s meant that the Community had to develop new ways of co-operation in foreign policy if it did not want to be only 'an economic giant but a political pygmy'.

The other important element of EPC was its impact on national foreign ministries and diplomats. This is known in the literature as the 'co-ordination reflex', in that any national foreign policy position has to cater for any impact it would have on the foreign policies of other members and, by implication, on the overall view of the Community. Whether an arrangement among all members could be found in EPC made all the difference between a clear European line (usually reinforcing the view of one – or more – state) and a diplomatic failure for the Community as a whole. Of course, failure to get EPC support did not mean the end of a national initiative, especially when it was made by a big state, but it did have a negative effect overall and a less than constructive impact on the emerging *acquis politique*, namely, EPC declarations, *communiqués*, and *démarches*. All this was of particular importance to the credibility of EPC in the latter part of its life, when more instruments were added to it, especially the use of economic sanctions to back the rhetoric. Indeed, the lack of a common stance meant a weakening of Europe's position on a given international issue and a return to more nationalistic positions. All this had a detrimental effect on integration, whether implicitly (the so-called 'footnote states' of the 1980s – Greece and Denmark – were not seen as convinced integrationists in other fields either) or explicitly (as was the case in the spring of 1982 when solidarity was seen as greatly damaged by Britain's insistence on obtaining political support in its efforts to regain the Falkland Islands, whereas it did not reciprocate in the Common Agricultural Policy (CAP) with its obstruction over agricultural prices).[7]

The overall impact of years of intergovernmental foreign policy-making and the careful avoidance of defence matters (although the economic and political aspects of security had been included in EPC as early as 1981) meant that some progress on a European voice in the world was made (especially in the CSCE, the Middle East and Central America), and an institutional structure had gradually developed, including European correspondents, COREU, emergency procedure and working groups. But somewhat paradoxically, the limits of such an exercise were also exposed: a distinctive structure with parallel foreign min-isterial meetings, a limited role for the Commission and the EP, and no defence dimension (see below). All this meant that in the run-up to the TEU, the new arrangements had to go one step beyond the existing mechanism if they were not to be seen as a total failure. But the lessons of the past had also been learned and no supranational/federal jump was seriously envisaged either (as the col-lapse of such an isolated effort by the Dutch Presidency as late as September 1991 had shown). This is clearly visible not only in the rather limited federalist aspects of the CFSP (the Commission's theoretical right to initiate debate and policies, the possible use of QMV in the Council over the implementation of Joint Actions, the possibility of using the Community budget for operational and administrative expenditure), but also in the limited changes that Amster-dam brought about in 1997 (see below).

In its most ambitious interpretation, the transition from EPC to the CFSP[8] had four main objectives in mind,[9] with the TEU itself largely approximating in the end a 'compromised structure':

- to 'integrate' the various external policies of the Union by weakening con-siderably, if not totally eliminating, the previously existing legal and *de facto* dichotomy between Community affairs (trade and aid policies) and EPC affairs (foreign policy);
- to facilitate the above by giving more powers to the Commission in what remains, even with Maastricht, mainly an intergovernmental pillar;
- to facilitate the emergence of common EU actions in foreign and security policy, by limiting the use of unanimity and of the national veto in the deci-sion-making process;
- to move towards overcoming at long last the distinction between, on the one hand, the economic and political aspects of European security, and on the other, its military component (defence).

With regard to the dichotomy between Community and EPC affairs, some progress can be found in the 'temple structure' of the TEU, although the dichotomy persists between its supranational (EC) and intergovernmental (CFSP and JHA) pillars. As for the Commission's role in the CFSP, some progress was made by the incorporation for the first time of a Commission right of co-initiative in second-pillar issues, although no exclusive competence was envisaged as is the case in the first pillar. The TEU deals with the third problem, by distinguishing between principles and Common Positions (Art. J2) on the one hand, and Joint Actions (Art. J3) on the other.[10] In the former case, decisions will still be taken by unanimity, but, once such decisions have been reached, their implementation would, if all states agree, come under QMV. Also, Maas-tricht adds a security–defence dimension to the Union, by allowing military issues to be discussed for the first time, albeit within the second pillar and its newly declared 'defence arm', namely the WEU. As for the Amsterdam CFSP revisions, there were rather limited overall, as the most important ones have been postponed. There is little change, as the Commission remains a junior partner. The so-called 'Mr CFSP' has now been named, and will be the Secretary General of the Council. To what extent this will help the identification of a visible and clear centre for the CFSP remains unclear, as this development affects the future structure of the Council Presidency, henceforth to consist of the current and next Presidencies, plus the Commission (new troika), with the assistance of 'Mr CFSP'. Early signs since Solana was appointed to the post in November 1999 pointed to increased tension with Patten, the (new) Commissioner for External Relations. Since then, there have been many efforts by all parties involved to try and play down this clash of prerogatives.

Some modifications have also been made regarding CFSP decision-making:

- 'Common Strategies' (a new concept) are to be defined by the European Council.
- Decisions are to be implemented by the Foreign Ministers' Council using QMV if needed (for both Common Positions and Joint Actions which have already been adopted). An 'emergency brake' is provided, allowing any member to oppose the adoption of a decision for important and stated reasons of national policy. In such cases, those members that wish the Union to act could, if they represented a QMV, refer the matter to the European Council for a decision by unanimity.
- 'Constructive abstention' is permitted and institutionalised. This could reduce the risk of deadlock.
- A policy planning and early warning unit led by the High Representative for the CFSP (with personnel drawn from the Council's General Secretariat, the member states, the Commission, and the WEU) is to be established in order to provide policy assessments and more focused input into policy formulation. The tasks of the unit include: monitoring and analysing developments in areas relevant to the CFSP; providing assessments of the Union's foreign and security policy interests and identifying areas on which the CFSP could focus in the future; providing timely assessments and early warning of events or situations which may have significant repercussions for the Union's foreign and security policy, including potential political crises; and producing at the request of either the Council or the Presidency, or its own initiative, argued policy options papers to be presented under the responsibility of the Presidency as a contribution to policy formulation.

There is, however, no real progress on the CFSP budget, which has dogged relations with the EP over recent years.[11] Some observers have argued that, as no 'contamination' has occurred, in the sense of an intergovernmentalisation of existing communitarian practices, this is a success for integration.[12] Such an approach fails to take into account that the *acquis politique*, as is the case with the *acquis communautaire*, is rarely reversed.

In terms of defence matters, the Petersberg tasks of the WEU have been inserted in the AMT and the word 'progressive' has replaced that of 'eventual' in the framing of a common defence policy and common defence. Where there is, however, great progress is after the December 1998 Franco-British Saint-Malo Declaration, which basically lays the foundations for a defence and military dimension within the Union. In practice, it puts an end to the WEU versus NATO debate on European defence, as the debate now is between the Union and NATO. It is important to analyse how the Union managed to move thus far. A number of WEU 'rebirths' in the early 1980s (over the 'euromissiles' and the 'space war' debates), and again in the early 1990s with Maastricht, but also over the 1991 Gulf War and in the mid-1990s in the Adriatic Sea over a naval embargo in the Balkans, had led many to believe that the future looked bright for this organisation. But the WEU became obsolete in November 2000 when it disbanded itself. After Saint-Malo, the Union had made major strides towards a ESDP. The WEU could no longer serve its main purpose as the Union itself had now become an alternative – in the long run – to NATO and national defence policies. However, a number of WEU arrangements remained in force, such as its Art. 5 provision, a shadow secretariat, and its Parliamentary Assembly (which has taken the name of an interim assembly). Other institutions or agencies have become, since 1 January 2002, EU agencies (the satellite centre in Torrejon, or the Institute for Security Studies in Paris). The EU has also created three new bodies to coordinate and develop the ESDP:

- a Political and Security Committee known as COPS (after its French acronym) which consists of senior officials from the fifteen member states based in their respective Permanent Representations. It deals with all aspects of the CFSP including the ESDP;
- a Military Committee which consists of the national Chiefs of Staff or their representatives;
- a Military Staff which provides military expertise and support to the ESDP.

These new structures came into action in an interim force in March 2000 and were confirmed as permanent organs after the December 2000 Nice European Council meeting. In addition, following the June 2000 Santa Maria de Feira European Council meeting and the November 2000 Capabilities Commitment Conference in Brussels, the foundation of the ERRF have been laid as follows:

Germany: 13,500 troops; 20 ships; 93 planes
Britain: 12,500 troops; 18 ships; 72 planes
France: 12,000 troops; 15 ships; 75 planes; Helios spy-planes
Spain: 6,000 troops; one ship unit including aircraft carrier; 40 planes
Italy: 6,000 troops
The Netherlands: 5,000 troops
Greece: 3,500 troops
Austria: 2,000 troops

Finland: 2,000 troops
Belgium: 1,000 (to 3,000 troops); 9 ships; 25 planes
Sweden: 1,500 troops
Portugal: 1,000 troops
Ireland: 1,000 troops
Luxembourg: 100 troops
Denmark: no contribution owing to the Amsterdam opt-out.

There are many problems one must mention at this stage: the national defence budgets have been falling dramatically in the past few years and it is only since the 11 September 2001 events that there has been some reversal of this trend, especially in the bigger countries. Several weaknesses have been identified with regards to lift capacities and satellite guidance systems. It is, therefore, unclear what impact the ERRF will have in the future. Moreover, the participation of non-EU NATO members has created friction (especially with Turkey) and the key issue will remain what relationship the ERRF will have with NATO (see also below). It is unclear if recent developments will lead to an 'autonomous' EU defence entity as the 'Europeanists' want (France, Belgium, Italy), or will instead reinforce NATO as the 'Atlanticists' (Britain, the Netherlands, Portugal) would prefer. But what is clear is that there are military officers working for the Union in Brussels now, and not only for NATO.

As for any 'lessons' for theory, one should stress the fact that European integration is a multifaceted, multiform process, which marries intergovernmental and federal arguments and processes. This is all the more so in the field of 'high politics'. A more 'sophisticated' approach, that of confederal consociation, might be more relevant here, not least because it is better equipped to offer a better explanation of why so much and no more integration has occurred in Western Europe in general, and in EPC/CFSP matters in particular. It also offers prescriptive views on the future development of an effective decision-making system in EU foreign policy.

Confederal consociation and European foreign policy

The approach in question, as argued in Chapter 2, has been developed since the early 1990s as an alternative to the rather sterile debate between intergovernmentalism and federalism (and all the variations in between). It has the double advantage of describing the process of integration in the past and of suggesting its limits in the future. As Church has summarised the confederal consociation thesis:

> Through the segmentation of the European populations, governance is left in the hands of a cartel of state elites in the Council of Ministers, with states securing their interests via proportionality and mutual veto in bargaining . . . Chryssochoou has built on this idea of Taylor (1993) to suggest that the fact that the EU is a Confederal Consociation is a direct cause of its lack of democracy.[13]

In our view, confederal consociation offers a better explanation of the 'hybridity' of the Union, in that its 'political constitution' comprises federal, confederal and consociational principles and procedures (see Chapter 2), while bringing in the additional question of democracy and foreign policy. The most important dimension of this approach for the decision-making process in the CFSP is to argue that the continued existence of the national veto and, hence, the need for consensus, reinforces not only the democratic element in the CFSP/ESDP (by respecting the wishes of the component national demoi as expressed through their elected representatives) but is also the best guarantee for the emergence of a truly common European foreign, security and, eventually, defence policy.[14] Such a normative statement differs starkly from the traditional federal view on foreign policy: instead of perceiving QMV as a panacea, confederal consociation takes it as a side-show that can be useful only in lesser issues such as the practical implementation of policies agreed on the basis of unanimity or consensus. The distinction between 'unanimity' and 'consensus' is important because it shows that the use of the national veto can only be a weapon of last resort. Within reasonable limits, the emergence of a true European identity should and must include all views and not exclude any particular position, especially on matters of vital national interest (which is by definition changing as it is largely decided by the government of the day). This will be especially relevant after the next enlargements.

Democracy and accountability in foreign and security policies are not seen as mutually exclusive but rather as prerequisites for the emergence of a European identity in the world. But all this is in the future and will take time. For the time being, the veto will remain for important matters of national sovereignty. EU institutions such as the Commission and the EP will try to accelerate the process towards a European demos, but there is no guarantee of success nor a clear timetable. What it means in terms of practical arrangements in CFSP decision-making is that there will be some advances on federalist means such as QMV in the implementation of Common Positions and Joint Actions, together with vetoes where necessary. 'Constructive abstention' is further evidence of progress in that direction, but the mere fact that abstention by one-third of EU members is acknowledged as a restriction on its use reflects the continued importance of intergovernmental practices. These restrictions fit quite well in the confederal consociation model, and could not therefore be described as evidence of obstinate and obsolete nationalism. It is hoped that the COPS and CFSP planning cells will also be used as the 'oil' necessary for the wheels to work more efficiently, but without undermining the importance of consensus.

In both theoretical and practical terms, there will be more of this multifaceted form of integration which, with or without the new fashionable name of 'flexibility', will produce progress in some areas and problems in others. In the latter category one could mention the eventual merging/absorbing of the WEU into the Union, especially now that 'old' neutrals and neutralists (Ireland and Denmark) have found new allies in the 1995 members (Sweden, Finland and Austria) and are bound to find even more diverging immediate security interests in the next newcomers as defined by the December 2001 Laeken European

Council meeting (all twelve states currently engaged in accession negotiations, except Bulgaria and Romania which have not been listed as joining by 2004, mainly on economic grounds).

To a large extent, the initial debate of 'small versus big states' has now been re-ignited. But as the international context (both world-wide and in Europe) has been dramatically and fundamentally altered, solutions that have been excluded in the past might now become more acceptable such as a European UN Security Council (*de facto* or *de jure*, with or without Russia, with or without the OSCE's blessing) and the Contact Group (which includes France, the UK, Germany and Russia) since the Bosnian phase of the Yugoslav crisis. Thus, good examples of the possible future 'turf wars' already occurred in the immediate aftermath of the 11 September events (see also Chapter 5), first on 19 October 2001 when a tripartite meeting between the French (Chirac/Jospin), the British (Blair) and the Germans (Schröder) took place just prior to the Ghent European Council meeting, and second on 5 November in London when another such meeting (in the form of an informal dinner this time) was 'gate-crashed' as a commentator put it, 'by Berlusconi, Aznar, Solana, Verhofstadt and Kok'. All these issues will be considered first during the European Convention (March 2002–March 2003) and second by the 2004 IGC, which had been announced in Nice in December 2000 to soothe German criticisms and which was confirmed by Laeken a year later. But let us now expand on the OSCE and NATO, whose development has impacted heavily on the construction of the institutional map of the European security and defence area. Discussion of the OSCE is brief and reflects its relatively limited role.

The Conference/Organisation on Security and Co-operation in Europe (C/OSCE)

The evolution of the C/OSCE did not progress as a kind of 'grand design' and was not implemented according to plans for a new security architecture. The transformation of the Helsinki Process was a response to acute needs and requirements, representing a continuous process of institutionalisation and adapting through manageable forms of creative development to the new political and security environment. It is the one forum that brings together all of Europe with the US and Canada, and its potential role is to provide a pan-European security framework. Recognised as a regional organisation under UN Chapter VIII, the Conference on Security and Co-operation in Europe (CSCE) function during the Cold War was ostensibly to bridge the European divide. Although in practice it mirrored the divide instead of overcoming it, the CSCE process did make important contributions to European security-building. The CSCE came into being in 1975, with thirty-five states signing the Helsinki Final Act, which comprised four sections or 'baskets'. The first section concerned security issues; the second, co-operation in economics; the third, humanitarian co-operation; and the final section included follow-up mechanisms. Although not formally institutionalised, it established a process of diplomatic engagements, conferences and reviews – the objective of the dialogue being to implement the Final Act.[15] The proceedings of the second 'follow-up' Conference that began in Madrid in 1980 were critically affected by the Soviet invasion of Afghanistan and the imposition of martial law in Poland in 1981. The Madrid sessions ended in 1983 with an agreement to convene specific working groups, including one in Stockholm on CSBMs and Disarmament in Europe, known as the Conference on Disarmament in Europe, and another in Ottawa on human rights. The latter failed to reach agreement, but Stockholm committed members to accepting specified notification, observation and verification procedures for military manoeuvres.[16] The third 'follow-up' meeting in Vienna lasted from November 1986 to January 1989. The Vienna talks secured agreement that NATO and the Warsaw Pact countries would commence Conventional Stability Talks (that led to the CFE) within the CSCE framework. The CSCE agreed to take further the Stockholm Document on CSBMs, human rights (the Human Dimension) and procedures for the peaceful settlement of disputes. Negotiations proceeded against the background of a changing European order that was in turn to change the CSCE.[17]

The CSCE Summit in Paris in November 1990 adopted the Charter of Paris for a New Europe. The Charter began the institutionalisation of the CSCE and established five bodies. The CSCE Council was founded, consisting of foreign ministers meeting (at least once) annually, supported by the Committee of Senior Officials (CSO). A CSCE Secretariat was established in Prague, an Office for Free Elections in Warsaw and a Conflict Prevention Centre in Vienna. The Charter also called for CSCE summits of heads of state and government every two years. The Charter, together with the conclusion of the CFE Treaty, marked a new stage in European security. The CSCE was developed further in meetings in Valletta, Moscow and Prague before the fourth 'follow-up' meeting in Helsinki in July 1992. At Valletta in February 1991 a 'mechanism' was adopted to settle disputes when the parties concerned were unable to resolve them by negotiation. The mechanism is obligatory, in that it can be requested by a party to a dispute, but its recommendations are not binding and even the initiating phase can be overridden. The 1991 Moscow meeting completed the work of the Conference on the Human Dimension, which commenced in Paris in 1989 and was taken forward at Copenhagen in 1990. The Copenhagen Conference concluded with a declaration guaranteeing the rights of citizens, committing governments to 'pluralistic democracy', the rule of law and the protection of national minorities. Minorities were to have the right to use their own language, observe their own religion and follow an appropriate education. The Moscow Conference went further and agreed that fact-finding teams could be sent to investigate alleged human rights abuses, whether or not the state in question agreed. The Prague Council in 1992 further developed CSCE institutions and procedures. The Warsaw Office for Free Elections was renamed the Office for

Democratic Institutions and Human Rights (ODIHR) and was assigned the task of overseeing the Human Dimension. The Prague Council confirmed the Moscow concept of 'consensus minus one'. Prague looked to enhance human rights, democracy and law, and decided that the CSCE could take political and peaceful action without the consent of the state concerned.[18]

The 1992 Helsinki Summit further institutionalised the CSCE, confirming the Prague decisions and widening the role of the CSO. Within the latter, an Economic Forum was created to review commitments under Basket II and with regard to market details. The ODIHR was also enhanced to monitor the Human Dimension and support the newly created High Commissioner on National Minorities (HCNM), which was seen as an institution to act at the earliest possible stage to resolve tensions involving national minority issues that had not developed into conflicts. The Helsinki Summit further created another institution, the Forum for Security Co-operation based in Vienna. It was entrusted with the negotiation of conventional disarmament measures; the promotion of CSBMs; and reducing the risk of conflict. The final innovation of the Summit was its adoption of peacekeeping, defined in accord with the classical UN understanding: a non-enforcement role, strict impartiality, and requiring the consent of all parties involved. CSCE peacekeeping operations would not proceed without an effective cease-fire in place and guarantees for the safety of personnel. Resources and expertise were to be drawn from NATO, the EC, WEU or the Commonwealth of Independent States (CIS). A more direct linkage to NATO was opposed by France, and the CSCE was to turn to NATO on a case-by-case basis. The Helsinki Document marked the transition of the CSCE from a forum for dialogue to an operational structure. Since 1995, the new OSCE has defined its role in the European security architecture by concentrating on conflict prevention in a broad sense: not only the immediate prevention of violent conflict but also long-term peace-building. Early warning, conflict prevention and crisis management have been identified as the institution's main activities.[19] Its involvement in conflict prevention was closely linked to the Human Dimension and the protection of minority rights. The HCNM has been involved in a number of cases, including the plight of ethnic Russians in Latvia and Estonia; the Hungarian minority in Slovakia; the Slovak minority in Hungary; the Hungarian minority in Romania; the Albanian minority in the former Yugoslav Republic of Macedonia; the Greek minority in Albania; and Ukraine–Crimean relations. Fact-finding missions were dispatched and augmented with CSCE 'good offices' on the ground, which sought, *inter alia*, to facilitate settlements in Moldova and Nagorno Karabakh.

At their Istanbul summit in November 1999, the leaders of the fifty-four OSCE member states signed the Charter for European Security. The Charter originated in the debate on developing a 'Common and Comprehensive Security Model for Europe for the 21st Century' – launched in March 1995, largely to calm Russian concerns about NATO's eastward enlargement. The OSCE Charter for European Security may not be revolutionary in nature but it should not be regarded as a mere empty shell either. It reviews the new risks and challenges to

European security in the post-Cold war strategic environment, reaffirms some basic general principles and provides for the strengthening of the OSCE's operational capacities in conflict prevention, crisis management and post-conflict rehabilitation. Finally, in the appended Platform for Co-operative Security, the Chapter proposes a set of arrangements for closer ties and co-operation between the OSCE and other international institutions, which, together with the operational guidelines for a more effective OSCE, are directly relevant to NATO's new role in Europe.[20] The Charter also considers the operational capacities of the OSCE from four different angles: field operations, peacekeeping operations, police operations and the Rapid Expert Assistance and Co-operation Teams (REACT) concept. The latter is of importance. Originally forged by the US, the REACT concept commits governments to develop at both national and OSCE levels the capacity to set up teams with a wide range of civilian expertise that the OSCE would be able to deploy in conflict prevention, crisis management and post-conflict rehabilitation. The general assessment to be made here is that we are witnessing an expansion of the operational role and capabilities of the OSCE.

There is no doubt that the OSCE did not, and does not, represent the often-called-for 'grand design' for the European security architecture; nor is it, or will it be in the foreseeable future, the central pillar of the European institutional structure. Perhaps its most important contribution in the new European security environment is the political legitimacy it can bestow on instruments or policies of its own, or of institutions like NATO.[21] By virtue of its membership and decision-making procedures, it can legitimise intervention aimed at ordering the European region. It has also been important in establishing a comprehensive approach to security, which includes human rights, economic and military dimensions at the point when European security has become more complex and multifaceted. Also, the OSCE can be conducive to the management of interregional and transregional relations by providing links to the emerging macro-regions of the world, and thus helping to shape an open regionalism, which may be of utmost importance for the future stability of the international system. However, the OSCE is a long way from becoming a security framework within which other organisations perform subfunctions delegated from above. Its weaknesses are its decision-making procedure and the mobilisation of consensus as well as the absence of an enforcement capability. In the field of the normative consensus, the OSCE has to be regarded, to a very large extent, as a forum of symbolic politics. Indeed, one can rightfully argue that the OSCE is basically not so much a community of values, but a quasi-legal community based on the principles of recognition of the given *status quo* and the commitment to peaceful change.[22]

NATO's rationale in the new European security environment

The evolution of NATO throughout the 1990s is a remarkable tale of survival and development in adverse conditions.[23] This section considers the institutional and strategic response of the Alliance to the geopolitical and security challenges of system change. Both NATO's origins and Cold War history are well known. What catalysed NATO was a strong desire to link Europe and the US (and Canada) in response to the Soviet threat. NATO mollified European concerns about a German threat; contributed to a greater sense of West European unity and security; and provided a mechanism for the US to participate in European economic and military reconstruction.

Following the accession of the Federal Republic of Germany to NATO, the pattern of West European security and co-operation was clarified. With the exception of the crisis surrounding French membership in 1966, the basic ratio-nale of the Alliance was set. The 1967 Harmel Report recommended that NATO co-ordinate a multilateral approach to bridging gaps between East and West, commit the major powers to full consultation with NATO allies on German reunification, overcome the division of Germany and foster European security, and co-ordinate and consult on arms control and mutual and balanced force reductions between East and West. The Report found that the Alliance had two main functions: 'Its first function is to maintain adequate military strength and political solidarity to deter aggression and other forms of pressure and to defend the territory of member countries from aggression should it occur.' The second function is 'to pursue the search for progress towards a more stable relationship in which the underlying political issues can be solved.'[24] In May 1989, the Alliance's Comprehensive Concept confirmed the continuing validity of the Harmel Report's objectives.

From 1954 the Alliance looked to nuclear deterrence as the basis of its defence to offset conventional inferiority in Europe. The Soviet acquisition of nuclear forces introduced problems concerning the credibility of American extended deterrence that were to plague NATO throughout the Cold War. By the late 1950s, the ultimate deterrent – i.e., the principle of Mutual Assured Destruction (MAD), which threatened massive retaliation by US nuclear forces in the event of a Soviet attack – was undermined by a fundamental challenge to collective defence. Would the US risk its own security now that the Soviet Union could threaten American soil? With nuclear parity emerging between the two superpowers, the concept of MAD actually increased the potential for a lower-level conventional attack in Europe, were the Soviet Union to test the US resolve to defend Western Europe. Indeed, the turbulent strategic environment tested the credibility of NATO's collective defence function and contributed to France's withdrawal from the integrated military command in 1966. Nevertheless, in the years that followed, the basic rationale of collective defence prevailed in the Atlantic Pact.[25]

The impact of *détente* did not change NATO's original rationale, not least because the emergence of strategic parity between the superpowers did not alter the European order. NATO did commit itself to the pursuit of European *détente*, albeit in addition to its military defence role. Ironically NATO strategy was crit-icised more as East–West relations deteriorated in the late 1970s. Public protest, parliamentary attention and the rebirth of the peace movement followed the (abortive) neutron bomb decision and the 1979 decision to deploy Cruise and Pershing II missiles. NATO came under a new public scrutiny in Western Europe. The Alliance had to defend its role and convince public opinion of its rationale. As European doubts and criticisms mounted, Congressional concerns regarding burden sharing were underlined. The INF Treaty of 1987 resolved the immediate issues in dispute but not the wider problems of the European balance of power.[26] The North Atlantic Council (NAC) continued to place its belief in the central importance of nuclear weapons. In its Brussels Declaration of 1988, NAC saw no alternative to a strategy of 'deterrence based upon an appropriate mix of adequate and effective nuclear and conventional forces'.[27] To that end, NAC further reasserted the importance of the American commitment to Europe. The Declaration asserted that 'the presence in Europe of the conventional and nuclear forces of the United States provides the essential linkage with the United States strategic deterrent . . . this presence must and will be maintained'. The Council identified the major imbalance of conventional forces in Europe as its central security concern. The Soviet Union and its allies enjoyed a clear advantage in numbers of key offensive systems, including main battle tanks, artillery and armoured troop carriers. NATO welcomed the signs of change in the policies of the Soviet Union following Gorbachev's leadership but 'witnessed no relaxation of the military effort pursued for years by the Soviet Union'. Indeed, in 1989, while NAC recognised the dramatic political changes in Eastern and Central Europe, it continued to stress its strategy of deterrence. Throughout the postwar years, as NATO's membership, organisational structure and list of responsibilities grew, two essential facts remained constant: NATO focused on the Soviet threat, and it performed both military and non-military functions for its members. Athough the degree of threat varied over time, for the Alliance the threat always was present.

The end of the Cold War and pace of change in the European order was, however, spectacular and it fundamentally challenged NATO's rationale and *raison d'être*. The Alliance responded by attempting to adapt to the new security environment, stressing its political role and reorienting its approach to issues of military doctrine, sufficiency and readiness. The process of change in the Alliance began in 1990. It was a process that would eventually result in significant reductions in funding and force levels for NATO's conventional and nuclear forces. Joint weapons programmes, annual military exercises, readiness, nuclear alert status and training have all been sharply reduced. In May 1990, NATO's Military Committee announced that it no longer considered the Warsaw Pact a threat to the alliance, which instead looked to 'seize the historic opportunities resulting from the profound changes in Europe to help build a new peaceful order in Europe'. The member states declared NATO as one of the principal architects of change in the new Europe and identified the need for adaptation. To that end, intra-Alliance co-operation, political consultation and co-ordination were underlined. The conclusion was that 'although the prevention of war will always remain (NATO's) fundamental task, the changing European environment now requires . . . a broader approach to security based as much on constructive peace building as on peace-keeping'.[28]

The London Declaration of the NATO Heads of State and Government in July 1990 confirmed that the Alliance 'must and will adapt'.[29] The Declaration stressed the continued institutional task of collective defence, acknowledging, however, that challenges to that mission had been radically transformed: 'security and stability do not lie solely in the military dimension, and we intend to enhance the political component of our Alliance'. Member states sought a new relationship with their former adversaries in Eastern Europe, thus inviting the Warsaw Pact powers to establish regular diplomatic liaison with NATO. The Declaration also envisaged changes in NATO's force structure as the CFE Treaty was implemented and Soviet troops left Eastern Europe. Strategy would change with the creation of true multinational units, moving away from the geographically based area defences of the past.[30]

A new Allied military strategy was to be prepared, which would move away from forward defence and modify 'flexible response' to reflect a reduced reliance on nuclear weapons. In June 1991, NATO began to define its 'Partnership with the Countries of Central and Eastern Europe'. NATO declared that it did 'not wish to isolate any country, nor to see a new division of the Continent', but to seek 'an architecture for the new Europe that is firmly based on the principles and promises of the Helsinki Final Act and the Charter of Paris'. The Alliance supported the adoption of democratic reforms and market economies in Central and Eastern Europe. It further identified a set of initiatives to develop its security partnership with its former enemies, including exchange of information and ideas on security policy; military doctrine and arms control; contact between senior military authorities and widening participation in Alliance activities, including scientific and environmental programmes.[31] NATO also began to recognise the emergence of a new European security architecture. NAC accepted that security in the new Europe had various dimensions – economic, political, ecological and defence – and found that the 'Alliance, the EC, the WEU, the CSCE and the Council of Europe are key institutions in this endeavour'. The Council believed that a transformed Alliance was an essential element in the new architecture, for an 'important basis for this transformation is the agreement of all Allies to enhance the role and responsibility of the European members'. The Council welcomed 'efforts further to strengthen the security dimension in the process of European integration and recognise the significance of the progress made by countries of the European Community towards the goal of political union, including the development of a common foreign and security policy'.[32] At the same time, it looked to the development of a European security identity to strengthen the European pillar within the Alliance. For the Council, such a process would 'underline the preparedness of the Europeans to take a greater share of responsibility for their security and will help to reinforce transatlantic solidarity'. While the Council accepted that institutions such as the

EC, WEU and CSCE have 'roles to play in accordance with their respective responsibilities and purposes', the 'extent of its membership and of its capabilities gives NATO a particular position'. Thus, the Alliance asserted its 'particular' role, by identifying four core security functions it would perform in the new Europe:[33]

- to provide one of the indispensable foundations for a stable security environment in Europe, based on the growth of democratic institutions and commitment to the peaceful resolution of disputes, in which no country would be able to intimidate or coerce any European nation or to impose hegemony through the threat or use of force;
- to serve, as provided for in Art. 4 of the North Atlantic Treaty, as a transatlantic forum for Allied consultations on any issues that affect their vital interests, including possible developments posing risks for members' security, and for appropriate co-ordination of their efforts in fields of common concern;
- to deter and defend against any threat of aggression against the territory of any NATO member state;
- to preserve the strategic balance within Europe.

Although the above represents classic *communiqué* language with nothing but platitudes, it meant that NATO was now seeking to anchor its position in the new European order and establish the complementary nature of other security institutions. In the words of Wörner, 'our future European architecture will rest on a system of different organisations, sometimes overlapping, but interlocking and, albeit with a different focus, complementary'. Accordingly, the challenge for NATO was to secure this relationship when, as Wörner recognised, 'all European institutions – the European Community, CSCE, Council of Europe and Western European Union – are equally in a phase of renewal and redefinition'.[34] Decisions taken (especially) in the second half of the 1990s advanced further the pace of change in the European security landscape. In June 1996, NATO's foreign ministers decided to adopt a European Security and Defence Identity (ESDI) 'within the Alliance' and to develop the Combined Joint Task Force (CJTF) concept. In May 1997, NATO and Russia agreed to establish a Joint Permanent Council. In June 1997, the EU completed the IGC and concluded the AMT. In July 1997 in Madrid, NATO agreed on the admission of three new members, and in April 1999, the Alliance adopted its Strategic Concept, while engaging in military action (Kosovo) for the first time in its fifty-year history. Almost at the same time, EU member states embarked upon their most serious attempt to 'Europeanise' security and defence, with a process starting at Saint-Malo and culminating in the decisions at the Nice Summit in December 2000.

The new strategic concept

Against this background, NATO's new Strategic Concept announced in Rome in November 1991 marked another turning point, as did the adoption of its first new military policy document in almost twenty years, the MC400 document. It was a major step towards the redefinition of the Alliance's role in the new Europe. The Council accepted that the end of the East–West confrontation had greatly reduced the risk of major conflict and that the notion of a 'predominant threat' had given way to 'risks'. The Strategic Concept found that risks to Allied security were less likely to result from calculated aggression against the territory of NATO members than from 'the adverse consequences of instabilities that may arise from the serious economic, social and political difficulties including ethnic rivalries and territorial disputes, which are faced by many countries in central and eastern Europe'. The Concept reaffirmed the four core functions of the Alliance declared in June 1991 and went further in a new broad approach to security. Security was seen to have political, economic, social, environmental, and defence dimensions. Allied security was now to adopt three mutually reinforcing elements: dialogue, co-operation and the maintenance of a collective defence capability.

In that context, the Concept stressed the new political approach and understanding of security in Europe. The Alliance recognised that the prevention of war in the post-Cold War European setting 'depends even more than in the past on the effectiveness of preventive diplomacy and the successful management of crises'. Under the new strategic circumstances, the Alliance planned to resolve crises at an early stage. It was recognised that this required a coherent strategy, which would co-ordinate a variety of conflict management measures. At the same time, it was anticipated that such a strategy would in turn require close control from the Alliance's political authorities. In June 1992, NATO announced it was willing to support, on a case-by-case basis, peacekeeping under the auspices of the CSCE, while in December 1992, it pledged to support peacekeeping under UNSC authorisation.

The Strategic Concept finally underlined the importance of collective defence. The Alliance will maintain an adequate military capability and a clear preparedness to act collectively in the common defence. A commitment was made to retain a mixture of nuclear and conventional forces, though at a much reduced level than in the past. NATO forces are, however, to be adapted to their new strategic roles. The overall size and readiness of forces was to be reduced. The maintenance of a linear defence in the Central European region was to be ended. The Strategic Concept stressed flexibility, mobility and an assured capability for augmentation. NATO forces are to be capable of responding to a wide variety of challenges and are to consist of rapid reaction and main defence components. The key element was that NATO forces should be able to 'respond flexibly to a wide range of possible contingencies'. The new strategic environment was seen to facilitate a significant reduction in substrategic nuclear forces, which were seen, however, as an important link with strategic nuclear forces, in particular American ones, which serve as the 'supreme guarantee' of Allied security.

The adoption of the Strategic Concept marked NATO's transition to the new European security environment, by reaffirming its security role and implementing the new broad approach to strategy. In the immediate post-Cold War era, NATO retained its position as the primary forum for security in the new architecture. The revived WEU complemented NATO's institutional development in this period. As p. 00 shows, WEU served to bridge NATO–EU relations and to resolve for the foreseeable future the tension between a European defence and security identity based upon the EU/WEU and the transatlantic basis that NATO provides. A second feature of the new security architecture was the overlap of security in terms of its broader political interpretation. The broad approach to security adopted by NATO in its New Strategic Concept was reflected in the response of other institutions to the changing European order. Preventive diplomacy, crisis management and peacekeeping are themes shared by NATO, the WEU, the Union and the OSCE. The latter had some recognition as the overarching organisation but was, and still is, a considerable distance from being Europe's security institution *par excellence.* Aspects of the OSCE role can also be seen in the EU's promotion of a European Stability Pact and the work of the North Atlantic Co-operation Council (NACC). While the lack of institutional definition within the new architecture was understandable, co-ordination remained imperative, and so was the need for a coherent and cohesive management of responses to crises, by implementing the broader political aspects of strategy in the new Europe. That was a challenge not just for the Alliance itself, but for the role and relationship of the 'interlocking institutions'.

Consolidating adaptation

With a mandate from the Alliance's Heads of State and Government, and in accordance with the terms of reference endorsed by NATO Foreign and Defence Ministers in December 1997, NATO's Policy Co-ordination Group (PCG) started examining the 1991 Alliance Strategic Concept with a view to updating it 'as necessary'. This process ended on 23–24 April 1999, with the approval by the Washington Summit of the new and by now forward-looking Strategic Concept. The latter was clearly the result of the consolidation of the strategic environment of the 1990s, the decisions taken at both national and international levels and the challenges that NATO had to face, mainly in Southeastern Europe throughout the decade. This new Strategic Concept was to guide the Alliance as it pursued this agenda. With this document, NATO stressed its role in consolidating and preserving the changes of the 1990s, and in meeting current and future security challenges. It clearly indicated a demanding agenda, in which NATO had to 'safeguard common security interests in an environment of further, often unpredictable change. It must maintain collective defence and reinforce the transatlantic link and ensure a balance that allows the European Allies to assume greater responsibility. It must deepen its relations with its partners and prepare for the accession of new members. It must, above all, maintain the political will and the military means required by the entire range of its missions.'[35]

In terms of threat perception, para. 24 represents an expansive list, which is directly linked with the new evolving security paradigm, by taking account of the post-Cold War global context, and by emphasising that Alliance security interests can be affected by other risks of a wider nature, including uncontrolled population mass movement, international terrorism, sabotage, international organised crime and the disruption of the flow of vital resources. Moreover, para. 20 indicates that NATO security remains subject to a wide variety of both military as well as non-military risks, which are multidirectional in nature and often difficult to predict. Such risks include uncertainty and instability in an around the Euro-Atlantic area, and the possibility of regional crises at its periphery, which could, para. 20 stresses, evolve rapidly. In short, both the definition of the risks and their geographic scope have been considerably expanded, while there is a growing recognition that most challenges are not likely to involve a direct military threat to NATO territory. Rather, they will involve non-Art. 5 'crisis response' operations.[36] The new Strategic Concept reflected this changed balance between collective defence and crisis response. NATO forces must be able to carry out a full range of missions as well as to contribute to conflict prevention and non-Art. 5 contigencies (para. 41). Thus, it laid the conceptual groundwork for the restructuring of NATO forces with the view to enhancing their power-projection capabilities. Particular emphasis was placed on deployability, mobility, and survivability of forces, together with their ability to operate 'out of area' (paras 53b and 53d). Improvements in these areas have been the main focus of the Defence Capabilities Initiative (DCI), also approved at the Washington Summit, which aims, in addition to enhancing the Alliance's power-projection capability, to increase interoperability.[37]

Another key issue that attracted attention before the Washington Summit was 'the mandate question' – i.e., whether NATO can take military action in non-self-defence situations, without the authorisation of the UN Security Council, as it did over Kosovo. The issue of the appropriate mandate did not arise until October 1998, when NATO threatened to use air power in Kosovo. In Bosnia, NATO entered by invitation. An Art. 5 mission would be covered by Art. 51 of the UN Charter, which provides:

> Nothing in the present Charter shall impair the inherent right of individual or collective self-defence if an armed attack occurs against a Member of the United Nations, until the Security Council has taken measures necessary to maintain international peace and security. Measures taken by Members in the exercise of these rights of self-defence shall be immediately reported to the Security Council and shall not in any way affect the authority and responsibility of the Security Council under the present Charter to take at any time such action as it deems necessary in order to maintain or restore international peace and security.

The European views, strongly supported by Russia, were that non-Art. 5 missions must always be authorised by the UN Security Council. The US and the British rejected this view, basing their argument on the evolving principles of humanitarian law and the danger of large-scale humanitarian catastrophe in the case of Kosovo,[38] and more generally on the legal principles in the UN

Charter regarding the maintenance of international peace and security.[39] The practical issue in the minds of US policy-makers has been the risk that a non-Art. 5 action could be vetoed in the UNSC by Russia or China. The view in Washington is that NATO members cannot allow their chosen course of action in a peace-support crisis to be blocked by a non-member. Many of the allies nevertheless do believe that it is necessary for future non-Art. 5 crisis management and peace-support operations to be based on a sound international legal framework.

The solution found at the Washington Summit was more indirect than expected,[40] and confirmed the trend – a result of the Kosovo war – towards seeing certain humanitarian and legal norms inescapably bound up with conceptions of national interest.[41] The Concept very briefly stressed that the UNSC 'has the primary responsibility for the maintenance of international peace and security and, as such, plays a crucial role in contributing to security and stability in the Euro-Atlantic area' (para. 15). The absence of a direct reference to a mandate has been interpreted as a rejection of legally generated or self-imposed political limits. The criteria, thus, are whether there is a 'threat' – though defined very widely – to the Euro-Atlantic area. For many, it was highly problematic that there was no attempt towards formulating more general rules in a possible emerging legality of humanitarian intervention, thus sending a signal to China and Russia that NATO has not given itself the right to attack sovereign nations at whim, even when there is strong moral justification.[42] Apart from the norms and thresholds of intervention, all the above, as well as several other issues addressed in the new Strategic Concept, clearly reveal the dominant trend in NATO: from defence of territory to defence of interests and values. In this context, the issue of roles and distribution of responsibilities within the Alliance acquired greater salience, especially after the renewed effort on the part of the Union to proceed to a more defence- and security-oriented institutional structure.

WEU and ESDI

NATO's evolving role in security management has not only emerged from the necessity of utilising its integrated military command structure, but also as a result of the policy adjustment of its members to the new security paradigm. Since 1991, the Alliance has been adjusting its force structures to acquire higher levels of flexibility and mobility with multinational formations. The product of this process has been the development of ESDI within the Alliance. The aim was to respond to the old/new debate on 'burden-sharing' and distribution of labour, by increasing the capabilities of the European Allies in crisis management operations, where the US may allow the use of NATO assets, but might not wish to be the leader.[43] The ESDI concept means a greater European capacity for autonomous military action, in part thanks to deeper political cohesion.[44] But the ESDI concept is not linked to a single institutional framework. Multiple organisations and efforts are involved, including bilateral initiatives (notably Franco-German and Franco-British co-operative frameworks) and trilateral endeavours (for instance, those involving French, Italian and Spanish forces in joint exercises and training). EU members engaged in a limited foreign and security policy co-operation from the early 1970s (with the EPC format), and by the late 1980s they were actively considering a more explicit engagement in defence matters, by utilising the WEU framework.[45] Actually, it was the French that launched the idea of an – autonomous from NATO – ESDI back in 1991, by attempting to establish an organic link between the Union and the WEU in the Maastricht Treaty.

The WEU, like NATO, did undergo a major transformation during the 1990s, until the decision by the Union to absorb it at the Cologne European Council in June 1999. During the Cold War, WEU military functions were largely eclipsed by NATO. The development of EPC in the early 1970s also overtook the WEU's political functions. The WEU lost a further role when Britain joined the Community and no longer needed a 'bridge' to the Six. It was not until the mid-1980s that the WEU was reborn, when France and West Germany looked to it to provide a forum for strategic discussion. The context was the launch of the Strategic Defence Initiative (SDI) and the Intermediate-range Nuclear Force (INF) crisis in Europe. France sought a 'Europeanisation' of security policy without the price of reintegration into the military command structure of NATO and Bonn aimed to increase public support for Europe's role in Western security policy.[46] Arguably, the major cause underlying these developments was Europe's need to have a more unified voice in defence matters in order to overcome the inertia of not being able to contribute to security and defence decisions reached in Washington.[47]

In October 1984 the foreign and defence ministers of the WEU convened an extraordinary session in Rome, underlying their determination to make better use of the WEU framework in order to increase co-operation between the member states in the field of security policy. The belief was that a 'better utilisation of the WEU would not only contribute to the security of Western Europe but also to an improvement in the common defence of all the countries of the Atlantic Alliance'.[48] Furthermore, the Rome Declaration led to institutional reform, with the WEU Council henceforth meeting twice a year and the work of the Permanent Council being intensified. Institutional change continued in 1985 with the WEU Bonn agreement to establish three new agencies to study arms control and disarmament, security and defence questions and co-operation in the field of armaments.[49] The potential role of the WEU in European integration was also identified in the 1987 Luxembourg and Hague Council meetings. In The Hague, the commitment 'to build a European Union in accordance with the Single European Act' was recalled, and it was declared that 'the construction of an integrated Europe will remain incomplete as long as it does not include security and defence'.[50] But the WEU remained committed to NATO, recognising that, under the (then) military balance in Europe, 'the security of the Western European countries can only be ensured in close association with our North American allies'. WEU members looked to a more integrated Europe to further their role in the Atlantic

Alliance and the European pillar, so that a more balanced partnership would emerge with the US.[51]

A further impetus to the development of the WEU was provided by crises in the Persian Gulf in the late 1980s and early 1990s. In 1987 and 1988 during the Iran–Iraq war, the WEU co-ordinated the member states' responses to the threat posed by mines in the Gulf. While co-operation in the naval clearance operation was not perfect, the WEU established a three-tier co-ordination framework comprising high-level consultation, involving political and military experts from foreign and defence ministries; meetings of officers serving as contact points within admiralties; and regular contacts between task force commanders on the spot.[52] A similar framework was established in 1990 to co-ordinate the WEU member states' implementation of UN Security Council resolutions. The WEU Ministerial Meeting on 21 August 1990 sought the most effective co-ordination in capitals and in the region, including areas of operation, sharing of tasks, logistical support and exchange of intelligence.[53] While NATO proved to be an important forum, its foreign ministers decided on 10 August 1990 not to proceed with military co-ordination under the integrated command structure. Each member of the Alliance was to contribute in its own way to the Gulf operation, although an attack on Turkey would invoke Art. 5. Thus the WEU had a clear field to provide 'out-of-area' co-ordination. Its role pertained largely to the naval embargo, and the US took effective command of fighting the land war.[54]

The Union, in contrast to the WEU, did not prove to be an effective body for the co-ordination of policy towards Iraq. Although it supported UN sanctions, froze Iraqi assets and suspended co-operation with Iraq, divergences in the Union emerged as the likelihood of military action increased. It was against this background and in the context of the emergent new European order that the role of the WEU in general, and particularly its relationship with the Union, emerged as important policy issues in the context of the IGC 1990/91. A number of different national positions regarding security policy were also presented at the IGC. More specifically, France and Germany envisaged a decisive move towards common defence and proposed the integration of the WEU into the Union. The US responded to the Franco-German initiative by insisting that all decisions to commit an ESDI to out-of-area activity involve consultation with Washington. Moreover, the US signalled its strong opposition to the prospect of a WEU integrated command structure duplicating that of NATO, as well as to any 'backdoor' security commitment to Central and Eastern Europe via WEU enlargement that implicitly extended the US commitment to NATO.[55]

In an attempt to reach a compromise, a joint British–Italian declaration proposed that the WEU should act as both the defence component of the Union and the European pillar of NATO. In contrast, the final Franco-German declaration envisaged the WEU as an integral part of the Union and identified a joint military force, which could form the basis of a Euro-Corps. The latter was a clear rebuttal of Anglo-Italian plans for a WEU force to act 'outside of area' and the

NATO Rapid Reaction Corps for Allied Command Europe under British command.[56] The final settlement left defence as a possible area of future development for the Union. Contrary to the desires of France and Germany, the WEU was not brought within the Union but was made an organisation that could be called upon by EU members to act on their behalf. The European Council was accorded ill-defined powers to 'request the Western European Union . . . to elaborate and implement discussions and actions of the Union which have defence implications' (Art. J4.2 TEU). Therefore, the WEU was not subordinated to the Union, but rather saw itself as 'the defence component of the European Union and as a means to strengthen the European pillar of the Atlantic Alliance'. At Maastricht, the nine-strong WEU (Spain and Portugal joined in 1990; Greece in 1992; Denmark and Ireland became observers in 1992; and Iceland, Norway and Turkey associate members) identified measures to develop closer relationships with both the Union and NATO. The WEU envisaged harmonisation of meetings and venues with the Union and close co-operation between the decision-making bodies and secretariats of both organisations. With reference to NATO, the WEU pledged to strengthen working links and the role, responsibilities and contributions of its member states within the Atlantic Alliance. This was to be undertaken 'on the basis of the necessary transparency and complementarily between the emerging European Security and Defence Identity and the Alliance'.[57] The WEU moreover committed itself to act in conformity with positions adopted by NATO, while it adopted a series of commitments to enhance its operational identity. A call was made for a planning cell, closer military co-operation, meetings of Chiefs of Staff and military units answerable to the WEU. The WEU Council and Secretariat were transferred from London to Brussels, and other EU members were invited to join.

The outcome of the Maastricht Treaty was an effective compromise giving the WEU a pivotal role in the new European security architecture. At the same time, it reflected the limit to which the British were prepared to go. Europe's newly instituted CFSP declared that the development of a defence policy was to be a clear objective of the Union, yet the wording of the Treaty was left deliberately vague and only stated, courtesy of Art. J4.1 TEU, that this 'might in time lead to a common defence'. The Maastricht outcome was thus an attempt to reconcile the contending perspectives of the major European powers. The WEU was declared to be both the defence arm of the Union and the European pillar of NATO, thus being left equidistant between the two organisations.[58] The WEU Petersberg Declaration in 1992 confirmed its dual role and the important NATO seal of approval was given by its Heads of State and Government in January 1994. The NATO Summit welcomed the Maastricht Treaty and the launch of the European Union. Full support was given to the development of a European Security and Defence Identity. The latter, according to NATO – in language complementary to the WEU's – will 'strengthen the European pillar of the Alliance while reinforcing the transatlantic link and will enable European Allies to take greater responsibility for their common security and defence'. But the

NATO declaration went further to proclaim that the 'Alliance and the European Union share common strategic interests', while it welcomed both co-operation and consultation with the WEU. Significantly, the Summit agreed to 'make [the] collective assets of the Alliance available, on the basis of consultations in the North Atlantic Council, for WEU operations undertaken by the European Allies in pursuit of their Common Foreign and Security Policy'. With American support, the Alliance envisaged the development of 'separable but not separate capabilities which could respond to European requirements and contribute to Alliance Security'.[59] As part of the process, the Summit endorsed the CJTF concept as a means of facilitating contingency operations.

The January 1994 Brussels Summit directly facilitated the development of the WEU's role. During the same year, the latter's preliminary conclusions on a ESDP reflected the new relationship between NATO and the WEU.[60] By then, a common perception had emerged that, both institutionally and substantively, the development of a common European defence policy had to be seen in the wider context of broader European and transatlantic relationships. The envisaged policy was further to lead to 'an increased European contribution to the objectives of collective defence and a new sharing of responsibilities, which should not only be compatible with NATO's defence policy but should also be a means of strengthening and renewing the transatlantic partnership'. Five levels of European interest and responsibility were identified in the field of defence, where it was agreed that WEU governments:

- have a direct responsibility for security and defence of their own peoples and territories;
- have a responsibility to project the security and stability presently enjoyed in the West throughout the whole of Europe;
- have a strong interest, in order to reinforce European security, in fostering stability in the southern Mediterranean countries;
- are ready to take on their share of the responsibility for the promotion of security, stability and the values of democracy in the wider world, including the execution of peacekeeping and other crisis management measures under the authority of the UN Security Council or the CSCE, acting either independently or through the WEU or NATO;
- are ready to address new security challenges such as humanitarian emergencies; proliferation; terrorism; international crime and environmental risks, including those related to disarmament and the destruction of nuclear and chemical weapons.[61]

The WEU Council of Ministers recognised the need for the WEU to strengthen its operational capabilities in order to fulfil its defence roles. Ministers identified several needs: access to more information on emerging and ongoing crises; a more systematic approach to identifying and meeting contingencies for European military deployments; and appropriate mechanisms for political decision-making, as well as military command and control. They also recorded

the need for 'appropriate information and consultation mechanisms and procedures and more support, in particular to enable prompt reactions to crises, *inter
alia* through a politico-military working group in Brussels which can be reinforced as necessary according to the specific nature of the contingency'. Finally,
the importance of a European armaments policy to the development of a
common defence policy was identified. In 1996, the WEU was to contribute to
the EU's review conference, but its Council of Ministers had already decided that
'whatever the outcome of the IGC will be, the intrinsic link between a common
European defence policy and NATO will remain'. Given the gradual realisation of
the limits of an ESDI, largely forged by the experience of the Bosnian crisis and
the consistent pressure to achieve reductions in defence expenditure,[62] it was only
natural that the WEU should develop 'in harmony with, not in competition to,
the wider framework of transatlantic defence cooperation in NATO'.[63]

Atlantic dominance: ESDI within the Alliance

Pivotal to most, if not all, of the policy developments in the latter half of the
1990s was the NAC Ministerial Meeting in June 1996 in Berlin. The meeting
marked a watershed in the development of US policy towards a more coherent
European role in the Alliance. It was then that the ESDI was clarified and the
European security architecture seemed to be coming together. 'The [US] Administration had clearly gone on the record as supporting a stronger European
pillar.'[64] By 1996, NATO had exemplified a transition from the Cold War structures, and from contained confrontation between the two superpowers to a new
configuration better adapted to the new geostrategic situation in Europe and the
world at large. The crisis in former Yugoslavia gave the Alliance an opportunity
to demonstrate that it can exercise its military prowess provided that it has the
firm political resolve of governments behind it, and that their objectives are
clearly stated. Involvement in former Yugoslavia had a dramatic impact on
NATO. As already mentioned, the new Strategic Concept acknowledged the need
to adapt the Alliance to the new security demands including risks emerging
beyond NATO borders, among other other challenges short of major war fighting contigencies. But it was operations in former Yugoslavia that gave the immediate impetus for NATO's increased emphasis on peacekeeping and 'out-of-area'
operations.[65] The success of missions assigned to the Implementation Force
(IFOR), together with work undertaken within the Partnership for Peace (PfP)
framework, were evidence of the Alliance's ability to deal with present-day
challenges and thus contribute to the political stability of the continent.[66]

In Berlin, the idea was finally accepted of establishing ESDI within NATO,
and the latter's most radical plan, the CJTF concept – first introduced at the January 1994 Brussels Summit – was refined and its development was authorised.[67]
The Berlin outcome was a major turning point in the post-Cold War European
security, for it settled the fundamental issues affecting the transatlantic bargaining: the primacy of NATO; US leadership in security and defence matters; the
contribution of the Europeans, and as a result – the short- and medium-term –

prospects of a self-contained ESDI. The communiqué endorsed the continuing 'internal adaptation' of NATO and defined the CJTF concept as 'central to our approach for assembling forces for (NATO) contigency operations' and 'operations led by the WEU'. Moreover, it stated that the whole adaptation process would be 'consistent with the goal of building [ESDI] within NATO', enabling 'all European Allies to play a larger role in NATO's military and command structures and, as appropriate, in contigency operations undertaken by the Alliance', while it also referred to 'a continued involvement of the North American Allies across the command and force structure', with the clear aim of preserving and reinforcing the transatlantic link.

What happened in Berlin was that NATO acquired even more credibility, in matters of security and defence, than any conceivable rival. With an ESDI within NATO, it became possible for the US to reconcile the strategic desire for primacy in Europe and the domestic political pressures for operational and financial burden-sharing. Strong US leadership expressed not only in the Alliance's post-Cold War adaptation drive, but also in the forceful US commitment to the Dayton process and in the subsequent performance of IFOR, made NATO increasingly attractive to almost every participant in the European security debate, including the French,[68] thus repositioning it firmly as the dominant actor in the new European security setting. Indeed, the Bosnian campaign made evident that the Europeans were incapable of any meaningful stabilising military intervention without the US leadership. The fundamental objective was, as always, the development of ESDI within NATO. CJTF would be a vital tool, leading to the 'creation of military coherent and effective forces capable of operating under the political control and strategic direction of the WEU'. A CJTF is a multinational, multiservice, task-tailored force consisting of NATO and possibly non-NATO forces; being capable of rapid deployment to conduct limited-duration 'out-of-area' peace operations, it would be under the control of either NATO's integrated command structure or under WEU. The aim is to open up multinational command and control outside the traditional NATO framework. The primary intent of the CJTF concept was to give NATO military forces the mobility and flexibility needed to execute the new security management tasks of the Alliance. Once fully in place, the new capabilities will at last fulfil the 1991 Strategic Concept's call for military authorities to design smaller, more mobile and more flexible forces. CJTF is a purely military concept, a technique long being used by many forces in the conduct of contigency warfare. NATO has been institutionalising the task force concept in order to make it more effective in the conduct of multilateral operations.[69] It is obvious that CJTF has been instrumental in combining ESDI with NATO's capabilities. The purpose was to give the WEU the necessary military capability to conduct Petersberg-type operations. In fact, deploying CJTF was intended to become the primary military doctrine of NATO in peacetime,[70] for it would provide flexibility to respond to new missions in or around Europe, facilitate the dual use of allied command structures for NATO and/or WEU operations and permit PfP countries to integrate into NATO-led operations.[71] In terms of the utilisation of NATO's integrated command structure for non-Art. 5 operations, it should be noted that within the three NATO Commands of Allied Forces Central Europe (AFCENT), Allied Forces Southern Europe (AFSOUTH) and Allied Command Atlantic (ACLANT), there are also three CJTF nuclei Headquarters (HQs), in place since the late 1990s.[72]

For the US, the realisation of the CJTF concept was always going to be instrumental in ensuring that NATO remains the core security and defence transatlantic, and for that matter European, institution, while refashioning the 'burden-sharing' debate by allowing Europeans to assume greater responsibility. Cornish, in an attempt to 'deconstruct' the CJTF concept, successfully identifies the constituent elements of its nature and political significance.[73] First, Berlin shows clearly that NATO has firm ambitions to be a crisis manager and peacekeeper in its own right, with the appropriate UN or OSCE mandate. CJTF is a means to achieve this goal. To that end, the idea of a division of labour between NATO and the WEU, with the former responsible for collective defence operations (Art. 5) and the latter for lower-scale missions (non-Art. 5). If there is to be such a division of labour it could only be *within* the non-Art. 5 category, with NATO taking 'hard' missions with fighting potential and the WEU dealing with 'soft' humanitarian and rescue tasks. In other words, non-Art. 5 operations were not the exclusive preserve of WEU. Second, CJTF is not simply 'a Euro-friendly afterthought in NATO's restructuring process, but lies at the heart of that process'.[74] It aims at providing an appropriate response capability across the spectrum of possible military tasks, ranging from the admittedly unlikely collective defence to non-Art. 5 needs for action. Third, via the NATO–WEU diplomatic relationship, CJTF is the practical means by which the ESDI within the Alliance was to be given operational expression. In political terms, it meant that CJTF, as a US-approved and NATO-sponsored idea, enabled a US-controlled development and implementation of ESDI. The key arrangement was the decisions for ESDI 'separable but not separate capabilities'. This meant that NATO had full control over the development of WEU-led operations. In the words of Cornish, 'it is most unlikely that a serious rival to NATO could now develop'.[75] This was confirmed in Amsterdam, where the WEU was recognised as 'an integral part of the development of the Union', and shall support the EU 'in framing the defence aspects of the common foreign security policy . . . with a view to the possibility of the integration of the WEU into the Union, should the European Council so decide' (Art. J7.1 TEU). It is obvious, though, that integrationist expectations have been reduced to hollow political rhetoric. The main significance of the WEU has been that it enabled a working compromise to be struck between integration and intergovernmentalism, Atlanticism and Europeanism.[76] What followed with the development of ESDP was made possible only after NATO's dominance seemed assured (especially by the British) and confirmed this compromise by further institutionalising a US-led, transatlantic division of labour.

European security and defence policy and US response

Two things emerged from the Franco-British Saint-Malo initiative. First, the WEU would be absorbed into the Union and placed under the CFSP. Second, the collective defence provision of Article V of the Brussels Treaty would be retained.[77] NATO's Washington Summit acknowledged the continuation of the Berlin decisions, including the implementation of CJTF, the creation of CJTF nuclei HQs, and the role of the Deputy Supreme Allied Command Europe (SACEUR) in overseeing the use of NATO assets by WEU-led operations. The Summit also acknowledged that the Union might at some point take over the role of the WEU in the existing NATO–WEU framework planning capabilities.

The Union's inability to tackle the build-up of the crisis in Kosovo and the ambivalence and delays in US policy were vital factors in creating a European demand for a new security and defence initiative. In Kosovo it was American plans that came into action, rather than those of NATO. It would not be far from the truth to note that the Kosovo war was a US operation under a NATO flag. That reality has been very uncomfortable both for the US and for NATO's European members.[78] The experience was instrumental in putting enough pressure on the EU members to move the debate radically forward.[79] Operation Allied Force consisted mainly of air operations. While non-US aircraft carried out over 15,000 sorties, about 39 per cent of the total, US aircraft delivered over 80 per cent of the weapons. The June 1999 Cologne European Council indicated the Union's willingness to provide the institutional framework for a future 'autonomous' European military contribution to international security and emphasised the two ways in which the Union could conduct Petersberg-type operations. One, by using NATO means and capabilities, including European command and control. In this case, the decisions taken in Berlin (1996) and Washington (1999) by the NAC are to be carried out. The other, EU-led operations without reliance on NATO assets and force structures could be conducted by European national or multinational means, which are pre-identified (or pre-designated in NATO terms) by the member states. In such cases either the national command structures, which provide for a multinational representation in the HQs or in the existing command structures within the multinational forces would have to be used for an effective conduct of EU-led operations.[80]

The US has welcomed the Union's ESDP initiative, but obviously this project holds implications for Washington. Hardly surprisingly, it requires a close relationship between the Union and NATO. American policy-makers and commentators have viewed the project in an ambivalent fashion. Officials within the Clinton administration were often at pains to offer their support, publicly welcoming the potential of ESDP to take on conflict management tasks the US would prefer to avoid. Yet, as the momentum of ESDP has gathered pace, anxieties in Washington were increasingly aired. Initially, during the Clinton administration, Secretary of State Albright, phrased these in December 1998 as the 'three Ds': the triple dangers of a decoupling (of European and Alliance decision-making), duplication (of defence resources) and discrimination (against non-EU NATO members). In a sincere attempt to ameliorate the anxieties, the 1999 Washington NAC Summit agreed on the so-called 'Berlin-Plus' compromise. For NAC, 'a stronger European role will help contribute to the vitality of our Alliance'. In this regard, 'we are determined that the decisions taken in Berlin in 1996, including the concept of using separable but not separate NATO assets and capabilities for WEU-led operations, should be further developed'.[81] American concerns, however, persisted. During the week of the Nice European Council, the outgoing US Secretary of Defense, Cohen, warned that NATO could become 'a relic' if the Union were to develop a military planning capability that duplicated NATO, and if resource commitments to ESDP detracted from force improvements slated under NATO's own DCI. To its credit, the G. W. Bush administration has tried to dispel most of these apprehensions, and it has nearly stopped making disparaging remarks about the credibility of European security and defence efforts, without, however, stopping voicing concern. Rumsfeld, the new Secretary of Defense, noted in February 2001 that he was 'worried' by a ESDP that might undermine NATO owing to a 'confusing duplication' of efforts, although Powell's first comments as Secretary of State were less alarmist. These broadsides against ESDP have galvanised the Union, by adding urgency to the creation of an efficient institutional interface with NATO and to the definition of mechanisms by which European operations will enjoy access to NATO assets.

The capabilities and responsibilities gap

It is clear that the US and the Union have been trying to define the new transatlantic bargain that would balance the latter's desire for a broader and more independent political role with its continued reliance on American and NATO military capabilities. There are quite a few practical steps to be taken in that direction. A crucial one concerns the way in which the Union enhances its military capabilities for projecting and sustaining power that is addressing the defence capabilities gap that divides its members from the US. The defence capabilities gap means that there is a danger of ending up with a two-tier alliance – one in which the US and perhaps a few European allies are able to conduct high-intensity operations, while the rest of the allies focus on the low end of the military spectrum. This would not strengthen NATO, but weaken it. Accordingly, the defence capabilities gap could result in a quite harmful division of labour for the cohesion of the transatlantic community, whereby the Union would take primary responsibility for conflict management and low-intensity peacekeeping, while the US would take the lead in high-intensity warfare.

In the near term, such a development could contribute to overall NATO capabilities if it were accompanied by an increase in European defence capabilities. Moreover, such a division of labour is consistent with the political desire on the part of the Union to take the lead on lower-end peacekeeping and conflict prevention tasks and also accords with US reluctance to get involved in every such contigency. Over the longer term, however, this kind of division of labour and 'mission specialisation' could undermine the cohesion of the

Alliance, for it would result in allies incapable of contributing to the Art. 5 collective defence commitments, or of conducting high-intensity joint operations 'out of area', thus raising questions about the ability of US and European forces to operate together in more demanding environments.

The debate after the Kosovo war as well as during the Afghanistan and the global anti-terrorism US campaign is revealing. The growing capabilities gap and the emerging division of labour inspires acrimonious debates about burden-sharing, and provides a constant source of friction in the transatlantic relationship. Because Europe is such a dwarf in security and defence issues, the US does not treat the European allies as genuine partners in the development and implementation of security and defence policies. As a result Americans and Europeans are growing resentful of each other in ways and at a pace that soon will become difficult to reverse.

Closing the capabilities gap, without undercutting the Alliance, is among the most urgent and difficult challenges NATO faces in the coming years. EU members should invest more on their defence capacity if they want to be able to exercise some control over American unilateralist tendencies especially after 11 September 2001. The interests of both the US and the Union would be served by developing a strong and effective ESDP. A Europe that remains allied to the US because of its own weakness is of limited value in the current turbulent strategic environment, and probably unsustainable politically. To preserve and advance transatlantic co-operation, NATO needs a bargain that shares more equitably the responsibilities of common interests. A stronger and more assertive Union is by far the more attractive partner for the US. In such a situation, the US would be more attentive to European concerns and more multilateralist than at present. American respect for ESDP would increase, making it easier for Washington to compromise for common transatlantic endeavours.[82]

Why NATO endures

The discussion above has been mainly about NATO's response and adaptation to the new European security environment, the development of its strategies towards the new challenges and its success in formulating effective policies. The issues were and still remain particularly salient, given the new strategic landscape. At the heart of the problem lies the pressing need for the Alliance to redefine its rationale, no longer in terms of identifying a unifying threat, but in terms of combining the capabilities of its members in a way that furthers their post-Cold War interests, while consolidating NATO as a device to the making of substantive agreements in world politics by providing rules, norms, principles and procedures that help state actors to realise those interests collectively. The challenge was enormous as the possibility of deterioration and dissolution became real. Alliances deteriorate and dissolve for several reasons, of which the most obvious and important is a change in the identity or nature of the threat that produced the original association. But NATO endured. Its durability and persistence has many sources.

First, there is a leader, the US, strongly committed to preserving the relationship and willing to expend the effort needed to keep its allies from straying. As Chapter 5 suggested, American leadership is not on the wane but has been exercised effectively through credible institutional structures. Second, NATO has become a symbol of credibility and resolve. The US decision to intervene in Bosnia, as well as its more recent resolute military response to the Kosovo crisis, appears to have been motivated by the fear that failure to act would cast doubt on its reliability and, hence, on NATO's future itself. Third, the high level of institutionalisation of NATO has created capabilities that are certainly worth preserving, despite the extensive change in the array of external threats, especially since it costs less to maintain them than it did to establish them in the first place. As Walt has indicated, 'the 1991 Gulf War could not have been fought without NATO assets, and the 1995 intervention in Bosnia relied on a similar base of infrastructure, military assets and joint decision-making procedures'.[83] Third, the high level of institutionalisation within NATO worked most powerfully because it had created capacities that are highly adaptable. As the foregoing discussion shows, NATO's durability increased since its institutional profile was instrumental in amending doctrines and organisational forms in response to external developments, making it easier to adapt to the new post-bipolar conditions. Fourth, ideological solidarity and a commitment to similar basic goals significantly helped to reduce intra-Alliance conflicts and to sustain it long after its original rationale had gone. Also, the fact that NATO has resulted in its members seeing themselves as integral parts of a larger (Atlantic) political community, reflecting or even creating a sense of common identity, means that the Alliance is undeniably appealing and, therefore, extremely robust.

Although neither the history of the past fifty years nor the public statements of contemporary national leaders offer an absolutely reliable guide for the future, the geostrategic developments and institutional dynamics of the 1990s resulted in NATO remaining the landmark of post-Cold War European security. NATO is still preparing to deal with threats in true realist fashion, even though their identities are increasingly in dispute or uncertain. What NATO has done in response – to realist and neo-realist surprise – is to expand its relationship to other international institutions, such as the WEU and the Union, 'as part of an effort to embed itself further into the framework of European, and to a lesser extent trans-Atlantic, relations. In so doing, NATO has demonstrated the flexibility expected of both organisations and international institutions.'[84] One can easily imagine that these factors, which safeguarded NATO's efficient political and institutional adjustment, led to the decisions that were (or were not) taken in Amsterdam. These decisions cast serious doubts as to whether 'the project of a true common European defence is still a real political objective being pursued by all governments of the relevant European countries',[85] and once again fuelled debate about the Union's role in world affairs and its nature as a global actor. The final section below offers a theoretical understanding of this debate.

Instead of a conclusion: the Union in world affairs

This section tries to identify what the Union is in terms of its international behaviour: an 'international actor', a 'global power', an 'economic power/bloc', a 'civilian power' or a 'superpower in the making'? These terms entail different descriptive and normative implications for European foreign policy. The same applies to what kind of European security superstructure should exist. There is little doubt from the existing literature that the Union (and before it the Community) has now acquired an international role, even if its legal status remains unclear.[86] There is in fact general agreement that all EU institutions have acquired such a role. This is particularly true of the Commission and the EP, but generally speaking this is due to the emergence of the Union as an international actor.[87]

A study undertaken in 1977 by Sjostedt, posing the question 'to what degree the EC is an international actor at a given time',[88] concluded that the Community was 'some sort of half developed international actor'.[89] As for the future, Sjostedt presented a series of possible developments without committing himself to any particular option. He also warned, quite correctly, of the difficulties inherent in any prediction in the social sciences.[90] In his view, an international actor is an acting unit in the international system, which possesses the quality of 'actor capability'. The latter was in turn defined as having a double characteristic: first, that unit 'is discernible from the external environment', in that 'it has a minimum degree of separateness'; second, that 'it has a minimal degree of internal cohesion'.[91] The Union has come some way from the time when Sjostedt could rightly claim that in the mid-1970s the Commission's role in 'high politics' was non-existent and that there was hardly ever '[a] common behaviour in the "high policy" field areas, to which foreign policy belongs *par excellence*'.[92] There is no doubt that the Commission played an important role in EPC, if only by being represented at all EPC meetings.[93] This is all the more so since the coming into force of the TEU, which gave the Commission a right of co-initiative, at least theoretically. Hence the general assessment that the Community/Union has emerged as a distinct entity on the international scene.

According to Kirchner, '[w]hereas in the 1970's there was a belief that the EC was mostly reactive or more affected by international events than vice versa, the Community can now be described as becoming more active in the international field and attractive to other international actors'.[94] Ginsberg has gone even further by arguing that the number of foreign policy 'actions' has increased over the years, claiming that the new logic behind such actions is what he calls 'self-styled' actions as opposed to the previous logics of integration or interdependence.[95] In certain areas, there seems to be a common European stance. De Schoutheete identified nine issue-areas where '*quelques résultats*' could be identified in the EPC framework: the CSCE, East–West relations, Cyprus, the Middle East, Africa, Latin America, the US, the Council of Europe and human rights. Januzzi identifies at least seven areas where there has been a common stance:

Eastern Europe, the Middle East, Afghanistan, Latin America, South Africa, terrorism and human rights.[96] Similarly, the Union possesses observer status in many international organisations, starting with the UN, and many non-member states have diplomatic relations and representation with it. From the perspective of third countries, they 'so often perceive the Twelve [now Fifteen] in EPC as being more united and stronger than the member states themselves are ready to admit'.[97] The additional requirement of Art. 30.5 SEA that EPC and the Community's external policy must coincide has added to this trend because the external economic relations of the Community, as well as its development and aid policy, have proved extremely important. Such a requirement is repeated both in the TEU and the AMT.[98]

A high degree of 'co-ordination reflex' has also developed among the foreign ministries of all the member states. Regelsberger has pointed out that a flexible frame of mind is more rewarding in understanding the nature of EPC than is any traditional foreign policy theory.[99] Rummel concurs: if '[t]he aggregation of (EPC) positions and activities ... does not yet constitute the foreign policy *of* the European Community and its member states, it at least represents a foreign policy *for* them.'[100] Thus both of Sjostedt's criteria (minimum degree of separateness and of internal cohesion) seemed to have been satisfied since he first used these terms. Although the CFSP (and EPC before it) has not amounted to a truly common European foreign policy, it would be incorrect to ignore its role in international relations. Even if one takes a minimalist approach, it is possible to identify a 'European' line on most international relations issues.

Moreover, the Union's own perception of being an international actor is evident in the many official statements on its international role. Europe as a distinct entity was also one of the original underpinnings of the integration process after the Second World War, based on a sense of common identity. The setting up of EPC was agreed upon at a time when the Community had 'arrived at a turning point in its history', when there was a need for Europe 'to establish its position in the world as a distinct entity'.[101] Such a position culminated in the Document on European Identity published by the (then) Nine as early as December 1973.[102] A good way of defining Europe's sense of distinctiveness can be summed up as follows: it is not based on the use of force; it both involves the peoples of Europe and implies their backing; it purports to set up a Europe which is not dominated by any one of its constituent parts (no empire-building). In short, the international actions of the Union can be described as those of a 'Civilian Power Europe'. This term was first coined in the 1970s at a time when economic power seemed to be more important in international affairs than traditional military power. In Duchêne's words, a civilian power is 'a civilian group of countries long on economic power and relatively short on armed force'. It is also 'a force for the international diffusion of civilian and democratic standards'.[103] Twitchett defines it as 'an international polity as yet possessing no military dimension, but able to exercise influence on states, global and regional organisations, international corporations and other transnational bodies through diplomatic, economic and legal factors'. This definition must be contrasted with that of a 'superpower' which possesses power and influence, and the means to implement them in the following fields: ideology, politics, economics, finance and the military, especially in nuclear technology. There also exists a sphere of influence where the superpower has almost unlimited control or dominance.

In the existing literature, two kinds of early criticisms have been made: the realists who deny the very existence of the concept itself, in that it amounts to nothing but a 'contradiction in terms'.[104] Ifestos adds that 'the turbulences of the 1970's and first half of the 1980's ... [have] tended to discredit [the civilian power Europe approach]'.[105] Pijpers went further in the late 1980s: 'EPC has some striking deficiencies in the field of security', stressing the lack of crisis management arrangements and the lack of co-ordination in the field of arms trade policy.[106] A second, more limited, attack came from a left-wing inspired critique of capitalism. Galtung claimed that a civilian power Europe represented only an alternative to American hegemony in his *The European Community: A Superpower in the Making.*[107]

Another relevant approach covers institutional arrangements, with the view to explaining what the Union is or is not in world affairs. There is no point in repeating the CFSP decision-making process at this stage; suffice it to say that whether or not the Union achieves a common stance on international affairs also has an impact on how close this entity is to a federal, confederal or *sui generis* model. This picture is further complicated by 'domestic sources' of foreign policy which tend to affect foreign policy in variable ways according to the issue at hand, the country concerned, and in relation to EU foreign policy developments. This is not the place to develop this point further but simply to say that a clear federalist–intergovernmentalist divide reminiscent of the formative debates can be found.

Despite the above, a more liberal view has tried to use the concept of a civilian power Europe in order to understand what the Union is in world affairs and, by implication, what its internal structure is. Rummel states: 'When compared to the superpowers, Western Europe stresses moral persuasion, the "good example", and unconditional help and de-emphasises ideological warfare, the selections of proxies, and the "projection of power."'[108] Hill identifies several reasons for applying the phrase 'Civilian Power' to Europe: first, because international politics is not exclusively about military power; second, because the use of military force to intervene in third countries 'has a dubious record'; third, because it is true to say that 'the record of civilian power in action is not insubstantial'; fourth, because Duchêne's original preoccupation was with the process of European integration, and particularly the Franco-German reconciliation, which has been 'gloriously' successful; and fifth, because a Civilian Power Europe is more desirable than a superpower Europe.[109] In that respect, Hill agrees with Duchêne's original view that the Community should not become a superpower because that would go against its intrinsic nature.

More recently, Buchan, in a journalistic effort, argued that the Union was a 'strange superpower'.[110] Thus, he views the Union not as a conventional super-power because of its mainly economic power, and he concludes that in the post-Cold War era this is an advantage as 'economic problems [are] back at the top of the international agenda'.[111] But he also stresses the current shortcomings of European integration and contrasts the advances on monetary union with the lack of a coherent foreign and security policy. As for Piening, he concluded that the Union was a 'global power'.[112] He takes a more practical and less normative view to argue that Europe is now a 'global' power of 'a class of its own'.[113] He sees this development as a direct result of internal integration and argues that the major changes have occurred 'at almost breakneck speed'.[114] Buchan and Pien-ing concentrate on the size of the market, the population, and the economy of the Union, rather than on any 'domestic peace'. Whereas the latter falls into the category of intra-democratic peace,[115] these most recent studies focus on eco-nomic power within an ever-interdependent and globalising world. They also both show some scepticism about future developments, especially on the impact of enlargements to come and of waning popular support, but neither offers a prescription to that effect, nor considers at length the implications for the future of European integration theory and practice.

Even more recently, and mainly owing to the *de facto* militarisation of the Union, two more opposing views have emerged about the continued usefulness of the concept of a civilian power.[116] Zielonka, Whitman and Smith have called for its demise. They all consider that a civilian power cannot become militarised and use military means without losing its *raison d'être*.[117] A minority view, first applied to Germany after its participation in NATO's bombing of Kosovo and Serbia,[118] considers on the contrary that military power will at long last offer the Union the means to act like a civilian power in the world, that is to say as a force for the projection of democratic and other human rights principles.[119] So, in short, the jury is still out about what kind of an international actor the Union is. Future deepening and widening will make its role in world affairs all the more relevant and important for further analyses.

The debate on the Union's identity and role in international affairs, while focusing on failings and dilemmas and on persistent limitations, does not ignore the progress European unity has made thus far. Bouts of expansion in both geo-graphical and functional scope have marked its history, and periods of pessimism and showdowns have almost never led to regressions. Hoffmann uses the image of Sisyphus only to suggest that the present shape of the Union 'is quite different from the supranational dream of its founders and that each leap forward brings with it problems as well as reminders of constant handicaps'.[120] However, prophe-cies of lethal break-ups have not been fulfilled. Instead, it seems that Europeans, following Haas' suggestions,[121] try to 'learn' and to 'revalue' themselves by at least safeguarding their laboriously evolving *acquis*. And this process of 'learning' and 're-evaluation' does lead to – painful and slow – institutional adaptation and policy innovation. As for now, the Union is a necessary and, in some respects, a leading part of the European political and security landscape, as well as a subtle, if often shaky, actor in international geopolitics.

Notes

1 On the EDC, see Edward Furdson, *The European Defence Community: A History*, London: Macmillan, 1980. On the Fouchet Plans, see Susan Bodenheimer, *Political Union: A Microcosm of European Politics 1960–1966*, Leyden: Sitjhoff, 1967.
2 This was also the case during the 'Empty Chair' crisis of 1965.
3 This phenomenon occurred again in the early 1980s, with Spain and Portugal doing the same in general foreign policy matters, but more particularly on Mediterranean and Central American issues.
4 Paul Taylor, *The Limits of European Integration*, New York: Columbia University Press, 1983.
5 Jacob Øhrgaard, '"Less than Supranational, More than Intergovernmental": European Political Co-operation and the Dynamics of Intergovernmental Integration', *Millennium*, 26:1, 1997, pp. 1–29; the quotes are on p. 27 and their order has been reversed.
6 The decision-making machinery was kept separate: the Paris and Rome Treaties (ECSC, EEC, Euratom) and the SEA covered the external economic relations (trade and development policies), whereas EPC was based on a series of Reports and on Title III of the SEA. See Simon Nuttall, *European Political Co-operation*, Oxford: Clarendon, 1992, pp. 51–259.
7 For more on this question, see Stelios Stavridis and Christopher Hill (eds), *Domestic Sources of Foreign Policy: West European Reactions to the Falklands Conflict*, Oxford: Berg, 1996.
8 As we are assessing a relatively short period of time, any such assessment can be only of an interim kind.
9 This draws on Stelios Stavridis, 'The Common Foreign and Security Policy of the European Union: Why Institutional Arrangements Are Not Enough', in S. Stavridis, E. Mossialos, R. Morgan and H. Machin (eds), *New Challenges to the European Union: Policies and Policy-Making*, Aldershot: Dartmouth, 1997, pp. 87–122.
10 Old EPC declarations and *communiqués* are replaced by CFSP statements.
11 Jörg Monar, 'The Financial Dimension of the CFSP', in Martin Holland (ed.), *Common Foreign and Security Policy – The Record and Reforms*, London: Pinter, 1997, pp. 34–51.
12 Simon Nuttall, 'The CFSP Provisions of the Amsterdam Treaty: An Exercise in Collusive Ambiguity', *CFSP Forum*, 3/97, p. 3.
13 Clive Church, *European Integration Theory in the 1990s*, European Dossier Series, No. 33, University of North London 1996, p. 33.
14 For more details, see Stelios Stavridis, 'The Democratic Control of the EU's Foreign and Security Policy after Amsterdam and Nice', *Current Politics and Economics of Europe*, 10:3, 2001, pp. 289–311.
15 Fergus Carr and Kostas Ifantis, *NATO in the New European Order*, London: Macmillan/St Martin's Press, 1996, p. 65.
16 *Ibid.*, p. 66.
17 *Ibid.*
18 *Ibid.*, p. 67.
19 *Ibid.*, p. 68.
20 See Victor-Yves Ghebali, 'The OSCE's Istanbul Charter for European Security', *NATO Review*, 48, Spring–Summer 2000, p. 23.
21 Carr and Ifantis, *NATO*, p. 69.

22 Gerhard Kummel, 'From Yesterday to Tomorrow – CSCE/OSCE at Twenty: Achieve-ments of the Past and Challenges of the Future', *OSCE ODIHR Bulletin*, 4:1, Winter 1995/96, p. 13.

23 Stuart Croft, Jolyon Howorth, Terry Terrif and Mark Webber, 'NATO's Triple Challenge', *International Affairs*, 76:3, July 2000, p. 495.

24 See NATO, *NATO Facts and Figures*, Brussels, NATO Information Office, 1989, pp. 402–4.

25 See R. Hunter, *Security in Europe*, London: Elek Books, 1969. Also, J. Wyllie, *European Security in the Nuclear Age*, Oxford: Basil Blackwell, 1986.

26 Carr and Ifantis, *NATO*, p. 61.

27 NATO, 'Declaration of the Heads of States and Governments Participating in the Meet-ing of the North Atlantic Council in Brussels', Brussels, NATO Information Service, 1988.

28 North Atlantic Council, 'Ministerial Meeting at Turnberry, 1990', *NATO Review*, 38:3, 1990.

29 NATO, 'The London Declaration on a Transformed North Atlantic Alliance', Brussels, NATO Information Service, 1990.

30 'NATO will field smaller and restructured active forces. These forces will be highly mobile and versatile so that Allied leaders will have maximum flexibility in deciding how to respond to a crisis. It will rely increasingly on multinational corps made up of national units. NATO will scale back the readiness of its active units, reducing training require-ments and the number of exercises. NATO will rely more heavily on the ability to build up larger forces if and when they might be needed.' See *ibid.*

31 North Atlantic Council, 'Partnership with the Countries of Central and Eastern Europe', NATO Press Communiqué, M-1(91)44, 1991.

32 North Atlantic Council, 'Ministerial Meeting, Denmark', *NATO Review*, 39:3, 1991.

33 *Ibid.*

34 Manfred Wörner, 'The Atlantic Alliance in the New Era', *NATO Review*, 39:1, 1991.

35 NATO, 'The Alliance's Strategic Concept', Press Release NAC-S(99)65, 24 April 1999, para. 4.

36 Ian Lesser, Jerrold Green, F. Stephen Larrabee and Michele Zanini, *The Future of NATO's Mediterranean Initiative: Evolution and Next Steps*, Santa Monica: RAND, 2000, pp. 20–1.

37 *Ibid.*

38 See Adam Roberts, 'NATO's "Humanitarian War" over Kosovo', *Survival*, 41:3, Autumn 1999, pp. 102–23.

39 Andrew J. Pierre, *NATO at Fifty: New Challenges, Future Uncertainties*, United States Institute for Peace (USIP) Special Report, 22 March 1999, p. 7.

40 Ole Waever and Barry Buzan, 'An Inter-Regional Analysis: NATO's New Strategic Con-cept and the Theory of Security Complexes', in Sven Behrendt and Christian-Peter Hanelt (eds), *Bound to Cooperate: Europe and the Middle East*, Gutersloh: Bertelsmann Foundation Publishers, 2000, pp. 92–3.

41 Roberts, 'NATO's "Humanitarian War"', p. 120.

42 Waever and Buzan, 'An Inter-Regional Analysis', p. 93

43 Gulnur Aybet, *NATO's Developing Role in Collective Security*, SAM Papers No. 4/99, Ankara: Center for Strategic Research, 1999, pp. 45–6.

44 David S. Yost, *NATO Transformed: The Alliance's New Roles in International Security*, Washington, DC: United Institute for Peace, 1998, p. 77.

45 *Ibid.*

46 Carr and Ifantis, *NATO*, pp. 76–7.

47 Aybet, *NATO's Developing Role*, p. 47.

48 WEU, The *Reactivation of the WEU, Statements and Communiqués, 1984 to 1987*, WEU Press and Information Service, 1988.

49 *Ibid.*
50 Carr and Ifantis, *NATO*, p. 70.
51 WEU, *Platform on European Security Interests*, The Hague, 1987, in WEU, *The Reactivation of the WEU*.
52 W. V. Eekelen, 'WEU and the Gulf Crisis', *Survival*, 32:6, 1990, p. 524.
53 *Ibid.*, p. 525.
54 Carr and Ifantis, *NATO*, p. 71.
55 Sean Kay, *NATO and the Future of European Security*, Oxford: Rowman & Littlefield, 1998, p. 126.
56 Carr and Ifantis, *NATO*, p. 71.
57 WEU, *Related Texts Adopted at the EC Summit Maastricht*, WEU Press and Information Service, 1991.
58 G. Wyn Rees, 'Constructing a European Defence Identity: The Perspectives of Britain, France and Germany', *European Foreign Affairs Review*, 1:2, November 1996, p. 236.
59 North Atlantic Council, *Declaration of Heads of State and Government January 1994*, NATO Press Communiqué, M-1(94)3, 1994.
60 WEU, *Preliminary Conclusions on the Formulation of a Common European Defence Policy*, WEU Press and Information Service, 1994.
61 *Ibid.*
62 Rees, 'Constructing a European Defence Identity', p. 146.
63 *Ibid.*
64 Stanley R. Sloan, *The United States and European Defense*, Chaillot Papers, 39, Institute for Security Studies, Western European Union, Paris, April 2000, p. 13.
65 Gregory L. Schulte, 'Former Yugoslavia and the New NATO', *Survival*, 39:1, Spring 1997, p. 27.
66 Assembly of WEU, *The Future Role of WEU*, Draft Report, A/WEU/POL(96)25, Paris, 11 November 1996.
67 North Atlantic Council, 'Berlin Communiqué', Berlin, 3 June 1996, *NATO Review*, 44:4, July 1996. A lengthy document, the Berlin Communiqué touched upon all the main issues facing NATO: the situation in former Yugoslavia and the conduct of IFOR; the spread of nuclear, biological and chemical weapons of mass destruction; outreach through NACC and PfP, and the enlargement timetable; relations with Russia and Ukraine; the role of the OSCE; the Middle East peace process; and disarmament and arms control.
68 France's so-called *rapprochement* with NATO is an important explanation for the Berlin outcome. In February 1991, France announced its decision to take part in NATO's Strategy Review Group. Four years later, in December 1995, following NATO's decision to send 60,000-strong force to Bosnia–Herzegovina to replace UNPROFOR and the Anglo-French Rapid Reaction Force, France initiated its return to the alliance. French chiefs of staff would take part in NATO's Military Committee, would improve their relations with NATO's military staff and would work more closely with NATO's European command structure at SHAPE.
69 See Charles L. Barry, 'NATO's CJTF Concept and the WEU's Role in Crisis Response', paper presented at the WEU Athens Seminar, 1–3 May 1997.
70 Barry, 'NATO's CJTF Concept'.
71 Kay, *NATO and the Future of European Security*, p. 133.
72 This arrangement meant that in a time of crisis if an operation was to be headed by the WEU, the double hatted staff who serve as NATO HQ staff and the CJTF nuclei HQ staff would form the core of the CJTF HQ for that operation, augmented by experts and staff from NATO and WEU and other countries. The actual execution of such an operation was envisaged to fall on the Deputy SACEUR, who is usually a British officer. He would oversee the transformation of a CJTF nuclei HQ into deployable HQ under the WEU to

be strengthened by commanders of the forces assigned by NATO and WEU member states for that mission. With this arrangement, the Deputy SACEUR has formed the key point of contact between NATO and WEU. A key role also falls on the Combined Joint Planning Staff (CJPS), which consists of joint staff working for both SACEUR and SACLANT, therefore covering all the land- and sea-based CJTF HQs. The CJPS was formed as the planning body responsible for the implementation of the CJTF concept. Now it is also the obvious planning source of European-led non-Art. 5 contingencies. See Aybet, *NATO's Developing Role,* p. 51.

73 Paul Cornish, 'European Security: The End of Architecture and the New NATO', *International Affairs,* 72:4, October 1996, pp. 762–4.

74 According to Wörner, the concept is 'the next logical step in the adaptation of our force structures'. Quoted in Cornish, 'European Security', p. 763.

75 *Ibid.,* p. 764.

76 *Ibid.,* p. 768.

77 Aybet, *NATO's Developing Role,* pp. 52–3.

78 Stuart Croft, 'Guaranteeing Europe's Security? Enlarging NATO Again', *International Affairs,* 78:1, January 2002, p. 108.

79 See Paul Cornish and Geoffrey Edwards, 'Beyond the EU/NATO Dichotomy: the Beginnings of a European Strategic Culture', *International Affairs,* 77:3, July 2001, p. 588.

80 See Declaration of the European Council on 'Strengthening the Common European Policy on Security and Defense', Cologne European Council, 3–4 June 1999.

81 North Atlantic Council, 'Washington Summit Communiqué: An Alliance for the 21st Century', NAC-S(99)64, 24 April 1999, para. 9.

82 Kori Schake, Amaya Bloch-Laine and Charles Grant, 'Building a European Defense Capability', *Survival,* 41:1, Spring 1999, pp. 21–2.

83 Stephen M. Walt, 'Why Alliances Endure or Collapse', *Survival,* 39:1, Spring 1997, p. 167.

84 Robert B. McCalla, 'NATO's Persistence After the Cold War', *International Organisation,* 50:3, Summer 1996, p. 470.

85 Assembly of the WEU, *WEU After Amsterdam: The European Security and Defence Identity and the Application of Article V of the Modified Brussels Treaty – Reply to the Annual Report of the Council,* Draft Report, A/WE/POL(97)10, Paris, 4 November 1997, p. 20.

86 See the AMT of October 1997.

87 What follows draws on Stelios Stavridis, 'Foreign Policy and Democratic Principles: The Case of European Political Cooperation', unpublished PhD thesis, London: LSE, 1991, pp. 22–7. There is, however, a vast literature on the subject. See, for instance, David Allen *et al.* (eds), *European Political Cooperation,* London: Butterworths, 1982; Christopher Hill (ed.), *National Foreign Policies and European Political Cooperation,* London: George Allen & Unwin, 1983; and Christopher Hill (ed.), *The Actors in Europe's Foreign Policy,* London: Routledge, 1996.

88 Gunnar Sjostedt, *The External Role of the European Community,* Farnborough: Saxon House 1977, p. 6.

89 *Ibid.,* p. 112.

90 *Ibid.,* see Part II, especially pp. 133–6.

91 *Ibid.,* p. 13.

92 *Ibid.,* p. 14.

93 For details, see Simon Nuttall, 'Where the European Commission Comes In', in Alfred Pijpers *et al.* (eds), *European Political Cooperation in the 1980's: A Common Foreign Policy for Western Europe?,* Dordrecht: Martinus Nijhoff, 1988, pp. 104–17.

94 Emil Kirchner, 'Has the Single European Act Opened the Door for a European Security Policy?', *Journal of European Integration,* 13:1, Autumn 1989, p. 11. See also Corinne Covillers, *Y-a-t-il une politique extérieure des Communautés Européennes?,* Paris: PUF, 1987, pp. 47–86; Panayiotis Ifestos, *European Political Cooperation: Towards a Frame-*

work of Supranational Diplomacy?, Aldershot: Gower, 1987, pp. 584–5; and Christopher Hill, 'European Foreign Policy: Power Bloc, Civilian Power – or Flop?', in Reinhart Rummel (ed.), The Evolution of an International Actor: Western Europe's New Assertiveness, Boulder: Westview, 1990, p. 35.

95 Roy Ginsberg, Foreign Policy Actions of the European Community – The Politics of Scale, Boulder: Lynne Rienner, 1989.

96 See, respectively, Philippe De Schoutheete, La Coopération politique européenne, 2nd edn, Brussels: Labor, 1986, pp. 67–8; Gianni Januzzi, 'European Political Cooperation and the Single European Act', in Panos Tsakaloyannis (ed.), Western European Security in a Changing World: From the Reactivation of the WEU to the Single European Act, Maastricht: EIPA, 1988, p. 106.

97 Reinhart Rummel, 'Speaking with One Voice – and Beyond', in A. Pijpers (ed.), European Political Cooperation in the 1980s: A Common Foreign Policy for Europe?, Dordrecht: Martinus Nijhoff, 1988, p. 140.

98 Art. C in both the Maastricht Treaty and the AMT.

99 Elfriede Regelsberger, 'EPC in the 1980s: Reaching another Plateau?', in Pijpers (ed.), European Political Cooperation, p. 37.

100 Rummel, 'Speaking with One Voice', p. 129.

101 The Hague Communiqué, point 3, December 1969, and the July 1973 Copenhagen Report, Part 1, in European Political Co-operation, Bonn: Press and Information Office of the Federal Government, 5th edition, 1988, pp. 22, 36.

102 European Political Co-operation, Bonn: Press and Information Office of the Federal Government, 1982, p. 58.

103 See Hedley Bull, 'Civilian Power Europe: A Contradiction in Terms', in Loukas Tsoukalis (ed.), The European Community: Past, Present and Future, Oxford: Basil Blackwell, 1983, p. 149.

104 Hedley Bull's verdict in the early 1980s, ibid., pp. 149–64.

105 Ifestos, European Political Cooperation, p. 68.

106 Alfred Pijpers, 'The Twelve Out-of-Area: A Civilian Power in an Uncivil World?', in Pijpers (ed.), European Political Cooperation, p. 157.

107 Johan Galtung, The European Community: A Superpower in the Making, London: George Allen & Unwin, 1973.

108 Rummel, 'Speaking with One Voice', p. 130.

109 Hill, 'European Foreign Policy', pp. 43–4.

110 David Buchan, Europe: The Strange Superpower, Aldershot: Dartmouth, 1993.

111 Ibid., p. 7.

112 Christopher Piening, Global Europe – The European Union in World Affairs, Boulder: Lynne Rienner, 1997. Piening uses a regional approach first taken by Geoffrey Edwards and Elfriede Regelsberger (eds), Europe's Global Links: The European Community and Inter-regional Co-operation, London: Pinter, 1990.

113 Piening, Global Europe, p. 196.

114 Ibid., p. 197.

115 See Nils Petter Gleditsch and Thomas Risse-Kappen (eds), 'Democracy and Peace', European Journal of International Relations, Special Edition, 1:4, December 1995.

116 For more see Stelios Stavridis, 'The Militarizing of the EU and the Concept of a "Civilian Power Europe" Revisited', The International Spectator, 36:4, 2001, pp. 43–50.

117 See Jan Zielonka, Explaining Euro-Paralysis: Why Europe is Unable to Act in International Politics, Macmillan: Basingstoke, 1998; Richard Whitman, From Civilian Power to Superpower? The International Identity of the European Union, Macmillan, Basingstoke, 1998; and Karen Smith, 'The End of Civilian Power Europe: A Welcome Demise or Cause for Concern?', The International Spectator, 35:2, 2000, pp. 11–28.

118 Hans Maull, 'Germany and the Use of Force: Still a Civilian Power?', Survival, 42:2, 2000, pp. 56–80.

119 Stavridis, 'The Militarizing of the EU'.
120 Stanley Hoffmann, *The European Sisyphus: Essays on Europe, 1964–1994*, Boulder: Westview, 1995, p. 6.
121 See Ernst B. Haas, *When Knowledge is Power: Three Models of Change in International Organizations*, Berkeley: University of California Press, 1990.

7

Debating the future of Europe
New polity dynamics

Introduction

The principal purpose of this study has been to provide an overview of the important political and institutional developments in the Union and to link such developments with relevant theory discourses; the most prominent of which being the relationship between theory and reform in the evolving political constitution of the Union. As the discussion in Chapter 2 suggested from a normative standpoint, it is possible to accept that the coming into being of the TEU in 1993, assisted by further treaty reforms, paved the way for a new integrative stage, best captured by the term 'nascent *Gemeinschaft*'. This is not to negate the usage of the term 'integration' in capturing the dynamics of the regional process, as it is still useful in the vocabulary of EU studies, insofar as it attempts to explain the joining together of previously independent entities under a new centre, whether or not federally organised. Yet, the point has been clearly made that 'polity-formation' is better equipped – both conceptually and operationally – to capturing the constitutive nature of European governance. Indeed, the dynamism of EU polity-building over the 1990s has provided some of the necessary infrastructure for the emergence of a 'constitutive' European polity that derives its legitimacy both from the component polities and the member demoi, emphasising the need for greater civic deliberation and participation.

It is not so much the actual provisions stemming from successive treaty reforms or for that matter the way in which they will be carried out that warrant our closer attention, as are the new European polity dynamics, in that questions of democracy, citizenship, rights (and duties) are now an integral part of the Union's agenda. Although a managerial-type reform has largely prevailed since the prolonged course of the IGC 1996/97 and the even more arduous IGC 2000, there is still hope that a more 'democentric' process of union will come about and, with it, a European public sphere founded upon a deliberative politics. This is the task of a newly-instituted 'Convention on the Future of Europe',[1] following the December 2001 Laeken Declaration and, before that, the initiative taken by the Swedish Presidency on 7 March 2001 to launch a European-wide consultation process to canvass opinion from political, business, academic and civil society circles. This quasi-formal, pre-reform process is intended to lead to yet another review conference in 2004. Its justification lies in the long-standing need to transform the Union into a more participatory system of deliberative governance based on the institutions and practices of civic inclusion, as opposed to the existing forms of executive elite dominance. Arguably, the latter emerges as a chronic malaise of the general system, which recent treaty reforms have failed to address properly. The rationale underpinning this critical assertion is that successive waves of formal constitutional review have fallen short of transforming a shadowy political space into a purposeful *res publica*: a composite polity able to navigate the normative orientations of European civic society, by means of harnessing its deliberative potential, and by elevating its members into a governing and politically self-conscious transnational demos. As for now, however, it could be safely argued that European integration is not about the subordination of states to a federally constituted centre, but rather about the preservation of those qualities that allow the segments – as distinct historically constituted nation-states – to survive as separate collectivities, while engaging themselves in a polity-formation process that transforms their traditional patterns of interaction. Whatever the end result of this elaborate exercise might be, this study has tried to illustrate that the new challenges confronting the Union are not without profound implications for both its present and future theorising.

Amsterdam and Nice in perspective

To start with the moderate treaty reforms embedded in the AMT, it is fair to suggest that the European construction has been 'stirred' rather than 'shaken'. Hailed by some as a 'reasonable step', and criticised by others as lacking ambition and vision, the AMT preserves the Union's three-pillar structure with its two separate legal methods. Some areas previously falling under the third pillar (and thus the intergovernmental method) will be gradually transferred to the first pillar, while the Schengen Agreement is now fully incorporated into the Union (with Britain and Ireland having secured an opt-out).

At the institutional level, it is agreed that at the first enlargement the big countries will lose their second Commissioner, provided that they are compensated through a reweighting of votes in the Council (see below). A final decision has been deferred until a new IGC is convened at least one year before EU membership exceeds twenty. Majority voting has been extended in the fields of research, customs co-operation and fraud, and so has the (now simplified) 'co-decision procedure' in the areas of employment (incentive measures), social policy (equal opportunities and treatment), public health, transparency (general principles), statistics and data protection (independent advisory authority). The legislative procedures involving the EP are reduced to three: co-decision, consultation and assent.

Moreover, a Chapter on Fundamental Rights and Nondiscrimination has been inserted in the AMT to strengthen the Union's 'human face', safeguard the protection of human rights and, in short, redress the fast-growing 'credibility gap' between EU 'decision-makers' and 'decision-receivers'. Still though, as Shaw rightly argues, the AMT 'is more about "managing" reactions to the Community/Union than it is about seeking to engage in citizen participation'.[2] Further, a new protocol is enshrined in the Treaty in an attempt to define more precisely the criteria for applying the principles of subsidiarity and proportionality. According to the Treaty: 'In exercising the powers conferred on it, each institution shall ensure that the principle of subsidiarity is complied with'; 'any action of the Community shall not go beyond any action necessary for the attainment of the objectives of the Treaty.' It is also stated that these principles should respect the *acquis communautaire* and the institutional balance, also taking into account that 'the Union shall provide itself with the means necessary to attain its objectives and carry through its policies'. Yet, there is a presumption of competence to the states (but not to subnational units), in that the Community has to justify compliance of proposed legislation to these principles (see below).

As suggested in Chapter 3, flexibility was finally included in the AMT though in a way that precludes the creation of a Europe *à la carte* by introducing stringent conditions for its application. More specifically, such 'reinforced co-operation' should further the objectives of the Union and protect its interests; respect the principles of the Treaties and the single institutional framework; be used only as a last resort; concern at least a majority of EU members; respect the *acquis communautaire*; not affect the competences, rights, obligations and interests of those members that do not wish to participate therein; remain open to all member states; and be authorised by the Council. However, the Treaty precludes member states from initiating flexible arrangements in areas which fall within the exclusive competences of the Community; affect the Community policies, actions or programmes; concern Union citizenship or discriminate between member state nationals; fall outside the limits of the powers conferred upon the Community by the Treaty; and constitute discrimination or restrict trade and/or distort competition between member states. Authorisation for such 'flexible' schemes 'shall be granted by the Council, acting by a qualified majority on a proposal by the Commission and after consulting the EP'. Any objection by a member state on grounds of 'important and stated reasons' results in the whole matter being referred to the European Council for a decision by unanimity. This points to yet another accommodationist-type arrangement that arguably strengthens the Union's consociational properties.

But the question that still remains to be addressed concerns the appropriate institutional structure to sustain successive waves of enlargement in the twenty-first century. On the basis of the (largely incomplete) outcome of the IGC

1996/97, there has clearly been a preference for a managerial type of reform to improve the effectiveness in policy output. Flexibility has been partially elevated to a *modus operandi* of the system, whereas the deepening of integration has been referred *ad calendas Graecas*. In any case, there is evidence to suggest that these moderate trends in treaty reform reinforce the point made earlier in this study about the reversal of the Mitranian logic to international integration, in that function follows form, rather than being followed by it. Interestingly, this is the opposite of what neofunctionalists had hoped to achieve: instead of politicisation (the process of linking the management of integration with the daily lives of EU citizens) becoming an additional weapon in the strategic arsenal of pro-integrationist forces, it is increasingly used by the more sceptical actors, often by means of resorting to nationalistic sentiments, thus making it difficult to mobilise the constituent publics in favour of higher levels of integration and, eventually, towards a 'complete equilibrium' among different levels of authority. Such a development, by contesting the idea that European polity-formation is a linear process towards a clearly discernible federal end, may lead to Schmitter's imaginative depiction of a condominium-type organisation (see Chapter 2), characterised by 'multiple flexible equilibria'.

In the CFSP, as mentioned earlier in this study, the Treaty provides for a limited extension of majority voting for detailed policy implementation; the appointment of a 'High Representative'; the creation of an 'early warning and planning unit'; and the possibility of 'constructive abstention' in Joint Actions. But the outcome of the Amsterdam process shows that Europe did not manage to develop an independent capability within the Union. Yet this is not to say that European states confronted with a choice between national action and integration have chosen the former.[3] In the first place, in opting against an exclusively EU security and defence component, they are opting for strengthening institutionalised co-operation within NATO. Moreover, regional security and defence co-operation shows no immediate signs of lessening in intensity outside the Union's formal institutional structures. Many co-operative ventures have been launched: the European Arms Agency; Eurofor and Euromarfor; the Franco-British Joint Air Command; the Eurocorps, and so on. That this co-operation took place outside the framework of integration is explicable by two factors, as the discussion in Chapters 5 and 6 has shown. First, the very existence of an alternative and highly successful framework tends to divert attention and resources away from the idea of linking defence with the Union. The fact that NATO exists and works cannot be underestimated. Second, states tend jealously to guard their autonomy over public policy unless compelling reasons exist for them to turn to integration as a solution. Even in areas where the Union nominally enjoys a great deal of influence over policy, the member states have been anxious to preserve their freedom of manoeuvre. This is all the more true for defence and security. Moreover, the absence of a direct threat weakens any rationale for agreeing to a higher level of integration in defence matters. In this context, it was not the debate on the Union but that on NATO and its role that was conceived as the most crucial issue affecting the physiognomy of any prospective security restructuring in Europe, for it related to multiple and inter-connected international relations issues: change in the world security polarity; core–periphery relations; definition of threat as a precondition of security configuration; fragmentation and integration; redefinition of power and its effectiveness; redefinition of national visions, preferences and interests; re-eval-uation of US leadership and EU strategy; and re-assessment of institutions and demands for international regimes.[4] Finally, as discussed in Chapter 6, the December 2000 Nice European Council formalised developments in EU secu-rity and defence by setting up an ESDP within the CFSP as well as a planned ERRF, which is to become 'operational' in 2003.

Turning in greater detail to the Nice treaty-amending process, after four-day marathon talks, an agreement was finally reached that the larger states will retain their second Commissioner until 2005, while each member state may nominate one Commissioner until the time when the Union expands to twenty-seven members (initially, IGC discussions included Turkey, but it was felt that its sheer size, among other issues, might complicate the negotiations). It was also agreed that the four largest states will each have 29 instead of 10 votes in the Council (which means that three large states and a small one could form a blocking minority, whose threshold was raised to circa 73 per cent), while the small- and medium-sized members will each have between 3 and 13 votes (which means that while the larger states' votes have increased threefold, those of the smaller states have only doubled). Also, the threshold of seats in the EP has been raised to 732 in an enlarged EU of twenty-seven members – Turkey was originally included in the logistics but was then dropped owing to its sheer size and controversy surrounding its eventual accession – thus exceeding the 700-seat threshold agreed in Amsterdam. QMV, as in earlier revisions, has been extended to largely non-controversial areas (save for the appointment of the Commission President), including international trade agreements (services, investment and intellectual rights), external border controls and certain visa rules, freedom of movement for non-EU nationals, treatment of illegal immi-grants, judicial co-operation in civil cases, emergency supplies in times of crisis and natural disasters, social exclusion and social welfare modernisation, state aid for industry, regional subsidies, financial and technical co-operation with non-EU members, etc.

Other changes included the possibility of applying flexible integration schemes within the Community pillar, but with the Commission's involvement, and under new decision rules in the European Council – i.e., by revising the 'emergency brake' procedure – provided, however, that at least eight states, instead of a majority, were willing to participate. Moreover, the work of the Court of First Instance was linked to the activities of the newly-instituted Judi-cial Panels, which, courtesy of Art. 225a EC, were authorised to deal with rele-vant cases. Finally, a fresh round of institutional reforms was agreed to take place in 2004, a time when Poland, Hungary and the Czech Republic (among others like Slovenia, Slovakia and Cyprus) are expected to join, covering, *inter alia*, the division of competences between the Union, the states and possibly subnational authorities; the status of the Charter of Fundamental Rights; the simplification of the Treaties; and the role of national parliaments in the integration process (see below).

In a high-stakes endgame, which undoubtedly brought on a flash of *déjà vu*, the NIT clearly lacked a departure of substance for the creation of 'norms of polity' centred on the specific constructions of legitimate governance. As the *Guardian* succinctly put it: 'At every stage of the prolonged negotiation, raw national interest has overshadowed the broader vision.'[5] Or, as *The Times* remarked: 'It is, at best, a ramshackle palace that has been cobbled together.'[6] As a result, Nice failed to discover 'a sense of process' (and purpose) over the transformation of a plurality of demoi into a pluralistic demos and, hence, the emergence of a new *pouvoir constituant* as 'the ultimate legitimising referent of the [Euro-] polity'.[7] This is linked to yet another crucial transformation the Union ought to undertake, 'from an ethics of integration to an ethics of participation': 'a deliberative process whereby citizens reach mutually acceptable agreements that balance their various communitarian commitments in ways that reflect a cosmopolitan regard for fairness.'[8] In Mény's words: 'There is a need for a new civic culture ... which allows for multiple allegiances, which combines the "right to roots" with the "right to options".'[9]

Following Dehousse's analysis of the Union's 'unstable equilibrium', 'although the parliamentary system remains by far the dominant paradigm in the discourse on the reform of European institutions, the last decade has witnessed a gradual emergence of issues and instruments which do not correspond to the parliamentary tradition'.[10] As Kohler-Koch put it, 'the EU is not just institutionally retired, but lives in a social environment that does not fulfil the prerequisites for representative democracy'.[11] Arguably, recent reforms have placed the EP closer to the *locus decidendi* of the system by extending the scope of co-decision and by simplifying the procedures therein (by changing the 'default condition' in the conciliation procedure). Although these reforms sought to address the Union's 'parliamentary deficit' by facilitating the emergence of a *de facto* European bicameral system, increased co-decision was not always linked with greater QMV,[12] nor has the EP's right of assent been extended to legislation in third-pillar issues, to decisions over the Community's 'own resources',[13] and to formal treaty reform.

Moving on to the issue of transparency, a principle inspired by notions of 'open government', Amsterdam succeeded in providing European citizens with a (conditional) right of information, by covering, in Dehousse's words, 'the practical modalities of [public] access' to official EU documents.[14] But it failed to contribute to a more comprehensible Treaty, as the simplification of some legislative procedures like co-decision was coupled with the institutionalisation (or even instrumentalisation) of other practices like flexibility, exceptions, reservations, safeguards, protocols, declarations and the rest which, taken together, arguably represent an exercise in 'cognitive difficulty'.[15] On balance, however, a formalisation of transparency procedures has taken place: their *de jure* incorporation into the Treaty. Whereas previously such procedures were determined by interinstitutional arrangements and rules of procedure, the ECJ can now monitor the implementation of a 'norm' of legislative openness as an operational principle of European governance. For all their shortcomings, the new transparency rules are now part of the EU's 'primary law'.[16] Yet, as Cram *et al.* categorically asserted, 'the post-Amsterdam EU is even more arcane and complex than its already impenetrable predecessor'.[17]

Regardless of one's pro/contra integrationist convictions, there is evidence to suggest that the phasing-in of questions of democracy and legitimacy in the Union's public agenda has not yet transcended the anxiety of states, both individually and collectively, to safeguard their own prerogatives, even when these questions became crucial to the political viability of the general system. Instead of focusing on issues that constitute the essence of any well-thought-out process of democratic reform, the largely unimaginative quality of proposals submitted to the review conferences, both of which were assigned the task of preparing the central institutions of governance for further waves of enlargement, highlighted in a most clear and tenacious way the absence of a clear democratic vision to take the European construction dynamically into the new millennium. As Weiler rightly suggests, '[w]hereas in its founding period Europe was positioned as a *response* to a crisis of confidence, fifty years later it has shifted to become one of the causes of that crisis'.[18] Both the Amsterdam and Nice reforms failed on the above accounts, not least because they lacked a kind of 'innovative reflection' on the possibilities of constructing a European civic space out of the segments' varied traditions. Instead, both processes focused on 'distributive compromises',[19] with a view to embodying the particularistic attitudes and claims of self-interested actors in negotiated package deals. This outcome is in line with the EU's *modus consociandi*, resulting in a sacrifice in democratic input for greater efficiency in output.

Indeed, the largest deficiency of both Amsterdam and Nice was their emphasis on policy rather than polity, efficiency rather than democracy, distributive compromise rather than integrative accommodation, functionalist structures rather than shared normative commitments and, above all, the rationalist exercise of competences rather than symbiotic legitimation. In particular, the areas upon which these reforms focused concerned the rationalisation and simplification of decision-making procedures (co-decision), voting adjustments (re-weighting of votes) and voting mechanisms (extension of QMV) and, in general, measures concerning the effectiveness of EU decision-making as a precondition for the future functioning, but not legitimation, of the general system. Ironically, this elaborate exercise in rationalised institutionalism originally aimed at rectifying a long-standing criticism of the Community as a 'joint decision-system', in that it tends to produce suboptimal policy outputs and, at the level of negotiated package deals, an inequitable *status quo*. For these reasons, both revision processes emerge as managerial types of reform, where affective/identitive politics still remains without reach. Their core principles rest not on the need for cementing the constitutive (even dialectical) norms of a polycentric civic space as a precondition for deliberative equity and substantive public engagement, but rather on a politics of consensus elite government determined by suboptimal exchanges within an overly complex negotiation system. Not surprisingly, then, the general assessment is that a European civic space based on the co-constitution of normative structures has yet to emerge.

Reflections on the future of Europe

The intense debate during the period leading to the AMT continued with the occasion of a publication by the Commission under the title 'Agenda 2000'.[20] It is worth looking at the content of this initiative as it constituted the prelude to a more engaging debate that was to follow a few years later on the future of Europe. The Commission put forward in the report its views on the future development of the Union ahead of the enlargement negotiations with each of the applicant countries. In particular, it 'outlines in a single framework the broad perspectives for the development of the EU and its policies beyond the turn of the century, the horizontal issues related to enlargement, and the future financial framework beyond 2000 . . . in an enlarged EU'. The report is divided into two parts, dealing with internal and enlargement issues, respectively. Internally, it sets four priority areas for action. The first concerned the setting of the conditions for sustainable employment and intensive growth, prescribing all those initiatives where priority is given either *de facto* or by choice of policy. Thus EMU and the introduction of the Euro on 1 January 1999 within the European banking system (for public use since January 2002), together with accompanying and/or supportive measures such as the Stability and Growth Pact (SGP), and the Action Plan endorsed in Amsterdam (emphasising rule simplification and the consolidation of the single market programme).[21] Competition rules were to be simplified and surveillance and enforcement structures modernised in partnership between national and central levels of governance. Priority was also given to the small and medium-sized enterprises (SMEs), and measures were proposed to facilitate their performance.[22] Sustainable development, which became part of the Union's objectives with the AMT, was expected to enhance the competitiveness of the European industry and services if reflected in environmentally sustainable production and consumption patterns and if the newest technologies were incorporated into the Union's environmental policy. Trans-European networks were given priority 'to enhance both the sustainable development and the internal cohesion of the Union,'[23] with the new rounds of enlargement also in mind. The second area was the placement of knowledge and technology at the forefront. Here, the Commission proclaims that research, innovation, education and training are of 'decisive importance for the development of the Union'.[24] Priority was given to research and technological development, focusing on ways of enhancing European competitiveness and creating jobs. Education and training received priority status, too, with emphasis on the exchange of personnel. The third area related to the modernisation of employment systems. Labour market and employment policies were to achieve maximum flexibility for the enterprises and maximum security for individuals in conjunction with the new Title on Employment in the AMT. Issues such as investment in the skills of the existing workforce, increase in participation rates, encouragement of mobility and dialogues between the workforce and management in anticipation of restructuring of the enterprises receive added currency. Reform of pensions and healthcare systems in view of adverse demographic developments represented another major challenge in the Commission's report. These were to be reconciled with budgetary rectitude, with the Union acting in a co-ordinating capacity, serving as a forum for promoting better mutual understanding of long-term perspectives and for identifying common challenges.[25] The fourth area finally related to the improvement of living conditions. Expected growth was linked with the promotion of a more cohesive and inclusive European society, with the Union intensifying its efforts to combat all forms of social exclusion and discrimination. Public health, the environment, the free movement of people, adequate levels of security and justice, the fight against fraud, crime, corruption and so on – all add up to a quality of life problem for post-materialist European societies, and have to be addressed as a priority, in light of increased public awareness.

With reference to the Union's external relations, the Commission's slogans were 'a stable Europe that is open to the world' and 'a strong and coherent Europe'. Relations with Russia, mainly owing to the eastward enlargement of NATO and of the Union itself with the possible inclusion of populations of ethnic Russian origin, mainly in Latvia and Estonia, were singled out for improvement, as were those with the Balkan countries that have signed association agreements with the Union. The latter, provided that it does not repeat the CFSP fiasco of the Yugoslav civil war, can become a stabilising force in the wider area, as these countries are actively seeking to become its members. The democratic reform process in these countries, currently in severe financial difficulties (especially Romania, Albania and Bulgaria), should be kept alive with the active support of the Union. The report also stresses the importance for the Union of the south Mediterranean area in relation to the Barcelona Process: a partnership agreement between the Union and the twelve non-EU Mediterranean countries (including the Palestinian Authority) covering political (security), economic (free trade area and financial projects) and sociocultural (civil society and intercultural dialogue) issues.[26] Development co-operation constituted the third major item in the Commission's agenda, and a new but unspecified form of partnership between the Union and the African, Caribbean and Pacific (ACP) countries was put forward, although, surprisingly, relations with Latin American countries, but also with the US, were somewhat downgraded in the report.

For the more effective intervention of the Union in international affairs, the report suggested that a more integrated approach should be built, meaning, and rightly so, that the artificial distinction between external economic and external political affairs be gradually phased out with more use of QMV. But all the above are more easily said than done, as successive treaty reforms have time and again reminded us. Thus, if the Union is going to move where the Agenda 2000 report wishes, it will need all the stamina and courage it can mobilise to persuade both its member states and demoi that this course of action is the best way forward.

But what might the best way forward be for the fledging European polity? A positive attempt at defining the new challenges confronting integration post-Nice can be attributed to the Commission's White Paper on European Governance, published in July 2001.[27] In it, the Commission identified the reasons for reforming existing modes of European governance and ascertained those principles of good governance that should guide the formulation and delivery of common policies and regulations. Among these principles, openess, transparency, participation, accountability, effectiveness and coherence – all of which are also linked to proportionality, subsidiarity and flexibility – figured prominently in the Commission's reformist menu, which represented a comprehensive approach to the challenges of complex institutional restructuring and positive European awareness-formation at the grassroots (with renewed emphasis on the future role of civil society representatives in EU policy-initiation). The White Paper formed part of a long-awaited European public debate, effectively launched with the address of German Foreign Minister Fischer to Humbold University in Berlin on 12 May 2000.

In particular, Fischer's *Vom Staatenverbund zur Föderation*,[28] by embodying a strong normative orientation towards some prototype European *Bundesrepublik* – i.e., to the extent that the end product will also be democratically structured – was instrumental in reviving European public debate and in some instances re-activating dormant national reflexes about the *finalité* of the Union. Likewise, it ignited the interest of both academic and policy communities about the future political – and, this time in more explicit terms than hitherto – constitutional evolution of the European polity. The timing of Fischer's federalist blueprint was rather strategically calculated, as it was launched three months after the IGC 2000 had been formally inaugurated and only three days after the fiftieth anniversary of the Schuman Plan. Although the then ongoing review conference was generally regarded as dealing with the 'Amsterdam leftovers', as opposed to being a self-conscious attempt at polity transformation through a substantive constitutional re-ordering or even re-design, the 'Fischer debate' – taken as a debate on good European governance – received a warm welcome, least of all by integration scholarship, as it signalled 'a truly bright and refreshing breath of fresh air in today's politics'.[29] Whether 'an unconventional type of political act', Fischer's address inspired, if not nurtured, a shift in emphasis from the unimaginative language often articulated by high-ranking technocrats to a more accessible terminology, mirroring some fundamental – and conceptual – challenges and dilemmas confronting European political society.

More specifically, in his capacity as a European and German parliamentarian, rather than as the official foreign representative of the German federal government, Fischer posed the question *Quo vadis Europa?* In the interests of economy, we offer a summative account of the normative underpinnings of his answer, which are to be found in his deontological call for a European constitutional treaty or *Verfassungsvertrag* centred around basic human rights; shared sovereignty; a division of competences between the Union and the states via a *Kompetenzkatalog*; a clear division of powers among the central institutions, including full parliamentarisation through the institutionalisation of a European bicameral structure – leaving, however, the option for the nature and composition of the upper house open between a US-inspired Senate model of directly elected members and a German-type chamber of state representatives with different numbers of votes; and a European Government formed either by the unit governments (thus developing the European Council into a government proper) or by a directly elected Commission President with extensive executive and administrative powers (thus transforming the existing Commission into a hierarchical structure of government). Far from encouraging the abolition of the member states, not least owing to the richness and diversity of their historically constituted cultures and traditions, his vision encompasses the notion of a lean but fully fledged European federation.

In response to Fischer's proposals, a clear, albeit qualified, federalist orientation was also recorded from many high-ranking figures like Rau, Schröder, Verhofstadt, Barnier, Bayrou, Prodi and Simitis; Chirac and Blair, opting for rather less federalist polity ideas and assorted policy *menus* that strengthen national statehood (envisioning an enhanced Council Secretariat, greater agenda powers for the Council and a Senate composed of national parliamentarians); and Jospin, influenced by Delors' preference for a 'mixed' system of governance (favouring greater central powers and even a directly elected President, but rejecting both the ideas for a second chamber and a federal core). But there has also been some justified criticism by EU scholarship regarding the emphasis placed in Fischer's federalist blueprint on the division, rather than the sharing, of sovereignty rights between the Union and the states. Börzel and Risse make the point well: 'Fischer still thinks in categories of the hierarchically structured nation-state with its exclusive authority over power and territory, including the legitimate monopoly over the use of (internal and external) force.'[30] Instead, they conceptualise a European federal order from the perspective of multilevel governance, stressing the importance of distinguishing between 'formal' and 'material' sovereignty: the former, they claim, is already divided, but also shared, between EU and nation-state authorities, whilst the latter is defined in degrees of the capacity for autonomous action.[31] Material sovereignty is central to understanding the Union as a multilevel system of governance, in that it 'does not easily translate into a constitutional language, which should delineate who is in charge of what and when, and thus, should define structures of formal sovereignty'.[32]

Thus depicted, the present-day European polity encompasses subnational, national, supranational and transnational institutions and processes, public, semi-public and private interests, as well as a plethora of 'governance arenas', 'negotiating networks', 'functional regimes' and the like, within which material sovereignty is shared across and between levels by a multiplicity of actors that interact regularly in the determination of policy outcomes. A further line of criticism was directed against Fischer's conceptual typology, in that his envisaged *finalité* amounted to a European federation but not a federal state, thus on the one hand attempting to escape the confines of classical constitutional theory without, on the other, formulating a conceptual alternative. Even the term he uses to describe the Union, *Staatenverbund* – a term inspired by the *Bundesverfassungsgericht* in its oft-quoted 'Maastricht ruling' – is, according to von Boyme,[33] practically untranslatable in all but the Swedish language, courtesy of the term *Statsförbundet*. If, then, such is the confusion over the Union's present stance, and for that matter Fischer's conceptual departure, and if no alternative term is offered for the imagined end state, how can one conceptualise Fischer's 'third-way' construct of 'federation without a state'? A plausible answer is offered by Leben, who notes that federation *à la* Fischer might have been influenced by Schmitt's ideas on a 'federative pact', aiming to reconcile seemingly irreconcilable elements, by advancing a public law conception of the federation, whereby the member states, both as the authors of the pact as well as constitutive units, retain their sovereignty.[34] Yet, whichever direction the constitutional development of the Union takes, Fischer's blueprint requires, in his own words, 'a deliberative political act to re-establish Europe'. This observation has fundamental implications for the emergence of a genuine European public sphere in the sense of becoming something more than the Europeanisation of the component political spaces. The institutionalisation of the envisaged composite public sphere lies, in our view, at the heart of any substantive move towards a qualitatively new European polity characterised by symbiotic legitimation, accountability, and communicative structures. In Olsen's words:

> A *public* discourse about the adequacy, or inadequacy, of existing institutional arrangements can be a process of civic education through which European citizens develop an understanding of what constitutes a good society and system of governance, ie, the legitimate constitutional principles of authority, power and accountability, and the normative-ethical basis, and value commitments and beliefs, of the polity.[35]

In this civic conception of the European polity, the constituent publics, in the form of a transnational civic demos, are capable of directing their democratic claims to, and via, the central institutions, through free public deliberation. In this context, democratic deliberation takes precedence over interest aggregation, as does civic over state/Union competence, and social over empirical legitimacy.

Finally, and whether or not further integration is to be pursued through 'a Hayekian discovery procedure' or through a 'pre-thought-out blueprint',[36] the search for legitimate forms of collective governance in Europe is central to the construction of a political community founded on more active and inclusionary virtues of belonging such as civic self-reliance and institutionalised participation: a European *res publica*, that is, composed of constitutive but equally sovereign citizens. The task at hand requires also a fundamental change in the current philosophy of European governance, in the sense of moving away from output-oriented, utilitarian, task-driven and cost-effective/reducing problem-solving modes of collective action, embracing instead the long-standing need to call greater attention to the relationship between the Union and 'the civic', with the view to transforming the governing capacity of its nascent demos into a system-steering agency. For ultimately, it is within this embracing civic space that a feature central to the democratic process – national or transnational – becomes crucial, that of 'civic competence': the institutional capacity of citizens *qua* social equals to enter the realm of political influence and sustain a vital public sphere – 'a network that gives citizens . . . an equal opportunity to take part in an encompassing process of focused political communication'.[37] Here, the pairing of 'civic' and 'competence' does not embody a category mistake, but rather acts in the interests of engaging the demos in the management of public affairs, institutionalising, through the granting of substantive civic entitlements, a normative commitment to core democratic values, while giving an institutional face to a central task of legitimate public life: active civic participation in the governance of the polity.

The above discussion brings to the fore the question of strengthening common citizenship rights and duties: a debate, however, which needs to be linked with the prospects for constitutionalisating the Charter of Fundamental rights. Indeed, the IGC 2004 offers an excellent opportunity for adding to the existing corpus of EU citizenship rights with a view to elevating this novel *status civitatis* to an independent sphere of civic entitlements. The need for positive action in that regard is urgent, especially in view of the importance of providing a sense of civic attachment to the collectivity and a shared sense of the public good that transcends the nationally determined fix between norms of citizenship and the (territorial) state. But this requires in turn a certain dosage of determination by the Union to redress effectively its constitutional shortcomings and to strengthen the range and depth of civic participation (deliberative or other) in the exercise of political authority. Out of a voluminous set of measures to build on the development of a transnational civic demos, the following merit our attention: institutionalising at Union level the notion of civic competence, thus adding it to the more conventional way of thinking about competences as statutory guarantees or the capacity for authoritative action; extending the right to vote and to stand as a candidate at national elections for citizens residing in a member state other than their own; introducing the right of European citizens to hold public office anywhere within the Union; enshrining the citizens' right to information on all EU issues, while making all the official documents of the Union available to the public; introducing the right of European citizens, individually or collectively, to be informed when a decision of the Union impinges on specific interests; recognising full political rights to legally resident third-country nationals (denizens), thus transcending any liberal–statist norms of civic inclusion and rejecting a 'dissociational-type democracy' at Union level; and codifying the principles of additionality and non-regression so that Union citizenship rights are established in addition to national ones, while ensuring that existing rights are not reduced.

At a more general level, the distinction between an extra-treaty arrangement – i.e., an EU Charter that provides only for a standard for fundamental rights – and a legally binding instrument that provides for a set of basic rights guarantees is vital, for in the latter case, a Charter incorporated into the Treaty would also be made subject to the jurisdiction of the ECJ. It would also grant the latter a crucial interpretative function with regard to human rights respect and protection throughout the Union. Also, with an internally justiciable Charter, the Union would make a positive as well as credible move towards what has been described as 'a more human rights-based constitutionalism'. Yet, a potential problem remains, as many legal experts were quick to point out: were the ECJ to be become the last instance of appeal in the Union for human rights issues, this might deprive its citizens of a final external appeal against violations of their fundamental rights. The only sensible way to avoid this predicament, as well as the possibility of two competing jurisdictions, is for the Union to accede to the European Convention on Human Rights (ECHR). In that way, it is claimed that ECJ rulings related to the ECHR would be made subject to the supervision of the ECHR, thus enhancing the accountability of the ECJ itself. This brings us to another complex legal issue, but with crucial political implications, not only for the quality of human rights protection and enforcement standards within the Union, but also for transnational demos-formation. Would a legally binding Charter have general application throughout the member states, or would it be restricted to fundamental rights protection only in the context of EU action? Put differently, would the Charter apply in cases of member state action (taken by central, regional or local authorities, or public organisations) that is not directly linked to the implementation of EU law, as Art. 51(1) of the Charter currently provides for? Assuming that the prevalent interpretation is that the Charter is indeed confined to EU action alone, and despite the drafters' *prima facie* intention to consolidate the current method of the ECJ to deal with questions of basic rights as 'general principles of Community law', given the nature and scope of the rights enshrined in the Charter, far more positive action is needed. Such action could take the form of amending Art. 51(1) with a view to extending the Charter's applicability to state action that is not linked directly to EU activities. Bold as this step may be, its case becomes even stronger if one links fundamental rights protection with the free movement of people within an integrated economic space operating under a single currency system. Taking rights (more) seriously, ascribes to the concept and process of 'Chartering Europe' their proper meaning, while endowing the Union with a political constitution proper. In line, finally, with a neo-republican approach to EU polity-building (see Chapter 2), the Charter attempts to bridge the long-standing rights/duties divide, by explicitly stating in the preamble that '[e]njoyment of these rights entail responsibilities and duties [especially the provisions on solidarity] with regard to other persons, the human community and to future generations'.

Arguably, all the above proposals are easier said than done. But if properly institutionalized, they would bring about an EU citizenship policy proper, as they ultimately depend on the political will of the member state executives, rather than on an overarching European *volonté générale* at the grassroots. In this way also, the Union would be equipped to allocate authoritatively, and not merely derivatively, rights (and values) within European civic society. The outcome would be not to create a 'community of fate' or *Schicksalsgemeinschaft* shaped by common descent, language, history and the like, but rather to 'democratise' the constitution of European citizenship and facilitate the horizontal integration of citizens in conformity to the norms and practices of EU-wide civic inclusion. It would also elevate its civic status to a distinctive form of 'meta-citizenship' and endow the Union with a distinctive political subject, whose collective civic identity exists independent of national public spheres, but whose 'politics' extends to both European and national civic arenas. Moreover, such a move would signal a shift in the basis of legitimation from a functionalist-driven, segmentary-type of (mainly) economic European civic body to a political community of free and equal citizens – i.e., a *populus liber* driven by a *charitas civicum*. Although such profound changes in the political constitution of Europe would almost certainly spark a series of substantive, and for some even unpleasant, amendments to national constitutions, basic laws or parliamentary statutes, for any well-thought-out and at the same time consequential debate on European democracy to come full circle – assuming of course that such a democracy will not go through all the developmental stages of Western liberal democracy – such proposals should be part of the discursive agenda on the constitutional (or other) future(s) of Europe, the member states and, crucially, the candidate countries. Such normative commitments at instituting a multilevel civic space within which the constituent publics are recognised as bearers of rights, freedoms and duties in relation, however, to the larger polity can also act as an antidote to the growing impoverishment of national public life, where an apparent decline in the quality of public discourse and civic participation is met by a shrinking (social) legitimacy of 'the political'.

Turning finally to the Charter's drafting process, and *pace* the absence of any formalised selection criteria, it has opened the way for a more visible, deliberative and inclusive method of EU polity-building – i.e., a European public process. Indeed, the symbolic importance attributed to the composition of the drafting Convention, but also of the new Convention in view of the IGC 2004, is that it marked a 'break point' in the politics of institutional representation at

Union level, particularly with reference to the transparency and social legitimacy of collective constitutional engineering (both elements were emphatically absent in previous treaty reforms, although during the IGC 2000 an abundance of related material became available in cyberspace). In addition, such a strategy has exemplified an acute and increasingly alarming 'democratic disjunction' between the state-controlled nature of treaty change (through unanimity and asymmetrically negotiated outcomes) and the impact of civil and civic society on the debate about the future of Europe. Accordingly, to ensure the pluralistic and participatory nature of the Charter's drafting formula, it would be desirable, at least from a political–constitutionalist perspective, to use its template for future treaty-amending processes. Should that prove too much for sovereignty-conscious states to digest, and there is an abundance of realist state-centric explanations and reasons why it should, an alternative, more pragmatic scenario would be for the EP to be granted constitutional competence over treaty reform through the assent procedure, acting by an absolute majority of its members. Having looked at the Charter, we can now turn to the remaining items on the IGC 2004 agenda: competence allocation, Treaty simplification, and the role of national parliaments.

Prospects for the IGC 2004

Allocating competences

Since this question is linked in both conceptual and operative terms with the governing structure of multilevel polities, some general observations are in order. To start with, multilevel polities perform functions that are either shared in common among different levels of decision-making, or are assigned to particular governmental settings that are seen as being either more legitimate or efficient structures for the performance of given tasks. Such polities are compound states based as much on informal and *ad hoc* arrangements of shared rule as on internal political pressures for self-governance. Hence, the search for appropriate forms and means of a division of competences is at the heart of the viability of composite systems aiming to reconcile what constitutes the cornerstone of all systems of dispersed authority: 'unity in diversity' and, at the level of joint decision-making, 'consensus in pluriformity'. A voluminous literature exists on both formal and informal constitutional and procedural mechanisms through which polity-builders attempt to transcend real or perceived divisions over what can be termed as 'capacity for governance'. Central to this issue is the distribution of formal legislative and executive authority, the form and range of such distribution, and the variegated possibilities for exclusive, concurrent or residual competences. In Western liberal polities, there is a strong predisposition to safeguard the essential norms of democratic governance, with the tensions between different levels of authority often being exacerbated by reference to their acclaimed 'democrativeness'. Such problems are compounded further by the extent to which the polity at hand is characterised by centralised or decentralised tendencies, symmetrical or asymmetrical relationships among the subunits, centripetal or centrifugal dynamics, and constitutional or less formalised guarantees for constituent autonomy. When the founding act of the polity is not a formal constitution accompanied by a supreme court, a system of rule based on Montesquieu's *trias politica* and a *Kompetenzkatalog*, but instead rests on a constituent act, pact, contract, convention or treaty, then the level of systemic ambiguity increases dramatically.

The Union is an excellent case for studying questions of multilevel competence allocation – and even of multilevel constitutionalism – owing to its in-built pluralism and variability. But the way in which subsidiarity operates in the Union chimes well with a consociationalist understanding of politics, as it justifies a potential flow of decision-making powers to nation-state authorities, thus offering a 'partial offset' to the quest for legislative autonomy within the component polities. This line of reasoning confirms the view that the principle resembles a kind of 'reserved powers' to the states: a self-defence mechanism against the accretion of competences to the centre. From this prism also, it is difficult to overlook signs of an inverse type of federalism, favouring the diffusion of power down to national tiers of governance, with the 'burden of proof' lying with the Community that has to justify through a public reason argument the compatibility of proposed legislation with the subsidiarity principle. Like previous references to the latter (a 'bottom-up' approach to fiscal federalism, or in the context of cross-frontier dimension effects, or as a policy instrument of economic intervention), there is no provision in the Treaties for the precise allocation of competences, nor is there any distinction between different types of competences – i.e., exclusive, concurrent and potential. This amounts to 'the problem of competence': the absence of an explicit formal mechanism for allocating responsibilities within the Union, outside the areas that, in principle, are considered to be its exclusive prerogative: the four freedoms of movement and the policies that are a corollary to them. It follows that the areas falling within the internal market sphere are not subject to the principle of subsidiarity, but are determined by the pre-emption doctrine, in that once the Community legislates in one area, then national action is being precluded. Accordingly, subsidiarity can be used as a rule for competence allocation only in cases of concurrence, or when the Community has for the first time passed legislation in a new field. In matters unaffected by Community law, the argument goes, it is presumed that the component states retain exclusive competence.

There is a case to be made for the powers specifically entrusted to the centre to be enlisted in the Treaty, as for instance the Australian Constitution does (Art. 51 stipulates thirty-nine areas which fall within the jurisdiction of the Federal Parliament); or that a clear mechanism to delegate specific competences to the centre be provided for, as in the case of the German *Grundgesetz* (Art. 72 II listing the conditions under which the *Bund* has the right to legislate); or that there is an explicit reference to the sovereignty of the parts as in the Swiss Constitution

(Art. 3 stating that the cantons are sovereign insofar as their sovereignty suffers no restriction from the federal constitution); or even that a 'residual clause' be included in a manner similar to the US Constitution (the Tenth Amendment of 1791 which created a sense of 'constitutive autonomy'). These polities, similarly to the Union, have followed, *ceteris paribus*, a pattern of competence attribution, where the emphasis was on specifying a limited set of central competences, with the residual powers resting with the subunits. Reflecting on their experience, the case for centralised governance has to be proved. This is justified on the grounds that the segments, in the form of previously independent polities, have preceded the creation of the federation. Such an approach falls within the logic of 'bottom-up' subsidiarity, derived from the Catholic social doctrine on the relationship between the individual, the state and society, as well as on a vertical division of power within federal polities. Although an ensemble *sui generis* formula should not be excluded for the Union, central to any constitutional settlement is the principle of proportionality, already an element of Community case law: 'Any action by the Community shall not go beyond what is necessary to achieve the objectives of this Treaty', a principle which does not alter the attribution of competence, but concerns the way in which central power should be exercised once the Community level has been authorised to take appropriate action. The rationale here is that central legislative action should not exceed what is necessary to meet the end in view. In other words, such action has to be *intra vires*.

In attempting to clarify the conditions for applying subsidiarity, the Commission has explicitly asserted the primacy of states, in that '[the] conferment of powers is a matter for the writers of our constitution, that is to say of the treaty. A consequence of this is that the powers conferred on the Community, in contrast to those reserved to the states, cannot be assumed.' The point here is that the states, as the conferring agency, could 'de-confer' if they wish to. In the end, the following criteria for central action were set out as guidelines on subsidiarity: whether the issue at hand has transnational effects that cannot be satisfactorily regulated by state action; whether state action or lack of Community action would conflict with Treaty requirements and significantly damage states' interests; whether the Council must be satisfied that Community action would produce clear benefits of scale or effects. Although these guidelines found their way into a detailed protocol agreed in Amsterdam, it is still the Community that has to justify compliance of proposed action to these principles. Moreover, there is no mention of substate units. *Ceteris paribus*, directives should be preferred to regulations, and so should framework directives (assigned the task of fixing objectives and guidelines) to detailed measures, thus leaving as much scope for national decision-making as possible. Although this may be revisited by the Convention and, eventually, by the 2004 IGC itself, it should be linked both to the preferred means of implementing and monitoring EU law (when different formulas are required according to different policy stages) and to the question of creating a hierarchy of Community Acts.

What still remains of crucial importance, however, is for a balance to be struck between state and EU competences on what level of aggregation should act on which types of issue. In view of the discussion above, and given the existing difficulties in implementing subsidiarity, a possible outline of action in relation to the IGC 2004 is to 'constitutionalise' the process of competence attribution, instead of delineating *expressis verbi* spheres of legislative authority and to set up a new instrument – i.e., a Committee of Competence Attribution – of a mixed composition (consisting of national representatives as well as members of the major EU institutions, including the CoR and the ECJ) that would provide complementary checks and balances to the existing framework by assessing disputed acts, should any of the actors involved in EU legislation call into question a proposal on the grounds of subsidiarity and proportionality. The proposed Committee would not have to be permanent (although that would help to develop its own institutional culture) and its rulings could take the form of recommendations. Given the immense complexities in the Union's legal system, the interconnectedness of national and collective modes of policy action, and the profound cross-border effects of joint decisions, it is fair to say that the idea of a *Kompetenzkatalog* is not the most productive way forward, as it could deprive integration from its inherent dynamism and flexibility. But equally problematic is Blair's view, as expressed in a speech delivered in Warsaw in October 2000, to contain a general delimitation of powers in a politically binding 'Statement of Principles'. Interesting as the idea of a Charter of Competences may be for future reference – i.e., on the eve of drafting a material European Constitution through a European Constituent Assembly – a more plausible alternative to those presented above is to enshrine in the Treaty, under the heading 'Competence Attribution', a core set of basic principles governing the attribution of competences within the Union, including also provisions for the active participation of subnational authorities. Such an arrangement, as noted earlier, should be seen within the wider context of framework directives becoming more widely used by the central authorities.

Pace the constitutional arrangements currently in place in some of its federal subsystems, and particularly the insistence of the *Länder* for a strict division of competences, one could legitimately argue that both the constitutional architecture and decision-making culture of the Union *qua* 'non-state polity' are not (as yet) in a position to resolve questions of competence allocation through an explicit delineation of legislative powers among the Union's constitutive levels of governance. Moreover, whether or not the existing *acquis* is inherently incompatible with the principle of subsidiarity, the fact remains that a system of delimited competences is prone to limit the future ambitions of the Union, not least of all in terms of extending its grip over new or relatively undeveloped policies (such as taxation and education); open the way for the re-nationalisaton of common policies (especially in agricultural matters); and create a complex world of 'micro-competences' that would deprive the Union of the levels of flexibility needed to deal effectively with new challenges (most notably in the social field). Thus, the drawing up of a set of governing principles (and mechanisms) for competence attribution within the Union, as opposed to a legally or politically binding Charter of Competences *à la* Fischer or Blair, fits better the current profile of the larger polity as a constitutional system *in statu nascendi*.

Simplifying the treaties

The perennial issue of simplifying the Treaties has been the subject of inquiry for some time. Most prominent among these studies has been the report commissioned to the EUI by the Commission. It appeared under the title 'Reorganisation of the Treaties' on 15 May 2000, that is, a few months after the IGC 2000 began its work and only three days after Fischer's address. The resulting draft was entitled 'Basic Treaty of the European Union' consisted of eight Titles and ninety-five Clauses (incorporating the major constitutive features of the Union), and demonstrated the feasibility of the exercise, as the task required a great amount of technical work, as well as its desirability, in that an exceedingly complex set of Treaty provisions would become simpler, more readable and, hence, more accessible to both European citizens and the candidate publics. Hardly surprisingly, the work of the drafting group revealed numerous ambiguities, inconsistencies, lacunae and contradictions inherent, to borrow a metaphor, in the 'loose and baroque structure' of the existing Treaties and subsidiary texts. *Pace* its limited mandate – i.e., it had to avoid any changes to legal status or substantive provisions – by dividing and re-classifying in a consistent manner the whole primary law of the Union, the group paved the way for a more apparent, comprehensible and transparent basic instrument. It also linked the project of 'rationalisation through simplification' with the future of Europe debate. Modest in ambition, as it was an exercise *à droit contant*, the Basic Treaty managed in the end to achieve its near-impossible objective: 'to restructure without modifying' the Union's *acquis constitutionnel*. Short of a European Constitution, at least with reference to statist analogies, the EUI brought to the fore the tension between legal and political arguments for and against a substantive reshuffling of the Union's constitutional basis.

Grosso modo, the restructuring operation aimed at preserving three types of balances, summarised by Mény thus: the *grands équilibres* among Community policies; the balance between substantive and institutional law; and that between Community action in the first pillar and intergovernmentalism in the remaining two.[38] A similar suggestion was made by the EP, in that the Treaties should be split into two parts: a constitutional part (enshrining fundamental principles and procedures) and an operational part (incorporating policy issues). Patterned on the TEU model, the Basic Treaty, which effectively replaces the TEU as amended by the AMT, remains a 'framework treaty' and covers all EU activities. Hence its equally flexible nature, also evident in the tripartite structure of the TEU. Although he EUI report did not make it to the negotiating table at Nice, it has both a symbolic and identity-creating impact, as the Convention can use it as a good starting point for the search of a truly intelligible basic instrument – i.e., a constitutional treaty. An important issue that merits our attention concerns the setting up of different and less cumbersome procedures for revising the Treaties. The EUI report took notice of this point by suggesting that present treaty-amending processes should be eased in future Treaty negotiations. Few would disagree that the traditional exclusionary and sovereignty-cautious method of 'qualified unanimity' for reforming the Treaties, as epitomised in Art. 48 TEU – i.e., unanimity between the member states and adoption by the latter according to their constitutional requirements – has clearly reached its limits, especially with the Nice experience, where even relatively small and, logically, less conflict-prone amendments became troublesome to negotiate and agree upon. But what alternatives are there for a more inclusive and at the same time efficient process of EU constitutional change?

To start with, the drafting group's recommendation for changing the rules guiding treaty reform – produced in a separate report envisaging greater parliamentary input, was for different procedures to apply to different Treaty provisions according to the relative political importance and/or sensitivity of the issues at hand. Incidentally, a similar proposal is found in the report drafted at the Commission's request prior to the IGC 2000 by the three 'Wise Men' (Simon, Dehaene and Weizsäcker). Doubtless, one could envisage numerous scenarios based on a distinction between 'major' and 'minor', or indeed 'constitutional' and 'non-constitutional' amendments, with each category guided by different revision rules: the former dealing only with issues regarding the re-allocation of competences within the Union (and between the central institutions) through some form of legislative co-determination between the Council and the EP, and conditional upon the ratification of a majority of, say, at least three-quarters of the member states, or even without any ratification obligations; the latter, requiring a more vigorous fourth-fifths majority in the Council, the assent of the EP through an absolute majority of its members, and conditional upon the ratification of, say, at least four-fifths of the member states. Other amending procedures could involve various combinations, including the conduct of European-wide referenda, especially if the underlying objective is to move towards the further politicisation of treaty revisions. The same, of course, applies to the process of initiating treaty reforms or for that matter the idea of a European Constitution proper, say, on the joint initiative of certain central institutions (through some form of majority) – i.e., the Council, the EP (with or without prior consultation with national parliaments) and/or the Commission acting as a 'college' – or 'by popular demand' after a general referendum, or by a combination of both. These formulas for treaty-amendment are merely to indicate the wide range of possibility according to different logics (and motives) of EU constitutional reform.

Yet, functional differentiation in amending the Treaties, especially in areas where the constituent units strive for higher levels of integration and, hence, are prepared to make greater use of QMV (and also extend it to all areas of parliamentary co-decision, which could in turn be applied to cover most EU decision-making), may not always act in the interests of a more 'user-friendly' Treaty. But it would most likely reduce the sheer volume and inordinate complexity of asymmetrically negotiated outcomes – usually producing an inequitable *status quo* among small(er) and large(r) states, as the Nice process has so dramatically exemplified – through the traditional intergovernmental practices of horse-trading, log-rolling, side-payments, and the like – all of which, are part of what essentially constitutes the EU's *acquis conferenciel*. Be that as it may, post-Nice, the European polity is once again in search of new procedures to inflict upon its still uncrystallised political constitution the appropriate dosage of democracy and efficiency. In the hope that the end product of the IGC 2004 will not result in a deadly mix, we shift our emphasis to the last substantive item that appears on the Union's reformist agenda.

Remodelling the legislature

Much like the debate on the reorganisation of the Union's primary law and the apparent wealth of constitutional choices between 'soft' and 'hard' methods for amending the Treaties, the questions of how best to remodel the European legislature and what input (in terms of powers and functions) there should be from national legislative bodies have no easy answers. For one thing, there is an *a priori* normative choice to be made between a clear-cut European bicameral structure patterned on some federal-type legislature or other (and likely to involve national parliamentarians) and building on the existing quasi-federal (the other half being presumably confederal) constitutional architecture of the Union, by means of developing further the co-legislative (and controlling) powers of the EP, but without formally incorporating national parliaments into the EU legislative process. Opting for the first choice implies, *inter alia*, either the establishment of a new upper house composed solely of representatives of national parliaments, or the creation of a 'mixed' legislative body consisting partly of national parliamentary deputies and partly of Council members. Opting for the second choice means that new checks and balances would have to be found in the current (and not so co-equal) process of legislative co-determination between the Council and the EP (with the former reforming its internal structure).

Little doubt exists that European integration has strengthened the executive branches of the member polities (especially in terms of national parliaments holding ministers to account on their EU actions or inaction), even to the extent that some confidently point to the 'de-parliamentarisation' of national political systems. The combined effects of national parliaments' inability to exercise effective control over both their government and the Brussels apparatus, along with the transfer of national legislative powers to a Council that – to this day – remains collectively unaccountable, has resulted in a dual, if not multilevel, 'democratic deficit' in the Union. But the Nice mandate for further reforms carefully camouflages the seriousness of the situation by simply referring to the role of national parliaments in the integration process. Our previous analysis has touched upon the different (and often differing) views expressed by various EU leaders in the context of the 'Fischer debate'. As Duff put it:

> Mr Blair apparently wants to introduce a third chamber into the legislature of the Union, composed, like the old European Parliament, of national MPs. Mr Verhofstadt seems to have the US Senate in mind when he looks at the future of the EU's Council of Ministers; Mr Schröder, the Bundesrat. Other luminaries, like Mr Fischer, just seem muddled, and national parliaments themselves differ widely in their reaction to the perceived problem.[39]

The problem, however, is compounded further by the failure of past initiatives, like the 'Assizes' (a forum bringing together more than 300 national and European parliamentarians), courtesy of TEU Declaration 14, as it was convened only once in November 1990 in Rome. Also, although Protocol 13 of the AMT granted Treaty status to the Conference of European Affairs Committees (COSAC) – first set up in 1989 following the initiative of the French Presidency – acknowledging its role in commenting on various pieces of EU legislation, this mechanism reflected a compromise between those who wanted its formal institutionalisation along the lines of an upper house (and, hence, its incorporation into the EU legislative process), and those who hailed its informality as its crucial property. (During the IGC 1996/97, there were voices arguing the case for COSAC to become a kind of second EP, rather than EU, chamber representing the national parliaments.) This proposal, however, would require the existing EP structure to be split into two constituent bodies (though not necessarily on an equal basis), whose members would be elected through national and EP elections. The point to make here is that the original role envisaged for COSAC was to engage national parliamentarians in dialogue, something that could be institutionalised more vigorously in the existing institutional setting, and even linked with the creation of a new Inter-Parliamentary Committee (composed of an equal number of COSAC and EP members) without, though, altering the present representative (and legitimising) function of the EP. At a speech given in Paris in May 2001, Jospin called for a similar body in the form of a permanent Congress of Parliaments to hold annual debates on the 'State of the Union', to make sure that the principle of subsidiarity is being observed, and to be involved in the modification of technical or procedural rules in certain policies. The new institution could be involved in certain fields of EU legislation, either by means of performing political review functions, or by monitoring policy implementation. The same could easily apply to the Commission's annual legislative programme and, as suggested by Jospin, to a multiannual programme that the European Council could adopt. In this way, the EP would get involved in the day-to-day negotiations with the Council and the Commission, and the Committee would thus provide additional democratic oversight. This depiction also preserves the foundations of the EU's double democratic legitimacy, with the EP representing the constituent publics directly and the Council, the member governments.

It is important to stress that various other institutional improvements could be introduced to the existing quasi-bicameral structure, which could prove more significant to the democratisation of the Union – in both political and operational terms – as compared with a radical remodelling of its legislature and, hence, either the restructuring of the EP into a lower house of a mixed composition as suggested by Blair, or the transformation of the Council into a *Bundesrat*-like assembly – what Schröder called a European Chamber of States – to sit beside the EP. In terms of improving the present institutional system, the EP should be granted full co-legislative powers with the Council, including the area of compulsory expenditure, as well as the right to co-initiate legislation with the Commission. Simplifying further the co-decision procedure is crucial in terms of increasing visibility and public awareness over joint decision-making. In relation finally to the Council, a new European Affairs Council (EAC) could be set up composed of Ministers for European Affairs. This body should remain distinct from the Foreign Affairs Council which, in turn, should be made responsible only for second-pillar issues.[40] As the General Affairs Council is presently overloaded, it experiences grave difficulties in performing effectively both legislative (including preparatory) and co-ordination functions. Furthermore, there is a missing link between the COREPER and the European Council that the proposed EAC could fill, while at the same time becoming more involved in the preparatory work of the European Council, and co-ordinating the activity of all other Councils to provide additional coherence.

The philosophy underlying the preferred means of associating national parliaments with the EU political system is neither through the creation of a new upper house, nor through the reconstitution of the lower chamber, but rather through the setting up of an Inter-Parliamentary Committee to provide additional checks and balances in the process of scrutinising EU legislation, the equalisation of legislative powers between Council and the EP (combined with a further simplification of co-decision), and the internal restructuring of the Council through the establishment of the EAC to enable it to cope more effectively with an ever-more complex interinstitutional apparatus, as well as with an ever-expanding and increasingly state-like EU agenda. To the above list one could add measures such as the reduction of Council-formations (by grouping together some policy areas), the generalisation of QMV, increased transparency in Council meetings (especially when it meets as a legislature), greater involvement of the CoR in those areas of EU legislation that affect subnational units more closely and importantly (including the observation of subsidiarity), the active involvement of the Council's Secretariat in the preparatory work of the Council Presidency (so as to relieve the latter of a variety of time-consuming and technical tasks), the assignment of greater implementation responsibility to the Commission but with enhanced national parliamentary oversight, and so on.

Having examined several possibilities for further institutional reform, and before turning to the final section of this study in an attempt to summarise the limits of institutionalising democratic norm-orientation in the Union, it is worth recalling Olsen's architectural analogy on EU institution-building:

> Building European institutions of governance may be compared to building San Pietro in Vatican – Saint Peter's Basilica. Some trace its history nearly two thousand years back, and even the current (new) Basilica took generations to build. There have been many builders, popes and architects, as well as artists and workers. Plans have been made, modified and rejected. There have been conflicts over designs and over the use of resources. There have been shifting economic and political conditions and changing cultural norms, including religious beliefs and fashions of architecture. Such factors have affected both the motivation and ability to develop the Basilica. Yet, as parts have been added, modified and even demolished, the project has had a dynamic of its own, constraining both the physical development, the use of, and meaning of, the Basilica.[41]

Concluding remarks

At a time when the Union remains much of an unspecified entity, and in Delors' words *un objet politique non-identifié*, its dynamism is caught between federalist aspirations of becoming a more congruent polity and a modified type of inter-governmentalism, currently in the form of confederal consociation (see Chapter 2), confirming the centrality of states in the general system, by retaining ultimate control over both system-wide constitutional choice and change. In support of state-centrism also comes the view that even the recently observed dialectic between sovereignty and integration, carrying with it the implication of an explicit right to political co-determination, has failed to produce credible commitments towards a common strategy for democratising the collectivity by means of strengthening European civic competence. Arguably, however, in the midst of a near-chaotic state of theorising the EU polity-building, the normative agents of legitimate governance, 'post-national constitutionalism',[42] and the gradual but steadfast Europeanisation of civil society have raised the expectations of successive treaty amendments in endowing the Union with a clearer constitutional physiognomy and civic identity. Yet, by consolidating national autonomy, and by acknowledging the innate need of states to retain their formal sovereignty by continuing to act as *Herren der Verträge*, the limits of treaty reform in the late 1990s and early 2000s represent a clear illustration of the limits of EU polity-building itself.

Another important implication is the perception that because the recent review conferences carried a mandate for limited reforms, the development of European citizenship and corollary democratic concerns would be dealt with at a later stage. Judging, however, from the end product of Amsterdam and Nice processes, it is not certain that the IGC 2004 will be equipped with the necessary mandate for establishing conditions of legitimate governance based on an extensive 'deepening' of common citizenship rights and the emergence of a new balancing act between social norms of legitimacy and actual policy performance. Particularly with reference to the recent Nice reforms, far from representing a *cause célèbre* for a substantive re-ordering of civic spaces and public spheres, they amount to a cautiously negotiated deal of 'partial offsets' to key democratic problems facing the Union. Hence, a new dynamic tension between the promise of democratising the collectivity and the actual management of integration manifested itself not only after Nice but, crucially, because of Nice. What the latter failed in the end to produce was not only a common democratic vision *per se*, but rather a belief that such a vision remains without reach, at least for the foreseeable future. This critical assertion is justified further by perceiving the NIT as the product of a predominantly utilitarian, cost–benefit calculus among divergent and often ambivalent national interests along the lines of an overall rationalist settlement.

To the above, one could add that it is hardly possible to introduce substantive democratic reforms without civic participation, now that the once unquestionable 'permissive consensus' cannot generate the necessary public commitment to an EU politics where 'the provision of public welfare is best met through the process of elite-led, regional integration'.[43] If anything, the exclusion of citizens from European governance, compounded by their lack of effective civic competence, is at the expense of popular fragmentation itself. But it is also against the interests of better equipping citizens to become agents of civic change within a nascent pluralist order composed of increasingly entangled arenas for action. Like any other polity that aspires to becoming a democracy, the Union has to engage itself in a constitutive process based on a deliberative rather than aggregative model of governance, thus instituting a new framework of politics that embraces the virtues of civic freedom and civic solidarity, by means of inventing and, whenever necessary, re-inventing a sense of European *res publica*. After all, as Bellamy insightfully argues, 'Europe long ceased to be Holy, but its future may be Roman'.[44]

Notes

1   Following the Laeken Declaration of 15 December 2001, and in addition to its Chairman (d'Estaing) and Vice Chairmen (Amato and Dehaene), the Convention will be composed of fifteen representatives of the Heads of State and Government of the member states, thirty members of national parliaments (two per member state), sixteen members of the EP, and two Commission representatives. Accession candidate states will also be represented in the same way as the current member states, without however being allowed to prevent any consensus which may arise among the member states. Regarding its working method, it is worth noting that the Convention's discussions and all official documents will be in the public domain.

2   J. Shaw, 'The Treaty of Amsterdam: Challenges of Flexibility and Legitimacy', *European Law Journal*, 4:1, 1998, p. 85.

3   A. Menon, 'Defence Policy and Integration in Western Europe', *Contemporary Security Policy*, 17:2, 1996, p. 279.

4 See Fergus Carr and Kostos Ifantis, *NATO in the New European Order*, London: Macmillan/St Martin's Press, 1996, p. 154.

5 *Guardian*, 11 December 2000.

6 *The Times*, 12 December 2000, p. 23.

7 J. H. H . Weiler, 'Legitimacy and Democracy of Union Governance', in G. Edwards and A. Pijpers (eds), *The Politics of European Treaty Reform: The 1996 Intergovernmental Conference and Beyond*, London: Pinter, 1997, p. 250.

8 R. Bellamy and A. Warleigh, 'From an Ethics of Integration to an Ethics of Participation: Citizenship and the Future of the European Union', *Millennium*, 27:3, 1998, p. 448.

9 Y. Mény, *The People, the Elites and the Populist Challenge*, Jean Monnet Chair Paper RSC, No. 98/47, European University Institute, 1998, p. 9.

10 R. Dehousse, *European Institutional Architecture after Amsterdam: Parliamentary System or Regulatory Structure?*, EUI Working Paper RSC, No. 98/11, 1998, p. 13.

11 B. Kohler-Koch, *Europe in Search of Legitimate Governance*, ARENA Working Papers, WP 99/27, 1999, p. 9.

12 A. Duff, (ed.), *The Treaty of Amsterdam: Text and Commentary*, London: Sweet & Maxwell, 1997, pp. 145, 152–3.

13 *Ibid*, pp. xxxvi–xlii, 143.

14 Dehousse, *European Institutional Architecture*, p. 10.

15 Robert A. Dahl, *The Future of Democratic Theory*, Estudios Working Papers, No. 90, 1996, pp. 13–14.

16 M. Nentwich and G. Falkner, *The Treaty of Amsterdam: Towards a New Institutional Balance*, European Integration Online Papers, 1:015, 1997, p. 11.

17 L. Cram, D. Dinan and N. Nugent, 'The Evolving European Union', in L. Cram, D. Dinan and N. Nugent (eds), *Developments in the European Union*, London: Macmillan, 1999, p. 363.

18 J. H. H. Weiler, 'Bread and Circus: The State of European Union', *The Columbia Journal of European Law*, 4, 1998, p. 230.

19 R. Bellamy and M. Hollis, 'Consensus, Neutrality and Compromise', *Critical Review of International Social and Political Philosophy*, 1:3, 1998, p. 63.

20 See European Commission, 'Agenda 2000: For a Stronger and Wider Union', COM(97) 2000 Final, Vols 1 and 2, Brussels, 15 July 1997.

21 On this see 'The 1996 Single Market Review', Commission Communication to the Council and the European Parliament, COM(96) 520 Final, 30 October 1996.

22 'Agenda 2000', p. 11.

23 *Ibid.*, p. 11.

24 *Ibid.*, p. 12.

25 *Ibid.*

26 For a comprehensive account of the Euro-Mediterranean Partnership see D. K. Xenakis and D. N. Chryssochoou, *The Emerging Euro-Mediterranean System*, Manchester and New York: Manchester University Press, 2001.

27 European Commission, 'European Governance: A White Paper', COM(2001) 428 Final, Brussels, 25 July 2001.

28 Speech by J. Fischer, 'From Confederacy to Federation: Thoughts on the Finality of European Integration', in C. Joerges, Y. Mény and J. H. H. Weiler (eds), *What Kind of Constitution for What Kind of Polity?*, Badia Fiesolana, FI: European University Institute, 2000, pp. 19–30. See also Stelios Stavridis, *Confederal Consociation and the Future of the European Union*, ELIAMEP Occasional Papers, OP01/09, 2001.

29 C. Joerges, Y. Mény and J. H. H. Weiler, 'The Fischer Debate: The Bright Side', in Joerges *et al.* (eds), *What Kind of Constitution?*, p. 1.

30 T. Börzel and T. Risse, 'Who is Afraid of a European Federation? How to Constitutionalise a Multi-level Governance System', in Joerges *et al.* (eds), *What Kind of Constitution?*, p. 48.

31 *Ibid.*, p. 49.
32 *Ibid.*, p. 50.
33 K. Von Boyme, 'Fischer's Move towards a European Constitution', in Joerges *et al.* (eds), *What Kind of Constitution?*, p. 77.
34 C. Leben, 'A Federation of Nation-States or a Federal State?', in Joerges *et al* (eds), *What Kind of Constitution?*, p. 110.
35 J. P. Olsen, 'How, Then, Does One Get There?', in Joerges *et al.* (eds), *What Kind of Constitution?*, p. 175.
36 Joerges *et al.*, *What Kind of Constitution?*, p. 4.
37 Jürgen Habermas, 'Why Europe Needs a Constitution', *New Left Review*, 11, 2001, p. 17.
38 Yves Mény, 'A Basic Treaty of the European Union: The EUI's Draft', in Kim Feus (ed.), *A Simplified Treaty for the European Union?*, London: Federal Trust, 2001, p. 34.
39 Andrew Duff, 'Constitution or Bust: The Laeken Declaration', in Martin Bond and Kim Feus (eds), *The Treaty of Nice Explained*, London: Federal Trust, 2001, p. 239.
40 For more on this see G. Durand, 'The Need for Council Reform', Working Paper, European Policy Centre, Brussels, October 2001.
41 J. Olsen, 'Organising European Institutions of Governance: A Prelude to an Institutional Account of Political Integration', ARENA Working Papers, WP 00/2, 2000, pp. 20–1.
42 Jo Shaw, 'Postnational Constitutionalism in the European Union', *Journal of European Public Policy*, 6:4, 1999, pp. 63–86.
43 Bellamy and Warleigh, 'From an Ethics of Integration', p. 453.
44 Richard Bellamy, 'Una Republica Europea?', *Europa*, Anno VII, 2000, pp. 5–21.

BIBLIOGRAPHY

Adonis, Andrew, 'Subsidiarity: Myth, Reality and the Community's Future', House of Lords Select Committee on the European Communities, London, June 1990.

Albertini, Mario, 'The Ventotene Manifesto: The Only Road to Follow', in Lucio Levi (ed.), *Altiero Spinelli and Federalism in Europe and in the World*, Milan: FrancoAngeli, 1990.

Allen, David *et al.* (eds), *European Political Cooperation*, London: Butterworths, 1982.

Anderson, Jeffrey J. and Goodman, John B., 'Mars or Minerva? A United Germany in a Post-Cold War Europe', in R. O. Keohane, J. Nye and S. Hoffmann (eds), *After the Cold War: International Institutions and State Strategies in Europe, 1989–1991*, Cambridge, MA.: Harvard University Press, 1993.

Anderson, M., den Boer, M. and Miller, G., 'European Citizenship and Cooperation in Justice and Home Affairs', in Andrew Duff *et al.* (eds), *Maastricht and Beyond: Building the European Union*, London: Routledge, 1994.

Archer, Clive, *International Organisations*, 2nd edn, London: Routledge, 1992.

Assembly of WEU, *The Future Role of WEU*, Draft Report, A/WEU/POL(96)25, Paris, 11 November 1996.

—— *WEU After Amsterdam: The European Security and Defence Identity and the Application of Article V of the Modified Brussels Treaty – Reply to the Annual Report of the Council*, Draft Report, A/WEU/POL(97)10, Paris, 4 November 1997.

Aybet, Gulnur, *NATO's Developing Role in Collective Security*, SAM Papers, No. 4/99, Ankara: Center for Strategic Research, 1999.

Bailey, Sydney D., *United Europe: A Short History of the Idea*, London: National News-Letter, 1948.

Barry, Charles L., 'NATO's CJTF Concept and the WEU's Role in Crisis Response', paper presented at the WEU Athens Seminar, 1–3 May 1997.

Bellamy, Richard, 'Una Republica Europea?', *Europa*, Anno VII, 2000.

Bellamy, Richard and Castiglione, Dario, 'Building the Union: The Nature of Sovereignty in the Political Architecture of Europe', *Law and Philosophy*, 16:4, 1997.

—— 'Democracy, Sovereignty and the Constitution of the European Union: The Republican Alternative to Liberalism', in Z. Bañkowski and A. Scott (eds), *The European Union and its Order* London: Blackwell, 2000.

Bellamy, R., and Hollis, M., 'Consensus, Neutrality and Compromise', *Critical Review of International Social and Political Philosophy*, 1:3, 1998.

Bellamy, R. and Warleigh, A., 'From an Ethics of Integration to an Ethics of Participation: Citizenship and the Future of the European Union', *Millennium*, 27:3, 1998.

Beloff, Max, 'False Analogies from Federal Example of the United States', *The Times*, 4 May 1950.

Bodenheimer, Susan, *Political Union: A Microcosm of European Politics 1960–1966*, Leyden: Sitjhoff, 1967.

Booth, Kenneth, 'Security and Emancipation', *Review of International Studies*, 17, 1991, pp. 313–26.

Börzel T., and Risse, T., 'Who is Afraid of a European Federation? How to Constitution-alise a Multi-level Governance System', in C. Joerges, Y. Mény and J. H. H. Weiler (eds), *What Kind of Constitution for What Kind of Polity?*, Badia Fiesolana, FI: European University Institute, 2000.

Bosco, Andrea (ed.), *The Federal Idea: The History of Federalism from the Enlightenment to 1945*, Vol. I, London and New York: Lothian Foundation Press, 1991.

—— 'The Federalist Project and Resistance in Continental Europe', in Andrea Bosco (ed.), *The Federal Idea: The History of Federalism Since 1945*, Vol. II, London and New York: Lothian Foundation Press, 1992.

—— 'What is Federalism?', paper presented at the 2nd ECSA World Conference, Brussels, 4–6 May 1994.

Bowie, Robert R., 'The Process of Federating Europe', in A. W. Macmahon (ed.), *Federalism: Mature and Emergent*, New York: Garden City, 1987.

Von Boyme, K., 'Fischer's Move towards a European Constitution', in C. Joerges, Y. Mény and J. H. H. Weiler (eds), *What Kind of Constitution for What Kind of Polity?*, Badia Fiesolana, FI: European University Institute, 2000.

Bozo, Frederic, 'French Security Policy and the New European Order', in Colin McInnes (ed.), *Security and Strategy in the New Europe*, London: Routledge, 1992.

te Brake, Wayne, *Shaping History: Ordinary People in European Politics, 1500-1700*, Berkeley and Los Angeles: University of California Press, 1998.

Breckinridge, Robert E., 'Reassessing Regimes: The International Regime Aspects of the European Union', *Journal of Common Market Studies*, June 1997.

Brenner, Michael J., 'EC: Confidence Lost', *Foreign Policy*, 91, Summer 1993.

Brewin, C., 'The European Community: A Union of States without Unity of Govern-ment', *Journal of Common Market Studies*, 26:1 1987.

Brzezinski, Z., *The Grand Chessboard: American Primacy and its Geostrategic Imperatives*, New York: Basic Books, 1997.

Buchan, David, *Europe: The Strange Superpower*, Aldershot: Dartmouth, 1993.

Bull, Hedley, 'Civilian Power Europe: A Contradiction in Terms', in Loukas Tsoukalis (ed.), *The European Community: Past, Present and Future*, Oxford: Basil Blackwell, 1983.

Bulmer, Simon, 'The Governance of the European Union: A New Institutionalist Approach', *Journal of Public Policy*, 13:4, 1993.

Bulmer, Simon and Scott, Andrew, 'Introduction', in Simon Bulmer and Andrew Scott (eds), *Economic and Political Integration in Europe: Internal Dynamics and Global Context*, Oxford: Basil Blackwell, 1994.

Bulmer, Simon and Wessels, Wolfgang, *The European Council: Decision-Making in European Politics*, London: Macmillan, 1988.

Burgess, Michael, 'Federal Ideas in the European Community: Altiero Spinelli and European Union', *Government and Opposition*, Summer 1984.

—— 'Federalism as Political Ideology: Interests, Benefits and Beneficiaries in Federalism and Federation', in Michael Burgess and A.-G. Gagnon (eds), *Comparative Federalism and Federation*, New York: Harvester Wheatsheaf, 1993.

Bush, Kenneth D. and Keyman, E. Fuat, 'Identity-Based Conflict: Rethinking Security in a Post-Cold War World', *Global Governance*, 3:3, September–December 1997.

Buzan, Barry, *People, States and Fear: An Agenda for International Security Studies in the Post-Cold War Era*, 2nd edn, New York: Harvester Wheatsheaf, 1991.

—— 'Rethinking Security After the Cold War', *Cooperation and Conflict*, 32:1, 1997.

Calleo, David P., 'America's Federal Nation State: A Crisis of Post-Imperial Viability', *Political Studies*, 42, 1994.

Cameron, David M. (ed.), *Regionalism and Supranationalism: Challenges and Alternatives to the Nation-State in Canada and Europe*, London: The Institute for Research on Public Polity, 1981.

Caporaso, James, 'The European Union and Forms of State: Westphalian, Regulatory or Post-Modern?', *Journal of Common Market Studies*, March 1996.

Carr, Fergus and Ifantis, Kostas, *NATO in the New European Order*, London: Macmillan/St Martin's Press, 1996.

Chipman, J., 'The Military Balance Press Conference', 18 October 2001.

Christiansen, Thomas, 'European Integration Between Political Science and International Relations Theory: The End of Sovereignty?', EUI Working Paper, No. 94/4, San Domenico: Badia Fiesolana, FI, 1994.

Christiansen, Thomas, Jørgensen, Knud E. and Wiener, Antje, 'The Social Construction of Europe', *Journal of European Public Policy*, 6:4, 1999.

Chryssochoou, Dimitris N., 'Democracy and Symbiosis in the European Union: Towards a Confederal Consociation?', *West European Politics*, October 1994.

—— *Democracy in the European Union*, London and New York: I. B. Tauris, 1998.

—— 'European Union and the Dynamics of Confederal Consociation: Problems and Prospects for a Democratic Future', *Journal of European Integration*, 18:2–3, Winter/Spring 1996.

—— 'Europe's "Could-be Demos": Recasting the Debate', *West European Politics*, October 1996.

—— 'Federalism and Democracy Reconsidered', *Regional and Federal Studies*, Summer 1998.

—— 'Metatheory and the Study of the European Union: Capturing the Normative Turn', *Journal of European Integration*. 22:2, 2000, pp. 123–44.

—— 'New Challenges to the Study of European Integration: Implications for Theory-Building', *Journal of Common Market Studies*, December 1998, pp. 521–42.

—— 'Rethinking Democracy in the European Union: The Case for a "Transnational Demos"', in Stelios Stavridis *et al.* (eds), *New Challenges to the European Union: Policies and Policy-Making*, Aldershot: Dartmouth, 1997.

—— *Theorizing European Integration*, London: Sage, 2001.

Church, Clive H., *European Integration Theory in the 1990s*, European Dossier Series, No. 33, University of North London, 1996.

—— 'The Not so Model Republic? The Relevance of Swiss Federalism to the European Community', Leicester University Discussion Papers in Federal Studies, No. FS93/4, November 1994.

Church, Clive H. and Phinnemore, David, *European Union and European Community. A Handbook and Commentary of the Post-Maastricht Treaties*, London: Harvester Wheatsheaf, 1994.

Cimbala, Stephen J., *US Military Strategy and the Cold War Endgame*, London: Frank Cass, 1995.

Commission of the EC, 'Agenda 2000: For a Stronger and Wider Union', COM(97) 2000 Final, Vols 1 and 2, Brussels, 15 July 1997.

—— 'Report on the Functioning of the Treaty on the European Union', SEC (95)731 Final, 10 May 1995.

—— 'The 1996 Single Market Review', Commission Communication to the Council and the European Parliament, COM(96) 520 Final, 30 October 1996.

Cornish, Paul, 'European Security: The End of Architecture and the New NATO', *International Affairs*, 72:4, October 1996.

Cornish Paul and Edwards, Geoffrey, 'Beyond the EU/NATO Dichotomy: The Beginnings of a European Strategic Culture', *International Affairs*, 77:3, July 2001.

Covillers, Corinne, *Y-a-t-il une politique extérieure des Communautés Européennes?*, Paris: PUF, 1987.

Cox, Robert W., *Approaches to World Order*, Cambridge: Cambridge University Press, 1996.

—— 'Global Restructuring: Making Sense of the Changing International Political Economy', in Richard Stubbs and Geoffrey R. D. Underhill (eds), *Political Economy and the Changing Global Order*, London: Macmillan, 1994.

—— 'Multilateralism and World Order', *Review of International Studies*, 18:2, 1992.

—— 'Social Forces, States and World Orders: Beyond International Relations Theory', *Millennium*, 10:2, Summer 1981.

—— 'States, Social Forces and World Order: Beyond International Relations Theory', in Robert Keohane (ed.), *Neorealism and its Critics*, New York: Columbia University Press, 1986.

Craig, Paul P., 'Democracy and Rule-making within the EC: An Empirical and Normative Assessment', *European Law Journal*, 3:2, 1977.

Cram, L., Dinan, D. and Nugent, N., 'The Evolving European Union', in L. Cram, D. Dinan and N. Nugent (eds), *Developments in the European Union*, London: Macmillan, 1999.

Croft, Stuart, 'Guaranteeing Europe's Security? Enlarging NATO Again', *International Affairs*, 78:1, January 2002.

Croft, Stuart, Howorth, Jolyon, Terrif, Terry and Webber, Mark, 'NATO's Triple Challenge', *International Affairs*, 76:3, July 2000.

Daalder, Ivo H., 'Are the United States and Europe Heading for Divorce?', *International Affairs*, 77:3, 2001.

Dahl, Robert A., *A Preface to Democratic Theory*, Chicago: University of Chicago Press, 1956.

—— *The Future of Democratic Theory*, Estudios Working Papers, No. 90, 1996.

Dahrendorf, Ralph, *Reflections on the Revolution in Europe*, Boulder: Westview Press, 1991.

Dehousse, R., *European Institutional Architecture after Amsterdam: Parliamentary System or Regulatory Structure?*, EUI Working Paper RSC, No. 98/11, 1998, p. 13.

Demaret, Paul, 'The Treaty Framework', in D. O'Keeffe and P. M. Twomey (eds), *Legal Issues of the Maastricht Treaty*, London: Wiley Chancery Law, 1994.

De Rougemont, Denis, 'The Campaign of European Congresses', in Ghita Ionescu (ed.), *The New Politics of European Integration*, London: Macmillan, 1972.

De Schoutheete, Philippe, *La coopération politique européenne*, 2nd edn, Brussels: Labor, 1986.

Deutsch, Karl W., *Political Community and the North Atlantic Area*, Princeton: Princeton University Press, 1957.

Dewitt, David B., 'Introduction: The New Global Order and the Challenges of International Security', in David Dewitt, David Haglund and John Kirton (eds), *Building a New Global Order: Emerging Trends in International Security*, Toronto: Oxford University Press, 1993.

Duff, Andrew, 'Constitution or Bust: The Laeken Declaration', in Martin Bond and Kim Feus (eds), *The Treaty of Nice Explained*, London: Federal Trust, 2001.

—— (ed.), *The Treaty of Amsterdam: Text and Commentary*, London: Sweet & Maxwell, 1997.

Durand, G., 'The Need for Council Reform', Working Paper, European Policy Centre, Brussels, October 2001.

Edwards, Geoffrey and Regelsberger, Elfriede (eds), *Europe's Global Links: The European Community and Inter-regional Co-operation*, London: Pinter, 1990.

Eekelen, W. V., 'WEU and the Gulf Crisis', *Survival*, 32:6, 1990.

Elazar, Daniel J., *Exploring Federalism*, Tuscaloosa: The University of Alabama Press, 1987.

—— *et al.*, *Federal Systems of the World: A Handbook of Federal, Confederal and Autonomy Arrangements*, 2nd edn, London: Longman Current Affairs, 1994.

EU, *Draft Treaty of Amsterdam*, 19 June 1997, CONF/4001/97.

—— *Treaty on European Union*, Brussels, Office for the Official Publications of the European Communities, 1992.

European Commission, 'Agenda 2000: For a Stronger and Wider Union', COM(97) 2000 Final, Vols 1 and 2, Brussels, 15 July 1997.

—— 'European Governance: A White Paper', COM(2001) 428 Final, Brussels, 25 July 2001.

European Commission, 'Report on the Functioning of the Treaty on the European Union', SEC(95)73/1 Final, 10 May 1995.

European Council, Declaration on 'Strengthening the Common European Policy on Security and Defense', Cologne European Council, 3–4 June 1999.

European Policy Centre, *Making Sense of the Amsterdam Treaty*, Brussels, 1997.

European Political Co-operation, Bonn: Press and Information Office of the Federal Government, 1982.

Featherstone, Kevin and Ginsberg, Roy H., *The United States and the European Community in the 1990s: Partners in Transition*, London: Macmillan/St Martin's Press, 1993.

Fischer, J., 'From Confederacy to Federation: Thoughts on the Finality of European Integration', in C. Joerges, Y. Mény and J. H. H. Weiler (eds), *What Kind of Constitution for What Kind of Polity?*, Badia Fiesolana, FI: European University Institute, 2000.

Forsyth, Murray 'Federalism and Confederalism', in Chris Bacon (ed.), *Political Restructuring in Europe: Ethical Perspectives*, London and New York: Routledge, 1994.

—— *Political Science, Federalism and Europe*, Discussion Papers in Federal Studies, No. FS95/2, University of Leicester, 1995.

—— 'Towards a New Concept of Confederation', European Commission for Democracy Through Law, Council of Europe, 1994.

—— *Unions of States: The Theory and Practice of Confederation*, Leicester: Leicester University Press, 1981.

Friedrich, Carl J., *Trends of Federalism in Theory and Practice*, London: Pall Mall Press, 1968.

Fukuyama, F., 'History is Still Going Our Way: Liberal Democracy will Inevitably Prevail', *Wall Street Journal*, 5 October 2001.

—— 'The End of History?', *National Interest*, 1:3, 1989.

—— *The End of History and the Last Man*, New York, Free Press, 1992.

Furdson, Edward, *The European Defence Community: A History*, London: Macmillan, 1980.

Galtung, Johan, *The European Community: A Superpower in the Making*, London: George Allen & Unwin, 1973.

Ghebali, Victor-Yves, 'The OSCE's Istanbul Charter for European Security', *NATO Review*, 48, Spring–Summer-2000.

Ginsberg, Roy, *Foreign Policy Actions of the European Community – The Politics of Scale*, Boulder: Lynne Rienner, 1989.

Gleditsch, Nils P. and Risse-Kappen, Thomas (eds), 'Democracy and Peace', *European Journal of International Relations*, Special Issue, 1:4, December 1995.

Groom, A. J. R., 'The European Community: Building Up, Building Down, and Building Across', in Conference Proceedings, *People's Rights and European Structures*, Manresa, September 1993.

Haas, Ernst B., *Beyond the Nation-State: Functionalism and International Organization*, Stanford: Stanford University Press, 1964.

—— *The Obsolescence of Regional Integration Theory*, Berkeley, CA: Institute of International Studies, 1975.

—— 'The Study of Regional Integration: Reflections on the Joy and Anguish of Pretheorising', *International Organization*, 24:4, 1970.

—— *The Uniting of Europe: Political, Social and Economic Forces 1950–1957*, London: Stevens & Sons, 1958.

—— *When Knowledge is Power: Three Models of Change in International Organizations*, Berkeley: University of California Press, 1990.

Habermas, Jürgen, 'Why Europe Needs a Constitution', *New Left Review*, 11, 2001.

Hall, John A., *International Orders*, Cambridge: Polity Press, 1996.

Hallenbeck, Ralph A., Molino, Thomas and Roller, Kevin, *Preventive Defence: A New Framework for US–European Security Cooperation?*, Wilton Park: The Center for Global Security and Cooperation, July 1997.

Harrison, Reginald J., *Europe in Question: Theories of Regional International Integration*, London: Allen & Unwin, 1974.

—— 'Neo-functionalism', in A. J. R. Groom and Paul Taylor (eds), *Frameworks for International Co-operation*, London: Pinter, 1990.

Hassner, Pierre, 'Obstinate and Obsolete: Non-Territorial Transnational Forces versus the European Territorial State', in Ola Tunander, Pavel Baev and Victoria Ingrid Einagel (eds), *Geopolitics in Post-Wall Europe: Security, Territory and Identity*, London: Sage/Oslo: International Peace Research Institute, 1997.

Held, David, *Modern State and Political Theory*, Stanford: Stanford University Press, 1992.

Hill, Christopher, 'European Foreign Policy: Power Bloc, Civilian Power – or Flop?', in Reinhart Rummel (ed.), *The Evolution of an International Actor – Western Europe's New Assertiveness*, Boulder: Westview, 1990.

—— (ed.), *National Foreign Policies and European Political Cooperation*, London: George Allen & Unwin, 1983.

—— (ed.), *The Actors in Europe's Foreign Policy*, London: Routledge, 1996.

Hirst, Paul, *Associative Democracy: New Forms of Economic and Social Governance*, Cambridge: Polity, 1994.

Hoffmann, Stanley, 'America and Europe in an Era of Revolutionary Change', in Helga Hoftendorn and Christian Tuschhoff (eds), *America and Europe in an Era of Change*, Boulder: Westview, 1993.

—— 'French Dilemmas and Strategies in the New Europe', in R. O. Keohane, J. S. Nye and S. Hoffmann (eds), *After the Cold War: International Institutions and State Strategies in Europe, 1989–1991*, Cambridge, MA: Harvard University Press, 1993.

—— 'Obstinate or Obsolete? The Fate of the Nation State in Western Europe', *Daedalus*, Summer 1966.

—— *The European Sisyphus: Essays on Europe, 1964–1994*, Boulder: Westview Press, 1995.

Hoftendorn, Helga, 'The Security Puzzle: Theory-Building and Discipline-Building in International Security', *International Studies Quarterly*, 35, 1991.

Hunter, Robert E., *Security in Europe*, London: Elek Books, 1969.

—— 'Starting at Zero: US Foreign Policy for the 1990s', in Brad Roberts (ed.), *US Foreign Policy After the Cold War*, Cambridge, MA: MIT Press, 1992.

Huntington, S. P., 'The Clash of Civilizations?', *Foreign Affairs* 72:3, 1993.

—— *The Clash of Civilizations and the Remaking of World Order*, London, Touchstone, 1996.

Ifestos, Panayiotis, *European Political Cooperation: Towards a Framework of Supranational Diplomacy?*, Aldershot: Gower, 1987.

Ikenberry, G. John, 'The Future of International Leadership', in Demetrios James Caraley and Bonnie B. Hartman (eds), *American Leadership, Ethnic Conflict, and the New World Politics*, New York: The Academy of Political Science, 1997.

—— 'The State and Strategies of International Adjustment', *World Politics*, 39:1, 1986.

Ionescu, Ghita (ed.), *The New Politics of European Integration*, London: Macmillan, 1972.

Januzzi, Gianni, 'European Political Co-operation and the Single European Act', in Panos Tsakaloyannis (ed.), *Western European Security in a Changing World: From the Reactivation of the WEU to the Single European Act*, Maastricht: EIPA, 1988.

Jervis, R., 'Security Regimes', in Stephen D. Krasner (ed.), *International Regimes*, Ithaca: Cornell University Press, 1983.

Joerges, C., Mény, Y. and Weiler, J. H. H., 'The Fischer Debate: The Bright Side', in C. Joerges, Y. Mény and J. H. H. Weiler (eds), *What Kind of Constitution for What Kind of Polity?*, Badia Fiesolana, FI: European University Institute, 2000.

Kamenka, Eugene, *Bureaucracy*, Oxford: Basil Blackwell, 1989.

Kay, Sean, *NATO and the Future of European Security*, Oxford: Rowman & Littlefield, 1998.

Keohane, Robert O., *After Hegemony: Cooperation and Discord in the World Political Economy*, Princeton: Princeton University Press, 1984.

—— 'Institutional Change in Europe in the 1980s', in Robert O. Keohane and Stanley Hoffmann (eds), *The New European Community: Decisionmaking and Change*, Boulder: Westview, 1991.

—— 'The Diplomacy of Structural Change: Multilateral Institutions and State Strategies', in Helga Hoftendorn and Christian Tuschhoff (eds), *America and Europe in an Era of Change*, Boulder: Westview Press, 1993.

Keohane, Robert and Hoffmann, Stanley, 'Conclusions', in William Wallace (ed.), *The Dynamics of European Integration*, London: Royal Institute of International Affairs, 1990.

King, Preston, *Federalism and Federation*, London: Croom Helm, 1982.

—— 'Federation and Representation', in Michael Burgess and A.-G. Gagnon (eds), *Comparative Federalism and Federation*, New York: Harvester Wheatsheaf, 1993.

Kirchner, Emil J., *Decision Making in the European Community*, Manchester: Manchester University Press, 1992.

—— 'Has the Single European Act Opened the Door for a European Security Policy?', *Journal of European Integration*, 13:1, Autumn 1989.

Kissinger, Henry, *Diplomacy*, New York: Simon & Schuster, 1994.

Kitzinger, Uwe, *The European Common Market and Community*, London: Routledge, 1967.

—— 'Time-Lags in Political Psychology', in James Barber and Bruce Reeds (eds), *European Community: Vision and Reality*, London: Croom Helm, 1973.

Klare, Michael and Thomas, Daniel (eds), *World Security: Challenges for a New Century*, New York: St Martin's Press, 1994.

Kohler-Koch, B., *Europe in Search of Legitimate Governance*, ARENA Working Papers, WP 99/27, 1999.

Kolodziej, Edward, 'Renaissance in Security Studies? Caveat Lector!', *International Studies Quarterly*, 36, 1992.

Krasner, Stephen D., 'Power, Polarity and the Challenge of Disintegration', in Helga Hoftendorn and Christian Tuschhoff (eds), *America and Europe in an Era of Change*, Boulder: Westview Press, 1993.

—— 'Structural Causes and Regime Consequences: Regimes as Intervening Variables', in Stephen D. Krasner (ed.), *International Regimes*, Ithaca: Cornell University Press, 1983.

Kummel, Gerhard, 'From Yesterday to Tomorrow – CSCE/OSCE at Twenty: Achievements of the Past and Challenges of the Future', *OSCE ODIHR Bulletin*, 4:1, Winter 1995/96.

Laidi, Zaki, 'Introduction: Imagining the Post-Cold War Era', in Zaki Laidi (ed.), *Power and Purpose After the Cold War*, Oxford: Berg, 1994.

—— 'Power and Purpose in the International System', in Zaki Laidi (ed.), *Power and Purpose After the Cold War*, Oxford: Berg, 1994.

Lavdas, Kostas A., 'Republican Europe and Multicultural Citizenship', *Politics*, 21:1, 2001.

Layne, C. and Schwartz, B., 'American Hegemony – Without an Enemy', *Foreign Policy*, 92, Autumn 1993.

Leben, C., 'A Federation of Nation-States or a Federal State?', in C. Joerges, Y. Mény and J. H. H. Weiler (eds), *What Kind of Constitution for What Kind of Polity?*, Badia Fiesolana, FI: European University Institute, 2000.

Lemaître, P., 'Des dispositions trop timorées pour les négotiateurs français du traité', *Le Monde*, 2 January 1998.

Lesser, Ian, Green, Jerrold, Larrabee, F. Stephen and Zanini, Michele, *The Future of NATO's Mediterranean Initiative: Evolution and Next Steps*, Santa Monica: RAND, 2000.

Levi, Lucio, 'Altiero Spinelli, Mario Albertini and the Italian Federalist School: Federalism as Ideology', in Andrea Bosco (ed.), *The Federal Idea: The History of Federalism Since 1945*, Vol. II, London and New York: Lothian Foundation Press, 1992.

—— 'Recent developments in Federalist Theory', in Lucio Levi (ed.), *Altiero Spinelli and Federalism in Europe and the World*, Milan: FrancoAngeli, 1990.

Lijphart, Arend, 'Consociation and Federation: Conceptual and Empirical Links', *Canadian Journal of Political Science*, September 1979.

Lindberg, Leon N. and Stuart A. Scheingold, *Europe's Would-Be Polity: Patterns of Change in the European Community*, Englewood Cliffs, NJ: Prentice-Hall, 1970.

Livingston, R. G., 'United Germany: Bigger and Better', *Foreign Policy*, 87, Summer 1992.

McCalla, Robert B., 'NATO's Persistence After the Cold War', *International Organisation*, 50:3, Summer 1996.

MacCormick, Neil, 'Democracy, Subsidiarity, and Citizenship in the "European Commonwealth"', *Law and Philosophy*, 16, 1997.

MacFarquhar, Roderick, 'The Community, the Nation-State and the Regions', in B. Burrows *et al.* (eds), *Federal Solutions to European Issues*, London: Macmillan, 1978.

MacIver, R. M., *Community: A Sociological Study*, London: Macmillan, 1936.

McKay, David, 'On the Origins of Political Unions', paper presented at the 2nd ECSA-World Conference, Brussels, 4–6 May 1994.

Marks, Gary, Hooghe, Leisbet and Blank, Kermit, 'European Integration from the 1980s: State-centric v. Multi-level Governance', *Journal of Common Market Studies*, September 1996.

Maull, Hans, 'Germany and the Use of Force: Still a Civilian Power?', *Survival*, 42:2, 2000.

Mearsheimer, John J., 'Back to the Future: Instability in Europe after the Cold War', *International Security*, 15:1, Summer 1990.

Menon, A., 'Defence Policy and Integration in Western Europe', *Contemporary Security Policy*, 17:2, August 1996.

Mény, Yves, 'A Basic Treaty of the European Union: The EUI's Draft', in Kim Feus (ed.), *A Simplified Treaty for the European Union?*, London: Federal Trust, 2001.

—— *The People, the Elites and the Populist Challenge*, Jean Monnet Chair Paper RSC, No. 98/47, European University Institute, 1998, p. 9.

Miller, Linda B., 'The Clinton Years: Reinventing US Foreign Policy?', *International Affairs*, 70:4, October 1994.

Milward, Alan S., *The European Rescue of the Nation State*, Berkeley, CA: California University Press, 1992.

Milward, Alan S. and Sørensen, Viebeke, 'Interdependence or Integration? A National Choice', in Alan S. Milward *et al.* (eds), *The Frontier of National Sovereignty: History and Theory 1945–1992*, London and New York: Routledge, 1993.

Mitrany, David, *A Working Peace System*, London: Royal Institute of International Affairs, 1943.

—— *The Functional Theory of Politics*, London: Martin Robertson, 1976.

Monar, J., 'The Financial Dimension of the CFSP', in M. Holland (ed.), *Common Foreign and Security Policy – The Record and Reforms*, London: Pinter, 1997.

Moravcsik, Andrew, 'Preferences and Power in the European Community: A Liberal Intergovernmentalist Approach', *Journal of Common Market Studies*, December 1993.

Mouffe, C., *The Return of the Political*, London: Verso, 1993.

Murphy, A., 'Belgium's Regional Divergence: Along the Road to Federation', in Graham Smith (ed.), *Federalism: The Multiethnic Challenge*, London and New York: Longman, 1995.

Mutimer, David, 'Theories of Political Integration', in Hans J. Michelmann and Panayotis Soldatos (eds), *European Integration: Theories and Approaches*, Lanham: University Press of America, 1994.

NATO, 'Declaration of the Heads of States and Governments Participating in the Meeting of the North Atlantic Council in Brussels', Brussels: NATO Information Service, 1988.

—— *NATO Facts and Figures*, Brussels: NATO Information Office, 1989.

—— 'The Alliance's New Strategic Concept', *NATO Review*, 39:6, 1991.

—— 'The Alliance's Strategic Concept', Press Release NAC-S(99)65, 24 April 1999.

—— 'The London Declaration on a Transformed North Atlantic Alliance', Brussels: NATO Information Service, 1990.

Nentwich M.. and Falkner, G., *The Treaty of Amsterdam: Towards a New Institutional Balance*, European Integration Online Papers, 1:015, 1997, p. 45.

Neunreither, Karlheinz, "The Syndrome of Democratic Deficit in the European Community", in G. Parry (ed.), *Politics in an Interdependent World: Essays Presented to Ghita Ionescu*, Aldershot: Edward Elgar, 1994.

North Atlantic Council, 'Berlin Communiqué', Berlin, 3 June 1996; *NATO Review*, 44:4, July 1996.

—— *Declaration of Heads of State and Government January 1994*, NATO Press Communiqué M-1(94)3, 1994.

—— 'Ministerial Meeting, Denmark', *NATO Review*, 39:3, 1991.

—— 'Ministerial Meeting at Turnberry, 1990', *NATO Review*, 38:3, 1990.

—— 'Partnership with the Countries of Central and Eastern Europe', NATO Press Communiqué, M-1(91)44, 1991.

—— 'Washington Summit Communiqué: An Alliance for the 21st Century', NAC-S(99)64, 24 April 1999.

Nuttall, Simon, *European Political Co-operation*, Oxford: Clarendon Press, 1992.

—— 'The CFSP Provisions of the Amsterdam Treaty: An Exercise in Collusive Ambiguity', *CFSP Forum*, 3/97.

—— 'Where the European Commission Comes In', in Alfred Pijpers *et al.* (eds), *European Political Co-operation in the 1980's: A Common Foreign Policy for Western Europe?*, Dordrecht: Martinus Nijhoff, 1988.

Nye, Joseph S. and Keohane, Robert O., 'The United States and International Institutions in Europe After the Cold War', in R. O. Keohane, J. S. Nye and S. Hoffmann (eds), *After the Cold War: International Institutions and State Strategies in Europe, 1989–1991*, Cambridge, MA: Harvard University Press, 1993.

Olsen, J. P., 'How, Then, Does One Get There?', in C. Joerges, Y. Mény and J. H. H. Weiler (eds), *What Kind of Constitution for What Kind of Polity?*, Badia Fiesolana, FI: European University Institute, 2000.

—— 'Organising European Institutions of Governance: A Prelude to an Institutional Account of Political Integration', ARENA Working Papers, WP 00/2, 2000.

Øhrgaard, Jacob, "'Less than Supranational, More than Intergovernmental": European Political Co-operation and the Dynamics of Intergovernmental Integration', *Millennium*, 26:1, 1997.

Pettit, Philip, *Republicanism: A Theory of Freedom and Government*, Oxford: Clarendon Press, 1997.

Piening, Christopher, *Global Europe – The European Union in World Affairs*, Boulder: Lynne Rienner, 1997.

Pierre, Andrew J., *NATO at Fifty: New Challenges, Future Uncertainties*, United States Institute for Peace (USIP) Special Report, 22 March 1999.

Pijpers, Alfred, 'The Twelve Out-of-Area: A Civilian Power in an Uncivil World?', in A. Pijpers (ed.), *European Political Cooperation in the 1980s: A Common Foreign Policy for Europe?*, Dordrecht: Martinus Nijhoff, 1988.

Pinder, J., 'The New European Federalism', in M. Burgess and A.-G. Gagnon (eds), *Comparative Federalism and Federation*, New York: Harvester Wheatsheaf, 1993.

Pistone, S., 'Altiero Spinelli and a Strategy for the United States of Europe', in A. Bosco (ed.), *The Federal Idea: The History of Federalism from the Enlightenment to 1945*, Vol. I, London and New York: Lothian Foundation Press, 1991.

Plant, Raymond, *Community and Ideology: An Essay in Applied Social Philosophy*,

London and Boston: Routledge & Kegan Paul, 1974.

Politi, Alessandro, *European Security: The New Transnational Risks*, Chaillot Papers, 29, WEU Institute for Security Studies, October 1997.

Preston, Christopher, *Enlargement and Integration in the European Union*, London: Routledge for UACES, 1997.

Pryce, Roy, 'The Maastricht Treaty and the New Europe', in Andrew Duff *et al.* (eds), *Maastricht and Beyond: Building the European Union*, London: Routledge, 1994.

Puchala, Donald J., 'Of Blind Men, Elephants and International Integration', *Journal of Common Market Studies*, December 1972.

—— 'The Integration Theorists and the Study of International Relations', in C. W. Kegley and E. Wittkopf (eds), *The Global Agenda: Issues and Perspectives*, New York: Random House, 1984.

Putnam, Robert D., 'Diplomacy and Domestic Politics: The Logic of Two-level Games', *International Organization*, 42:3, 1988, pp. 427–60.

Reflection Group, *Final Report*, SN 520/95 REVI, Brussels, 5 December 1995.

—— *Interim Report of the Chairman*, SN 509/95 REVI, Brussels, 24 August 1995.

Regelsberger, Elfriede, 'EPC in the 1980s: Reaching another Plateau?', in A. Pijpers (ed.), *European Political Co-operation in the 1980s: A Common Foreign Policy for Western Europe?*, Dordrecht: Martinus Nijhoff, 1988.

Ress, George, 'Democratic Decision-Making in the European Union and the Role of the European Parliament', in D. Curtin and T. Heukels (eds), *Institutional Dynamics of European Integration: Essays in Honour of Henry G. Schermers*, Vol. II, Dordrecht: Martinus Nijhoff, 1994.

Richardson, Luise, 'British State Strategies After the Cold War', in R. O. Keohane, J. S. Nye and S. Hoffmann (eds), *After the Cold War: International Institutions and State Strategies in Europe, 1989–1991*, Cambridge, MA: Harvard University Press, 1993.

Roberts, Adam, 'NATO's "Humanitarian War" over Kosovo', *Survival*, 41:3, Autumn 1999.

Roberts, Brad, 'Introduction', in Brad Roberts (ed.), *US Foreign Policy After the Cold War*, Cambridge, MA: MIT Press, 1992.

Robinson, K., 'Sixty Years of Federation in Australia', *Geographical Review*, 51:1, 1961.

Rosamond, Ben, *Theories of European Integration*, London: Palgrave, 2000.

Rosenau, James N. and Czempiel, Ernst-Otto (eds), *Governance Without Government: Order and Change in World Politics*, Cambridge: Cambridge University Press, 1992.

—— 'New Dimensions of Security: The Interaction of Globalising and Localising Dynamics', *Security Dialogue*, 25:3, September 1994.

Ruggie, J. G., *Constructing the World Polity: Essays on International Institutionalization*, New York: Routledge, 1998.

Rummel, Reinhart, 'Speaking with One Voice – and Beyond', in A. Pijpers (ed.), *European Political Cooperation in the 1980s: A Common Foreign Policy for Europe?*, Dordrecht: Martinus Nijhoff, 1988.

Sbragia, Alberta M., 'The European Community: A Balancing Act', *Publius*, Summer 1993.

—— 'Thinking about the European Future', in Alberta M. Sbragia (ed.), *Euro-Politics*, Washington, DC: The Brookings Institution, 1992.

Schake, Kori, Bloch-Laine, Amaya and Grant, Charles, 'Building a European Defense Capability', *Survival*, 41:1, Spring 1999.

Scharpf, Fritz W., 'The Joint-Decision Trap: Lessons from German Federalism and European Integration', *Public Administration*, Autumn 1988.

Schmitter, Philippe C., 'Some Alternative Futures for the European Polity and their Implications for European Public Policy', in Y. Mény *et al.* (eds), *Adjusting to Europe: The Impact of the European Union on National Institutions and Policies*, London and New York: Routledge, 1996.

—— 'The European Community as an Emergent and Novel Form of Political Domination', Estudio Working Paper, 26, 1996.

Schulte, Gregory L., 'Former Yugoslavia and the New NATO', *Survival*, 39:1, Spring 1997.

Sharma, B. M. and Choudhry, L. P., *Federal Policy*, London: Asia Publishing House, 1967.

Shaw, Jo, 'Postnational Constitutionalism in the European Union', *Journal of European Public Policy*, 6:4, 1999.

—— 'The Treaty of Amsterdam: Challenges of Flexibility and Legitimacy', *European Law Journal*, 4:1, 1998.

Shaw, Jo and Wiener, Antje, 'The Paradox of the "European Polity"', in M. Green Cowles and Michael Smith (eds), *State of the European Union, Volume 5: Risks, Reform, Resistance, and Revival*, Oxford: Oxford University Press, 2000.

Sjostedt, Gunnar, *The External Role of the European Community*, Farnborough: Saxon House, 1977.

Sloan, Stanley R., *The United States and European Defense*, Chaillot Papers 39, Institute for Security Studies, Western European Union, Paris, April 2000.

Smith, Anthony D., *National Identity*, Harmondsworth: Penguin Books, 1991.

Smith, Gordon, 'The Crisis of the Western European State', in David M. Cameron (ed.), *Regionalism and Supranationalism: Challenges and Alternatives to the Nation-State in Canada and Europe*, London: The Institute for Research on Public Polity, 1981.

Smith, Karen, 'The End of Civilian Power Europe: A Welcome Demise or Cause for Concern?', *The International Spectator*, 35:2, 2000.

Smith, Michael, 'Beyond the Stable State? Foreign Policy Challenges and Opportunities in the New Europe', in Walter Carlsnaes and Steve Smith (eds), *European Foreign Policy: The EC and Changing Perspectives in Europe*, London: Sage, 1994.

Spinelli, Altiero and Rossi, Ernesto, 'European Union in the Resistance', *Government and Opposition*, April–July 1967.

—— *Il Manifesto di Ventotene*, Pavia, 1944.

Stavridis, Stelios, *Confederal Consociation and the Future of the European Union*, ELIAMEP Occasional Papers, OP01/09, 2001.

—— 'Democracy in Europe: West and East', in Conference Proceedings, *People's Rights and European Structures*, Manresa, September 1993.

—— 'Foreign Policy and Democratic Principles: The Case of European Political Co-operation', unpublished PhD thesis, London: LSE, 1991.

—— 'The Common Foreign and Security Policy of the European Union: Why Institutional Arrangements Are Not Enough', in S. Stavridis, E. Mossialos, R. Morgan and H. Machin (eds), *New Challenges to the European Union: Policies and Policy Making*, Aldershot: Dartmouth, 1997.

—— 'The Democratic Control of European Foreign Policy: Whose Demos Is It Anyway?', paper presented to the Fifth Biennial ECSA–USA Conference in Seattle, Washington, 29 May–1 June 1997.

—— 'The Democratic Control of the EU's Foreign and Security Policy after Amsterdam and Nice', *Current Politics and Economics of Europe*, 10:3, 2001.

—— 'The Militarizing of the EU and the Concept of a "Civilian power Europe" Revisited', *The International Spectator*, 36:4, 2001.

—— 'The "Second" Democratic Deficit in the European Community: The Process of European Political Co-operation', in F. R. Pfetsch (ed.), *International Relations and Pan-Europe: Theoretical Approaches and Empirical Findings*, Münster: Lit Verlag, 1993.

Stavridis, Stelios and Hill, Christopher (eds), *Domestic Sources of Foreign Policy: West European Reactions to the Falklands Conflict*, Oxford: Berg, 1996.

Strange, Susan, *Casino Capitalism*, Oxford: Basil Blackwell, 1986.

Stubb, C.-G. A., 'A Categorization of Differentiated Integration', *Journal of Common Market Studies*, 34:2, 1996.

Tarrow, Sidney, 'Building a Composite Polity: Popular Contention in the European Union', Institute for European Studies Working Paper, No. 98/3, Cornell University, 1998.

Taylor, Paul, 'A Conceptual Typology of International Organisation', in A. J. R. Groom and Paul Taylor (eds), *Framework for International Co-operation*, London: Pinter, 1990.

—— 'Functionalism: The Approach of David Mitrany', in A. J. R. Groom and Paul Taylor (eds), *Frameworks for International Co-operation*, London: Pinter, 1990.

—— 'Interdependence and Autonomy in the European Communities: The Case of the European Monetary System', *Journal of Common Market Studies*, June 1980.

—— *International Co-operation Today: The European and the Universal Patterns*, London: Elek Books, 1971.

—— *International Organization in the Modern World: The Regional and the Global Process*, London: Pinter, 1993.

—— 'Prospects for the European Union', in Stelios Stavridis *et al.* (eds), *New Challenges to the European Union: Policies and Policy-Making*, Aldershot: Dartmouth, 1997.

—— 'The Concept of Community and the European Integration Process', *Journal of Common Market Studies*, December 1968.

—— *The Limits of European Integration*, New York: Columbia University Press, 1983.

—— 'The Politics of the European Communities: The Confederal Phase', *World Politics*, April 1975.

Tönnies, Ferdinand, *Community and Association*, translated and supplemented by Charles P. Loomis, London: Routledge & Kegan Paul, 1974.

Toth, A. G., 'The Principle of Subsidiarity in the Treaty of Maastricht', *Common Market Law Review*, 29, 1992.

Tranholm-Mikkelsen, J., 'Neo-Functionalism: Obstinate or Obsolete? A Reappraisal in the Light of the New Dynamism of the EC', *Millennium*, Spring 1991.

Treverton, Gregory F., 'America's Stakes and Choices in Europe', *Survival*, 34:3, Autumn 1992.

Treitschke, Heinrich von, 'State Confederations and Federated States', Book III, in Murray Forsyth *et al.* (eds), *The Theory of International Relations*, London: Allen & Unwin, 1970.

Tsembelis, George, 'The Power of the European Parliament as a Conditional Agenda-Setter', *American Political Science Review*, March 1992.

Tsinisizelis, Michael J. and Chryssochoou, Dimitris N., 'From "Gesellschaft" to "Gemein-schaft"? Confederal Consociation and Democracy in the European Union', *Current Politics and Economics of Europe*, 5:4, 1995, pp. 1–33.

Tucker, R. W., '1989 and All That', *Foreign Affairs*, 69:4, Autumn 1990.

Tupman, Bill and Tupman, Alison, *Policing in Europe: Uniform in Diversity*, Exeter: Intellect, 1999.

Vibert, Frank, *A Core Agenda for the 1996 Intergovernmental Conference*, European Policy Forum, London, 1995.

Wallace, Helen, 'European Governance in Turbulent Times', *Journal of Common Market Studies*, September 1993.

Wallace, W., 'Europe as a Confederation: The Community and the Nation-State', *Journal of Common Market Studies*, September–December 1982.

—— 'Less than a Federation, More than a Regime: The Community as a Political System', in Helen Wallace *et al.* (eds), *Policy-Making in the European Community*, Chichester: John Wiley, 1983.

—— 'Theory and Practice in European Integration', in Simon Bulmer and Andrew Scott (eds), *Economic and Political Integration in Europe: Internal Dynamics and Global Context*, Oxford: Basil Blackwell, 1994.

Walt, Stephen M., 'Why Alliances Endure or Collapse', *Survival*, 39:1, Spring 1997.

Watts, R. L., 'Federalism, Regionalism, and Political Integration', in David M. Cameron (ed.), *Regionalism and Supranationalism: Challenges and Alternatives to the Nation-State in Canada and Europe*, London: The Institute for Research on Public Policy, 1981.

Waever Ole, and Buzan, Barry, 'An Inter-Regional Analysis: NATO's New Strategic Concept and the Theory of Security Complexes', in Sven Behrendt and Christian-Peter Hanelt (eds), *Bound to Cooperate: Europe and the Middle East*, Gutersloh: Bertelsmann Foundation Publishers, 2000.

Webb, C., 'Theoretical Perspectives and Problems', in Helen Wallace *et al.* (eds), *Policy-Making in the European Community*, Chichester: John Wiley, 1983.

Weiler, J. H. H., 'Bread and Circus: The State of European Union', *The Columbia Journal of European Law*, 4, 1998.

—— 'Legitimacy and Democracy of Union Governance', in G. Edwards and A. Pijpers (eds), *The Politics of European Treaty Reform: The 1996 Intergovernmental Conference and Beyond*, London: Pinter, 1997.

Wessels, Wolfgang, 'An Ever Closer Fusion? A Dynamic Macropolitical View on Integration Processes', *Journal of Common Market Studies*, June 1997.

—— 'Nice Results: The Millenium IGC in the EU's Evolution', *Journal of Common Market Studies*, 39:2, 2001.

—— 'The Modern West European State. Democratic Erosion or a New Kind of Polity?', in S. S. Andersen and K. A. Elliassen (eds), *The European Union: How Democratic Is It?*, London: Sage, 1996.

WEU, *After Amsterdam: The European Security and Defence Identity and the Application of Article 5 of the Modified Brussels Treaty – Reply to the Annual Report of the Council*, Draft Report, A/WE/POL(97)10, Paris, 4 November 1997.

—— *European Security: A Common Concept of the 27 WEU Countries*, WEU Council of Ministers, Madrid, 14 November 1995.

—— *Platform on European Security Interests*, The Hague, 1987, in WEU, *The Reactivation of the WEU, Statements and Communiqués, 1984 to 1987*, WEU Press and Information Service, 1988.

—— *Preliminary Conclusions on the Formulation of a Common European Defence Policy*, WEU Press and Information Service, 1994.

—— *Related Texts Adopted at the EC Summit Maastricht*, WEU Press and Information Service, 1991.

—— *The Reactivation of the WEU, Statements and Communiqués, 1984 to 1987*, WEU Press and Information Service, 1988.

Whitman, Richard, *From Civilian Power to Superpower? The International Identity of the European Union*, Basingstoke: Macmillan, 1998.

Wörner, Manfred, 'The Atlantic Alliance in the New Era', *NATO Review*, 39:1, 1991.

Wyllie, J., *European Security in the Nuclear Age*, Oxford: Basil Blackwell, 1986.

Wyn Rees, G., 'Constructing a European Defence Identity: The Perspectives of Britain, France and Germany', *European Foreign Affairs Review*, 1:2, November 1996.

Xenakis, Dimitris K. and Chryssochoou, Dimitris N., *The Emerging Euro-Mediterranean System*, Manchester and New York: Manchester University Press, 2001.

Yost, David S., *NATO Transformed: The Alliance's New Roles in International Security*, Washington, DC: United Institute for Peace, 1998.

Young, Oran, *International Cooperation: Building Regimes for Natural Resources and the Environment*, Ithaca: Cornell University Press, 1989.

Zielonka, Jan *Explaining Euro-Paralysis: Why Europe is Unable to Act in International Politics*, Macmillan: Basingstoke, 1998.

Page references for tables are in *italics*; those for notes are followed by 'n'.